RACING & Out

RACING GUIDE
2003
Statistics • Results
Previews • Training centre reports

Contributors: Chris Cook, Nick Deacon, Steffan Edwards, Ken Hussey, Tony Jakobson, Michael McBriarty, Kel Mansfield, Steve Mellish, Peter Naughton, Dave Nevison, Ben Osborne, Colin Roberts, Graham Wheldon, Richard Williams.

Designed and edited by Chris Cook

Published in 2003 by Outlook Press
an imprint of Raceform Ltd,
Compton, Newbury, Berkshire RG20 6NL
Raceform Ltd is a Trinity-Mirror business

Copyright © Outlook Press 2003

All rights reserved. No part of this publication may be reproduced, stored in a retrieval system, or transmitted in any form or by any means, electronic, mechanical, photocopying, recording, or otherwise, without prior written permission of the publishers.

A catalogue record for this book is available from the British Library.

ISBN 1-904317-13-8

Printed by Cox & Wyman, Reading

RACING & FOOTBALL Outlook

Contents

Introduction	5
Profiles for punters — Andrew Balding	6
Ian Wood	10

2002 Review

News review	15
Five-year stats for 2002's top ten trainers	24
Season's statistics	44
Group 1 review	52
Two-year-old review	59
Ken Hussey	75

2003 Preview

Ante-post	80
Morning Mole	87
Racing & Football Outlook's horses to follow	91
Downsman (Lambourn)	99
Aborigine (Newmarket)	104
Jerry M (Ireland)	109
Borderer (North)	112
Hastings (West Country)	116
Southerner (South)	120
John Bull (Midlands)	124
Dave Nevison	127

Races and Racecourses

Fixtures	132
Big-race Dates	138
Big-race Records	143
By The Numbers	152
Track facts – Britain's flat courses	165
Betting guide	204
Competition	206
Horse index	207

RACING & FOOTBALL

Outlook

It costs justs £39.89 to subscribe to the RFO for 12 months. That works out at only 77p a copy! Save yourself some money by filling out the form below and returning it, along with a cheque made payable to 'Outlook Press', to:

RFM House, Compton, Berkshire. RG20 6NL.

Copies are despatched each Monday to reach most areas by Tuesday.

Subscribe by post for only 77p a week!

Alternatively, you can subscribe NOW by calling us on

01635 578080 (24 hours)

We accept major credit cards

A 26-week order for UK-based readers costs £20.50 and a 13-week trial is £10.58

```
NAME..................................................................
ADDRESS ............................................................
........................................................................
........................................................................
POSTCODE. .......................................................
TEL.....................................................................
```

Sponsored by Stan James

Outlook

Editor's introduction

YOU'VE GOT to be quick to win on the Flat.

Not just the horses – punters have to be quick on the uptake, must make immediate, accurate judgements about the relative weight of many bits of form. The turnover among Britain's racehorse population is so rapid on the Flat that, if you need to see a horse two or three times before forming a view, you'll just get washed away.

What you need to have half a chance of winning at this game is a running start, which is where we hope to help out.

The *Racing & Football Outlook* has been expanding in line with increasing circulation in recent years, and our annuals are keeping pace. We're proud to bring you the biggest ever *RFO Racing Guide* and you can be assured that we've redoubled our efforts to make sure you're fully apprised of everything you need to know ahead of the coming Flat season.

Usually, we kick off with a trainer interview in which the handler gets to brag about all his achievements to date. This time, there are two trainers and no small-talk – in our 'Profiles for punters', we ask the questions you'd ask if you could.

What are their qualifications to do this job? Are they any good? What kind of horses do they do well with? Do they bet?

Andrew Balding and Ian Wood are not yet household names but both have already proved themselves to be highly competent and we think you'll be interested by what they have to say.

At this point we usually look back at the last season, and what better way to start than by reminding ourselves of all the big news stories. In case some of the important stuff has slipped your mind, our inaugural News Review will bring you back up to speed.

Then, we've got a beefed-up array of stats; as well as the traditional five-year analysis of last year's winningmost trainers, we've got eight tables ranking last year's jockeys and trainers, with All-Weather racing treated as a separate discipline for the first time.

We've got a 100-race form guide to last year's two-year-olds, as per usual, to which we've added a Group 1 form book, allowing you to reflect in depth on the best performances of last year.

When it comes to looking forward to this year's action, we can offer our usual spread of strongly-held views and wise counsel. Dave Nevison and Morning Mole Steve Mellish mark your card about the animals they think could turn out to be a bit special, while Raceform's analyst Steffan Edwards takes a good hard look at the ante-post markets.

Our team of training centre reporters have been working their contacts and combing the form book. Their number is bolstered this time by the addition of Midlands man John Bull, giving RFO blanket coverage of the country; if there's a good horse out there, we'll hear about it, and so will you.

Our racecourse section includes three dimensional maps of all Britain's Flat courses, together with Graham 'Sprintline' Wheldon's draw analysis of each venue, so you can consider yourself fully briefed, no matter where you're punting.

And there's our final new feature – By The Numbers, presenting you with the data you'll need to crack some of the season's toughest puzzles.

Have a go at our competition (page 206) and you could be getting the RFO free to your door every Tuesday for six months. If you miss out, never fear – as you can see from the facing page, an annual subscription still costs just 77p per week and for that you'll get weekly access to the wit and wisdom of all our team.

Have a good season.

Sponsored by Stan James

Profiles for punters
Andrew Balding

HIS FAMOUS father Ian having bowed out, 30-year-old Andrew comes bounding onto stage. A strong performance can be expected – this lad's been rehearsing for years, has indeed been pulling a few of the old man's strings from behind the scenes for quite some time.

This is a role he was made for. Born the year after Balding Snr won the Derby and the Arc with Mill Reef, the young Andrew was at home in racing stables from his earliest days and knew from the age of seven or eight that there could be only one career path for him: "During my school years, all I did was read Timeform Annuals. While the other kids were learning their times tables, I could reel off a list of Derby winners."

During the holidays, he worked in the family's yard and others in the area, quietly absorbing the methods of various trainers. He rode as an amateur for a few years, getting "about 20 winners" before his apprenticeship started – first, a year with uncle Toby, then two Flat seasons working for legendary shrewdies Jack and Lynda Ramsden in Yorkshire, which he describes as "an exceptional experience."

"I think we had 50 winners both seasons

"I learned from the Ramsdens the importance of placing horses in their right level and also the importance, in this country more than anywhere, of a handicap rating for a horse's career"

I was there, which is an achievement from a 50-horse yard, and they were really good, fun years. It was a much more relaxed and laid-back yard than I was used to.

"They had a totally different approach to training from what I'd seen at home, I suppose a bit more scientific. I learned the importance of placing horses in their right level and also the importance, in this country more than anywhere, of a handicap rating for a horse's career."

For the 2000 season, he returned to his father's yard at Kingsclere, just outside Newbury. The yard was effectively split in two, Andrew taking full responsibility for the 40-odd horses housed in two of the four stable blocks.

The arrangement has worked well for the last three seasons. Though all the runners have been in his father's name, it was Andrew who patched up the nine-year-old Top Cees to become the oldest ever Cesarewitch winner, Andrew who landed a Group 2 at Newbury named after Mill Reef with the two-year-old Firebreak, Andrew who got Pentecost to win at Royal Ascot.

Most impressively, he trained the first two in the 2001 Cesarewitch, Distant Prospect and Palua beating 29 rivals in the fiercely competitive handicap.

At New Year, after almost 40 years in the game, Ian Balding retired and handed over the keys to Kingsclere. Balding Jnr has inherited a team of 110, including about 45 two-year-olds. When we spoke in early February, he'd already trained five winners in his own name, all on Lingfield's polytrack.

Understandably, he nominates the Surrey course as his favourite (for now) and enthuses about All-Weather racing; "I'd definitely like to see a few more Group 1 racecourses, like Newbury, install All-Weather tracks because it's the future; if racing in this country is to compete internationally, we've got to be racing 12 months of the year.

"The polytrack is the best All-Weather surface, it's so fair. It means that you can plan a race well in advance, knowing what the ground's going to be like and that, whatever draw you get on the day, there's no draw that's impossible to win from."

So, after such a promising start, what's the aim? "My ambition is to win big races, more than anything else, and have good horses. It's difficult, of course, but I'd like to get a win out of every horse I'm sent.

"It's too early to be thinking about specialising in particular kinds of races. So far, I've enjoyed success with a good two-year-old, adecent sprinter and some staying handicappers, so I've had a fair variety ofhorses already, although none of them were expensive. I'd love to train some really good horses."

He won't be financing any new stable blocks on the basis of his betting, though. He enjoys a bet "every once in a while, very unsuccessfully and mostly on football."

He feels no need forexcessive modesty and is not backward about coming forward with suggestions for the sport's future. "I think British racing could do with a two-tier system, where goodhorses can run against each other for good money and that can be the focus of public attention, rather than the situation just now, where you have three cards a day and two are crap.

"Obviously you have to cater for moderate horses, and we have some of them, but we should put the focus on the good horses. I can't help thinking how many people avoid racing because it seems so complicated – we need to present something more streamlined, in the way that football has with the Premiership."

Considering he has such a hard act to follow, Balding seems very poised. Does anything worry him? "I'm not daunted about taking over, unless they all start coughing in the spring. I'd say that's the only thing that can stop us having a good season."

Sponsored by Stan James

Balding's best

Three-year-olds

Rimrod
3yo bay colt
Danzig – Annie Edge (Nebbiolo)

Half-brother to Selkirk and an outstanding two-year-old, when he beat Oasis Dream in a 7f Sandown maiden and won a Listed race at Goodwood before running eighth of 16 in the Dewhurst. He's done very well through the winter, though he's just been cantering so far. The first target is the Poule d'Essai des Poulains at Longchamp in May – he might have a prep first. Then he'll probably go for the St James's Palace Stakes. He'll go on any ground but we have a theory that he might be better on a turning track, on the basis of what he showed as a juvenile.

Casual Look
3yo bay filly
Red Ransom – Style Setter (Manila)

Won her maiden over 1m on firm going at Bath, and was then second in both the Fillies' Mile and the Rockfel. Hopefully she'll be going for the 1,000 Guineas first time out and then the Oaks. Alternatively, there would be a lovely programme for her in France – we'll talk to the owner about which to go for. She'll stay 1m4f and handles fast ground well.

Oblige
3yo bay filly
Robellino – Acquiesce (Generous)

Won a Brighton maiden and a Haydock nursery before finishing a running-on fifth in the Fillies' Mile. She'll start off in the Masaka over 1m at Kempton in mid-April and the priority with her is to win a Listed race somewhere, so she can get some black type. It's quite possible we'll go abroad for that.

Speed Cop
3yo chestnut filly
Cadeaux Genereux – Blue Siren (Bluebird)

Won a Bath maiden and a Listed race at Newbury before making the frame in a couple of backend Group races, all over 5f. The programme for her this year is not great. Three-year-old fillies with her speed often struggle a bit until midsummer at least. She may go for the King's Stand at Royal Ascot and she'll probably stay in training as a four-year-old, which is more likely to be her year.

Opera Glass
3yo bay filly
Barathea – Optaria (Song)

She has some nice placed form, having been second or third in all three runs last season. She looks a sure-fire maiden winner and we'd hope she's even a bit better than that.

Arctic Desert
3yo bay colt
Desert Prince – Thamud (Lahib)

Ran third in a 21-runner maiden at Windsor and was then over the top by the time of his only other run, when sixth of 15 in a similar race at Newbury. He looks a very nice horse and should win a maiden at least.

Phoenix Reach
3yo bay colt
Alhaarth – Carroll's Canyon (Hatim)

Second in a 6f Salisbury maiden on his only start, beaten a head by Norse Dancer, who finished the season running in Group races. This one's from the same family as Arc winner Carroll House and could be useful. Unfortunately, he split a pastern after that run and it needed plating. He's back now, steady cantering, but we haven't put him under any pressure yet. We're aiming to have him back for May and then we'll see.

Older Horses

Dumaran
5yo bay gelding
Be My Chief – Pine Needle (Kris)

Won three decent, big-field handicaps last season. Has since had a disappointing campaign over hurdles and is being rested now. He's in the Lincoln and may well go for that. He's a nice horse round a turning track, though he's plenty high enough in the handicap just now.

Golden Chalice
4yo chestnut gelding
Selkirk – Special Oasis (Green Desert)

Finally won his maiden over 1m at Goodwood last summer after a frustrating run of four seconds and he was last seen winning

Sponsored by Stan James

a little handicap at Salisbury in July. He needs good or good to soft and 1m will always be right up his street. He's unexposed and I'm excited about his chances in the Lincoln.

Passing Glance
4yo brown colt
Polar Falcon – Spurned (Robellino)
Ultra-consistent but getting no slack from the handicapper and he's stuck unless he improves a lot. We've got no grand plans for him but he'll be in all the big handicaps around eight or nine furlongs. The Cambridgeshire might be his sort of race.

Vanderlin
4yo chestnut gelding
Halling – Massorah (Habitat)
Also handicapped to the hilt, so we'll be looking to run him in conditions and classified races, there are lots of chances to run him. He may go for the International Handicap at Ascot on King George day.

Pentecost
4yo chestnut gelding
Tagula – Boughtbyphone (Warning)
Won the Britannia Handicap at Royal Ascot but rather lost his way after that. He's done terribly well over the winter, though, and will be aimed at the Royal Hunt Cup.

Border Arrow
8yo chestnut gelding
Selkirk – Nibbs Point (Sure Blade)
Has narrowly won the last two runnings of Kempton's Listed Magnolia Stakes and will be going for the hat-trick on April 21. Handicaps are out of the question with him.

He's still enjoying it – as soon as that stops being true, we'll retire him.

Bourgainville
5yo bay gelding
Pivotal – Petonica (Petoski)
He's a lovely horse who could be Listed class if he improves a little bit. He'll be running over 1m to 1m2f and should win a nice race.

Distant Prospect
6yo bay gelding
Namaqualand – Ukraine's Affair (The Minstrel)
A smashing horse, won the 2001 Cesarewitch and made the frame last year off a 4lb higher mark. He'll have a similar campaign to last year, starting off in the Chester Cup. He needs ground on the soft side, which is a pity because it limits his chances through the summer – even so, he ran a big race in the 2001 Northumberland Plate on firm.

Lochridge
4yo chestnut filly
Indian Ridge – Lochsong (Song)
She could be the sort for the Wokingham or the Stewards' Cup. She's so well bred, it'd be lovely to get some black type for her. We'll see – she could be Group class.

Two-year-olds
We've got a nice bunch, though it's awfully early to be sure about any of them. The pick just now would be **Dandy Jim**, a son of Dashing Blade, who won four from five including the Dewhurst as a juvenile. Dandy Jim looks a lot like his dad, so you never know. He'll be out by June.

SUMMER SUCCESS: Pentecost (far right) wins the Britannia – he goes for the Hunt Cup

Profiles for punters
Ian Wood

IAN WOOD used to be a financial advisor. He must have been good at it because by the mid-1980s (when he was in his late 30s) he was able to start buying racehorses. By 1997, he could afford a whole stable and, in the short time since, he's developed a knack for training winners.

Born in Glasgow, he used to go racing at Ayr in the '70s and saw Roman Warrior win the Gold Cup there. His interest was caught and ever since he's been devoting more and more time to the sport, to the point where it has become his profession.

He can't recall ever deciding that he wanted to be a trainer but, once he'd bought the 75-box Neardown Stables in Lambourn from John Akehurst, it seemed a logical thing to try. He installed Kevin Bell at first and learnt rapidly as his assistant. After just two years, in October 1999, he took out a licence himself and hasn't looked back.

This season, if everything goes as it should, he'll train his hundredth career winner. For a man with no background in the sport, with no previous exposure to caring for horses and no experienced mentor, it's a sensational achievement (albeit not without precedent – Terry Mills is another recent example of the successful businessman turned successful trainer).

Wood puts his success down to "dedication, good staff and treating the horses as individuals," but, whatever the case, punters need to sit up and pay attention because this is a good yard to follow. As you'll see from our stats tables on the facing page, the unbelievable truth is that you could have made a profit backing every one of Wood's runners since he started training. The strike-rate has not been high but the winners have

Sponsored by Stan James

> *"They made a slow start in 2002. I don't know why – we had a winner in January and then we couldn't seem to do anything right until April. We have a much bigger team, of course, so I would expect to see more consistency this year"*

returned at healthy SPs, which must be at least partly due to the fact that, for most punters, his name is not familiar – not yet.

Asked if there's any area in which he has particular skill, he says he thinks he's been good at placing horses, and that he does well preparing two-year-olds. It's true - his strike-rate is indeed higher with juveniles than with older horses.

But his ambition isn't selective. "I want to train as many winners as possible," he says. "Everybody likes to have runners at the Grade A tracks but it doesn't bother me particularly where we go. We'll go up north if we need to, if that's what the horse needs."

"I've set a target of 40 winners this year and we should achieve it." Indeed they should – the target last year was 30 and they ended with 38, having started the season with about 30 horses in the yard. This time, there are over twice as many; the yard is almost at capacity and Wood is happy to contemplate the possibility of expansion.

For that reason, you can back his runners throughout the year, despite the fact that they made a slow start in 2002. "I don't know why that was. We had a winner in January and then we couldn't seem to do anything right until April. We have a much bigger team, of course, so I would expect to see more consistency this year."

As we go to press in February, there have already been five winners in 2003 and Wood is aiming for ten by the time of the Lincoln meeting.

His determination to give every runner the best chance it can have has so far led him away from using the celebrated stars of the weighing room.

"We had some success with Paul Doe last year, when we needed a lightweight jockey with plenty of strength. Ryan Moore also rode for us a lot – he appealed because he was a jockey who could claim a few pounds off a horse's back and yet still had the skill to ride well against veteran jockeys."

"This season, we have 19-year-old David Nolan riding for us as an apprentice and he's riding particularly well. He's a jockey who's got into problems with the stewards for his use of the stick in the past but I would say that that's not indicative of him, he's a pleasant young man who just needs to be managed and directed, and his agent and I are hoping to do that for him. He's got loads of potential."

Though he enjoyed a punt in his spectating days, Wood is a stranger to bookmakers now that he's a participant and says he wouldn't know what a betting exchange website would look like. *Outlook* readers, however, can expect to do well from backing the following horses, profiled for us by the trainer himself.

	Age	Ran	1st	2nd	3rd	Unpl	Win %	+/- to £1 stake
				Non-handicaps				
	2	97	11	11	6	69	11	-25.51
	3	64	4	5	4	51	6	+14.00
	4+	102	10	12	15	64	10	+15.25
				Handicaps				
	2	45	5	1	4	35	11	+49.00
	3	159	13	17	12	116	8	+27.25
	4+	299	33	23	24	217	11	+12.25
	Totals	766	76	69	65	552	10	+92.24

	Win	run	%	£1
Jan	7	72	10	-15.50
Feb	1	28	4	-25.25
Mar	0	23	0	-23.00
Apr	1	37	3	-33.00
May	5	56	9	+32.00
Jun	8	81	10	+17.00
Jul	16	96	17	+53.13
Aug	9	92	10	+9.00
Sep	12	78	15	+82.50
Oct	5	72	7	-29.75
Nov	5	68	7	-9.50
Dec	7	63	11	+34.63

Sponsored by Stan James

Wood's Winners

Three-year-olds

Bluegrass Beau
3yo chestnut colt
Bluegrass Prince – Blushing Belle (Local Suitor)
A nice three-year-old in the making, having won one of his ten starts at two, a 7f maiden auction race at Warwick, but I think he was unlucky at Brighton when he was beaten a short-head by Lady McNair, who won the next three. It was good to soft going that day and he could have done with it being good. He's wintered well and strengthened up, he looks magnificent. He'll start in handicaps over 1m and we'll assess him as we go but I would be looking to step him up in trip through the season.

Clann A Cougar
3yo chestnut gelding
Bahamian Bounty – Move Darling (Rock City)
Also had ten outings as a juvenile and won a maiden auction over 6f at Chepstow. He was last seen getting beaten just three lengths in a huge field for the £100,000 auction race at Newmarket in October. Willie Supple rode him for the first time that day and told me he'd make a real nice three-year-old. Right enough, he's going well on the gallops and you'll be seeing him running over 1m to 1m2f this year.

New Foundation
3yo bay filly
College Chapel – Island Desert (Green Desert)
She's just joined us, having had 10 runs for Richard Hannon last season. She won a 5f maiden at Warwick and kept good company after that, mostly running in Listed races, and she wasn't beaten far in the Group 2 Flying Childers. She'll be useful providing she's trained on, and she's showing us all the signs that she *has* trained on, though we haven't asked her any serious questions on the gallops yet.

Polka Princess
3yo bay filly
Makbul – Liberatrice (Assert)
We got her after she had won a couple of sellers for Dennis Coakley last summer and we won a couple of nurseries with her in August and September. She's a little pony but she's a battler, she's all heart and I'd like to think she could win some nice races as a three-year-old.

Riva Royale
3yo bay filly
Royal Applause – Regatta (Mtoto)
She's not long back from her winter break and I like the look of her a lot now. She won a 5f Yarmouth maiden from her five runs as a two-year-old and she's got tremendous natural speed. She'll be running over 5f and 6f and we might go abroad with her to win a little Listed race somewhere like Italy.

Special Ellie
3yo bay filly
by Celtic Swing – Recherchee
She's come to us unraced from Mick Channon. She's big and heavy-topped and it looks like she was always going to make a three-year-old. I like her a lot.

Older Horses

Jonny Ebeneezer
4yo bay gelding
Hurricane Sky – Leap Of Faith (Northiam)
A lovely horse, not far short of Listed class so far and there's a lot of improvement to come from him. We got a win out of him at two and then he landed three handicaps for us last season but he still had to fill out into his frame and I'd say even now he has a little way to go. He's versatile, too, having won from 5f to 7f in the soft and I hope he's going to be a star for us.

Most-Saucy
7yo brown mare
Most Welcome – So Saucy (Teenoso)
A favourite with many people, she was the one that got all the visitors during our Open Day last year and she took it all in her stride. She's been with us for some time now, winning four on the All-Weather as well as a handicap at Windsor last July. She's so game and consistent, she always runs her race and I could do with a yard full of horses like her. If she was a human, she'd be a fitness fanatic – if we only give her a single canter some morning, she lets us

Sponsored by Stan James

know she wants to do more, she'll be bucking and kicking. I'd hope she's got another couple of years racing but she's got the temperament to be a broodmare so it's quite possible she'll be retired for breeding at some point.

Pay The Silver
5yo grey gelding
Petong – Marjorie's Memory (Fairy King)
Joined us from Alan Jarvis at the start of the last turf season and did us proud, winning handicaps at Goodwood and Epsom. Strange as it may seem, it looks as if he's grown through the winter and he's looking the part, so I think we can even hope for some improvement. We were just starting to get the key to him last year.

Look First
5yo bay gelding
Namaqualand – Be Prepared (Be My Guest)
Another who joined us from Alan Jarvis last spring, he's progressing and I think he's going to be a seriously good horse. He's not the biggest but he can quicken off a fast pace and I'm thinking of aiming him at the Cesarewitch. I'll give him a little break at some point if that's to be the plan.

Debbie
4yo bay filly
Deploy – Elita (Sharpo)
She turned out for the first time at Newbury last October, finishing sixth of 17 and we've just given her a couple of runs on the sand for experience after that. A couple of those behind her at Newbury have won since and she's giving us all the signs that she's ready to win races this season.

Protectorate
4yo chestnut filly
Hector Protector – Possessive Lady (Dara Monarch)
She was second to Gossamer in a Group 3 at two and had a lot of potential but never really fulfilled it. She'll be covered and then she'll be back for a spring campaign.

Thesaurus
4yo grey gelding
Most Welcome – Red Embers (Saddlers' Hall)
Won a handicap at Goodwood before having a little setback last summer. He's not run since July but he's over it and back in work now. He's similar to Most-Saucy, Swynford Welcome and many others by Most Welcome in that he's game and hard, he's determined.

White Ledger
4yo chestnut gelding
Ali-Royal – Boranwood (Exhibitioner)
We've bought him out of Terry Mills's yard and he's shaping up real nice. He showed consistent form in handicaps last year and we like him a lot.

Telori
5yo chestnut mare
Muhtarram – Elita (Sharpo)
She won five times for us from June to December last year. She's tremendously game and always runs her heart out.

Eastborough
4yo bay gelding
Woodborough – Easter Girl (Efisio)
Won a handicap at 1m2f Warwick last season and is a lovely sort. You can expect a good season from him.

Two-year-olds

We have 31 for this season, a mixed bag as you'd expect. They're shaping up nicely, as I suspect any trainer would tell you, but they're unknown quantities at this time of year. The ones I like in particular are a Dracula colt, a Woodborough filly and a Cloudings filly that is particularly nice.

Look First: is he one for the Cesarewitch?
Sponsored by Stan James

Profiles by Chris Cook

Outlook

News Diary 2002

January

1 It's never too early to dream about the Derby – Kieren Fallon says the Queen's Right Approach is possibly the best colt he has ridden and a live contender for Epsom. Regarding his own hopes of retaining his champion jockey's title, he says: "I feel fresher and better than I have ever been and think I am riding as well as I have ever done."

2 Having just had a hectic year, Kevin Darley gives up the chance of a lucrative three-month contract to ride in Hong Kong. "I think I owe it to myself and my family just to spend a bit of time with them," he says.

Entries for the 2003 Derby are announced; they total 573, of which the Maktoum family have 136 and Coolmore 64.

5 For the second time in a week, weather conditions render Wolverhampton's 'All-Weather' track unraceable. Their 10-race card is switched to Southwell.

8 Dispol Evita edges across Battle Line in the final furlong at Lingfield. No riding offence was involved and Battle Line had looked unlikely to win anyway, so Dispol Evita is 1-12 in the ring to keep the race – but the stewards throw her out! Her trainer Andrew Reid describes the decision as madness and launches an appeal.

9 In Hong Kong, the equivalent of almost £11million is donated to charity by the local Jockey Club after an unknown punter fails to collect his spectacular Triple Trio win within the 60-day time limit.

Peter Savill is to continue as BHB Chairman until June 2004 to oversee negotiations for the sport's future funding.

10 Joe Naughton, trainer of multiple Group-winning sprinter Hever Golf Rose, retires due to "a combination of problems."

11 The decision of the Lingfield stewards to disqualify Dispol Evita three days before is overturned on appeal to the Jockey Club, leading to calls for a centralised system of stewarding. It's too late, though, for pro punter Chris Broom, who would have won a Jackpot pool of over £40,000 had she not been kicked out in the first place. No action is to be taken against the stewards.

13 Dubai Millennium's first foal is born in Kentucky. He is a chestnut colt out of Night Shift mare Zelanda.

15 German champion jockey Andrasch Starke receives a worldwide six-month riding ban from the Hong Kong stewards following a positive test for cocaine.

16 The International Classifications say Johannesburg was, in 2001, the best two-year-old since Xaar in 1997 and the best miler of any age in Europe. He is Aidan O'Brien's third successive champion juvenile. Sakhee is named top older horse, 4lb ahead of Fantastic Light.

The Hawk Wing hype starts here, when the Irish Turf Club's chief handicapper names the horse as having the potential to be the best horse at Ballydoyle since the days of Vincent O'Brien.

Unfuwain dies of a neurological condition, aged 17. Having run second in the King George and fourth in the Arc, he had sired Classic-winning fillies Petrushka, Lahan and Lailani.

Sponsored by Stan James

17 Bookmakers announce that, since betting tax was abolished 3 months before, turnover has increased by up to 48%. Tragically, it seems this has been accompanied by drastically reduced profit margins.

22 The cost to racing of the 2001 foot and mouth epidemic is assessed by the industry at £12.1 million.

29 Johannesburg is revealed to have topped the American equivalent of our Free Handicap.

30 Apprentice David Nolan gets a 13-day ban under the Jockey Club's totting-up procedure, having accumulated a total of 17 days in bans for whip offences over the previous year.

February

4 Arena Leisure is to seek more fixtures for Lingfield, where the new polytrack surface, first used in November 2001, is generally reckoned to have been a success.

7 Following allegations of neglect, five horses are removed from the Newmarket yard of Kamil Mahdi, who had been refused renewal of his licence to train a year before.

12 Ex-SAS officer Jeremy Phipps starts work as the Jockey Club's head of security. It seems he can take the job in his stride – "There really isn't an awful lot of crime out there," he opines.

At Preston Crown Court, Lee Ryder is jailed for two and a half years for his part in a betting scam. Victims were lured into sending money to various addresses with the promise that professional punters would invest their money in a "guaranteed" no-risk venture.

14 Planning permission is cleared for a proposed new racecourse at Great Leighs, Essex. Those behind the project, which will now be presented to the BHB, hope to stage All-Weather racing twice a week from mid-morning, but will also ask for six turf fixtures per year. However, BHB approval is not expected this year.

15 Jason Weaver retires from the saddle, having just turned 30. He rode more than 1,000 winners over 14 years, including a double-century when second in the 1994 jockeys' championship, but had battled with his weight and suffered a declining number of rides in recent years.

18 At America's Eclipse Awards, Johannesburg is named champion juvenile of 2001, while Banks Hill and Fantastic Light are honoured as the best of the year on turf.

20 For the second time in a week, the starting stalls fail at Lingfield. A flip start is used for a 16-runner 7f race. Two horses whip round and take no part but ugly scenes are avoided when 8-13 favourite Lakota Brave wins anyway.

24 Sakhee makes his seasonal debut, beating Atlantis Prince nine lengths over 1m2f at Nad Al Sheba.

26 The Jockey Club starts a new policy of random drug tests on training stables. Five jumps yards are first to be raided.

March

7 In America, The Thoroughbred Corporation pay $1.9million for Atlantic Ocean, setting a new record for a juvenile filly sold at auction. Though described by the purchasing agent as "kind of ugly", she becomes a multiple stakes winner and, as we go to press, is still racing.

11 Brett Doyle has lost his retainer with Brian Meehan after a year in the job. Meehan will not retain a jockey for the coming season but plans to use Pat Eddery whenever possible.

12 Returning from a fortnight off with a neck injury, Kieren Fallon is plainly untroubled when winning at Southwell on his first ride back.

16 Adiemus beats I Cried For You in

Lingfield's Winter Derby. He's 5-2 favourite to win the following week's Lincoln, but 11 horses need to come out before he'll get a run.

20 In a prep for his Kentucky Derby bid, Johannesburg is exercised around Lingfield's polytrack. He is joined in a 1m canter by others from Aidan O'Brien's yard, including Rock Of Gibraltar and Hawk Wing.

21 On the opening day of the turf season at Doncaster, Bill Turner wins his second Brocklesby with 13-2 shot The Lord.

23 David Arbuthnot's 33-1 shot Zucchero saves the bookies' bacon by beating ante-post plunge Adiemus a head for the Lincoln. The pair are drawn 7 and 6 in the 23-runner field.

24 Street Cry wins the Dubai World Cup. Sakhee, backed down to 2-5 in Britain, is beaten over eight lengths in third but Godolphin are unable to explain his poor showing.

Nayef wins the Dubai Sheema Classic, with Boreal and Marienbard among those that finish close behind.

April

2 Naheef wins Godolphin's trial of their best three-year-old colts and is now as short as 5-1 for the 2,000 Guineas. The much-vaunted Hawk Wing is favourite at a best price of 7-4 and it's 14-1 bar two.

7 Johannesburg is beaten at 1-3 on his seasonal debut in the Curragh's Gladness Stakes, a race which 17 of the last 18 favourites have now lost. Rebelline finishes fast and late to score at 8-1.

8 Newmarket announce they will take measures costing £3.5million to rectify their new Millennium Grandstand, which has been the subject of much criticism in the two years since it opened.

14 High Chaparral is an easy winner of Leopardstown's Listed Ballysax Stakes. The Tote cut him from 10-1 into 5-1 for the Derby, though Corals and Ladbrokes still go 8-1. Hype horse Hawk Wing heads the market at a general 5-1.

18 King Of Happiness wins Newmarket's Craven Stakes from Della Francesca and is now as short as 3-1 for the 2,000 Guineas.

At the same meeting, Mick Kinane is handed a seven-day ban for irresponsible riding that will prevent him from partnering Johannesburg in the Kentucky Derby.

21 Queen's Logic hardens into a best price of 9-4 for the 1,000 Guineas after a convincing win over Roundtree in Newbury's Fred Darling Stakes.

Redback wins the Greenham but the race is not thought to have been much of a Guineas trial and he remains on 33-1 with Hills for the first colts' Classic.

22 Ascot's management team reveal the course made a record pre-tax profit of £10.9million in 2001.

24 News breaks that the BBC's Panorama may investigate corruption in British racing. The Jockey Club writes to all racecourses with instructions that no documentary crew should be allowed to film on their premises without permission from Portman Square. Clearly, the sport has nothing to hide and no reason to fear.

30 Michael Roberts, champion jockey of 1992 and best known as the rider of dual Eclipse hero Mtoto, is forced to retire from the saddle as the result of a neck injury he sustained in a fall at Wolverhampton the previous September. He ends his career just 36 winners short of 4,000.

May

1 Attheraces, racing's newest television channel, goes live for the first time.

3 Having landed the Jockey Club Stakes by a neck from Millenary, Marienbard is to be aimed at the Yorkshire Cup, a race he won in 2001.

4 The 2,000 Guineas turns out to be a draw race. In a field of 22, the 9-1 Rock Of Gibraltar wins from stall 22, with Zipping (drawn 21) fourth at 40-1 and Twilight Blues (19) fifth at 50-1. The much-vaunted Hawk Wing (10), all on his own on the stands' side, is the only horse drawn outside the top seven boxes to make the first five. Punters who did their money on the 6-4 favourite share the sentiments of his jockey Jamie Spencer, caught on TV mouthing expletives to himself as he returned to unsaddle.

Johannesburg trails in eighth of 18 in the Kentucky Derby. Connections report that he may have got some dirt in his throat.

5 Godolphin and Frankie Dettori combine to land the 1,000 Guineas with the German-bred Kazzia, who returns at 14-1 in spite of her high-profile connections. The 11-8 favourite Gossamer does well to be eighth, considering she doesn't act on the good to firm going.

10 Concern is shown before the start of a race at Carlisle when jockey Paul Fessey appears unwell – trainer John Norton describes him as "incoherent". Fessey falls off Red River Rebel in the paddock and appears unsteady riding down to the start but the course doctor passes him fit to ride. Moments after the race starts, Fessey falls off again and is trampled. He is taken to hospital with back and neck injuries and will not ride for another two months.

12 High Chaparral fails to impress all observers in winning his final Derby prep at Leopardstown. The Tote push him out to 11-4 from 5-2 for the Epsom race.

15 At York's Dante meeting, Kieren Fallon claims he was verbally abused by a camera crew after riding in the Queen's colours. He is escorted around the course by security guards for the rest of the day.

17 Newbury's Listed Oaks trial is won by Monturani, with Protectress second. The finish is eerily similar to that of the same race six years before, in which Monturani's dam Mezzogiorno beat Quota, dam of Protectress.

18 Kentucky Derby winner War Emblem wins the Preakness, second leg of the American Triple Crown.

21 Trainer David Wintle tells the *Racing Post* that undercover BBC reporters bought and raced a horse with him three times. According to Wintle, they then confronted him with a camera at Stratford racecourse and accused him of race-fixing. Of course, the sport has nothing to hide, which is why the camera crew were escorted from the course immediately afterwards.

22 Dick Hern dies, aged 81. Four times champion trainer, he won every British Classic at least twice and built the careers of champion equines Brigadier Gerard, Troy, Nashwan and Dayjur during a training career of almost 40 years.

June

2 Pascal Bary wins his fourth French Derby in nine years when Sulamani (199-10 on the French PMU) beats the odds-on Act One.

5 Frankie Dettori is just one of many getting a bit carried away in the lead up to Saturday's Derby. He describes Naheef as "my best chance yet" of winning the race.

7 Kazzia (100-30f) adds the Oaks to her 1,000 Guineas triumph. After persistent rain, it's so soft that the field tacks over to the stands side up the straight. Kazzia grabs the fastest strip under the rail and holds off Aidan O'Brien's Quarter Moon (15-2) by a diminishing half-length.

It's a Group 1 double for German-breds after Peter Schiergen's Boreal beats Storming Home in the Coronation Cup.

9 A year after his first Derby win, 32-year-old Aidan O'Brien trains the first two home in the big race – but, for punters, they finish in the wrong order. The much-vaunted Hawk Wing (9-4f) cruises up to challenge High Chaparral (7-2) two furlongs out but falters and falls back into a two-length second, 12 lengths ahead of the third.

It's O'Brien's fifth British Classic out of the last seven, the other two having been won by Godolphin.

Appalled racegoers see Coshocton break his leg in front of the stands. He is put down on the racecourse – the cause of the injury is not established.

Bidding for the first American Triple Crown since 1978, War Emblem stumbles at the start and trails in eighth of 11 in the Belmont Stakes. The race is won by Sarava, who had run 13th of 14 in a Doncaster maiden the previous September, when trained by Brian Meehan.

11 The BBC screen an edition of cavalier investigative show Kenyon Confronts concerned with alleged corruption in horseracing. Three trainers are shown making various unguarded comments after prompting from undercover reporters. The producer seems naive, saying in the following day's *Racing Post* that "sport should not be about cheating," but Jockey Club PR man John Maxse sounds complacent when, in the same edition, he denies that punters are being deceived in any way.

18 On the opening day of Royal Ascot, Rock Of Gibraltar wins the St James's Palace Stakes, his fifth successive Group 1 triumph.

20 Royal Rebel (16-1) wins a second consecutive Ascot Gold Cup, but the moment is marred for jockey Johnny Murtagh when he gets a four-day ban for his use of the whip, ruling him out of the Irish Derby. Having suffered exactly the same fate on the same horse the previous year, he tells trainer Mark Johnston: "Don't ring me next year for him."

27 Ascot unveil plans for a £180million revamp aimed at creating the finest racecourse in the world, as befits the home of the Wokingham. But rather than cherishing his competitive handicaps, Lord Hartington (the Queen's rep at the track) says it would put Ascot in pole position for when the Breeders' Cup is held in Europe. Has anyone told the Americans about this?

31 High Chaparral (1-3f) wows the Curragh and becomes the 15th horse to complete the English-Irish Derby double. He leads home a 1-2-3 for Aidan O'Brien, the first time any trainer has so dominated the race.

July

6 Amazing scenes at Sandown as Hawk Wing wins a race. In perhaps the weakest Eclipse ever run, he beats stablemate and pacemaker Sholokhov, plus three also-rans. Afterwards, connections promised that his best was yet to come . . .

7 A spokesman for Victor Chandler claims that, until two years before, it had been common practice within the bookmaking industry to offer "free bets and similar arrangements" to trainers. The *Racing Post* quote him as saying: "The sport's betting industry relies heavily on information . . . this information helps us minimise our commercial risks." All other bookmakers strenuously deny that they have ever been involved in such practices.

9 Jockey Tony Culhane spectacularly throws away a race he should have won at Pontefract. Well clear at the furlong pole on 8-13 favourite True Courage, he drops his hands, pats the horse on the neck and eases him down. Only too late does he see that Ted Durcan is closing on Kahalah (4-1) and, though he tries to get True Courage going again, he is passed and beaten a length. "I messed up in a major way," he concedes, though neither this, nor the 21-day ban he gets, can mollify punters who lost an accumulated £25,000 on the horse.

10 Almost three months after her final outing, Queen's Logic is retired. A succession of ailments had ruled her out of various high-profile races at which she had been aimed.

11 Two past winners of the Ayr Gold Cup, Continent (12-1) and Bahamian Pirate (16-1), give trainer Dandy Nicholls a 1-2 in Newmarket's July Cup. Continent is the first gelding to win the Group 1 race for over 60 years.

Red-faced John Akehurst forgets to put the weight cloth on his charge Capricho before the Bunbury Cup. Running 9lb light, the horse dead-heats for first place but is, of course, disqualified.

12 Supposedly mistaking a tall spectator for the winning post, jockey J D Smith stops riding 50 yards before the line at Beverley. His horse is beaten just a short-head.

Bizarrely, the local stewards don't even hold an inquiry.

19 Nashwan dies after complications arise from surgery to a hind leg. A champion three-year-old (when he won the 2,000 Guineas, the Derby, the Eclipse and the King George), he went on to sire dual King George winner Swain.

27 Golan (11-2) pips Nayef (7-1) in Ascot's King George VI & Queen Elizabeth Diamond Stakes. The race comes just five days after the death of Lord Weinstock, owner-breeder of Golan. It was a training triumph for Sir Michael Stoute, this being the first time in 52 runnings that the race had been won by a horse making its seasonal debut.

31 The office of Deputy Prime Minister John Prescott rejects an appeal for planning permission for a new racecourse at Fairlop Waters. It had been hoped that the proposed site, 15 miles east of central London, could offer international-calibre All-Weather racing.

August

1 Johannesburg, unbeaten at two, is retired to stud in America after losing all three of his starts at three. Aidan O'Brien admits it had been a mistake to run the horse in May's Kentucky Derby, which, he says, "bottomed him out."

2 Coral, who run the UK's third-largest chain of betting shops, are bought for £860m by venture capitalists.

4 William Hill executive chairman John Brown accuses the government of a "dereliction of duty" in failing to regulate internet betting exchanges.

7 Rock Of Gibraltar is on Aidan O'Brien's sicklist, having started to cough. The brilliant miler will miss York's Ebor meeting.

9 The Malaysian Racing Association finds London-born jockey Gary Carter guilty of failing to obtain the best possible placing in a race in Singapore. He receives the minimum sentence they can mete out for the offence – a 12-month worldwide riding ban. On appeal, this is drastically reduced to 12 racing days.

10 For the first time, there is clear evidence of jockeys collaborating with each other at Ascot's Shergar Cup, in which the riders are split into two teams – Great Britain & Ireland v the Rest Of The World. Trainers afterwards complain that jockeys ignored their instructions and rode to give their team-mates the best chance, while punters are also in uproar. The Jockey Club condemns the use of team tactics and warns they will not be allowed the following year.

On his first run since March, reigning European champion Sakhee (1-5) is sensationally beaten by Wellbeing at Deauville.

12 Aidan O'Brien puts plans on hold for his entire string after discovering that coughing has spread to his two-year-olds. Although two of his juveniles finished first and second in the Pheonix Stakes the day before, one of his other runners, 11-10 favourite Hold That Tiger, finished last in a state of "respiratory distress."

17 After her stall opens fractionally before those of her rivals, Impressive Flight wins Newmarket's feature handicap by a neck. Amazingly, the stewards take no action, on the grounds that "no horse suffered a disadvantage."

19 Sunday Silence dies at the age of 16. Sold for $17,000 as a yearling, he won the Kentucky Derby and Breeders' Cup Classic in 1989 before becoming easily the most influential sire ever to stand in Japan, his progeny having won over $323million by the time of his death.

20 Nayef turns round the King George form, pipping Golan for the Juddmonte International at the start of York's Ebor meeting, while Bandari, Highest and Bollin Eric fight out a thrilling finish to the Great Voltigeur.

21 Hugs Dancer wins the Ebor to add to trainer James Given's growing reputation. Topweight Sarangani is put down after dislocating a joint.

Islington is an easy winner of the Yorkshire Oaks, the third Group 1 to be won by Lord Weinstock's colours since the owner-breeder's death in July, Islington having also won Goodwood's Nassau Stakes earlier in the month.

22 Kyllachy wins York's Nunthorpe under a tactically daring ride from Jamie Spencer. Starting from stall 15 of 17, he switches the horse across the entire track but gets up to beat Malhub, who runs straight from stall 16.

Russian Rhythm is cut to 5-2 (Tote) for the 1,000 Guineas after overcoming serious trouble in running to land the Lowther.

24 Terry Mills is fiercely critical of Richard Hughes after Goodwood's Celebration Mile, in which the Hughes-ridden Tillerman won by a neck, with the Mills-trained Where Or When a close fourth. Hughes had Where Or When boxed in around the furlong pole – when his rival pulled wide for racing room, he closed rapidly but couldn't get up in time.

After a stewards' inquiry, the placings remain unaltered.

25 Jockey Jimmy Mansell (19) suffers serious head injuries in a fall at Ballinrobe. His recuperative period will last many months and it is not known how complete the recovery will be.

Having been reluctant to enter the stalls and slowly away, Elusive City wins the Group 1 Prix Morny, earning quotes from 14-1 to 20s for the 2,000 Guineas.

29 British horseracing's share of the off-course betting market is at an all-time low of 59% according to Ladbrokes.

30 Richard Hughes loses an appeal against five-day riding ban, effectively ending his hopes of catching Kieren Fallon (nine winners ahead) in the race for the jockey's championship.

September

1 Marienbard elbows his way into the Arc picture by winning the Grosser Preis Von Baden ...

3 ... but, in a reversal of this good fortune for Godolphin, their Dubai World Cup winner Street Cry has to be retired after persistent ankle problems.

5 Kieren Fallon, 13 wins clear at the head of the jockeys' table, gets a 13-day suspension under the Jockey Club's totting-up guidelines. He remains odds-on to finish the season as champion, as short as 1-3 with Victor Chandlers.

7 For the second year running, Godolphin beats Ballydoyle in a thrilling finish to the Irish Champion Stakes at Leopardstown. Grandera (5-2) just gets up in a photo from the much-vaunted Hawk Wing (8-11f).

8 Rock Of Gibraltar beats Banks Hill and Gossamer to land the Prix Du Moulin at Longchamp. It's his seventh consecutive Group 1 triumph, breaking Mill Reef's record of six.

In Australia, Zafonic dies after a freak accident while galloping in his field. A brilliant 2,000 Guineas winner, he had been champion first-season sire just four years before.

Sponsored by Stan James

10 Kazzia is ruled out of a Triple Crown bid when it becomes clear she won't recover from a foot abscess before the St Leger.

14 Bollin Eric (7-1) is the first Yorkshire-based winner of the St Leger for 29 years. Trainer Tim Easterby tells reporters: "This feels like history."

In Ireland, Vinnie Roe (4-7f) wins a second consecutive Irish Leger.

16 Lee Newman, champion apprentice in 2000, is forced to quit the saddle at age 20 because of the increasing difficulties in keeping his weight down. His natural weight, he says, appears to be 10st.

21 It's an unbelievable hat-trick of wins in the Ayr Gold Cup for Dandy Nicholls, as Funfair Wane (16-1) beats 33-1 shots The Tatling and Abbajabba. Capricho, 15-2 jolly, finishes a close seventh. No runner from a single-figure draw makes the first nine in the 28-horse field.

28 Humiliation for the much-vaunted Hawk Wing (1-2f), as he is left eating the dust of Where Or When (7-1) in Ascot's QEII Stakes. An ebullient Terry Mills, winning his first Group 1 as a trainer, says "I can die a happy man now. I haven't slept for the last three nights."

But nothing can stop Aidan O'Brien and the Ballydoyle team in Canada, where Ballingarry wins the Canadian International at Woodbine. Mark Johnston's Yavana's Pace is third.

October

5 One of the gambles of the season goes badly astray when Zonergem (4-1f) finishes 13th of 30 in the Cambridgeshire. Bookies had been facing a seven-figure payout if the horse won but tragically it seems they will now be allowed to keep the money.

The race goes to Beauchamp Pilot (9-1). Runner-up Far Lane (12-1), running from stall two, is the only horse from a draw of less than 22 to make the first eight in the 30-runner event.

6 Back-to-back Arcs for Godolphin, as Marienbard – thought of as a Cup horse in 2001 – wins the Arc at 158-10 on the PMU. The winners of the French and English Derbys, Sulamani (7-2) and High Chaparral (22-10), finish within a length of him.

Panorama's investigation into racing is watched by 3.9 million people, four times as many as saw the Arc earlier in the day. Without proving any particular instances of corruption within the sport, the programme attacks the Jockey Club's ability to regulate it and manages to make the Club's head of security, Jeremy Phipps, look very silly.

9 Phipps resigns, describing himself as "the Jockey Club fall guy." Having been in the job for fully eight months, he was plainly responsible for any lapses in integrity the sport may have suffered, so no further response from the Club will be necessary.

10 The Jockey Club is described as "institutionally incompetent" by Rhydian Morgan-Jones, a BHB director and advisor to leading international owner Prince Khalid Abdullah. He calls for the Club's integrity responsibilities to be transferred to an "independent judiciary."

11 Mark Johnston begins his weekly *Racing Post* column with the words: "The Jockey Club must go."

14 Godolphin give up trying to restore Sakhee to his best and announce the retirement of the 2001 Arc winner. Hours later, they confirm that they have bought the French Derby winner of 2002, Sulamani, from the Niarchos family for an undisclosed sum. A spokesman says: "We're now looking forward to seeing him running in the top international races next year."

17 Godolphin, indulging in a vertiginous turnover of star racehorses this week, retire Marienbard. He will stand at stud in Japan.

19 Tout Seul is a 25-1 upset winner of the Dewhurst, giving Fulke Johnson Houghton his first Group 1 success since 1979. Afterwards, Fulke's daughter gives an avaricious sales pitch to the press: "Any offers are going to have to be serious," she says. "If they want the horse, they're going to have to give me serious money. It's got to be huge, and I'm talking mega-huge."

Martin Pipe trains first and third in the Cesarewitch, Miss Fara (12-1) winning under 19-year-old Ryan Moore. Tees Components (11-2f) can finish only 16th. Remarkably, the draw appears to affect the outcome of the 2m2f race; in a field of 36, the first two are drawn 36 and 35 respectively, while the third runs from stall 29.

25 The Breeders' Cup is staged at Arlington, Chicago, and witnesses an embarrassing end to Rock Of Gibraltar's unbeaten run. Entering the straight in the Mile, Mick Kinane has him positioned one from last and, though the odds-on favourite flies past most of the field, he's got too much to do and goes down by three-quarters of a length to Domedriver (26-1).

It's an appalling way for a champion's career to end. Respected US handicapper Andy Beyer is moved to describe European jockeys as "pinheads", while French trainer Andre Fabre also compares them unfavourably with US jockeys, who, he says, ride with more intelligence.

High Chaparral wins the Turf impressively to salvage something from the evening for Ballydoyle, while Volponi is a 40-1 shock winner in the Classic.

Sponsored by Stan James

November

5 Media Puzzle (11-2) gives Dermot Weld his second Melbourne Cup – Weld remains the only trainer from the northern hemisphere to win Australia's biggest race. Weld also has the fourth home, Vinnie Roe (9-2f), while Godolphin are responsible for third-placed Beekeeper.

It's a very poignant success for jockey Damien Oliver. He had endured the death of his brother Jason, following a racecourse accident, the week before.

9 On the final day of the turf season, Kieren Fallon is crowned champion jockey on 144 winners, 18 ahead of Richard Hughes. "Next year," he says, "I'll concentrate more on trying to get 200 winners again, like I've done three times before."

Mick Kinane is champion jockey in Ireland. He and Johnny Murtagh go into the final day level on 76 winners apiece, but Kinane rides a treble.

20 Five months after the Kenyon Confronts programme about racing was aired, Jockey Club justice roars into action. Trainer Ferdy Murphy, seen in a secretly filmed segment claiming that money had been made through the defeat of one of his horses, is fined £4,000 for bringing the sport into disrepute. It's an exemplary fine that will certainly ensure no trainer is tempted by foul play in future.

24 Frankie Dettori is "the happiest man in the world" after riding Italian raider Falbrav (195-10) to success in the Japan Cup at Nakayama. It is his native country's most important win in world racing since Tony Bin's Arc of 1988.

Golan is beaten less than four lengths in seventh place, running his final race before a stud career.

27 In a 2m race, Eddie Ahern rides a finish after just six furlongs of Lingfield's polytrack. The rest of the field swings out onto another circuit as he pulls up 25-1 shot Cool Bathwick. He offers no excuses and gets a 14-day riding ban.

29 Former jump jockey Graham Bradley is warned off for eight years by the Jockey Club, having been found guilty of a variety of offences, including passing on information in return for reward. He is to pursue an appeal, for which a hearing will not be held until March 2003 at the earliest.

December

12 Jamie Osborne is found guilty of bringing racing into disrepute, having been shown on the Kenyon Confronts programme telling an undercover reporter, whilst a hidden camera rolled, that he would be prepared to "cheat". He is fined £4,000 – the same weak punishment meted out to Ferdy Murphy a fortnight before.

17 The BBC will not show live coverage of the 2003 Dubai World Cup. It seems that England's game with Liechtenstein (football) matters more than the world's richest race.

Quotes of the Year

"When I'm good, I'm brilliant. When I'm bad, I'm crap"
Frankie Dettori

"The sky's the limit for this colt – Sheikh Mohammed might be on the phone tonight"
Peter Easterby, after his son Tim's Bollin Eric had finished second in the Dante

"Godolphin is only ten per cent of where we want to go. We want to go to the peak, then to another peak"
Sheikh Mohammed

"It's nice for me to win this, but there's so many million-dollar races now"
US trainer Bobby Frankel

Mark Johnston

All runners by race type

	Ran	1st	2nd	3rd	Unpl	Win %	£1 level stake
Non-handicaps							
2	782	135	126	103	414	17	-149.90
3	669	123	110	80	355	18	-108.50
4+	379	93	54	57	174	25	+38.17
Handicaps							
2	188	26	23	17	122	14	-35.33
3	990	140	108	85	648	14	-47.70
4+	837	103	105	84	542	12	-48.99
Totals	**3845**	**620**	**526**	**426**	**2255**	**16**	**-352.25**

Monthly breakdown

	Won	Ran	%	£1 Level Stake
Jan	22	126	18	-18.47
Feb	15	107	14	+4.50
Mar	16	96	17	-35.10
Apr	39	226	17	-44.25
May	62	483	13	-84.78
Jun	92	564	16	-42.44
Jul	119	577	21	+82.98
Aug	87	483	18	-59.53
Sep	78	500	16	-27.38
Oct	54	422	13	-42.13
Nov	27	198	14	-72.14
Dec	9	63	14	-13.42

Top dozen jockeys

	Won	Ran	%	£1 Level Stake
J Fanning	132	871	15	-193.60
D Holland	123	651	19	+0.34
K Darley	105	517	20	+8.93
K Dalgleish	87	503	17	+84.77
J Carroll	25	194	13	-76.07
R Ffrench	17	153	11	-63.26
K Fallon	13	43	30	+6.68
R Hills	13	74	18	+16.45
M Hills	11	85	13	-2.63
D McKeown	9	87	10	-30.09
M Roberts	8	65	12	-27.00
R Fitzpatrick	8	68	12	-9.87

IF THEY decided the trainers' championship by number of winners trained in a season, this man would be wearing the crown. This season, he's going for a new British record, his tenth consecutive season with 100 winners or more.

Over the last five years, as our stats show, his strongest rate of return has been with older horses outside of handicaps — remarkably, despite the yard's solid reputation, you can still make money backing such runners blindly.

Johnston's penchant for winning at Goodwood is well known but the profit he's generated there for his followers is still impressive, representing a 33% profit on turnover. Surprisingly, his record at Ascot is even better.

His runners seem to peak in July, between Royal Ascot and Glorious Goodwood, and he gets good use out of Keith Dalgleish.

Favourites

	Won	Ran	%	£1 Level Stake
Non-handicaps				
2	54	135	40	-19.20
3	40	123	33	-43.41
4+	38	107	36	-5.37
Handicaps				
2	9	34	27	-4.91
3	37	135	27	-34.21
4+	28	98	29	-5.57

Sponsored by Stan James

Course records

	W	R	%	Non-handicaps			Handicaps			£1 level stake
				2yo	3yo	4yo+	2yo	3yo	4yo+	
Ascot	37	182	20	9-28	2-25	8-28	1-5	10-44	7-52	+132.62
Wolver	33	207	16	4-31	8-38	7-20	1-9	7-52	6-57	-71.35
Newcastle	31	189	16	11-58	6-43	0-3	1-6	4-44	9-35	-27.03
Doncaster	30	211	14	9-47	7-39	3-24	0-19	9-38	2-44	-26.14
Hamilton	28	150	19	9-55	7-25	0-1	2-8	5-38	5-23	-36.11
Southwell	28	176	16	1-17	7-24	5-12	1-11	10-57	4-55	+2.84
Goodwood	27	143	19	5-20	2-15	5-15	2-7	6-43	7-43	+50.05
Ayr	27	174	16	14-60	7-23	1-2	1-17	1-39	3-33	-39.81
York	27	202	13	5-39	2-14	3-15	3-16	6-47	8-71	-8.17
Musselburgh	26	123	21	6-29	5-16	1-3	1-6	6-33	7-36	-1.78
Redcar	24	127	19	8-47	4-16	1-4	0-4	7-37	4-19	+16.02
Beverley	22	125	18	8-32	2-21	0-3	3-4	5-42	4-23	-10.91
Lingfield AW	22	164	13	1-15	11-40	2-10	2-11	5-47	1-41	-40.27
Ripon	21	133	16	5-30	8-33	2-4	0-0	5-41	1-25	-33.48
Newbury	18	72	25	2-10	4-10	5-11	1-4	2-16	4-21	+45.83
Haydock	18	140	13	2-27	1-20	3-15	0-2	9-46	3-30	-23.39
Pontefract	17	121	14	5-28	2-24	3-7	1-10	6-36	0-16	-23.01
Nmkt Rowley	17	148	12	2-33	2-26	6-19	1-7	4-41	2-32	-19.89
Thirsk	15	87	17	5-17	5-34	0-1	0-1	2-13	3-21	-40.11
Catterick	15	98	15	3-30	6-22	1-4	1-13	3-21	1-8	-47.01
Nmkt July	14	94	15	1-12	2-13	2-12	2-11	4-26	3-20	-1.03
Epsom	12	77	16	5-20	1-7	3-6	0-2	0-17	3-25	-17.80
Leicester	10	66	15	1-12	2-14	4-13	0-3	1-14	2-10	-1.48
Warwick	9	27	33	2-6	1-2	1-3	0-1	4-11	1-4	+12.42
Windsor	8	27	30	0-2	1-4	2-6	1-1	3-10	1-4	+34.83
Carlisle	7	53	13	1-13	2-9	1-3	0-0	2-23	1-5	-2.00
Chester	7	56	13	1-8	2-10	0-3	0-3	2-12	2-20	-22.56
Sandown	7	61	12	1-8	1-2	1-14	0-0	2-19	2-18	+2.50
Dusseldorf	6	17	35	0-0	2-6	4-11	0-0	0-0	0-0	-9.50
Lingfield	6	32	19	1-9	2-8	0-2	0-0	2-9	1-4	+6.75
Yarmouth	6	43	14	1-10	0-3	1-6	0-5	2-15	2-4	-22.08
Nottingham	5	57	9	3-12	2-10	0-7	0-1	0-20	0-7	-35.08
Chepstow	4	15	27	0-0	1-1	0-2	0-0	3-10	0-2	+0.88
Leopardstown	3	8	38	0-0	1-3	1-4	0-0	0-0	1-1	+4.25
Bath	3	18	17	0-4	1-4	0-0	0-0	1-5	1-5	-6.75
Kempton	3	30	10	2-7	0-5	0-3	0-0	0-6	1-9	-11.83
Ovrevoll	2	5	40	0-0	0-2	2-3	0-0	0-0	0-0	-3.00
Frauenfeld	2	6	33	0-0	0-3	2-3	0-0	0-0	0-0	-4.00
Folkestone	2	6	33	1-1	0-0	0-1	0-0	1-3	0-1	-1.43
Cologne	2	14	14	0-0	1-8	1-6	0-0	0-0	0-0	-0.50
Brighton	2	17	12	0-0	1-6	0-0	1-1	0-6	0-4	-9.50
Longchamp	2	18	11	0-1	0-5	2-12	0-0	0-0	0-0	+8.60

Sponsored by Stan James

Richard Hannon

All runners by race type

	Ran	1st	2nd	3rd	Unpl	Win %	£1 level stake
Non-handicaps							
2	1818	259	250	242	1064	14	-501.60
3	1004	116	140	134	611	12	-285.20
4+	354	46	48	42	218	13	-52.61
Handicaps							
2	425	45	28	35	316	11	-102.00
3	1308	97	116	99	995	7	-494.20
4+	601	43	39	52	467	7	-210.70
Totals	**5510**	**606**	**621**	**604**	**3671**	**11**	**-1646.31**

Monthly breakdown

	Won	Ran	%	£1 Level Stake
Jan	13	94	14	-36.59
Feb	2	42	5	-34.75
Mar	5	84	6	-51.50
Apr	33	358	9	-150.40
May	95	812	12	-216.70
Jun	97	870	11	-183.60
Jul	119	872	14	-202.40
Aug	85	769	11	-248.10
Sep	64	749	9	-304.30
Oct	47	577	8	-179.80
Nov	26	178	15	-37.89
Dec	20	105	19	+0.55

Top dozen jockeys

	Won	Ran	%	£1 Level Stake
D O'Neill	180	1636	11	-482.00
R Hughes	170	1292	13	-299.80
P Dobbs	40	379	11	-112.10
L Newman	36	368	10	-156.20
R Smith	30	283	11	-24.70
Pat Eddery	28	183	15	-38.54
P Fitzsimons	19	194	10	-63.76
J Fortune	11	96	12	-17.77
D Holland	9	54	17	-13.25
J Reid	9	66	14	-9.37
T Sprake	7	20	35	+10.83
K Fallon	7	42	17	-1.63

FOLLOWING RICHARD HANNON is a world of pain for punters. Although he gets plenty of winners, this is so widely appreciated that his horses are generally over-backed to the point where you're bound to lose most of your money backing his runners blindly.

His juvenile favourites have been profitable, however, which is hardly surprising, since they've maintained a strike-rate of about 40%. Even then, the profit generated by those running in non-handicaps is a miniscule percentage of turnover.

He had most runners in June and interestingly this is the time when it becomes least expensive to back his runners.

You wouldn't want to make a practice of backing the Hannon/O'Neill combo – together, they've come up with a net loss approaching 33% of total stakes. Richard Hughes fares better for this yard.

Favourites

	Won	Ran	%	£1 Level Stake
Non-handicaps				
2	117	277	42	+8.62
3	21	105	20	-47.65
4+	12	51	24	-15.76
Handicaps				
2	15	38	40	+14.32
3	16	73	22	-10.88
4+	6	38	16	-20.12

Sponsored by Stan James

Course records

	W	R	%	Non-handicaps			Handicaps			£1 level
				2yo	3yo	4yo+	2yo	3yo	4yo+	stake
Salisbury	53	365	15	24-138	11-67	3-14	0-3	15-113	0-30	-60.59
Windsor	50	394	13	24-162	7-53	2-20	2-22	7-91	8-46	-81.37
Brighton	39	263	15	19-78	7-52	0-11	1-23	9-72	3-27	-40.21
Lingfield AW	39	315	12	10-56	6-62	3-31	5-38	13-76	2-52	-117.70
Goodwood	33	400	8	13-130	7-61	0-18	7-38	4-92	2-61	-207.90
Newbury	33	430	8	15-169	8-80	2-21	1-22	5-83	2-55	-225.60
Kempton	30	286	11	13-97	6-56	3-11	0-6	3-69	5-47	-110.90
Lingfield	27	216	13	18-93	2-37	0-6	5-22	2-47	0-11	-72.92
Nmkt Rowley	27	308	9	10-74	8-63	3-26	1-31	5-89	0-25	-74.82
Leicester	25	167	15	11-57	4-44	1-10	1-13	6-32	2-11	+22.86
Wolves	24	123	20	5-24	3-20	2-10	4-16	4-33	6-20	+18.15
Sandown	23	245	9	12-74	2-21	3-21	1-13	4-83	1-33	-84.54
Ascot	23	252	9	12-101	4-40	3-16	3-11	0-54	1-30	+1.88
Nmkt July	23	298	8	6-89	4-54	4-18	3-32	5-80	1-25	-127.20
Epsom	21	146	14	7-36	7-31	1-13	2-11	3-43	1-12	-17.46
Bath	17	141	12	10-65	5-28	0-3	1-5	1-26	0-14	-54.85
York	14	109	13	4-34	6-13	1-11	0-9	0-21	3-21	+29.88
Chepstow	14	124	11	4-42	3-23	1-3	1-8	5-40	0-8	-33.97
Doncaster	13	187	7	4-59	1-28	4-14	1-39	2-21	1-26	-86.30
Warwick	12	83	15	8-33	3-19	1-6	0-6	0-16	0-3	-35.88
Chester	11	70	16	4-23	1-8	2-6	3-10	0-15	1-8	-7.87
Haydock	10	132	8	5-38	2-33	1-13	0-6	2-36	0-6	-84.88
Curragh	8	27	30	6-15	1-7	1-5	0-0	0-0	0-0	+11.85
Folkestone	7	85	8	1-32	3-23	1-7	0-5	0-10	2-8	-34.75
Nottingham	7	96	7	5-29	0-18	0-5	1-9	1-31	0-4	-35.63
Pontefract	4	36	11	2-10	1-8	0-0	0-8	0-6	1-4	-6.00
Deauville	3	18	17	0-4	1-7	2-7	0-0	0-0	0-0	-2.40
Southwell	3	24	13	0-5	2-5	0-3	0-4	0-2	1-5	-7.25
Yarmouth	3	45	7	1-10	0-10	1-5	1-9	0-8	0-3	-31.92
Newcastle	2	8	25	0-1	0-2	1-1	1-2	0-1	0-1	+4.00
Thirsk	2	11	18	1-2	1-3	0-1	0-0	0-4	0-1	-6.50

Sponsored by Stan James

Mick Channon

All runners by race type

	Ran	1st	2nd	3rd	Unpl	Win %	£1 level stake
Non-handicaps							
2	1324	199	192	162	770	15	-365.00
3	652	76	77	100	394	12	-158.10
4+	179	27	22	16	114	15	+10.75
Handicaps							
2	310	31	37	36	206	10	-64.38
3	732	39	67	58	568	5	-306.10
4+	726	63	66	64	532	9	-178.30
Totals	**3923**	**435**	**461**	**436**	**2584**	**11**	**-1061.13**

Monthly breakdown

	Won	Ran	%	£1 Level Stake
Jan	4	35	11	-18.25
Feb	2	33	6	-24.00
Mar	13	108	12	-19.42
Apr	39	334	12	-135.60
May	60	550	11	-159.50
Jun	64	562	11	-125.00
Jul	73	585	13	-179.90
Aug	65	564	12	-114.20
Sep	61	565	11	-113.40
Oct	34	426	8	-160.50
Nov	14	118	12	+4.25
Dec	6	43	14	-14.75

Top dozen jockeys

	Won	Ran	%	£1 Level Stake
S Drowne	99	906	11	-290.50
T Quinn	61	492	12	-107.60
C Williams	57	445	13	-1.92
C Catlin	27	253	11	-42.34
A Culhane	24	136	18	+7.51
A Mackay	23	271	9	-152.10
D Corby	20	189	11	+4.00
L Dettori	17	76	22	-11.33
T Durcan	8	52	15	-0.81
J Reid	7	56	13	-15.50
P Fessey	6	49	12	-20.77
W Supple	6	52	12	-14.09

IN A similar way to soundalike colleague Richard Hannon, Channon offers little hope of a level stakes return for faithful followers. He has a large, strong team, of course, but that means backers are always looking for a chance to back his horses, so they go off too short.

His strike-rates generally are surprisingly feeble, particularly in handicaps, perhaps reflecting a tendency to run his charges in competitive company.

One unexpected source of profit has been to follow his older horses. When he has a favourite in a handicap aged four or older, his strike-rate hits around 25% and his runners generate a profit of about 20% on turnover. This doesn't work in non-handicaps, though his older horses in general return a profit in such races, suggesting it's worth backing them when they're bigger prices. Why this should be is anyone's guess.

Favourites

	Won	Ran	%	£1 Level Stake
Non-handicaps				
2	84	211	40	+2.98
3	22	79	28	-31.54
4+	7	31	23	-7.25
Handicaps				
2	6	35	17	-13.38
3	3	43	7	-33.27
4+	13	53	25	+9.25

Sponsored by Stan James

Course records

	W	R	%	Non-handicaps 2yo	3yo	4yo+	Handicaps 2yo	3yo	4yo+	£1 level stake
Bath	25	176	14	11-67	4-23	5-12	0-6	2-27	3-41	-12.20
Brighton	22	151	15	11-50	5-27	2-6	2-14	1-25	1-29	-33.68
Newbury	21	234	9	13-92	2-43	0-4	2-23	2-30	2-42	-114.30
Goodwood	20	236	9	7-63	3-22	3-15	1-22	2-51	4-63	-63.13
Hamilton	18	54	33	8-17	4-13	0-1	3-3	1-7	2-13	+19.00
Salisbury	17	204	8	7-86	1-35	0-1	0-3	4-34	5-45	-85.70
Lingfield AW	16	121	13	4-27	2-23	4-14	1-7	1-23	4-27	-24.50
Nottingham	15	117	13	8-38	4-21	0-1	0-10	3-35	0-12	-41.02
Doncaster	14	158	9	3-51	4-19	3-12	1-14	0-25	3-37	-27.50
Haydock	13	78	17	6-22	2-14	0-4	0-5	3-22	2-11	+16.50
Ayr	13	78	17	5-28	3-9	1-2	3-12	0-17	1-10	-16.03
York	13	117	11	8-37	0-13	0-4	1-13	2-21	2-29	+4.00
Kempton	13	142	9	6-45	5-36	0-1	0-3	0-27	2-30	-7.06
Wolves	11	67	16	8-30	1-17	1-6	0-2	0-8	1-4	+2.50
Leicester	11	92	12	2-23	4-22	0-4	1-10	1-24	3-9	-19.92
Sandown	11	130	9	4-35	1-16	0-8	4-14	0-26	2-31	-62.10
Windsor	11	166	7	4-64	1-16	0-4	0-10	3-47	3-25	-53.67
Ascot	11	171	6	5-62	1-26	0-9	0-6	1-24	4-44	-77.75
Newcastle	10	46	22	5-16	4-11	0-0	0-3	0-7	1-9	-1.72
Thirsk	10	54	19	9-18	1-15	0-5	0-1	0-4	0-11	-10.99
Nmkt Rowley	10	161	6	5-47	0-26	1-11	2-20	2-36	0-21	-36.84
Chester	9	58	16	4-22	0-4	0-1	2-7	2-10	1-14	+1.00
Warwick	9	66	14	4-20	2-18	0-3	1-3	1-13	1-9	-9.13
Yarmouth	9	66	14	3-18	3-11	0-0	0-11	0-14	3-12	-7.84
Lingfield	9	116	8	4-44	1-15	2-4	1-18	0-26	1-9	-54.00
Redcar	8	38	21	5-12	0-5	0-1	0-5	0-4	3-11	+0.94
Ripon	8	49	16	2-13	2-9	0-0	0-3	2-15	2-9	+2.95
Folkestone	8	68	12	4-30	2-15	0-0	0-4	2-12	0-7	-30.25
Musselburgh	7	37	19	3-10	1-12	0-0	2-7	0-2	1-6	+3.85
Pontefract	7	66	11	2-15	3-18	0-3	0-8	0-8	2-14	-22.15
Curragh	6	30	20	3-18	0-7	3-5	0-0	0-0	0-0	+3.25
Beverley	6	51	12	3-21	2-5	0-0	0-6	0-13	1-6	-28.59
Southwell	6	63	10	4-22	1-15	0-1	0-2	0-13	1-10	-30.75
Epsom	6	91	7	2-14	0-13	1-4	2-6	1-24	0-30	-35.34
Catterick	5	41	12	3-12	1-1	0-3	0-13	0-5	1-7	-15.50
Chepstow	5	102	5	2-44	1-13	0-0	1-5	1-24	0-16	-68.75
Nmkt July	5	112	5	2-41	0-16	1-4	1-11	1-21	0-19	-62.50
Deauville	4	19	21	2-14	2-4	0-1	0-0	0-0	0-0	+11.20
San Siro	3	8	38	2-5	1-3	0-0	0-0	0-0	0-0	-3.30
Msns-Laffitte	2	6	33	2-4	0-1	0-1	0-0	0-0	0-0	-4.00
Baden Baden	2	7	29	2-4	0-2	0-1	0-0	0-0	0-0	-4.20

Sponsored by Stan James

Sir Michael Stoute

All runners by race type

	Ran	1st	2nd	3rd	Unpl	Win %	£1 level stake
Non-handicaps							
2	533	104	99	73	256	20	-129.10
3	966	228	173	126	436	24	-63.26
4+	222	44	31	33	114	20	-22.55
Handicaps							
2	14	1	0	3	10	7	-9.50
3	412	53	48	61	250	13	-143.90
4+	56	12	7	6	30	21	+25.75
Totals	**2203**	**442**	**358**	**302**	**1096**	**20**	**-342.56**

Monthly breakdown

	Won	Ran	%	£1 Level Stake
Jan		0		
Feb	1	2	50	-1.00
Mar	1	3	33	-2.00
Apr	22	132	17	-16.19
May	76	329	23	+44.82
Jun	84	361	23	-37.03
Jul	61	306	20	-72.69
Aug	86	391	22	-79.95
Sep	60	336	18	-83.56
Oct	46	298	15	-67.22
Nov	4	39	10	-23.53
Dec	1	6	17	-3.70

Top dozen jockeys

	Won	Ran	%	£1 Level Stake
K Fallon	120	568	21	-101.40
F Lynch	71	271	26	-14.53
P Eddery	36	163	22	-42.66
R Hills	26	106	25	-16.60
J Murtagh	22	112	20	+17.58
J Reid	22	156	14	-51.40
G Stevens	20	89	23	-18.80
W Swinburn	18	75	24	+10.78
W Ryan	13	43	30	+6.43
D Holland	12	63	19	+11.00
F Dettori	8	31	26	+0.25
J Fortune	8	40	20	+28.50

DOES SIR MICHAEL train them to peak in May? The stats would certainly suggest that he likes to have his team in good order by about the time of Newmarket's Guineas meeting.

Over the last five years, he's dramatically stepped up his number of entries from April to May, by about a factor of three, and yet his strike-rate has improved by about a third over the same period.

In general, as one would expect, his name is too well-known to generate straight profits, but his older horses still seem to be underestimated in handicaps; even the favourites can be backed blindly.

His association with Fallon will butter no punter's crumpets but surprisingly it seems his runners return a profit when Johnny Murtagh is in the plate, despite the well-known successes enjoyed by the pair in recent years.

Favourites

	Won	Ran	%	£1 Level Stake
Non-handicaps				
2	56	138	41	-24.41
3	118	261	45	-25.28
4+	18	57	32	-5.96
Handicaps				
2	0	1	0	-1.00
3	25	117	21	-29.52
4+	5	20	25	+4.25

Sponsored by Stan James

Course records

	W	R	%	Non-handicaps 2yo	3yo	4yo+	Handicaps 2yo	3yo	4yo+	£1 level stake
Sandown	29	119	25	7-19	13-48	4-20	0-0	3-25	2-6	+28.91
Windsor	28	103	27	0-8	22-71	2-7	0-0	4-17	0-0	+1.74
Ascot	26	158	17	3-26	10-50	6-31	0-0	3-38	4-13	+3.25
York	25	130	19	5-17	13-47	0-12	0-1	6-45	1-8	-30.91
Leicester	23	80	29	14-52	6-16	1-4	0-0	2-8	0-0	+20.06
Goodwood	22	107	21	3-10	12-46	1-9	0-1	5-33	1-8	-12.12
Rowley Mile	22	211	10	6-60	10-104	3-18	0-1	2-24	1-4	-77.75
July Course	20	147	14	9-62	7-41	3-14	0-1	0-25	1-4	-69.14
Haydock	18	73	25	4-11	8-36	2-8	0-1	4-17	0-0	-1.81
Doncaster	17	92	19	8-35	4-35	5-13	0-0	0-8	0-1	+5.61
Newcastle	14	52	27	4-11	7-19	0-3	0-0	3-17	0-2	-4.37
Yarmouth	14	69	20	4-34	8-26	1-1	0-1	1-7	0-0	-23.55
Newbury	13	87	15	2-19	6-38	3-17	0-2	2-11	0-0	-25.67
Kempton	13	89	15	4-32	7-40	0-2	0-0	1-13	1-2	-35.30
Chester	12	51	24	2-7	2-20	3-6	0-0	4-13	1-5	-3.47
Lingfield	11	43	26	5-23	6-19	0-0	0-0	0-1	0-0	-6.95
Pontefract	11	43	26	1-5	9-29	0-0	0-0	1-9	0-0	-0.12
Chepstow	10	28	36	4-8	6-18	0-1	0-0	0-1	0-0	-3.46
Thirsk	10	32	31	0-3	8-25	0-0	0-0	2-4	0-0	+12.57
Warwick	9	23	39	3-7	5-13	0-0	0-1	1-2	0-0	+19.80
Bath	9	37	24	0-0	9-33	0-0	0-0	0-4	0-0	+1.23
Beverley	8	32	25	1-12	6-10	0-0	0-0	1-10	0-0	-7.81
Nottingham	8	44	18	3-17	4-21	0-0	0-0	1-6	0-0	-2.90
Salisbury	8	45	18	2-12	5-24	0-0	0-0	1-9	0-0	-19.73
Ripon	7	42	17	0-2	5-28	0-0	0-0	2-12	0-0	-21.74
Catterick	6	14	43	2-4	4-6	0-0	0-0	0-4	0-0	+3.92
Wolves AW	6	22	27	1-6	3-6	0-0	0-0	2-10	0-0	-5.07
Hamilton	5	8	63	0-1	5-6	0-0	0-0	0-1	0-0	+3.49
Brighton	5	18	28	2-3	2-9	0-0	1-1	0-5	0-0	-4.17
Epsom	5	40	13	0-2	2-16	2-7	0-2	1-12	0-1	-22.88
Musselburgh	4	7	57	1-1	2-4	0-0	0-0	1-2	0-0	+3.75
Curragh	4	20	20	0-0	1-10	3-10	0-0	0-0	0-0	-6.2
Redcar	4	21	19	2-7	2-6	0-0	0-1	0-7	0-0	+1.23
Ayr	4	21	19	1-6	3-7	0-4	0-0	0-4	0-0	-7.25
Longchamp	3	17	18	0-1	2-10	1-6	0-0	0-0	0-0	-6.80
Nad Al Sheba	2	4	50	0-0	0-0	2-4	0-0	0-0	0-0	-2.00
Toulouse	1	1	100	0-0	1-1	0-0	0-0	0-0	0-0	+4.40
Southwell AW	1	3	33	0-0	1-2	0-0	0-0	0-1	0-0	+7.00
Sha Tin	1	4	25	0-0	0-0	1-4	0-0	0-0	0-0	-1.70
Carlisle	1	5	20	0-0	1-2	0-0	0-0	0-3	0-0	-3.09
Churchill D'ns	1	6	17	0-0	0-1	1-3	0-0	0-1	0-1	-0.40
Folkestone	1	12	8	0-2	1-9	0-0	0-0	0-1	0-0	-10.83
Lingfield AW	1	17	6	1-8	0-6	0-0	0-1	0-2	0-0	-14.75

Sponsored by Stan James

John Gosden

All runners by race type

	Ran	1st	2nd	3rd	Unpl	Win %	£1 level stake
Non-handicaps							
2	538	107	78	62	291	20	+.34
3	885	177	130	120	452	20	-101.60
4+	199	41	32	25	101	21	+6.67
Handicaps							
2	34	3	2	5	24	9	-16.00
3	330	37	43	26	221	11	-73.08
4+	142	17	19	19	85	12	-14.15
Totals	2128	382	304	257	1174	18	-197.82

Monthly breakdown

	Won	Ran	%	£1 Level Stake
Jan	0	2	0	-2.00
Feb	1	4	25	-1.50
Mar	1	10	10	-7.50
Apr	31	120	26	+13.98
May	45	298	15	-76.41
Jun	55	328	17	-48.77
Jul	61	278	22	-31.22
Aug	56	310	18	-61.62
Sep	66	364	18	-43.70
Oct	49	318	15	+54.99
Nov	16	83	19	+14.60
Dec	1	13	8	-8.67

Top dozen jockeys

	Won	Ran	%	£1 Level Stake
L Dettori	89	376	24	+17.73
J Fortune	83	427	20	-31.99
G Hind	33	179	18	+52.21
R Hills	32	151	21	+1.73
R Hughes	22	84	26	+23.48
R Havlin	22	164	13	-20.31
K Darley	17	84	20	-6.42
O Peslier	7	40	18	-4.50
J Carroll	7	52	14	-5.28
W Ryan	7	72	10	-45.83
K Fallon	6	23	26	+18.71
R Cochrane	4	22	18	-2.35

DON'T EXPECT John Gosden's runners to come bursting out of the traps and start setting course records in the opening weeks of the season.

Despite that level-stakes profit for April's runners, this is a slow-burning stable. For confirmation, look at the returns you'd have enjoyed by backing all their runners in October and November over the last five years.

This of course would be the time of year when he'd be unleashing his better two-year-olds. His juveniles just scrape into profit in non-handicaps but he doesn't seem the man to be with in the handicaps, producing poor returns in all departments.

By contrast, his older horses in non-handicaps show a nice profit of 17% on turnover and the yard does particularly well at Goodwood, Ascot and on the Rowley Mile (though, curiously, not the July Course).

Favourites

	Won	Ran	%	£1 Level Stake
Non-handicaps				
2	51	113	45	+6.18
3	82	217	38	-35.77
4+	13	49	27	-20.42
Handicaps				
2	1	5	20	-1.00
3	13	66	20	-23.08
4+	7	30	23	-6.15

Sponsored by Stan James

Course records

	W	R	%	Non-handicaps			Handicaps			£1 level
				2yo	3yo	4yo+	2yo	3yo	4yo+	stake
Goodwood	39	175	22	9-38	18-69	2-11	0-5	6-36	4-16	+33.55
Nmkt Rowley	30	173	17	12-61	14-72	1-12	0-2	2-17	1-9	+48.58
Nmkt July	29	160	18	8-55	15-53	3-16	0-1	3-28	0-7	-21.88
Ascot	26	174	15	4-27	12-61	2-19	0-0	3-38	5-29	+37.49
Newbury	25	152	16	7-38	13-70	2-10	0-1	3-22	0-11	-19.15
Doncaster	24	125	19	10-48	8-39	3-8	0-5	2-12	1-13	+1.99
Salisbury	20	81	25	8-28	9-37	1-3	1-1	1-9	0-3	-0.26
Nottingham	15	62	24	4-18	6-25	0-2	0-0	5-14	0-3	+10.40
Yarmouth	15	79	19	6-27	3-31	3-4	0-3	3-12	0-2	-10.31
Haydock	15	93	16	2-11	7-50	2-13	0-0	2-15	2-4	-7.90
Leicester	14	53	26	5-30	6-10	3-5	0-0	0-7	0-1	+2.97
Sandown	14	75	19	4-16	7-33	1-8	0-1	2-14	0-3	-14.76
Windsor	13	67	19	0-2	13-41	0-6	0-0	0-16	0-2	-31.51
Redcar	12	33	36	6-15	4-11	1-1	0-0	1-6	0-0	+25.90
Lingfield AW	10	51	20	3-21	6-18	0-0	0-4	0-7	1-1	+6.00
Kempton	9	53	17	4-20	4-19	0-1	0-0	1-7	0-6	-14.53
Deauville	8	26	31	2-7	3-10	3-9	0-0	0-0	0-0	+7.40
York	7	47	15	2-8	2-19	1-2	0-0	0-8	2-10	-15.75
Longchamp	7	59	12	1-11	3-28	3-20	0-0	0-0	0-0	-11.20
Chester	6	22	27	1-3	1-7	1-3	0-0	3-8	0-1	+11.44
Ayr	6	29	21	2-7	2-9	1-5	1-3	0-5	0-0	-15.05
Brighton	4	18	22	2-5	2-8	0-0	0-1	0-3	0-1	-8.40
Bath	4	49	8	1-6	3-30	0-1	0-2	0-8	0-2	-36.50
Thirsk	3	12	25	0-1	1-7	2-2	0-0	0-1	0-1	-6.87
Newcastle	3	22	14	1-5	1-9	1-2	0-0	0-3	0-3	-1.50
Epsom	3	24	13	0-2	1-9	1-3	0-1	0-4	1-5	-12.40
Chepstow	3	25	12	1-6	2-15	0-1	0-0	0-3	0-0	-16.38
Lingfield	3	26	12	1-5	1-14	0-2	1-2	0-3	0-0	-9.67
Ripon	3	26	12	0-3	3-13	0-2	0-1	0-7	0-0	-21.63
Wolves	2	8	25	0-0	1-4	1-1	0-0	0-2	0-1	-2.23
Msns-Laffitte	2	10	20	0-1	0-6	2-3	0-0	0-0	0-0	-7.60
Saint-Cloud	2	12	17	0-1	1-6	1-5	0-0	0-0	0-0	-7.40
Beverley	2	13	15	1-3	1-2	0-0	0-0	0-5	0-3	-6.00

Sponsored by Stan James

John Dunlop

All runners by race type

	Ran	1st	2nd	3rd	Unpl	Win %	£1 level stake
Non-handicaps							
2	937	150	133	123	530	16	-336.50
3	776	158	132	90	396	20	-41.28
4+	314	64	58	41	150	20	-4.01
Handicaps							
2	99	9	8	13	69	9	-45.25
3	832	133	103	82	507	16	-158.40
4+	208	31	22	23	132	15	-36.76
Totals	**3166**	**545**	**456**	**372**	**1784**	**17**	**-622.20**

Monthly breakdown

	Won	Ran	%	£1 Level Stake
Jan		0		
Feb		0		
Mar	10	41	24	-1.21
Apr	59	279	21	-5.91
May	78	428	18	-35.35
Jun	69	420	16	-137.40
Jul	86	433	20	-85.13
Aug	91	454	20	-59.13
Sep	77	502	15	-131.40
Oct	60	501	12	-137.70
Nov	15	106	14	-25.90
Dec	0	2	0	-2.00

Top dozen jockeys

	Won	Ran	%	£1 Level Stake
Pat Eddery	159	851	19	-116.50
T Quinn	75	381	20	-34.60
R Hills	70	373	19	-22.52
G Carter	44	291	15	-89.49
W Supple	32	141	23	-36.24
K Darley	27	135	20	-37.90
K Fallon	17	71	24	-15.96
S Sanders	10	83	12	-19.11
G Duffield	9	51	18	-9.50
B Doyle	6	34	18	+9.67
L Dettori	6	35	17	+15.00
J Reid	6	35	17	+4.20

THIS USED to be a yard famous for starting slowly and ending the season strongly, but that seems to have changed in recent times.

Whether by design or not, Dunlop now seems to get his share of winners in the early part of the new term. We speculated in this space last year that this may have something to do with the milder winters on the south coast (he trains at Arundel, Sussex) which may allow him to get a start on the weather-afflicted Lambourn and Newmarket yards.

Those seeking an easy profit should look elsewhere, though he also falls into the pattern of producing his best rate of return with older horses in non-handicaps.

Haydock has been a spectacularly successful hunting ground for some reason, while his stats at Thirsk and Longchamp are also worth a second look.

Favourites

	Won	Ran	%	£1 Level Stake
Non-handicaps				
2	85	197	43	-14.05
3	64	161	40	-5.64
4+	28	84	33	+9.74
Handicaps				
2	4	20	20	+0.25
3	66	204	32	-2.83
4+	9	45	20	-11.89

Sponsored by Stan James

Course records

	W	R	%	Non-handicaps			Handicaps			£1 level stake
				2yo	3yo	4yo+	2yo	3yo	4yo+	
Nmkt July	35	211	17	10-86	8-39	6-18	2-8	7-43	2-17	+7.76
Haydock	30	121	25	11-26	4-25	2-10	0-0	12-52	1-8	+50.53
Nottingham	30	149	20	8-50	8-41	1-4	0-4	11-46	2-4	-31.50
Doncaster	27	160	17	9-59	5-33	4-13	2-8	3-33	4-14	-44.36
Newbury	26	197	13	1-62	10-52	7-21	0-6	5-38	3-18	-43.68
Nmkt Rowley	26	260	10	9-76	6-70	4-34	1-9	4-53	2-18	-28.99
Salisbury	24	131	18	8-61	5-28	1-5	0-2	8-32	2-3	-29.36
Lingfield	22	118	19	11-53	6-26	1-4	0-11	3-20	1-4	-44.26
Leicester	20	157	13	7-82	4-32	0-3	0-5	9-34	0-1	-63.65
Goodwood	20	217	9	8-63	7-51	1-22	0-9	3-58	1-14	-104.40
Kempton	19	120	16	6-53	8-31	3-7	0-0	2-20	0-9	-40.91
Newcastle	17	62	27	5-11	6-16	0-4	0-1	6-26	0-4	-6.46
Ripon	17	66	26	4-4	5-18	1-1	0-3	7-34	0-6	-1.97
York	17	100	17	7-18	4-21	3-17	0-2	2-19	1-23	-13.40
Sandown	16	105	15	4-25	5-16	1-20	0-0	6-36	0-8	-12.70
Thirsk	15	35	43	0-7	10-14	0-0	0-0	5-14	0-0	+15.59
Beverley	15	45	31	2-12	2-6	0-0	0-2	8-23	2-2	+4.69
Ascot	14	140	10	3-14	4-39	4-35	1-1	2-30	0-21	-43.75
Chester	13	39	33	3-7	3-11	1-6	0-0	1-3	5-12	+10.22
Yarmouth	13	52	25	3-6	3-13	1-1	1-2	5-28	0-2	-9.71
Pontefract	12	48	25	3-7	4-9	1-5	0-2	4-24	0-1	-5.69
Windsor	12	98	12	3-26	4-27	1-2	1-3	2-37	1-3	-45.32
Chepstow	10	48	21	3-21	6-13	0-0	0-0	1-13	0-1	-14.15
Bath	10	54	19	0-9	5-16	1-2	0-2	4-22	0-3	+7.63
Brighton	10	55	18	3-14	3-12	0-0	1-8	3-20	0-1	-2.82
Warwick	9	31	29	2-11	2-6	0-0	0-1	3-11	2-2	-1.08
Redcar	9	56	16	6-19	1-7	0-0	0-2	1-24	1-4	-25.65
San Siro	8	31	26	4-11	3-14	1-6	0-0	0-0	0-0	-20.20
Epsom	8	40	20	0-6	3-14	3-7	0-2	1-9	1-2	-13.25
Ayr	7	28	25	4-10	0-1	1-2	0-4	2-8	0-3	-5.52
Longchamp	6	28	21	0-1	2-14	4-13	0-0	0-0	0-0	+19.30
Hamilton	3	6	50	2-3	0-1	1-1	0-0	0-1	0-0	-0.56
Chantilly	3	12	25	0-0	2-8	1-4	0-0	0-0	0-0	-4.20
Curragh	3	14	21	0-1	1-2	2-11	0-0	0-0	0-0	-0.50
Deauville	3	15	20	0-1	3-8	0-6	0-0	0-0	0-0	+4.80
Folkestone	3	37	8	1-14	1-12	0-1	0-1	1-9	0-0	-27.50
Cologne	2	6	33	0-1	0-0	2-5	0-0	0-0	0-0	-4.00
Capannelle	2	10	20	0-0	0-6	2-4	0-0	0-0	0-0	-8.00

Sponsored by Stan James

Tim Easterby

All runners by race type

	Ran	1st	2nd	3rd	Unpl	Win %	£1 level stake
Non-handicaps							
2	947	106	88	114	637	11	-325.70
3	407	38	38	45	286	9	-154.80
4+	122	21	11	20	70	17	-15.97
Handicaps							
2	275	28	31	15	200	10	-50.10
3	920	70	75	72	700	8	-389.50
4+	703	61	77	67	498	9	-201.10
Totals	**3374**	**324**	**320**	**333**	**2391**	**10**	**-1137.17**

Monthly breakdown

	Won	Ran	%	£1 Level Stake
Jan	1	21	5	-16.67
Feb	2	17	12	-3.75
Mar	4	72	6	-4.50
Apr	15	244	6	-137.10
May	41	537	8	-256.80
Jun	73	589	12	-151.90
Jul	65	628	10	-228.30
Aug	60	505	12	-53.32
Sep	34	425	8	-194.00
Oct	22	252	9	-49.50
Nov	7	68	10	-25.00
Dec	0	16	0	-16.00

Top dozen jockeys

	Won	Ran	%	£1 Level Stake
K Darley	58	415	14	-95.03
R Winston	41	471	9	-176.70
L Charnock	39	435	9	-162.20
W Supple	22	197	11	-20.89
J Carroll	16	205	8	-135.40
K Fallon	13	68	19	-1.67
J Fortune	13	85	15	+0.85
T Durcan	11	137	8	-49.50
T Quinn	9	34	27	+52.50
M Roberts	9	44	21	+14.41
J Weaver	8	50	16	+26.50
D Allan	7	89	8	-43.00

SOMETHING OF a devastated area for punters looking for a trainer to latch onto. Scour these pages though you may, you'll find plusses hard to locate in the stats relating to Tim Easterby's runners.

Why should this be? He gets a perfectly healthy strike-rate andh as had some n otable winners in good races yet has hardly become the most fashionable of trainers.

Once again, older horses in non-handicaps have generally performed well for him (presumably there must be some trainers out t here who finds uch races difficult) and those aged four or older have generally proved worthy favourites in handicaps.

Richard Quinn has been an infrequent employee but perhaps deserves more opportunities, given the success he's had for Easterby. The Yorkshire trainer's Musselburgh runners have amassed a good profit.

Favourites

	Won	Ran	%	£1 Level Stake
Non-handicaps				
2	38	85	45	+10.11
3	12	36	33	-9.29
4+	8	24	33	-7.47
Handicaps				
2	4	24	17	-9.09
3	19	64	30	-5.79
4+	18	75	24	+1.95

Course records

| | W | R | % | Non-handicaps | | | Handicaps | | | £1 level |
				2yo	3yo	4yo+	2yo	3yo	4yo+	stake
Beverley	50	384	13	17-122	6-40	3-6	4-22	12-116	8-78	-94.92
Thirsk	23	231	10	11-76	2-40	1-6	0-5	4-56	5-48	-123.50
Ripon	23	251	9	6-76	4-33	0-5	3-9	7-85	3-43	-131.90
York	23	265	9	10-72	0-15	4-15	5-34	2-54	2-75	-55.55
Haydock	22	242	9	5-83	2-26	4-14	0-9	6-62	5-48	-122.90
Catterick	21	160	13	3-42	4-30	1-6	3-24	8-33	2-25	+0.03
Newcastle	21	240	9	10-82	0-23	2-4	1-12	4-70	4-49	-101.30
Redcar	21	247	9	8-74	2-26	0-5	2-18	5-92	4-32	-63.20
Pontefract	18	198	9	9-61	3-33	0-4	0-21	2-40	4-39	-36.77
Doncaster	18	236	8	2-65	4-21	0-5	5-33	3-49	4-63	-102.40
Musselburgh	12	63	19	1-12	1-7	0-3	0-3	3-17	7-21	+11.33
Ayr	10	101	10	4-22	0-5	0-1	2-23	2-25	2-25	-26.88
Nottingham	9	85	11	1-21	0-9	2-6	1-10	4-31	1-8	Level
Carlisle	7	106	7	3-28	4-17	0-3	0-0	0-40	0-18	-78.98
Southwell	7	124	6	3-30	3-30	0-7	0-3	1-30	0-24	-50.42
Nmkt July	6	56	11	0-5	1-10	1-6	1-8	2-20	1-7	-16.00
Ascot	6	59	10	4-13	0-6	0-7	0-2	0-6	2-25	-12.13
Hamilton	5	38	13	2-11	0-2	1-1	0-5	0-11	2-8	-11.75
Chester	5	78	6	3-19	0-4	0-1	1-12	1-24	0-18	-58.50
Sandown	3	14	21	0-1	0-1	0-0	0-1	1-6	2-5	+5.75
Newbury	3	16	19	2-10	0-0	0-1	0-2	1-2	0-1	+0.20
Newmarket	3	51	6	0-5	0-5	1-3	0-9	1-17	1-12	-22.50
Goodwood	2	19	11	0-1	0-3	0-0	0-3	0-4	2-8	+30.00

Sponsored by Stan James

Barry Hills

All runners by race type

	Ran	1st	2nd	3rd	Unpl	Win %	£1 level stake
Non-handicaps							
2	961	154	168	122	516	16	-145.20
3	991	155	171	133	529	16	-238.90
4+	176	25	26	24	100	14	-74.91
Handicaps							
2	153	19	16	23	95	12	-36.63
3	778	61	58	57	599	8	-314.10
4+	482	43	40	34	363	9	-103.50
Totals	**3541**	**457**	**479**	**393**	**2202**	**12.91**	**-913.24**

Monthly breakdown

	Won	Ran	%	£1 Level Stake
Jan	4	33	12	-18.33
Feb	9	28	32	+2.23
Mar	15	81	19	-12.14
Apr	38	254	15	-24.97
May	51	472	11	-165.50
Jun	46	450	10	-172.70
Jul	81	514	16	-146.30
Aug	69	534	13	-207.20
Sep	61	529	12	-54.08
Oct	57	484	12	-113.50
Nov	23	131	18	+17.93
Dec	3	31	10	-18.25

Top dozen jockeys

	Won	Ran	%	£1 Level Stake
M Hills	179	1355	13	-273.30
R Hughes	37	194	19	-8.89
R Hills	34	249	14	-69.27
D Holland	32	211	15	-17.45
J D Smith	19	149	13	-47.32
Pat Eddery	15	105	14	-10.06
J Weaver	13	68	19	+5.57
A Culhane	12	42	29	+39.07
J Reid	11	109	10	-17.67
R Cochrane	8	44	18	+8.03
K Darley	8	66	12	-26.15
K Fallon	6	32	19	-4.67

NO PRIZES for guessing the course at which Mr Hills has enjoyed most success over the years. As is notorious, the Lambourn man can't resist plotting raids on Doncaster and is likely to have a handful ready for the opening meeting of the new turf season there at the end of March.

He seems more at home than some of his big-name fellow trainers in keeping his charges going through the winter, as high strike-rates in November and February testify (as well as that level-stakes profit at Wolverhampton), though his poor 2002 has contributed to the fact that he can't reliably be followed at any time of year.

His older horses have a poorer strike-rate than the upstarts but are a steady source of profit when favourites for handicaps. Tony Culhane has done well for the yard, with the notable exception of *that* race at Pontefract last July.

Favourites

	Won	Ran	%	£1 Level Stake
Non-handicaps				
2	67	188	36	-24.55
3	77	190	41	-29.76
4+	13	38	34	-11.16
Handicaps				
2	7	23	30	-1.64
3	15	71	21	-19.25
4+	10	39	26	+8.85

Course records

	W	R	%	Non-handicaps 2yo	3yo	4yo+	Handicaps 2yo	3yo	4yo+	£1 level stake
Doncaster	52	290	18	22-105	16-71	3-21	3-23	1-32	7-38	+23.33
Ayr	26	95	27	12-28	7-24	1-5	3-9	2-21	1-8	+5.00
Nmkt Rowley	26	329	8	9-85	6-90	2-24	0-15	5-75	4-40	-87.72
Chester	25	121	21	6-17	11-46	1-4	1-8	2-24	4-22	-3.27
Wolves	24	108	22	5-16	8-29	2-9	0-0	8-37	1-17	+19.35
Nmkt July	22	228	10	9-80	3-51	1-10	2-12	5-48	2-27	-76.71
Lingfield AW	21	108	19	6-27	8-31	0-5	1-7	5-33	1-5	-7.61
Ripon	16	69	23	2-5	11-29	1-1	0-1	1-22	1-11	-6.31
Newbury	16	251	6	7-100	3-56	1-12	1-5	0-37	4-41	-137.80
Haydock	15	111	14	3-24	7-35	0-4	0-1	4-33	1-14	-19.63
Bath	15	114	13	6-37	6-40	2-5	0-1	0-22	1-9	-4.69
Warwick	14	69	20	1-14	7-28	0-0	2-6	3-19	1-2	-1.60
Goodwood	14	163	9	7-37	1-29	0-8	1-7	3-45	2-37	-60.18
Lingfield	12	55	22	3-12	7-30	0-0	0-2	2-10	0-1	+4.11
Pontefract	12	78	15	5-19	4-24	0-0	0-6	1-18	2-11	+5.48
Sandown	12	93	13	3-32	2-12	1-4	0-3	4-29	2-13	-27.50
Southwell	11	56	20	5-11	3-14	0-1	0-3	2-15	1-12	-9.44
Salisbury	11	73	15	5-23	3-16	0-2	1-1	1-19	1-12	+6.13
Windsor	11	82	13	6-36	2-18	0-5	1-4	1-14	1-5	-14.00
Leicester	10	71	14	4-29	3-11	3-7	0-4	0-17	0-3	-27.70
York	10	182	6	3-40	0-35	1-9	1-12	2-41	3-45	-119.80
Thirsk	8	25	32	1-4	7-17	0-0	0-0	0-4	0-0	+0.44
Catterick	8	40	20	2-7	4-10	2-2	0-4	0-15	0-2	+1.37
Epsom	7	73	10	3-11	2-28	0-1	1-3	0-18	1-12	-24.62
Ascot	7	157	5	2-35	3-39	0-15	0-4	1-23	1-41	-92.13
Folkestone	6	31	19	2-10	3-11	0-0	0-2	0-7	1-1	+0.92
Yarmouth	6	36	17	2-15	2-15	0-0	0-1	2-5	0-0	-1.70
Newcastle	6	44	14	2-6	3-15	0-2	0-3	1-11	0-7	-26.59
Beverley	6	50	12	2-9	1-16	0-0	0-2	3-20	0-3	-23.70
Nottingham	6	58	10	3-20	2-15	1-2	0-0	0-12	0-9	-28.83
Brighton	5	44	11	1-9	4-15	0-1	0-2	0-11	0-6	-28.05
Kempton	5	106	5	3-30	1-34	0-3	1-1	0-16	0-22	-85.47
Curragh	4	18	22	0-6	2-7	2-5	0-0	0-0	0-0	+9.75
Redcar	2	24	8	1-7	0-6	1-1	0-0	0-7	0-3	-16.80

Sponsored by Stan James

David Nicholls

All runners by race type

	Ran	1st	2nd	3rd	Unpl	Win %	£1 level stake
Non-handicaps							
2	97	4	3	7	83	4	-58.20
3	129	7	7	11	103	5	-62.13
4+	625	90	82	70	380	14	-135.60
Handicaps							
2	19	1	2	3	13	5	-12.50
3	224	10	13	13	187	5	-133.70
4+	2138	199	145	151	1637	9	-473.20
Totals	**3232**	**311**	**252**	**255**	**2403**	**10**	**-875.33**

Monthly breakdown

	Won	Ran	%	£1 Level Stake
Jan	19	221	9	-138.70
Feb	14	109	13	+13.37
Mar	9	186	5	-101.40
Apr	18	256	7	-74.83
May	39	501	8	-149.70
Jun	48	495	10	-159.00
Jul	75	494	15	+30.11
Aug	41	365	11	-104.90
Sep	33	371	9	-45.16
Oct	11	162	7	-92.51
Nov	2	46	4	-35.00
Dec	2	26	8	-17.25

Top dozen jockeys

	Won	Ran	%	£1 Level Stake
Alex Greaves	73	737	10	-199.80
A Nicholls	43	582	7	-226.30
F Norton	24	284	9	-117.40
D Holland	17	61	28	+49.06
K Fallon	17	81	21	-11.25
Clare Roche	13	180	7	-75.00
T Hamilton	12	161	8	-54.50
O Pears	11	184	6	-33.25
S Sanders	8	33	24	+6.20
I Wands	8	51	16	+9.25
J D Smith	7	71	10	-35.05
K Darley	6	33	18	+6.50

OVER 80% of Dandy Nicholls's runners are older than three, and his strike-rate with his older horses is around double that he can achieve with the youngsters.

He won't have been given a great deal of youthful material to work with, in fairness, but such stats must give an understanding of the sort of races that occupy most of his attention.

It's a popular yard (his favourites score at a good rate but nonetheless cost punters money) that seems to reach its peak in July, the time of year when Nicholls enjoyed his most notable success to date in last term's July Cup.

Pontefract, Ayr, the July Course and Sandown appear to be his venues of choice. He's trained most winners at Southwell but they must have been poor prices because it would have cost you a lot if you'd followed his runners there.

Favourites

	Won	Ran	%	£1 Level Stake
Non-handicaps				
2	1	2	50	-0.20
3	0	5	0	-5.00
4+	38	125	30	-22.24
Handicaps				
2	0	1	0	-1.00
3	1	11	9	-6.67
4+	61	253	24	-23.56

Sponsored by Stan James

Course records

	W	R	%	Non-handicaps			Handicaps			£1 level stake
				2yo	3yo	4yo+	2yo	3yo	4yo+	
Southwell	32	378	9	2-8	1-35	11-97	0-2	0-34	18-202	-189.60
Catterick	25	163	15	0-6	2-8	12-53	1-3	1-7	9-86	-0.72
Goodwood	20	128	16	0-0	0-0	2-8	0-0	1-5	17-115	+12.38
Pontefract	20	156	13	1-8	1-6	4-22	0-1	0-8	14-111	+40.67
Thirsk	15	219	7	1-9	0-13	3-26	0-0	1-19	10-152	-85.18
Ayr	14	149	9	0-5	0-2	3-12	0-1	1-11	10-118	+47.50
Doncaster	14	218	6	0-7	0-11	1-30	0-3	1-8	12-159	-105.50
Wolves	13	105	12	0-1	2-6	4-33	0-0	0-8	7-57	-45.50
York	12	190	6	0-4	0-1	0-21	0-1	1-10	11-153	-35.50
Redcar	10	104	10	0-5	0-6	7-29	0-2	0-12	3-50	-42.76
Newcastle	10	139	7	0-3	0-3	0-17	0-0	1-8	9-108	-61.00
Epsom	9	61	15	0-0	0-0	4-10	0-0	0-0	5-51	-2.68
Beverley	8	127	6	0-9	0-9	0-23	0-2	2-8	6-76	-88.57
Ripon	8	134	6	0-8	0-5	2-19	0-0	0-14	6-88	-79.00
Nmkt July	7	43	16	0-0	0-2	1-5	0-0	0-2	6-34	+28.12
Lingfield AW	7	59	12	0-0	1-3	4-20	0-0	0-5	2-31	-1.01
Chester	7	73	10	0-1	0-4	1-7	0-1	0-8	6-52	-25.50
Lingfield	6	17	35	0-0	0-0	0-0	0-0	0-3	6-14	+13.41
Yarmouth	6	28	21	0-0	0-0	2-10	0-0	0-0	4-18	+0.12
Sandown	6	30	20	0-0	0-0	4-18	0-0	0-2	2-10	+28.75
Brighton	6	34	18	0-0	0-1	3-8	0-0	0-1	3-24	-3.00
Hamilton	6	61	10	0-4	0-0	4-13	0-0	0-1	2-43	-22.25
Musselburgh	6	106	6	0-10	0-2	3-20	0-2	0-13	3-59	-60.00
Haydock	5	68	7	0-2	0-1	0-8	0-0	0-8	5-49	-8.00
Carlisle	5	76	7	0-3	0-2	1-21	0-0	0-12	4-38	-46.75
Ascot	5	94	5	0-2	0-0	0-13	0-0	0-2	5-77	-36.50
Kempton	4	25	16	0-0	0-0	4-9	0-0	0-0	0-16	-8.63
Windsor	4	37	11	0-0	0-0	2-9	0-0	0-4	2-24	-22.12
Leopardstown	3	6	50	0-0	0-0	3-5	0-0	0-0	0-1	+12.00
Nmkt Rowley	3	67	5	0-0	0-2	1-15	0-0	1-5	1-45	-41.00
Chepstow	2	6	33	0-0	0-0	0-1	0-0	0-0	2-5	+6.50
Folkestone	2	8	25	0-0	0-1	0-2	0-0	0-0	2-5	-2.84
Salisbury	2	11	18	0-0	0-0	0-2	0-0	0-0	2-9	-0.50
Bath	2	17	12	0-0	0-0	1-3	0-0	0-0	1-14	-12.09
Leicester	2	25	8	0-0	0-4	0-7	0-1	0-0	2-13	-6.00

Sponsored by Stan James

Amanda Perrett

All runners by race type

	Ran	1st	2nd	3rd	Unpl	Win %	£1 level stake
Non-handicaps							
2	202	28	24	23	127	14	-42.04
3	271	62	41	42	124	23	+40.17
4+	99	17	14	13	55	17	+26.31
Handicaps							
2	9	0	0	0	9	0	-9.00
3	187	17	11	20	139	9	-61.45
4+	314	27	30	22	233	9	-88.59
Totals	**1082**	**151**	**120**	**120**	**687**	**14**	**-134.60**

Monthly breakdown

	Won	Ran	%	£1 Level Stake
Jan	1	9	11	+1.00
Feb	1	20	5	-7.00
Mar	2	14	14	-9.75
Apr	8	47	17	-1.75
May	17	120	14	+23.03
Jun	31	164	19	+3.74
Jul	23	153	15	+5.50
Aug	16	149	11	-52.20
Sep	29	184	16	-29.25
Oct	20	182	11	-52.68
Nov	1	23	4	-16.00
Dec	2	17	12	+0.75

A MUCH smaller stable than the others we've so far looked at, so Mrs Perrett deserves all the more praise for hunting them up so closely in the table of winners trained.

Her three-year-olds offer a level-stakes profit of about 15% in non-handicaps, while her older runners do the same at a rate of about 26%. Her record in handicaps is relatively feeble.

From the stats, it seems you could set your watch by her – her runners return consistent profits from May through July, while her favourites in non-handicaps have an admirable record, especially the three-year-olds. Bath has been a productive visit for her, while she's generated profits on turnover of around 100% at the glamour tracks of York, Kempton and Longchamp. This seems an under-rated yard and therefore worth any punter's attention.

Top dozen jockeys

	Won	Ran	%	£1 Level Stake
Pat Eddery	27	133	20	+21.48
T Quinn	22	132	17	-34.80
R Hughes	19	113	17	-2.01
S Sanders	15	69	22	+20.75
T Sprake	10	44	23	+59.50
W Ryan	9	82	11	-26.50
K Fallon	7	24	29	+7.25
M Kinane	7	33	21	+29.91
M Roberts	5	19	26	+17.25
S Drowne	5	26	19	+12.25
Darren Williams	3	25	12	-11.75
T Ashley	3	51	6	-32.00

Favourites

	Won	Ran	%	£1 Level Stake
Non-handicaps				
2	8	18	44	-0.54
3	26	52	50	+16.72
4+	7	25	28	+5.48
Handicaps				
2	0	1	0	-1.00
3	4	14	29	-0.95
4+	5	29	17	-3.17

Sponsored by Stan James

Course records

	W	R	%	Non-handicaps			Handicaps			£1 level stake
				2yo	3yo	4yo+	2yo	3yo	4yo+	
Bath	13	59	22	4-13	5-26	1-4	0-0	2-6	1-10	+23.38
Kempton	13	60	22	1-12	8-17	0-3	0-0	1-6	3-22	+56.33
Goodwood	13	115	11	2-16	4-30	3-8	0-2	4-36	0-23	-35.52
Leicester	9	42	21	5-19	2-10	1-3	0-1	0-5	1-4	+6.71
Salisbury	9	64	14	2-15	3-20	0-2	0-0	1-12	3-15	-12.00
Windsor	8	63	13	1-6	5-24	2-5	0-0	0-14	0-14	-20.04
Folkestone	7	28	25	2-9	4-6	0-4	0-0	0-2	1-7	-8.28
Sandown	7	57	12	2-9	2-10	2-7	0-0	1-15	0-16	-17.63
Newbury	7	65	11	1-10	3-15	0-4	0-0	1-15	2-21	-11.67
Lingfield AW	7	80	9	0-9	2-22	0-11	0-0	0-2	5-36	-16.25
Yarmouth	6	20	30	0-2	4-7	0-2	0-0	2-2	0-7	+0.05
Lingfield	6	45	13	1-11	4-11	0-3	0-0	1-5	0-15	-13.50
Nmkt July	6	47	13	1-12	4-8	0-3	0-1	0-6	1-17	-3.50
Ascot	6	55	11	0-2	1-7	0-8	0-0	2-11	3-27	-8.50
Nmkt Rowley	6	81	7	2-25	1-15	3-7	0-2	0-15	0-17	-27.17
Pontefract	4	12	33	1-2	3-5	0-0	0-0	0-1	0-4	-1.90
York	4	14	29	0-1	0-2	0-0	0-0	2-3	2-8	+20.33
Brighton	4	40	10	0-6	0-10	1-5	0-0	0-6	3-13	-18.25
Epsom	3	15	20	1-2	1-5	1-4	0-0	0-0	0-4	+2.41
Warwick	3	15	20	0-4	3-7	0-0	0-0	0-2	0-2	-1.00
Longchamp	2	5	40	0-0	0-0	2-5	0-0	0-0	0-0	+11.90

Sponsored by Stan James

Top Trainers by Winners (Turf)

All runs				First time out			Horses*		
Won	Ran	%	Trainer	Won	Ran	%	Won	Ran	%
116	642	18	M Johnston	21	129	16	63	129	49
113	994	11	R Hannon	22	169	13	76	169	45
110	940	12	M Channon	12	138	9	67	138	49
102	460	22	Sir M Stoute	32	146	22	79	146	54
81	348	23	J Gosden	27	123	22	61	123	50
79	569	14	J Dunlop	16	148	11	56	148	38
78	788	10	T Easterby	4	125	3	46	125	37
77	651	12	B Hills	8	148	5	55	148	37
64	629	10	D Nicholls	2	67	3	38	67	57
57	316	18	Mrs A Perrett	10	74	14	38	74	51
54	238	23	J Fanshawe	11	64	17	38	64	59
52	250	21	R Charlton	8	68	12	36	68	53
52	428	12	I Balding	5	77	6	27	77	35
51	420	12	P Cole	6	82	7	35	82	43
48	369	13	M Bell	9	74	12	37	74	50
46	314	15	M Jarvis	9	79	11	32	79	41
44	166	27	Sir M Prescott	6	30	20	19	30	63
44	336	13	R Fahey	3	48	6	25	48	52
38	356	11	P Harris	8	71	11	26	71	37
35	236	15	G A Butler	9	49	18	20	49	41
35	780	4	A Berry	4	93	4	27	93	29
34	228	15	W Haggas	7	51	14	25	51	49
34	280	12	K Ryan	2	39	5	17	39	44
34	441	8	B Meehan	5	87	6	27	87	31
33	189	17	N Callaghan	3	22	14	18	22	82
32	142	23	M Tregoning	8	54	15	25	54	46
32	750	4	J Bradley	0	75	0	20	75	27
31	171	18	A Stewart	9	39	23	18	39	46
31	395	8	E Dunlop	5	121	4	29	121	24
30	189	16	H Cecil	10	66	15	23	66	35
30	263	11	I A Wood	1	32	3	15	32	47
28	169	17	J Noseda	6	44	14	21	44	48
28	194	14	T Mills	2	26	8	14	26	54
27	282	10	T Barron	4	34	12	15	34	44
25	154	16	G Wragg	3	43	7	17	43	40
25	253	10	M Tompkins	2	47	4	19	47	40
25	330	8	N Littmoden	1	41	2	16	41	39
23	192	12	L Cumani	4	50	8	17	50	34
23	256	9	J Given	2	58	3	12	58	21
23	338	7	M W Easterby	2	67	3	16	67	24
21	88	24	S Bin Suroor	9	41	22	19	41	46
21	129	16	H Candy	5	27	19	13	27	48
21	205	10	J A Osborne	0	32	0	9	32	28
21	303	7	C Brittain	2	37	5	13	37	35
20	156	13	H Morrison	4	29	14	13	29	45
20	192	10	I Semple	3	28	11	11	28	39
20	243	8	J Hills	1	48	2	16	48	33
20	289	7	P Evans	3	36	8	9	36	25
19	173	11	Mrs J Ramsden	3	35	9	12	35	34

*Shows how many individual horses ran last season, how many won at least once, and percentage.

Sponsored by Stan James

Top Trainers by Prize Money (Turf)

Total prize money	Trainer	Win prize money	Wins	Class A-C Won	Class A-C Ran	Class A-C %	Class D-G Won	Class D-G Ran	Class D-G %
£2,708,427	A P O'Brien	£1,797,665	9	9	78	12	0	4	0
2,360,981	Sir M Stoute	1,536,030	102	31	200	16	71	260	27
2,195,179	M Johnston	1,586,901	116	54	279	19	62	363	17
1,851,266	R Hannon	901,648	113	43	365	12	70	629	11
1,601,643	S Bin Suroor	892,997	21	18	78	23	3	10	30
1,575,282	B Hills	966,369	77	28	274	10	49	377	13
1,419,557	J Dunlop	907,866	79	34	206	17	45	363	12
1,407,163	M Channon	806,667	110	32	373	9	78	566	14
1,395,845	T Easterby	995,251	78	26	227	11	52	561	9
1,247,274	J Gosden	834,999	81	22	127	17	59	221	27
1,077,762	M Tregoning	652,216	32	14	58	24	18	84	21
1,004,531	D Nicholls	657,843	64	15	254	6	49	375	13
770,664	Mrs A Perrett	503,463	57	14	86	16	43	230	19
727,066	J Fanshawe	508,580	54	19	97	20	35	141	25
715,091	I Balding	406,701	52	18	144	13	34	284	12
708,338	P Cole	445,773	51	20	155	13	31	265	12
655,350	T Mills	477,288	28	15	93	16	13	101	13
641,406	G A Butler	479,938	35	19	114	17	16	122	13
584,102	R Charlton	382,941	52	18	85	21	34	165	21
535,419	M Jarvis	306,860	46	16	152	11	30	162	19
519,201	J Given	373,115	23	10	82	12	13	174	7
507,068	B Meehan	257,274	34	14	178	8	20	263	8
506,769	D Elsworth	225,062	18	8	102	8	10	155	6
501,992	G Wragg	354,544	25	17	79	22	8	75	11
488,337	M Bell	281,484	48	8	111	7	40	258	16
483,863	R Fahey	392,552	44	12	80	15	32	256	13
478,142	J Noseda	293,684	28	10	73	14	18	96	19
476,903	W Haggas	342,744	34	12	57	21	22	171	13
436,923	P Harris	244,264	38	8	91	9	30	265	11
424,389	E Dunlop	199,164	31	4	118	3	27	277	10
399,308	H Candy	342,572	21	7	23	30	14	106	13
376,244	L Cumani	240,976	23	6	59	10	17	133	13
367,339	Sir M Prescott	236,717	44	6	37	16	38	129	29
358,043	H Cecil	215,443	30	9	62	15	21	127	17
348,252	C Brittain	158,993	21	8	117	7	13	186	7
333,140	R Johnson Houghton	230,330	13	6	34	18	7	109	6
328,653	A Berry	137,812	35	1	165	1	34	615	6
323,224	J Bradley	198,267	32	5	101	5	27	649	4
304,401	N Littmoden	164,329	25	7	103	7	18	227	8
281,952	K Ryan	197,799	34	7	74	9	27	206	13
279,240	D Loder	235,074	12	4	14	29	8	47	17
277,330	N Callaghan	178,959	33	11	64	17	22	125	18
263,179	M Tompkins	141,914	25	4	69	6	21	184	11
263,076	D Weld	153,700	3	3	17	18	0	0	0
250,754	H Morrison	152,615	20	8	49	16	12	107	11
244,072	I A Wood	183,285	30	4	44	9	26	219	12
238,943	A Stewart	165,471	31	6	48	13	25	123	20
236,053	B Smart	141,029	17	6	39	15	11	139	8
228,440	W Musson	174,340	18	5	51	10	13	116	11
226,585	J Goldie	123,688	17	6	83	7	11	218	5

Sponsored by Stan James

Top Trainers by Winners (AW)

All runs				First time out			Horses*		
Won	Ran	%	Trainer	Won	Ran	%	Won	Ran	%
54	368	15	N Littmoden	5	55	9	33	55	60
31	181	17	T Barron	8	38	21	20	38	53
27	118	23	G A Butler	9	32	28	20	32	63
27	155	17	J A Osborne	8	41	20	18	41	44
25	130	19	P Haslam	6	32	19	15	32	47
20	149	13	K Ryan	1	29	3	12	29	41
18	106	17	M Johnston	4	30	13	16	30	53
18	178	10	K Burke	3	38	8	9	38	24
18	276	7	Mrs N Macauley	2	32	6	10	32	31
17	119	14	G L Moore	3	29	10	10	29	34
17	131	13	A Jarvis	5	28	18	14	28	50
15	49	31	J Noseda	5	15	33	9	15	60
15	89	17	I Balding	2	21	10	10	21	48
15	206	7	D Shaw	5	37	14	11	37	30
14	109	13	I Semple	5	18	28	8	18	44
14	161	9	D Chapman	0	27	0	4	27	15
13	69	19	M Channon	2	12	17	10	12	83
13	89	15	Sir M Prescott	1	30	3	8	30	27
13	95	14	B Hills	1	15	7	9	15	60
13	98	13	Miss G Kelleway	0	15	0	6	15	40
13	104	13	B Meehan	1	17	6	12	17	71
13	151	9	S Bowring	1	24	4	6	24	25
12	118	10	W Muir	0	16	0	7	16	44
11	78	14	J R Poulton	2	20	10	8	20	40
11	89	12	J R Best	2	21	10	5	21	24
11	192	6	A Berry	0	35	0	7	35	20
10	56	18	P Cole	0	9	0	5	9	56
10	68	15	P Makin	3	10	30	6	10	60
10	69	14	B Smart	1	15	7	7	15	47
10	84	12	A Newcombe	3	25	12	6	25	24
10	100	10	C Brittain	3	22	14	7	22	32
10	127	8	R Wilman	5	31	16	6	31	19
10	144	7	M Polglase	1	25	4	6	25	24
10	187	5	P Evans	0	34	0	8	34	24
9	52	17	M A Buckley	2	7	29	4	7	57
9	69	13	W Haggas	4	14	29	6	14	43
9	103	9	P Hiatt	0	16	0	5	16	31
9	104	9	S Dow	2	24	8	7	24	29
9	119	8	A Reid	3	22	14	6	22	27
8	28	29	H Morrison	3	6	50	5	6	83
8	35	23	B Ellison	3	11	27	4	11	36
8	39	21	C Wall	2	15	13	8	15	53
8	40	20	M Jarvis	2	9	22	6	9	67
8	86	9	J Hills	2	22	9	7	22	32
8	105	8	R Hannon	2	18	11	5	18	28
8	144	6	I A Wood	2	24	8	6	24	25
7	36	19	D Morris	1	6	17	5	6	83
7	38	18	W Jarvis	3	11	27	6	11	55
7	49	14	T Mills	3	19	16	6	19	32

*Shows how many individual horses ran last season, how many won at least once, and percentage.

Top Trainers by Prize Money (AW)

Total prize money	Trainer	Win prize money	Wins	Class A-C Won	Class A-C Ran	Class A-C %	Class D-G Won	Class D-G Ran	Class D-G %
£312,585	N Littmoden	£224,790	54	10	53	19	44	315	14
159,511	G A Butler	122,759	27	3	22	14	24	96	25
137,002	T Barron	103,413	31	4	22	18	27	159	17
128,766	J Noseda	120,728	15	5	7	71	10	42	24
103,738	J A Osborne	79,141	27	2	10	20	25	145	17
101,853	Mrs N Macauley	61,360	18	2	21	10	16	255	6
94,381	M Channon	71,792	13	2	6	33	11	63	17
84,598	B Hills	56,522	13	1	10	10	12	85	14
84,007	K Burke	57,950	18	1	22	5	17	156	11
80,480	P Haslam	62,711	25	0	2	0	25	128	20
80,400	B Meehan	54,914	13	1	11	9	12	93	13
78,236	C Brittain	59,779	10	4	19	21	6	81	7
75,525	M Johnston	53,213	18	0	8	0	18	98	18
74,525	S Dow	46,908	9	2	17	12	7	87	8
73,004	K Ryan	55,466	20	0	4	0	20	145	14
69,291	A Jarvis	49,941	17	1	11	9	16	120	13
68,447	I Balding	53,551	15	0	4	0	15	85	18
68,139	G L Moore	49,411	17	0	6	0	17	113	15
63,995	Miss G Kelleway	42,579	13	0	4	0	13	94	14
61,178	S Bowring	40,060	13	0	3	0	13	148	9
59,991	A Newcombe	40,029	10	2	13	15	8	71	11
59,940	R Hannon	25,272	8	0	12	0	8	93	9
59,313	I Semple	40,037	14	0	5	0	14	104	13
58,648	J R Best	46,828	11	2	5	40	9	84	11
57,035	D Shaw	37,209	15	0	5	0	15	201	7
56,771	P Cole	42,385	10	1	8	13	9	48	19
56,556	P Evans	24,912	10	0	5	0	10	182	5
56,185	D Chapman	43,278	14	0	9	0	14	152	8
55,405	W Muir	34,148	12	0	5	0	12	113	11
54,019	J R Poulton	38,996	11	1	4	25	10	74	14
53,203	W Haggas	28,884	9	0	7	0	9	62	15
52,864	Sir M Prescott	43,075	13	0	1	0	13	88	15
48,864	S Kirk	24,681	7	0	4	0	7	91	8
48,603	M Polglase	28,265	10	0	12	0	10	132	8
47,773	A Berry	32,867	11	0	8	0	11	184	6
45,404	I A Wood	20,953	8	0	4	0	8	140	6
45,352	M Jarvis	33,124	9	0	7	0	8	33	24
45,004	P Hiatt	30,450	9	0	6	0	9	97	9
44,639	B Smart	34,843	10	0	3	0	10	66	15
43,382	T Mills	26,127	7	0	5	0	7	44	16
42,050	R Wilman	28,417	10	0	4	0	10	123	8
40,538	P Mitchell	27,771	7	1	5	20	6	58	10
40,379	J Hills	27,044	8	0	3	0	8	83	10
39,673	M A Buckley	32,190	9	0	1	0	9	51	18
37,946	P Makin	25,952	10	0	6	0	10	62	16
37,912	M Tompkins	29,025	7	1	8	13	6	45	13
37,877	R Guest	23,777	6	0	6	0	6	40	15
36,793	A Reid	23,631	9	0	2	0	9	117	8
36,077	P Harris	20,808	6	0	4	0	6	46	13
35,289	J Balding	22,352	7	0	3	0	7	85	8

Sponsored by Stan James

Top Jockeys (Turf)

W	R	%	Jockey & Weight	Best Trainer	W	R	%
136	715	19	K Fallon 8-4	Sir M Stoute	34	141	24
121	746	16	R Hughes 8-5	R Hannon	31	213	15
108	770	14	K Darley 8-4	M Johnston	45	223	20
106	704	15	S Sanders 8-4	Sir M Prescott	14	42	33
100	712	14	T Quinn 8-4	H Cecil	22	136	16
89	693	13	Pat Eddery 8-4	J Dunlop	18	142	13
85	697	12	D Holland 8-4	G Wragg	19	115	17
80	438	18	R Hills 8-3	M Tregoning	15	53	28
79	606	13	J P Spencer 8-5	L Cumani	15	111	14
79	610	13	F Lynch 8-5	Sir M Stoute	22	66	33
78	591	13	J Fortune 8-6	J Gosden	31	116	27
72	716	10	S Drowne 8-3	M Channon	32	290	11
67	347	19	L Dettori 8-0	S Bin Suroor	15	51	29
65	585	11	W Supple 7-13	J Dunlop	11	49	22
60	438	14	M Hills 8-4	B Hills	39	277	14
59	613	10	G Duffield 8-0	Sir M Prescott	23	95	24
58	625	9	Martin Dwyer 7-12	I Balding	26	196	13
57	499	11	A Culhane 8-5	M Channon	20	90	22
57	544	10	K Dalgleish 7-10	M Johnston	29	199	15
56	564	10	E Ahern 8-1	G A Butler	25	148	17
54	517	10	T E Durcan 8-2	M Tompkins	20	154	13
53	483	11	J Fanning 8-1	M Johnston	16	100	16
51	519	10	M Fenton 8-3	M Bell	21	154	14
51	530	10	R Winston 8-4	T Easterby	19	211	9
49	475	10	P Robinson 8-1	M Jarvis	33	216	15
46	557	8	Dane O'Neill 8-4	R Hannon	26	234	11
46	682	7	C Catlin 7-10	M Channon	22	234	9
37	244	15	O Urbina 8-3	J Fanshawe	31	121	26
37	508	7	J Quinn 7-10	M Blanshard	5	90	6
35	454	8	J Carroll 8-3	J Noseda	3	4	75
31	560	6	F Norton 7-12	A Berry	18	245	7
29	335	9	N Callan 8-5	D Morris	7	51	14
27	423	6	J Mackay 7-7	J Spearing	5	31	16
26	346	8	Dean McKeown 8-3	T Barron	7	46	15
25	322	8	J F Egan 8-0	P D'Arcy	6	37	16
23	293	8	S W Kelly 8-5	J Noseda	5	38	13
23	341	7	I Mongan 8-3	N Littmoden	15	144	10
22	213	10	W Ryan 8-3	H Cecil	8	45	18
22	233	9	R Ffrench 7-12	A Stewart	10	59	17
22	334	7	S Carson 8-0	G Balding	6	43	14
22	359	6	P Doe 7-13	I A Wood	7	56	13
21	313	7	A Nicholls 7-11	D Nicholls	15	155	10
21	429	5	Dale Gibson 7-10	M W Easterby	9	130	7
20	227	9	M Henry 7-10	R Cowell	4	24	17
19	289	7	G Gibbons 7-12	R Hollinshead	7	161	4
17	317	5	D Sweeney 8-4	R Beckett	5	57	9
16	129	12	Alex Greaves 8-12	D Nicholls	16	128	13
16	219	7	M Tebbutt 8-6	W Jarvis	6	45	13
16	239	7	C Rutter 7-12	H Candy	11	67	16
15	122	12	J Murtagh 8-5	Sir M Stoute	7	35	20
15	368	4	T Williams 7-9	D Barker	4	56	7

Sponsored by Stan James

Top Jockeys (AW)

W	R	%	Jockey & Weight	Best Trainer	W	R	%
64	600	11	**J Quinn** 7-10	Mrs L Pearce	6	22	27
59	415	14	**I Mongan** 8-3	N Littmoden	28	149	19
47	336	14	**Martin Dwyer** 7-12	I Balding	10	36	28
32	263	12	**S Drowne** 8-3	M Channon	7	33	21
28	160	18	**E Ahern** 8-1	G A Butler	17	57	30
28	279	10	**S Whitworth** 8-1	A Newcombe	6	43	14
27	150	18	**D Holland** 8-4	J Noseda	5	12	42
27	196	14	**L Enstone** 7-13	P Haslam	14	74	19
26	247	11	**G Gibbons** 7-12	D Shaw	13	78	17
24	172	14	**A Culhane** 8-5	D Chapman	11	63	17
24	251	10	**Dane O'Neill** 8-4	R Hannon	5	26	19
24	276	9	**M Fenton** 8-3	E Alston	5	31	16
23	197	12	**J Fanning** 8-1	M Johnston	8	53	15
23	234	10	**N Callan** 8-5	A Jarvis	5	28	18
21	145	14	**F Lynch** 8-5	K Ryan	10	54	19
21	362	6	**C Catlin** 7-10	S Dow	5	51	10
20	159	13	**S W Kelly** 8-5	J A Osborne	9	60	15
19	175	11	**J Bramhill** 7-10	S Bowring	12	72	17
19	194	10	**L Fletcher** 8-0	M Polglase	7	83	8
18	141	13	**Dean McKeown** 8-3	T Barron	9	34	26
18	175	10	**P Doe** 7-13	J Akehurst	5	12	42
18	198	9	**D Sweeney** 8-4	K Burke	4	18	22
17	128	13	**S Sanders** 8-4	Sir M Prescott	7	22	32
15	95	16	**K Fallon** 8-4	G A Butler	2	4	50
15	200	8	**K Dalgleish** 7-10	M Johnston	5	21	24
14	149	9	**J Fortune** 8-6	T Mills	3	9	33
12	127	9	**G Baker** 8-0	C Wall	2	3	67
12	218	6	**Joanna Badger** 7-5	Mrs N Macauley	5	81	6
11	129	9	**A Clark** 8-2	P Makin	5	22	23
11	137	8	**R Mullen** 8-1	W Muir	6	27	22
10	74	14	**Pat Eddery** 8-4	B Meehan	4	16	25
10	99	10	**G Duffield** 8-0	Sir M Prescott	4	26	15
10	117	9	**D Mernagh** 7-10	T Barron	9	67	13
10	131	8	**N Pollard** 8-1	A Jarvis	5	45	11
10	150	7	**T G McLaughlin** 8-8	Mrs L Stubbs	2	18	11
9	46	20	**J-P Guillambert** 7-13	N Littmoden	6	31	19
9	123	7	**S Carson** 8-0	B Powell	3	21	14
9	199	5	**D Kinsella** 7-5	M Blanshard	3	12	25
8	62	13	**R Winston** 8-4	P Evans	3	8	38
8	75	11	**M Tebbutt** 8-6	M Channon	1	1	100
8	124	6	**F Norton** 7-12	A Berry	4	49	8
7	52	13	**J P Spencer** 8-5	D Loder	1	1	100
7	54	13	**M Worrell** 8-2	D Cantillon	2	5	40
7	56	13	**N Chalmers** 7-9	I Balding	2	16	13
7	57	12	**D Corby** 8-0	A Reid	2	14	14
7	61	11	**B Reilly** 7-11	J A Gilbert	5	18	28
7	64	11	**O Urbina** 8-3	J Fanshawe	4	15	27
7	110	6	**M Henry** 7-10	M Jarvis	2	8	25
7	118	6	**Darren Williams** 8-2	K Burke	4	49	8
6	42	14	**Paul Scallan** 8-4	W Jarvis	2	3	67
6	57	11	**R Smith** 7-12	R Hannon	3	18	17

Sponsored by Stan James

Top Apprentices

W	R		Jockey & Weight	Best Trainer	W	R	%
84	730	12	P Hanagan 7-10	R Fahey	28	190	15
44	448	10	L Enstone 7-13	P Haslam	23	148	16
42	412	10	D Corby 8-0	M Channon	20	162	12
39	385	10	R L Moore 7-11	I A Wood	7	35	20
30	314	10	L Keniry 7-13	I Balding	13	85	15
30	547	5	D Kinsella 7-5	M Blanshard	4	44	9
26	345	8	L Fletcher 8-0	M Polglase	10	146	7
26	385	7	Darren Williams 8-2	K Burke	9	128	7
23	277	8	G Baker 8-0	J R Best	4	16	25
23	336	7	D Allan 7-9	T Easterby	8	102	8
23	343	7	F P Ferris 7-5	P Evans	9	126	7
23	378	6	P Fitzsimons 7-13	J Bradley	18	265	7
22	251	9	P Dobbs 8-4	R Hannon	7	75	9
18	185	10	B Reilly 7-11	J A Gilbert	6	43	14
15	203	7	Lisa Jones 7-3	W Musson	8	46	17
14	138	10	Claire Stretton 7-5	Mrs P Dutfield	4	24	17
14	173	8	T Eaves 8-2	Mrs M Reveley	4	57	7
14	193	7	D McGaffin 8-5	I Semple	5	56	9
14	434	3	S Hitchcott 7-6	M W Easterby	5	103	5
13	196	7	G Sparkes 7-7	T Clement	2	6	33
13	200	7	N Mackay 7-3	Miss J Feilden	3	7	43
12	78	15	R Miles 7-12	T Mills	10	53	19
11	87	13	M Worrell 8-2	Sir M Prescott	6	31	19
11	179	6	J F McDonald 7-3	I A Wood	4	23	17
10	77	13	J-P Guillambert 7-13	N Littmoden	6	41	15
10	143	7	T Hamilton 7-10	D Nicholls	8	83	10
10	219	5	D Nolan 8-1	I A Wood	2	23	9
9	94	10	Hayley Turner 7-5	M Bell	3	19	16
9	102	9	P Goode 8-2	P Hiatt	4	14	29
8	109	7	P Mulrennan 8-4	P Haslam	5	39	13
8	114	7	N Chalmers 7-9	I Balding	3	28	11
7	79	9	Clare Roche 7-3	W Storey	3	9	33
7	79	9	Leanne Kershaw 7-6	J O'Keeffe	6	46	13
7	174	4	M Savage 8-1	J Bradley	4	140	3
6	126	5	R Thomas 7-5	R J Price	2	13	15
6	197	3	P Bradley 7-12	Ron Thompson	2	19	11
5	40	13	R Cody-Boutcher 8-3	P Harris	4	34	12
5	44	11	A Quinn 8-2	G Enright	2	4	50
5	90	6	N Farmer 7-12	W G M Turner	4	52	8
5	97	5	C Poste 7-5	R Fahey	4	64	6
5	129	4	D Fox 7-3	G L Moore	1	1	100
4	25	16	M Howard 7-6	J Akehurst	2	14	14
4	32	13	L Branch 8-5	B Smart	3	16	19
4	105	4	C Cogan 7-7	N Littmoden	2	36	6
3	70	4	S Crawford 7-7	J A Osborne	3	38	8
3	85	4	Kristin Stubbs 7-3	R Dickin	1	3	33
2	11	18	Laura-Jayne Crawford 8-4	D Barker	1	2	50
2	12	17	Joan Flynn 7-4	K Ryan	2	9	22
2	22	9	W Hogg 7-5	M Johnston	2	13	15
3	70	4	S Crawford 7-7	J A Osborne	3	38	8
2	67	3	Natalia Gemelova 7-3	Mrs L Pearce	1	2	50

Sponsored by Stan James

Top Owners

Owner	Best earner	W-R	Winners-runners	2nd	3rd	Prize-money
Hamdan Al Maktoum	Nayef	96-495	72-156	79	74	£2,223,274
Godolphin	Kazzia	21-88	19-41	17	12	1,601,643
Khalid Abdulla	Tillerman	76-358	60-111	70	48	1,240,533
Michael Tabor & Susan Magnier	High Chaparral	4-27	4-15	2	0	1,065,761
Maktoum Al Maktoum	Storming Home	36-211	24-71	27	22	913,884
The late Lord Weinstock	Golan	5-28	4-14	5	3	807,866
Susan Magnier	Hawk Wing	3-12	3-8	5	0	793,341
Cheveley Park Stud	Russian Rhythm	46-191	31-53	30	22	615,309
Lucayan Stud	Continent	19-181	14-28	21	13	531,239
Sir Alex Ferguson & Susan Magnier	Rock Of Gibraltar	3-3	1-1	0	0	495,401
Major A M Everett	Presto Vento	5-26	2-4	2	1	360,061
Abdulla BuHaleeba	Zindabad	9-52	6-16	13	11	355,680
Sir Neil Westbrook	Bollin Eric	3-19	3-4	6	4	340,310
J C Smith	Persian Punch	21-130	13-27	16	22	329,012
Sheikh Ahmed Al Maktoum	Araam	29-229	21-55	32	28	324,235
Paul J Dixon	Red Wine	50-425	21-47	38	26	306,181
Highclere Thor'ghbreds	Highest	16-94	10-17	12	12	296,426
H H Aga Khan	Balakheri	17-89	14-27	22	15	292,112
Sheikh Mohammed	Dublin	27-111	20-52	13	13	277,302
Susan Magnier & Michael Tabor	Tomahawk	2-30	2-15	5	4	238,104
Saeed Manana	Warrsan	13-128	8-21	20	18	225,479
Eden Racing	Tout Seul	4-16	1-2	3	2	224,959
John Humphreys Ltd	Where Or When	2-9	1-2	0	0	223,468
Erik Penser	Beauchamp Pilot	12-73	7-13	7	7	223,441
Legard Sidebottom & Sykes	Somnus	4-5	1-1	0	0	221,827
Prince A A Faisal	Invincible Spirit	5-22	4-7	1	4	221,040
Jaber Abdullah	Zafeen	15-79	10-16	18	10	217,761
Peter Savill	Royal Rebel	10-109	7-19	10	10	217,395
Elite Racing Club	Soviet Song	11-59	5-14	6	6	207,210
Terry Mills	Norton	12-58	5-10	11	10	199,379
M J Dawson	Mine	11-95	7-15	8	13	189,178
R C Bond	Bond Boy	17-88	8-12	7	3	188,719
Abdulla Al Khalifa	Nayyir	11-34	4-7	6	2	177,509
J G White	Hugs Dancer	3-9	1-2	1	0	171,905
L Neil Jones	Millenary	3-11	2-3	3	1	162,429
Aston House Stud	Boreas	2-5	1-1	2	0	159,775
Gestut Ammerland	Boreal	1-2	1-1	0	0	159,500
The late R Hitchins	Dumaran	7-48	5-8	9	4	152,751
J Raw	Crystal Castle	2-3	1-1	0	0	149,815
Mollers Racing	Island House	7-39	4-8	6	3	146,272
K Rausing	Frosty Welcome	14-72	7-15	12	10	143,613
The Thoroughbred Corp.	Elusive City	10-54	7-20	5	12	143,399
J C Parsons	Vintage Premium	3-12	1-2	2	1	140,174
Saeed Suhail	First Charter	8-43	7-13	3	10	139,651
Tina Miller	Sharplaw Venture	2-4	1-1	1	0	136,475

Sponsored by Stan James

Outlook

Group 1 Review
Britain & Ireland, 2002

For two-year-old Group 1s, see 'Two-year-old Review', page 59

1 **Sagitta 2,000 Guineas Stakes (1m)**
Newmarket May 4 (Gd to Firm)

1 **Rock Of Gibraltar** 9-0   J Murtagh
2 **Hawk Wing** 9-0   J P Spencer
3 **Redback** 9-0   D Holland
9-1, 6-4f, 25-1. nk, 1¼ ml. 22 ran. 1m 36.5 (b7.42)
Sir Alex Ferguson & Mrs John Magnier (A P O'Brien, Ireland).

Running on the faster side of the track, the winner had other horses to race against, whereas Hawk Wing was clear on the slower side for the final furlong and should have won.

2 **Sagitta 1,000 Guineas Stakes (1m)**
Newmarket May 5 (Gd to Firm)

1 **Kazzia** 9-0   L Dettori
2 **Snowfire** 9-0   Pat Eddery
3 **Alasha** 9-0   J Murtagh
14-1, 28-1, 6-1. nk, nk. 17 ran. 1m 37.9 (b6.07)
Godolphin (S Bin Suroor, Newmarket).

Prominent throughout, Kazzia galloped right to the line and looked a potential stayer. Favourite Gossamer hated the fast ground.

3 **Juddmonte Lockinge Stakes (1m)**
Newbury May 18 (Gd to Firm)

1 **Keltos** 9-0   O Peslier
2 **Noverre** 9-0   J P Spencer
3 **Olden Times** 9-0   M J Kinane
9-1, 5-6f, 8-1. 3½l, 1½l. 10 ran. 1m 38.7 (b4.11)
Mr Gary A Tanaka (C Laffon-Parias, France).

Despite trouble in running, Keltos quickened well to win this impressively but it proved to be his last race, as he was retired following injury problems. Noverre appeared to try to bite the winner as he went past.

4 **Entenmann's Irish 2,000 Guineas (1m) Curragh May 25 (Soft)**

1 **Rock Of Gibraltar** 9-0   M J Kinane
2 **Century City** 9-0   J A Heffernan
3 **Della Francesca** 9-0   C O'Donoghue
4-7f, 6-1, 20-1. 1½l, 3l. 7 ran. 1m 47.3 (a2.75)
Sir Alex Ferguson (A P O'Brien, Ireland).

A much more clear-cut win for the Rock, though this Guineas was a lot weaker than the Newmarket version. For the second year running, O'Brien saddled the first three.

5 **Entenmann's Irish 1,000 Guineas (1m) Curragh May 26 (Soft)**

1 **Gossamer** 9-0   J P Spencer
2 **Quarter Moon** 9-0   M J Kinane
3 **Starbourne** 9-0   C O'Donoghue
4-1f, 9-2, 20-1. 4¼l, 1l. 15 ran. 1m 45.5 (a0.95)
Gerald W Leigh – CancerBACUP (L Cumani, Newmarket).

Very easy for Gossamer, who had finisehd behind Quarter Moon at Newmarket and is clearly a much better horse with ease in the ground. The first three were all by Sadler's Wells, while Aidan O'Brien's five runners all made the first seven.

6 **Tattersalls Gold Cup (1m2f110yds) Curragh May 26 (Soft)**

1 **Rebelline** 8-11   D P McDonogh
2 **Bach** 9-0   M J Kinane
3 **Nayef** 9-0   R Hills
7-1, 7-1, 8-11f. 2l, 2¼l. 8 ran. 2m 22.2 (b3.83)
Lady O'Reilly (K Prendergast, Ireland).

With conditions in her favour, Rebelline beat a couple of consistent types. It was her last run, as she was later retired with muscle problems.

7 Vodafone Coronation Cup (1m4f10yds) Epsom June 7 (Soft)

1 **Boreal** 9-0   K Fallon
2 **Storming Home** 9-0   M Hills
3 **Zindabad** 9-0   K Darley
4-1, 7-2, 9-1. 3½l, 6l. 6 ran. 2m 45.0 (b1.34)
Gestut Ammerland (P Schiergen, Germany).

Persistent rain and the outrageous camber of this course meant that the ground up the inside rail of the straight was a quagmire, whereas there was a narrow strip of much better ground up the stands side. Runners in all races on this card tacked over to the stands side on entering the straight but it proved difficult to overtake a leader who grabbed the rail first. So it proved here, with Fallon the jockey most alert to the importance of the stands rail, which he seized at the top of the straight. Storming Home, fourth at the turn for home, chased him all the way but never looked like making up the ground.

8 Vodafone Oaks (1m4f10yds) Epsom June 7 (Soft)

1 **Kazzia** 9-0   L Dettori
2 **Quarter Moon** 9-0   M J Kinane
3 **Shadow Dancing** 9-0   Martin Dwyer
10-3f, 15-2, 14-1. ½l, 14l. 14 ran. 2m 44.5 (b1.83)
Godolphin (S Bin Suroor, Newmarket).

A tremendously game effort from Kazzia, who made all. Having seen off the challenge of **Islington** at the top of the straight, she ran right to the line but was assisted in holding off Quarter Moon's challenge by having the better strip under the stands rail. The runner-up, who'd seemed wound up in the preliminaries, was closing all the way to the post but had had to give up the best ground and race on the camber in order to try to pass Kazzia, and couldn't quite pull it off. The pair finished well clear, with Islington tiring into eighth.

9 Vodafone Derby (1m4f10yds) Epsom June 8 (Gd to Soft)

1 **High Chaparral** 9-0   J Murtagh
2 **Hawk Wing** 9-0   M J Kinane
3 **Moon Ballad** 9-0   J P Spencer
7-2, 9-4f, 20-1. 2l, 12l. 12 ran. 2m 39.5 (b6.90)
Mr M Tabor & Mrs John Magnier (A P O'Brien, Ireland).

A triumph for O'Brien, whose pair dominated as he won the principal Classic for the second successive year. Though less favoured in the betting, High Chaparral was the one with the right background for 1m4f on soft ground, having won over 1m2f and being by Sadler's Wells out of a Darshaan mare, whereas Hawk Wing had never raced beyond 1m and was by Woodman. Though he was under pressure even before the turn for home, High Chaparral was always going to keep going. He hit the front with over two furlongs to go and was quickly joined by his stablemate, who was travelling very easily. It's impossible to be sure whether Hawk Wing failed for want of stamina or lack of guts but, either way, he went from travelling smoothly to looking held in a matter of strides and fell back into second place. Mark Johnston's pair **Fight Your Corner** and **Bandari** were disappointing but the first-named was then found to have sustained a fractured hind cannon-bone in the race. He underwent successful surgery and may race again in 2004. Not so fortunate was **Coshocton**, who broke a leg inside the final furlong. The incidence of injury in this race leaves the course with questions to answer, but they have shown no sign of addressing the issue.

10 St James's Palace Stakes (1m) Ascot June 18 (Gd)

1 **Rock Of Gibraltar** 9-0   M J Kinane
2 **Landseer** 9-0   J Murtagh
3 **Aramram** 9-0   S Drowne
4-5f, 13-2, 20-1. 1¾l, 4l. 9 ran. 1m 40.9 (b6.37)
Sir Alex Ferguson & Mrs John Magnier (A P O'Brien, Ireland).

The Rock became the first 2,000 Guineas winner to land this since 1981. He won emphatically, with those behind him including the winners of the French, Italian and German Guineas. Landseer gave Aidan O'Brien another Group 1 one-two.

11 Prince Of Wales's Stakes (1m2f) Ascot June 19 (Gd)

1 **Grandera** 9-0   L Dettori
2 **Indian Creek** 9-0   T Quinn
3 **Banks Hill** 8-11   O Peslier
4-1, 25-1, 7-2f. 5l, ¾l. 12 ran. 2m 4.4 (b11.57)
Godolphin (S Bin Suroor, Newmarket).

Impressive stuff from Grandera, of whom Dettori said "He wants fast ground, a strong pace and a mile and a quarter." Not for the first time, Indian Creek ran above himself on fast ground, passing most of the field in the last furlong. Banks Hill and **Nayef** finished tired.

Sponsored by Stan James

12 Gold Cup (2m4f) Ascot June 20 (Gd to Firm)

1	**Royal Rebel** 9-2	J Murtagh
2	**Vinnie Roe** 9-0	P J Smullen
3	**Wareed** 9-0	L Dettori

16-1, 5-2f, 13-2. nk, 1l. 15 ran. 4m 25.6 (b6.36)
Mr P D Savill (M Johnston, Middleham).

In a repeat of his form the previous year, Royal Rebel warmed up with two bad runs and then bounced back to his best for the big one.

13 Coronation Stakes (1m) Ascot June 21 (Gd to Firm)

1	**Sophisticat** 9-0	M J Kinane
2	**Zenda** 9-0	R Hughes
3	**Dolores** 9-0	T Quinn

11-2, 7-1, 5-1. nk, 2½l. 11 ran. 1m 41.6 (b5.69)
Mr M Tabor & Mrs John Magnier (A P O'Brien, Ireland).

Beaten a length by Zenda in the French 1,000 Guineas when suffering interference, Sophisticat again met trouble in running but flew home, making up four lengths in the last furlong.

14 Golden Jubilee Cork & Orrery Stakes (6f) Ascot June 22 (Gd to Firm)

1	**Malhub** 9-4	K Darley
2	**Danehurst** 9-1	S Sanders
3	**Three Points** 9-4	L Dettori

16-1, 13-2, 4-1. 1¼l, ½l. 12 ran. 1m 14.3 (b6.48)
Mr Hamdan Al Maktoum (J Gosden, Manton).

Malhub carried his owner's third colours after a low-key prep winning a four-runner affair at Yarmouth. He ran on strongly to beat Danehurst, who would have preferred more give. Continent stayed on into fifth but **Johannesburg** was never going and this was his last race.

15 Budweiser Irish Derby (1m4f) Curragh June 30 (Gd)

1	**High Chaparral** 9-0	M J Kinane
2	**Sholokhov** 9-0	P J Scallan
3	**Ballingarry** 9-0	J A Heffernan

1-3f, 200-1, 12-1. 3½l, 1½l. 9 ran. 2m 32.2 (b6.13)
Michael Tabor (A P O'Brien, Ireland).

Another Classic 1-2-3 for O'Brien and a lap of honour for High Chaparral. Champion sire Sadler's Wells had four sons in the race, and they filled the first four places.

16 Coral Eurobet Eclipse Stakes, (1m2f7yds) Sandown July 6 (Gd to Soft)

1	**Hawk Wing** 8-10	M J Kinane
2	**Sholokhov** 8-10	Paul Scallan
3	**Equerry** 9-7	L Dettori

8-15f, 14-1, 4-1. 2½l, 2½l. 5 ran. 2m 13.3 (b0.79)
Mrs John Magnier (A P O'Brien, Ireland).

Despite the achievements of stablemates Rock Of Gibraltar and High Chaparral, both of whom were multiple Group 1 winners by this point, Hawk Wing continued to receive rather more than his share of hype. Unlucky in the Guineas but fairly beaten at Epsom, this horse had fans who seemed to expect him to turn out the best of his generation. This race at last got him off the mark as a three-year-old but proved little as to the extent of his ability, since he beat perhaps the weakest field ever assembled for the Eclipse. The runner-up was his pacemaker, while none of the others had won in better than Group 3 company.

17 Darley July Cup (6f) Newmarket July 11 (Gd to Soft)

1	**Continent** 9-5	D Holland
2	**Bahamian Pirate** 9-5	R Hughes
3	**Danehurst** 9-2	G Duffield

12-1, 16-1, 5-2f. ½l, 1¼l. 14 ran. 1m 13.0 (b2.90)
Lucayan Stud (D Nicholls, Thirsk).

A tremendous training performance by Dandy Nicholls, whose two runners fought out the finish. Both were past winners of the Ayr Gold Cup but had proved hard to place since – indeed, Continent had not won in nine runs since, though he'd looked progressive in Group races earlier this term. Danehurst had almost her ideal conditions but had no excuses in what was reckoned to be a sub-standard renewal and the likelihood is that she's just not up to winning at Group 1 level.

18 Darley Irish Oaks (1m4f) Curragh July 14 (Soft)

1	**Margarula** 9-0	K J Manning
2	**Quarter Moon** 9-0	M J Kinane
3	**Lady's Secret** 9-0	M Hills

33-1, 4-5f, 16-1. 1l, 6l. 12 ran. 2m 27.4 (b10.93)
Mrs J S Bolger (J Bolger, Ireland).

This really ought to have been a coronation for Epsom Oaks second Quarter Moon but the suspicion had been brewing that she has a difficult temperament and she confirmed this by getting thoroughly stewed up in the preliminaries. The race went to plan up to the final furlong, as she cruised to the lead and went clear, but she was then a sitting duck for Margarula and went under quite tamely when that one challenged. Since the winner's only other successes came in handicaps and she was well beaten in her only two subsequent efforts, it's hard to have much respect for the form.

19 King George VI & Queen Elizabeth Diamond Stakes (1m4f) Ascot July 27 (Gd to Firm)

1 **Golan** 9-7   K Fallon
2 **Nayef** 9-7   R Hills
3 **Zindabad** 9-7   K Darley
11-2, 7-1, 11-2. hd, 3½l. 9 ran. 2m 29.7 (b11.82)
Exors of the late Lord Weinstock (Sir M Stoute, Newmarket).

Golan hadn't been seen since his sixth in the Japan Cup the previous November, so this was quite an achievement, even allowing for the fact that he'd won the previous year's 2,000 Guineas on his seasonal reappearance. **Grandera** was sent off favourite but ran flat over a trip at which he had lost in both previous attempts, while the proximity of Zindabad suggests this was not a vintage renewal.

20 Sussex Stakes (1m) Goodwood July 31 (Gd)

1 **Rock Of Gibraltar** 8-13   M J Kinane
2 **Noverre** 9-7   L Dettori
3 **Reel Buddy** 9-7   R Hughes
8-13f, 3-1, 33-1. 2l, 2l. 5 ran. 1m 38.3 (b1.79)
Sir Alex Ferguson & Mrs John Magnier (A P O'Brien, Ireland).

The most impressive performance yet from Rock Of Gibraltar, who was taking on older horses for the first time. He fairly cruised past Noverre, who had looked a good winner in the previous year's renewal. The race came at a time when O'Brien's horses were under a cloud.

21 Vodafone Nassau Stakes (1m1f192yds) Goodwood August 3 (Gd to Firm)

1 **Islington** 8-6   K Fallon
2 **Sulk** 8-6   R Hughes
3 **Quarter Moon** 8-6   M J Kinane
10-3, 33-1, 9-4f. 4l, ½l. 10 ran. 2m 4.7 (b8.10)
Exors of the late Lord Weinstock (Sir M Stoute, Newmarket).

Given the way she lay down in the Irish Oaks, Quarter Moon did not deserve to be favourite for this and she was duly put in her place by Islington, who was bouncing back from her exhausted defeat in the Epsom Oaks. Taking it up two furlongs out, she was soon clear and looked in a different league to these.

22 Juddmonte International Stakes (1m2f85yds) York August 20 (Gd)

1 **Nayef** 9-5   R Hills
2 **Golan** 9-5   K Fallon
3 **Noverre** 9-5   L Dettori
6-4f, 9-4, 7-2. ½l, 1½l. 7 ran. 2m 8.7 (b11.16)
Mr Hamdan Al Maktoum (M Tregoning, Lambourn).

Beaten a head at Ascot, Nayef turned the form round with his King George conqueror over a quarter-mile less. Taking it up two out, he was forced to battle but was always just holding on and the suspicion must be that Golan is better at further. This was the winner's last run of the season, but he is expected back as a five-year-old. Noverre was stepping up in trip but the steady early pace meant his stamina was not tested.

23 Aston Upthorpe Yorkshire Oaks (1m3f195yds) York August 21 (Gd)

1 **Islington** 8-8   K Fallon
2 **Guadalupe** 8-8   Andreas Suborics
3 **Sulk** 8-8   R Hughes
2-1, 20-1, 16-1. 5l, hd. 11 ran. 2m 26.7 (b15.15)
Exors of the late Lord Weinstock (Sir M Stoute, Newmarket).

Kazzia was sent off favourite but could have used faster ground and was apparently short of peak fitness. Islington beat a good field impressively and could have won further.

24 Victor Chandler Nunthorpe Stakes (5f) York August 22 (Gd to Firm)

1 **Kyllachy** 9-11   J P Spencer
2 **Malhub** 9-11   R Hills
3 **Indian Prince** 9-11   K Fallon
3-1f, 15-2, 33-1. ½l, ½l. 17 ran. 58.1 (b1.90)
Thurloe T'breds V & Cheveley Park Stud (H Candy, Wantage).

Having decided that the far rail was the place to be, Jamie Spencer took Kyllachy right across the course early on and was last after a furlong, but the horse ran on well. Whether the tactic was entirely justified must be moot, however, since runner-up Malhub ran from the adjacent stall, kept straight and was only col-

25 Stanley Leisure Sprint Cup (6f) Haydock September 7 (Gd to Firm)

1 **Invincible Spirit** 9-0	J Carroll
2 **Malhub** 9-0	R Hills
3 **Three Points** 9-0	K Darley

25-1, 11-2, 12-1. shd, 2l. 14 ran. 1m 12.4 (b2.56)
Prince A A Faisal (J Dunlop, Arundel).

Quite a turn up, since the winner had never won above Group 3 company before, though he had some form claims. With the going in his favour, he got up in a bobbing finish. **Orientor** was finishing strongly in fourth, while **Continent** was also nearest at the finish in sixth, about three lengths off Invincible Spirit. **Nayyir** was sent off favourite but was tapped for speed over such a fast 6f, while **Danehurst** couldn't cope with the lively ground.

26 Ireland The Food Island Champion Stakes (1m2f) Leopardstown September 7 (Gd)

1 **Grandera** 9-4	L Dettori
2 **Hawk Wing** 8-11	M J Kinane
3 **Best Of The Bests** 9-4	J P Spencer

5-2, 8-11f, 12-1. shd, nk. 7 ran. 2m 4.7 (b9.56)
Godolphin (S Bin Suroor, Newmarket).

A glorious finish to a race that usually produces excitement. **Sholokhov**, once more on pace-setting duties for Hawk Wing, was allowed to go clear and was 15 lengths up at the top of the straight. Best Of The Bests passed him a furlong out but was collared by Hawk Wing close to the line, only for Godolphin to produce another trump in the form of Grandera, who hit the front in the final stride.

27 Jefferson Smurfit Memorial Irish St. Leger (1m6f) Curragh September 14 (Gd to Firm)

1 **Vinnie Roe** 9-9	P J Smullen
2 **Pugin** 9-9	J P Murtagh
3 **Ballingarry** 8-12	J A Heffernan

4-7f, 10-1, 8-1. 1½l, 1l. 8 ran. 2m 59.0 (b4.18)
Seamus Sheridan (D Weld, Ireland).

The winner of six of his previous seven outings, Vinnie Roe's only defeat in over a year was by quarter of a length in the Ascot Gold Cup to a dual winner of that race. The race panned out well for him, as he tracked the leader, moved easily to the front and kept going on ground a bit too lively for him. The form received a huge compliment when Ballingarry won the Canadian International two weeks later.

28 Rothmans Royals St Leger Stakes (Showcase Race) (1m6f132yds) Doncaster September 14 (Gd to Firm)

1 **Bollin Eric** 9-0	K Darley
2 **Highest** 9-0	D Holland
3 **Bandari** 9-0	R Hills

7-1, 10-1, 13-8f. 1¼l, 2l. 8 ran. 3m 2.9 (b25.42)
Sir Neil Westbrook (T Easterby, Malton).

Bollin Eric hadn't won in five outings at three but Time Easterby had declared himself "sure he's a St Leger horse" after he was second in the King Edward at Royal Ascot and the horse did this well, galloping on strongly from off a strong pace. The first three had fought out the Great Voltigeur the month before, but their placings were reversed this time, with Bandari not quite seeing out the trip.

29 Netjets Queen Elizabeth II Stakes (1m) Ascot September 28 (Gd to Firm)

1 **Where Or When** 8-11	K Darley
2 **Hawk Wing** 8-11	M J Kinane
3 **Tillerman** 9-1	K Fallon

7-1, 1-2f, 10-1. 2l, 3l. 5 ran. 1m 41.4 (b5.91)
John Humphreys (Turf Accountants) Ltd (T Mills, Epsom).

Hawk Wing started a warm favourite, as he had for all four previous runs this season, but for the fourth time he was beaten. He had no excuses – **Sholokhov** set the race up for him, he hit the front a furlong out and simply had no answer when Where Or When accelerated past. The winner had previously put up some sound efforts in good company but nothing to suggest he could win one like this.

30 Emirates Airline Champion Stakes (1m2f) Newmarket October 19 (Gd)

1 **Storming Home** 9-2	M Hills
2 **Moon Ballad** 8-11	J P Spencer
3 **Noverre** 9-2	L Dettori

8-1, 5-2f, 9-2. ½l, ¾l. 11 ran. 2m 1.4 (b10.28)
Maktoum Al Maktoum (B Hills, Lambourn).

Storming Home hadn't tackled a trip this short since he was third in the Dante 17 months before but he showed improved form, which Barry Hills attributed to the fitting of sheepskin cheekpieces. Hills also felt his horses were only starting to come right at the very end of the season. Moon Ballad appeared to become unbalanced in The Dip and was finishing well up the hill. He could be the sort to make further progress as a four-year-old.

THE CHAMP: Rock Of Gibraltar, who won five of six races in 2002, all at Group 1 level
Sponsored by Stan James

Group 1 index

All horses placed or commented on in our Group 1 review section, with race numbers

Horse	Races	Horse	Races
Alasha	2	Keltos	3
Aramram	10	Kyllachy	24
Bach	6	Lady's Secret	18
Bahamian Pirate	17	Landseer	10
Ballingarry	15, 27	Malhub	14, 24, 25
Bandari	9, 28	Margarula	18
Banks Hill	11	Moon Ballad	9, 30
Best Of The Bests	26	Nayef	6, 11, 19, 22
Bollin Eric	28	Nayyir	25
Boreal	7	Noverre	3, 20, 22, 30
Century City	4	Olden Times	3
Continent	17, 25	Orientor	25
Coshocton	9	Pugin	27
Danehurst	14, 17, 25	Quarter Moon	5, 8, 18, 21
Della Francesca	4	Rebelline	6
Dolores	13	Redback	1
Equerry	16	Reel Buddy	20
Fight Your Corner	9	Rock Of Gibraltar	1, 4, 10, 20
Golan	19, 22	Royal Rebel	12
Gossamer	5	Shadow Dancing	8
Grandera	11, 19, 26	Sholokhov	15, 16, 26, 29
Guadalupe	23	Snowfire	2
Hawk Wing	1, 9, 16, 26, 29	Sophisticat	13
High Chaparral	9, 15	Starbourne	5
Highest	28	Storming Home	7, 30
Indian Creek	11	Sulk	21, 23
Indian Prince	24	Three Points	14, 25
Invincible Spirit	25	Tillerman	29
Islington	21, 23	Vinnie Roe	12, 27
Johannesburg	14	Wareed	12
Kazzia	2, 8, 23		

THE CHUMPS' CHAMP: Hawk Wing was a beaten favourite four times in the last season

Sponsored by Stan James

Outlook

Two-year-old Review
Britain & Ireland, 2003

1 Sara Lee Marble Hill Stakes (Listed), (5f) Curragh May 25 (Soft)

1 **Marino Marini** 9-0 M J Kinane
2 **Luminata** 8-11 K J Manning
3 **Petite Histoire** 8-11 D P McDonogh
4-6f, 9-1, 13-8. 2½l, 2½l. 4 ran. 1m 4.8 (a2.12)
Mrs John Magnier (A P O'Brien, Ireland).
Petite Histoire, a winner of two minor races already, led at a good pace but had no answer and looked tired when the first two went past. The winner had won a 6f Cork maiden on his only previous start and won with authority, while the second was making her debut.

2 Swordlestown Stud Sprint Stakes (Listed), (6f) Naas June 3 (Soft)

1 **Rag Top** 8-9 D O'Neill
2 **Luminata** 8-9 K J Manning
3 **Tus Maith** 8-9 D J Moran
2-1f, 7-2, 33-1. 1l, shd. 11 ran. 1m 18.8 (a6.13)
Fergus Jones (R Hannon, Marlborough).
After two wins over 5f on fast ground in England, Rag Top made all and landed this in grand style. She was value for a good bit more than the official margin, being eased down close home. Tus Maith met trouble in running, while **Yesterday** (eighth) was never in it.

3 Vodafone Woodcote Stakes (Listed), (6f) Epsom June 8 (Gd to Soft)

1 **The Bonus King** 9-0 K Darley
2 **Monsieur Boulanger** 9-0 J Fortune
3 **One Last Time** 9-0 Dane O'Neill
11-8f, 10-1, 3-1. ½l, ½l. 6 ran. 1m 12.7 (a0.41)
Mrs Mo Done (M Johnston, Middleham).
Already a winner of a 5f Ripon maiden, The Bonus King made all and held on grittily. One Last Time ran a more eyecatching race, though, losing his chance with a very slow start and then flying home in the final furlong.

Sponsored by Stan James

4 Rochestown Stakes, (6f) Leopardstown June 12 (Soft)

1 **Akanti** 8-12 W J Smith
2 **Benicio** 8-12 K J Manning
3 **Catcher In The Rye** 8-12 M J Kinane
5-1, 7-1, 4-5f. 1l, ½l. 6 ran. 1m 19.6 (a3.41)
Third Avenue Syndicate (G Lyons, Ireland).
A first pattern winner on the Flat for Lyons, who reckoned this one would prove better on better ground, though in the event he was not seen again. Previously the winner of a maiden here and runner-up to Spartacus at Gowran Park, he made all this time.

5 Coventry Stakes (Group 3), (6f) Ascot June 18 (Gd)

1 **Statue Of Liberty** 8-12 M J Kinane
2 **Pakhoes** 8-12 P J Smullen
3 **Kawagino** 8-12 P Doe
5-2f, 16-1, 33-1. nk, 3½l. 16 ran. 1m 15.7 (b5.09)
Mr M Tabor & Mrs John Magnier (A P O'Brien, Ireland).
Run at a predictably strong pace, this ended with the first two pulling clear and they look useful prospects, though as it turned out the winner was not seen again. Pushed along early, Statue Of Liberty produced potent acceleration at the point when it was most needed, allowing him to take a gap ahead of the better-placed Pakhoes. After that, he always looked like finding enough to hold on. Kawagino stayed on well, having been last at halfway, while the O'Brien second-string **Spartacus** was also nearest at the finish.

6 Queen Mary Stakes (Group 3), (5f) Ascot June 19 (Gd)

1 **Romantic Liason** 8-8 Pat Eddery
2 **Never A Doubt** 8-8 M Hills
3 **Rag Top** 8-8 Dane O'Neill
16-1, 12-1, 6-1f. 3¹/2l, nk. 19 ran. 1m 0.6 (b4.44)

Sheikh Mohammed (B Meehan, Upper Lambourn).

This had looked a strong field, with 13 winners, of whom five were unbeaten, so it was impressive that Romantic Liason could win so emphatically, and after a less than ideal prep (a bout of coughing meant her only prep run was on the sand at Lingfield, in which she only got up by a head). Her half-sister also won this, but never won again.

7 Chesham Stakes (Listed), (7f) Ascot June 19 (Gd to Firm)

1 **Helm Bank** 9-0   K Dalgleish
2 **Tomahawk** 9-2   M J Kinane
3 **Celtic Sapphire** 8-7   K Darley
25-1, 1-2f, 11-1. shd, nk. 12 ran. 1m 29.0 (b5.57)
Mr & Mrs G Middlebrook (M Johnston, Middleham).

Helm Bank stepped up on the form of his debut win in an Ayr novice to take quite a scalp here – someone from the Ballydoyle camp told Mark Johnston before the race that they thought Tomahawk was unbeatable. The winner showed plenty of guts to hold on under pressure for the last quarter-mile, despite having been up there throughout, but Tomahawk may not have been comfortable on such firm ground.

8 Norfolk Stakes (Group 3), (5f) Ascot June 20 (Gd to Firm)

1 **Baron's Pit** 8-12   R Hughes
2 **The Bonus King** 8-12   K Darley
3 **Marino Marini** 8-12   M J Kinane
12-1, 10-1, 4-7f. hd, 3l. 12 ran. 1m 1.9 (b3.13)
J T & K M Thomas (R Hannon, Marlborough).

A full second slower than the fillies had managed in the Queen Mary. The trainer's son reported that most of the yard were gutted and skint after Baron's Pit had lost his debut at Kempton to Among Friends. He looked like he was going to win this well until The Bonus King kept rallying and pressed him all the way, the pair finishing clear. Marino Marini didn't cope well when let down on the fast going, while **Greek Revival** (sixth) showed some good pace and was reportedly well thought-of at home.

9 Windsor Castle Stakes (Conditions Race), (5f) Ascot June 21 (Gd to Firm)

1 **Revenue** 8-11   J Murtagh
2 **One Last Time** 8-13   Dane O'Neill
3 **Sir Albert** 8-13   D Holland
14-1, 7-2, 5-1. 1¼l, shd. 14 ran. 1m 2.1 (b2.91)
The Royal Ascot Racing Club (M Bell, Newmarket).

This form ties in with the Norfolk, since One Last Time had last been seen running a one-length third to The Bonus King at Epsom (3), suggesting that the worth of the two races is similar. Revenue was a three-times raced maiden but the advantage was he came into this unpenalised, whereas fourth-placed **Ontario** (another beaten O'Brien-trained juvenile favourite at this meeting) had an extra 4lb for having won a maiden at the Curragh. The first four finished almost three lengths clear.

10 Henry Carnarvon Albany Stakes (Listed Fillies), (6f) Ascot June 22 (Gd to Firm)

1 **Duty Paid** 8-11   T Quinn
2 **Luvah Girl** 8-11   K Darley
3 **Pearl Dance** 8-11   L Dettori
11-1, 12-1, 5-1f. hd, hd. 19 ran. 1m 15.9 (b4.92)
Mr J C Smith (D Elsworth, Whitsbury).

Duty Paid needed nearly every yard to hit the front, having dwelt in the stall and given up five lengths to everything else. The first three were drawn 19, 18 and 14, while the fifth ran from 16, suggesting that the fourth-placed **Mail The Desert** (broke from three) ran very well in adverse circumstances.

11 Goffs 2YO Challenge, (6f) Curragh June 28 (Gd)

1 **Hurricane Alan** 9-0   R Hughes
2 **Hazelhatch** 9-0   P Shanahan
3 **Bronntanas** 8-9   K J Manning
11-10f, 12-1, 10-1. 3½l, ½l. 14 ran. 1m 16.1 (a0.01)
I A N Wight (R Hannon, Marlborough).

The winner had scored twice over 5f at Brighton and Bath so this was a serious step up but he did it well. The trainer's son revealed (afterwards) that the horse was thought of as Group class at home and was as good as the yard's Royal Ascot runners.

12 Anheuser Busch Railway Stakes (Group 3), (6f) Curragh June 30 (Gd)

1 **Hold That Tiger** 8-10   M J Kinane
2 **Pakhoes** 8-10   P J Smullen
3 **Luminata** 8-7   K J Manning
5-4, 11-10f, 7-1. nk, 1l. 4 ran. 1m 17.0 (a0.91)
Michael Tabor (A P O'Brien, Ireland).

O'Brien also fielded the fourth, **Newfoundland**, who set a steady pace from which Hold That Tiger quickened impressively. This was his second win from two, as he'd previously flown home over a soft-ground 6f at Leopardstown. A half-brother to a Belmont Stakes winner, he's sure to stay further in time.

13 Dragon Stakes (Listed), (5f6yds) Sandown July 6 (Gd to Soft)

1 **Bella Tusa** 8-7 — T Quinn
2 **Queen's Victory** 8-7 — S Drowne
3 **Arran Pilot** 8-12 — M J Kinane
10-1, 11-4, 10-1. 1¾l, 2½l. 5 ran. 1m 4.5 (a0.11)
Mr Ettore Landi (C Wall, Newmarket).

Bella Tusa had just won a maiden at the third time of asking, over a firmish 6f at Goodwood for which the form was not all that taking, but she was the best here just the same and seemed if anything more suited by some give. Queen's Victory had been fifth in the Queen Mary (6). The Mark Johnston-trained favourite **Royal Beacon** finished last of the five – it was reported that connections felt he ran too freely but the Royal Applause colt never reproduced the promise of his fifth in the Coventry Stakes (5).

14 Kleinwort Benson Private Bank Cherry Hinton Stakes (Group 2), (6f) Newmarket July 9 (Gd to Soft)

1 **Spinola** 8-9 — T Quinn
2 **Cassis** 8-9 — D Holland
3 **Pearl Dance** 8-9 — R Hughes
7-1, 7-2f, 4-1. shd, hd. 9 ran. 1m 15.6 (b0.32)
The Winning Set (P Harris, Berkhamsted).

With a moderate time and a close finish, this didn't look anything special and the race has suffered a declining reputation in recent years, in terms of producing future stars. Spinola looks unlikely to fare better than recent winners; she had one more run at two, when seventh of eight in a Group 3 at Goodwood.

15 TNT July Stakes (Group 3), (6f) Newmarket July 10 (Gd to Soft)

1 **Mister Links** 8-10 — R Hughes
2 **Tacitus** 8-10 — Dane O'Neill
3 **The Bonus King** 8-13 — K Dalgleish
2-1f, 7-1, 10-3. ½l, ¾l. 10 ran. 1m 14.3 (b1.62)
Coriolan Links Partnership III (R Hannon, Marlborough).

The first seven were covered by about four lengths at the finish, so this seems an unlikely source of champions but Mister Links was making it three from three, albeit he needed to step up on previous form to do so. The Bonus King put up a game effort in trying to give weight all round but again his proximity tends to devalue the form. Fifth-placed **Tizzy May** was the unlucky one in the race, getting badly squeezed on the inside rail during the final furlong, but for which she would have finished close to The Bonus King.

16 Weatherbys Superlative Stakes (Listed), (7f) Newmarket July 11 (Gd to Soft)

1 **Surbiton** 8-11 — M Hills
2 **Magistretti** 8-11 — K Fallon
3 **Celtic Sapphire** 8-6 — K Dalgleish
16-1, 13-8f, 4-1. 5l, 1¾l. 7 ran. 1m 27.0 (b3.48)
Mrs Belinda Harvey (B Hills, Lambourn).

Magistretti came into this with a big reputation based on good looks and a win in a four-runner Sandown maiden but he couldn't cope when Surbiton stepped up the pace. The winner had been 12th in the Coventry (5). This improved form may have been down to the longer trip, the easier ground or the stable's better form.

17 Anglesey Stakes (Group 3), (6f63yds) Curragh July 13 (Soft)

1 **Ontario** 8-10 — M J Kinane
2 **Spartacus** 8-10 — C O'Donoghue
3 **Benicio** 8-10 — K J Manning
4-6f, 10-3, 5-1. 1½l, 2l. 4 ran. 1m 20.7 (a0.49)
Michael Tabor (A P O'Brien, Ireland).

Mick Kinane chose Ontario of O'Brien's two in a poor turnout. Stablemate Spartacus set the pace and Ontario quickened past nicely, showing the turn of foot that had won him a 5f maiden.

18 Vodafone Silver Flash Stakes (Listed), (6f) Leopardstown July 17 (Gd)

1 **Luminata** 8-9 — K J Manning
2 **Daganya** 8-9 — T P O'Shea
3 **New Design** 8-9 — W M Lordan
5-4f, 7-2, 8-1. nk, 3½l. 6 ran. 1m 15.2 (b0.99)
D H W Dobson (J Bolger, Ireland).

A game performance from Luminata, as she hit the front about two furlongs out and then came under strong pressure from previous winner Daganya. The runner-up was in front entering the last furlong but Luminata battled back well. She'd been placed three times in Group company before landing her maiden but this was her last win of the season.

19 Cantor Sport-Spread Free Rose Bowl Stakes (Listed), (6f8yds) Newbury July 19 (Gd to Firm)

1 **Deportivo** 9-0 — R Hughes
2 **Checkit** 9-0 — S Drowne
3 **Silca Boo** 8-6 — Pat Eddery
2-1, 11-2, 16-1. 1¼l, ½l. 5 ran. 1m 12.3 (b4.70)
Mr K Abdulla (R Charlton, Beckhampton).

All five were previous winners but Deportivo put the others firmly in their places with some eye-catching acceleration. The consistent Checkit gives the form a solid look. **Greek**

Revival was sent off the 4-5 favourite, having won a novice race at Newmarket the week before but he never looked comfortable on the fast ground.

20 Weatherbys Super Sprint, (5f34yds) Newbury July 20 (Gd to Firm)

1 **Presto Vento** 8-9 — E Ahern
2 **Wunders Dream** 8-0 — P Hanagan
3 **Sir Edwin Landseer** 9-1 — K Darley
6-1, 9-2j, 10-1. 2½l, shd. 24 ran. 1m 1.1 (b2.21) Major A M Everett (R Hannon, Marlborough).

Despite a historical bias in favour of those drawn high here, all but three went over to the far rail. That was a mistake – Presto Vento was slowly away and didn't have much to race against for important sections of the contest on the stands side but was in front a furlong out and won cosily. She wasn't beaten far when seventh of nine to Spinola in the Cherry Hinton (14), but the trainer reckoned her defeat there was due to the hold-up instructions he gave in what turned out to be a slowly-run race. He has a fine record in this, and kept it up here – from six runners, he also had the fourth, sixth and eighth.Not surprisingly, James Given, trainer of Wunders Dream, blamed the draw. She was prominent throughout and won the race on her side, having missed Royal Ascot through coughing. Kevin Darley gave up what had looked a good draw (18) to send Sir Edwin Landseer up the middle and that one ran a fine race under top weight, considering.

21 Milcars Star Stakes (Listed), (7f16yds) Sandown July 25 (Gd to Firm)

1 **Sister Bluebird** 8-9 — Pat Eddery
2 **Ribbons And Bows** 8-9 — S Sanders
3 **Mail The Desert** 8-12 — S Drowne
14-1, 25-1, 4-1. shd, ½l. 9 ran. 1m 30.6 (b2.51) O'Reilly Hyland & Pidgley Partnership (B Meehan, Upper Lambourn).

A shock on the face of it, but Brian Meehan had thought a fair bit of the winner earlier in the season. After she disappointed in maidens, he gave her a two-month break before picking up a nursery at Salisbury and this was a confirmation of the ability she'd previously hinted at. Ribbons And Bows had been last behind Surbiton (16) last time out but appreciated the better ground here.

22 Princess Margaret Stakes (Group 3), (6f) Ascot July 27 (Gd to Firm)

1 **Russian Rhythm** 8-9 — K Fallon
2 **Luvah Girl** 8-9 — K Darley
3 **Nasij** 8-9 — R Hills
evensf, 4-1, 3-1. 1¼l, 5l. 6 ran. 1m 15.3 (b5.52) Cheveley Park Stud (Sir M Stoute, Newmarket).

A taste of the drama that was to come at York, as Russian Rhythm was held up at the back for the first half-mile before progressing smoothly past everything else to win as she pleased.

23 Flame Of Tara Tyros Stakes (Listed), (7f) Curragh July 27 (Gd)

1 **Van Nistelrooy** 8-12 — M J Kinane
2 **Etruscan King** 8-12 — N G McCullagh
3 **Chappel Cresent** 8-12 — F M Berry
4-6f, 10-1, 10-1. hd, hd. 6 ran. 1m 32.7 (a3.71) Mrs John Magnier (A P O'Brien, Ireland).

A fortnight after winning his maiden over course and distance, Van Nistelrooy was back for more experience. With no stablemate to set the pace, he was held up off a steady gallop and struggled to get up, something he would not have managed on a softer surface. Even so, the bare form is meaningless, as the winner is undoubtedly capable of much better in better company.

24 Prix Robert Papin (Group 2), (5f110yds) Maisons-Laffitte July 28 (Gd)

1 **Never A Doubt** 8-13 — M Hills
2 **Zinziberine** 8-13 — O Peslier
3 **Ela Merici** 8-13 — D Boeuf
11-1, 9-1, 3-1. hd, 1½l. 9 ran. 0.0 Mr D M James (B Hills, Lambourn).

Never A Doubt came into this on one win from five but Barry Hills rated her an unlucky fourth in the Cherry Hinton (14), when she was beaten about two lengths after meeting interference close home. She was under a strong drive from some way out but took it up inside the last half-furlong and hung on well from a runner-up who went on to frank the form with two Group wins on the same course later in the season. Never A Doubt was not seen out again.

25 Gerrard Investment Management Richmond Stakes (Group 2), (6f) Goodwood July 30 (Gd to Firm)

1 **Elusive City** 8-11 — K Fallon
2 **Revenue** 8-11 — D Holland
3 **Checkit** 8-11 — S Drowne
9-2, 12-1, 20-1. 3l, 1l. 9 ran. 1m 10.8 (b0.42) The Thoroughbred Corporation (G A Butler, Blewbury).

Elusive City had won his debut on the All-

Weather at Lingfield but this was a classy-looking effort, the horse running green before powering past the field. He was unruly in the stalls and seems to be a tough horse to calm down but there's clearly no shortage of ability. He beat some reliable yardsticks here, including **Hurricane Alan** (fourth) and **The Bonus King** (sixth) but was unfortunately disqualified from this and his previous win, since a prohibited substance (a medication used for treating ulcers) was found in his sample.

26 Champagne Victor Vintage Stakes (Group 3), (7f) Goodwood July 31 (Gd)

1 **Dublin** 8-11 J P Spencer
2 **Bourbonnais** 8-11 K Darley
3 **Sarayat** 8-11 P Robinson
11-1, 6-1, 10-1. 1¼l, ½l. 10 ran. 1m 27.6 (b1.81) Sheikh Mohammed (D Loder, Newmarket).

Three from three for Dublin, one of three in the first four here who'd been unbeaten before. He looks progressive.

27 betfair.com Molecomb Stakes (Group 3), (5f) Goodwood August 1 (Gd)

1 **Wunders Dream** 8-7 M Fenton
2 **Sir Edwin Landseer** 8-12 K Fallon
3 **Folio** 8-12 T Quinn
8-1, 5-2f, 20-1. 2l, shd. 13 ran. 58.3 (b1.47) Mr J Ellis (J Given, Gainsborough).

Revenge for Wunders Dream, who seemed to have come on a lot for the Newbury race (20), confirming form with the second and turning it round comprehensively with **Presto Vento**, who could only run sixth after falling out of the stalls.

28 Prix De Cabourg (Group 3), (6f) Deauville August 3 (Soft)

1 **Loving Kindness** 8-8 T Thulliez
2 **Together** 8-8 D Sicaud
3 **Pleasure Place** 8-8 T Jarnet
11-10f, 20-1, 9-2. 4l, 5l. 7 ran. 1m 11.2 (a2.70) Famille Niarchos (P Bary, France).

Straightforward stuff for Loving Kindness, though she could hardly have been more impressive, taking it up two out and scoring in untroubled fashion. Talk of the 1,000 Guineas was in the air immediately afterwards, though the strength of the form was unclear.

29 British Red Cross Shergar Cup Juvenile (Auction Race), (7f) Ascot August 10 (Soft)

1 **Tout Seul** 9-1 K Fallon
2 **Devious Boy** 8-12 D Flores
3 **Iron Lad** 8-12 G Mosse
9-2f, 6-1, 25-1. 2½l, 9l. 10 ran. 1m 32.2 (b2.37) Eden Racing (R Johnson Houghton, Didcot).

The field finished very spaced out on this unseasonably soft going and it would probably be a mistake to put a great deal of faith in the form. Even so, Tout Seul showed a pleasing determination in landing his third win from four starts, his one defeat coming on the one occasion when he came up against firm going.

30 Milcars Sweet Solera Stakes (Listed), (7f) Newmarket August 10 (Soft)

1 **Soviet Song** 8-8 O Urbina
2 **Summitville** 8-8 M Fenton
3 **Miss Assertive** 8-8 I Mongan
4-1, 6-1, 33-1. 3l, 5l. 8 ran. 1m 30.0 (b0.46) Elite Racing Club (J Fanshawe, Newmarket).

A performance which had James Fanshawe drooling "She really, really travelled today." Summitville, previously a course and distance winner, went off in front but was effortlessly outclassed by Soviet Song, who just cruised clear. The runner-up put a deal of distance between herself and the third, giving hope that the form may turn out every bit as impressive as it seemed.

31 Independent Waterford Wedgwood Phoenix Stakes (Group 1), (6f) Curragh August 11 (Soft)

1 **Spartacus** 9-0 C O'Donoghue
2 **Marino Marini** 9-0 J A Heffernan
3 **Polar Force** 9-0 K P Darley
16-1, 7-2, 25-1. ¼l, shd. 9 ran. 1m 15.1 (b0.99) Mrs John Magnier (A P O'Brien, Ireland).

What chance do punters have when it seems that even connections as clued-up as Ballydoyle can't tell which is their best in the race? O'Brien ran four here, of which Spartacus was the rank outsider. **Hold That Tiger** was the 11-10 favourite, a position which he belied by trailing in last – it was later reported that he finished in a state of respiratory distress. Spartacus made nearly all and held on dourly. O'Brien reckoned he'd had no chance, in hindsight, on the firm ground at Ascot and that he must have progressed for his last run (17). Why he was able to turn the form round so readily with **Ontario** (fifth) was not clear.

32 Robert H. Griffin Debutante Stakes (Group 3), (7f) Curragh August 11 (Soft)

1 **Rainbows For All** 8-10 W J Smith
2 **Yesterday** 8-10 M J Kinane
3 **Rapid Ransom** 8-10 D P McDonogh
14-1, 5-4f, 7-2. 1¼l, 1½l. 9 ran. 1m 28.7 (b0.29)

Lady O'Reilly (K Prendergast, Ireland).

Two fillies who both looked decent prospects fought this out. Yesterday, the O'Brien-trained runner with the reputation, came there a furlong out looking the likely winner but, though she battled well, Rainbows For All was able to maintain a strong gallop from start to finish and would not be passed.

33 Scottish & Newcastle Washington Singer Stakes (Listed), (7f) Newbury August 16 (Gd to Firm)

1 **Muqbil** 8-8 — R Hills
2 **Pinkerton** 8-11 — Dane O'Neill
3 **La Mouline** 8-3 — E Ahern
4-1, 7-4f, 2-1. 5l, ½l. 6 ran. 1m 26.6 (b4.32) Mr Hamdan Al Maktoum (J Dunlop, Arundel).

This race has quite a reputation for producing future champions, though recent winners have hardly been uniformly brilliant. The bare form is suspect because of a false pace, whereas most of these looked middle-distance sorts in the making, but Muqbil scored in taking style to give Swain his first winner as a sire.

34 Stan James St Hugh's Stakes (Listed), (5f34yds) Newbury August 17 (Gd to Firm)

1 **Speed Cop** 8-8 — Martin Dwyer
2 **Wimple** 8-8 — B Doyle
3 **Topkamp** 8-8 — M Fenton
7-4f, 7-1, 7-1. nk, ¾l. 9 ran. 1m 0.8 (b2.54) Mr J C Smith (I Balding, Kingsclere).

Fourth in both the Queen Mary and the Molecomb, Listed success seemed assured for Speed Cop and she showed her experience in landing this, requiring only to be shaken up to repel the challenge of Wimple, who finished midfield in the Ascot race after traffic problems.

35 Paradime Acomb Stakes (Listed), (6f214yds) York August 20 (Gd)

1 **Bourbonnais** 8-13 — K Darley
2 **Salcombe** 8-13 — R Hughes
3 **Wahsheeq** 8-13 — M J Kinane
5-6f, 6-1, 7-2. ¾l, nk. 6 ran. 1m 25.7 (b4.52) Sheikh Mohammed (M Johnston, Middleham).

Not much of a field for the prize, with the most major stables unrepresented, and they finished in a heap, so again it seems we'll look in vain for a champion among these. On the other hand, Bourbonnais seemed to have plenty of scope for improvement (Johnston wouldn't have put him among his top 20 juveniles in May) and is bred to make a three-year-old. It was his last outing of the year – he was subsequently sold to Godolphin.

36 Scottish Equitable Gimcrack Stakes (Group 2), (6f) York August 21 (Gd)

1 **Country Reel** 8-11 — L Dettori
2 **Mister Links** 9-0 — R Hughes
3 **Membership** 8-11 — B Doyle
3-1f, 5-1, 20-1. ½l, 1l. 11 ran. 1m 12.6 (b2.99) Maktoum Al Maktoum (D Loder, Newmarket).

Loder and co seemed pleased with their winner, but he looked a two-year-old and if there is one to take from this race it's more likely to be Mister Links, who has the greater scope for growth and was bumped during the race.

37 Costcutter Roses Stakes (Listed), (5f) York August 21 (Gd)

1 **Sir Albert** 8-11 — O Peslier
2 **Cumbrian Venture** 8-11 — R Winston
3 **Bond Becks** 8-11 — Paul Eddery
6-1, 9-2, 10-1. 1l, ½l. 10 ran. 59.6 (b0.41) Lucayan Stud (J Noseda, Newmarket).

The winner had done nothing wrong before and was beaten under two lengths in the Windsor Castle (9) – he showed good speed to take this but his season went south afterwards. **Sir Edwin Landseer** (fifth) was a disappointment.

38 Convivial Maiden Stakes, (6f) York August 21 (Gd)

1 **Court Masterpiece** 9-0 — R Hughes
2 **Arctic Burst** 9-0 — M Hills
3 **Weavers Pride** 9-0 — R Hills
5-2, 7-4f, 9-2. shd, 1¼l. 6 ran. 1m 13.3 (b2.26) Maktoum Al Maktoum (E Dunlop, Newmarket).

A finish fought out by two of the three with racecourse experience, neither of whom had any claims to greatness. **Governor Brown** ran on pleasingly in fourth.

39 Peugeot Lowther Stakes (Group 2), (6f) York August 22 (Gd to Firm)

1 **Russian Rhythm** 9-0 — K Fallon
2 **Danaskaya** 8-11 — K J Manning
3 **Romantic Liason** 9-0 — L Dettori
8-13f, 11-1, 5-2. 1¼l, nk. 5 ran. 1m 11.1 (b4.55) Cheveley Park Stud (Sir M Stoute, Newmarket).

An amazing performance from the winner against quality rivals. Russian Rhythm was completely squeezed out on the rail and had to be pulled three wide but then flew past them all looking an exceptionally talented filly.

Sponsored by Stan James

40 Galileo E.B.F. Futurity Stakes (Group 2), (7f) Curragh August 24 (Gd to Soft)

1 **Van Nistelrooy** 8-12   M J Kinane
2 **Chappel Cresent** 8-12   F M Berry
3 **Wilful** 8-12   K Dalgleish
1-1f, 7-1, 7-2. nk, nk. 8 ran. 1m 24.3 (b4.69)
Mrs John Magnier (A P O'Brien, Ireland).

An uninspiring win, though Van Nistelrooy is said to be a lazy type – Kinane expected him to win by two lengths until the final furlong. Given that this came at a time when most of the O'Brien juveniles were reportedly sick, it's hard to crab his effort.

41 Tattersalls Breeders Stakes, (6f) Curragh August 24 (Gd to Soft)

1 **Tout Seul** 8-12   S Carson
2 **Cosmo** 8-12   M J Kinane
3 **Zaby** 8-12   J P Murtagh
3-1f, 7-2, 16-1. 1½l, shd. 25 ran. 1m 12.7 (b3.39)
Eden Racing (R Johnson Houghton, Didcot).

On 3lb better terms, Tout Seul got his revenge on Cosmo for inflicting his only defeat to date. Both look very useful but there's more than a suspicion that the draw played a part here, with the first three running from stalls 25, 22 and 20.

42 Prix Morny Casinos Barriere (Group 1), (6f) Deauville August 25 (Gd to Soft)

1 **Elusive City** 9-0   K Fallon
2 **Zafeen** 9-0   S Drowne
3 **Loving Kindness** 8-10   T Thulliez
15-8, 11-1, evensf. ¾l, 2½l. 6 ran. 0.0 (b1m8.50)
The Thoroughbred Corporation (G A Butler, Blewbury).

The only one of three wins at two that Elusive City was allowed to keep, this was most impressive. Again unruly at the start, he raced with enthusiasm, accelerating between rivals of proven quality to go clear.

43 Touchdown In Malaysia Prestige Stakes (Group 3), (7f) Goodwood August 25 (Gd to Firm)

1 **Geminiani** 8-9   M Hills
2 **Mail The Desert** 8-9   D Holland
3 **Huja** 8-9   R Hills
3-1f, 14-1, 7-2. 1¼l, hd. 8 ran. 1m 26.8 (b2.64)
Mrs E Roberts (B Hills, Lambourn).

Geminiani won both her races last year, both over this course and distance on fast ground, but she's reckoned likely to prove better on good and a flatter track, in which case this clear-cut victory was the more meritorious.

44 Betfair.com Ripon Champion 2YO Trophy 2002 (Listed), (6f) Ripon August 26 (Gd)

1 **Cool Question** 8-9   G Duffield
2 **Harb** 8-11   R Hills
3 **Polar Force** 8-11   A Culhane
4-1, 2-1, 13-8f. ½l, ¾l. 7 ran. 1m 15.7 (b0.80)
Lady Fairhaven (Sir M Prescott, Newmarket).

Black type was the stated aim for this one after she'd won both her previous races over the minimum trip, and she achieved that here in a race that barely deserved Listed status. Polar Force won one from 11 last year, while Harb won only a Nottingham maiden. Cool Question was well beaten in both starts after.

45 Del Mar Debutante Stakes, (7f) Del Mar August 31 (Standard)

1 **Miss Houdini** 8-3   E Delahoussaye
2 **Santa Catarina** 8-3   M Smith
3 **Indy Groove** 8-3   J L Castanon
11-1, 9-10f, 12-1. nk, 9½l. 8 ran. 1m 23.4
Bo Hirsch (Warren Stute).

Saratoga lived up to its rep as a bad place for favourite-backers as Santa Catarina was edged out of this. Eighty-year-old trainer Warren Stute was winning this prize for the second time, having landed the inaugural running – 51 years ago.

46 Iveco Daily Solario Stakes (Group 3), (7f 16yds) Sandown August 31 (Gd to Firm)

1 **Foss Way** 8-11   J Fortune
2 **Sweet Return** 8-11   J Quinn
3 **Dhabyan** 8-11   R Hills
11-2, 33-1, 12-1. hd, ¾l. 11 ran. 1m 29.5 (b3.58)
Sheikh Mohammed (J Gosden, Manton).

Foss Way showed a nice attitude to keep galloping despite meeting traffic problems here, finding reserves of speed to get up in the dying strides. Gosden put his debut defeat down to soft ground, since when he'd won a moderate Goodwood maiden. **St Pancras** was staying on well in fourth.

47 Go And Go Round Tower Stakes (Listed), (6f) Curragh September 1 (Gd)

1 **Walayef** 8-9   D P McDonogh
2 **Mombassa** 8-12   J P Murtagh
3 **Daganya** 8-9   T P O'Shea
11-10f, 7-1, 3-1. 1½l, 1l. 7 ran. 1m 12.5 (b3.59)
Hamdan Al Maktoum (K Prendergast, Ireland).

Two from two over the track and trip for this winner, though it's hard to see that the form is any more than average for the level.

48 Moyglare Stud Stakes (Group 1), (7f) Curragh September 1 (Gd)

1 **Mail The Desert** 8-11   S Drowne
2 **Luminata** 8-11   J A Heffernan
3 **Pearl Dance** 8-11   R Hughes
8-1, 6-1, 11-4. hd, nk. 9 ran. 1m 25.5 (b3.49)
John Livock (M Channon, West Ilsley).

A Group 1 pinched by Mick Channon with a horse who, having been no better than third in four successive Listed races, had been second in a Group 3 the week before. Though she was undoubtedly on the upgrade, this win surely flatters her; it was her last run in 2002.

49 Sirenia Stakes (Listed), (6f) Kempton September 8 (Gd to Firm)

1 **Sir Edwin Landseer** 8-11   S Drowne
2 **Hurricane Alan** 8-11   D Holland
3 **Membership** 8-11   P Robinson
6-1, 4-1, 7-2f. shd, ½l. 8 ran. 1m 11.0 (b7.20)
Richard Green (Fine Paintings) (P Cole, Whatcombe).

Though Sir Edwin Landseer had disappointed at York, his earlier form, most notably in the Weatherbys Super Sprint, was solid and he was entitled to land this. Hurricane Alan upheld the Richmond form, while Membership was proving hard to win with.

50 £200,000 St Leger Yearling Stakes, (6f) Doncaster September 11 (Gd)

1 **Somnus** 8-11   T E Durcan
2 **Mister Links** 9-4   R Hughes
3 **Crimson Silk** 8-11   Paul Eddery
10-1, 4-1j, 14-1. ½l, shd. 21 ran. 1m 11.6 (b7.12)
Legard Sidebottom & Sykes (T Easterby, Malton).

Somnus deserves great credit for winning a really tough renewal, with a lot of good winning form represented by the also-rans, though the draw played its part, with the first five running from stalls 17, 18, 21, 20 and 19.

51 Prix D'Arenberg (Group 3), (5f110yds) Maisons-Laffitte September 11 (Gd)

1 **Pleasure Place** 8-8   T Jarnet
2 **Zinziberine** 8-8   O Plaais
3 **Traou Mad** 8-8   D Bonilla
17-2, 9-10f, 5-2. shd, 1¼l. 6 ran. 1m 5.9
Razza dell'Olmo (R Menichetti).

Well held over 6f on soft when last seen (28), Pleasure Place found this test of speed much more to her liking, scooting off in front and just holding off the runner-up's late challenge. For the consistent Zinziberine, this was a fourth successive game run in defeat.

52 Ralph Raper Memorial Prince Of Wales Cup (Showcase Handicap), (1m) Doncaster September 12 (Gd to Firm)

1 **Mysterinch** 9-1   I Mongan
2 **Go Tech** 9-0   Pat Eddery
3 **Tusk** 8-0   A Nicholls
4 **Pure Speculation** 8-3   J Mackay
11-1, 10-1, 40-1, 9-1. 1¼l, 1¼l, shd. 18 ran. 1m 38.1 (b9.73)
Colin & Melanie Moore (N Littmoden, Newmarket).

Draw analysts had a tricky week at Doncaster but this was definitely a race in which to be low, the first two (who'd been first and second in a similar race at Newcastle last time out) coming from traps one and two.

53 Rothmans Royals May Hill Stakes (Group 3), (1m) Doncaster September 12 (Gd to Firm)

1 **Summitville** 8-9   M Fenton
2 **Approach** 8-9   G Duffield
3 **Nasij** 8-9   R Hills
11-2, 7-2, 6-1. 1½l, 1¼l. 9 ran. 1m 38.5 (b9.36)
Mountain High Partnership (J Given, Gainsborough).

Given a soft lead, Summitville was also allowed to dictate when to up the pace. Sent on two out, she was always in control. The only horse to have beaten her in three runs so far is Soviet Song (30).

54 Rothmans Royals Champagne Stakes (Group 2), (7f) Doncaster September 13 (Gd to Firm)

1 **Almushahar** 8-10   L Dettori
2 **St Pancras** 8-10   K Darley
3 **Wizard Of Noz** 8-10   S W Kelly
8-11f, 25-1, 10-1. 1¼l, ½l. 11 ran. 1m 24.1 (b8.72)
Mr Hamdan Al Maktoum (D Loder, Newmarket).

It was 9-1 bar one and the greatest excitement here was generated by the quotes afterwards, most notably Loder comparing the winner favourably with Dubai Millennium.

55 DBS St Leger Yearling Stakes, (6f) Doncaster September 13 (Gd to Firm)

1 **Fleetwood Bay** 8-11   S Drowne
2 **Queen Of Night** 8-6   G Faulkner
3 **Danehill Stroller** 8-11   D Sweeney
25-1, 10-1, 20-1. shd, ¾l. 22 ran. 1m 12.5 (b6.25)
Mrs Julie Gavin (B Millman, Cullompton).

This was Fleetwood Bay's first win from eight starts, which probably says it all. Only one of those from a single-figure draw made the first ten – **Helms Deep**, seventh from box seven.

Sponsored by Stan James

56 Stardom Stakes (Listed), (1m) Goodwood September 13 (Gd)

1 **Rimrod** 8-11 — Martin Dwyer
2 **Rainwashed Gold** 8-11 — J P Spencer
3 **Makhlab** 8-11 — R Hills
9-4, 5-1, 11-8f. 1¼l, 6l. 5 ran. 1m 38.2 (b1.90)
Mr George Strawbridge (I Balding, Kingsclere).

Rimrod broke the course record set 13 years before by his half-brother Selkirk, thanks to **Naahy**, who paid for setting a strong pace by finishing last. The winner looks on the upgrade and appreciated the step up to a mile, while the form is worthy of respect.

57 Polypipe Flying Childers Stakes (Group 2), (5f) Doncaster September 14 (Gd to Firm)

1 **Wunders Dream** 8-12 — M Fenton
2 **Revenue** 8-12 — D Holland
3 **Speed Cop** 8-7 — Martin Dwyer
9-2, 7-1, 8-1. 1l, hd. 14 ran. 59.0 (b6.45)
Mr J Ellis (J Given, Gainsborough).

Russian Rhythm's reputation swelled while she stood in her box as one of those she beat in the Lowther made all to beat a good field. Wunders Dream is wonderfully consistent and probably just found the 6f at York a bit far. Speed Cop also holds her form well, albeit at a lesser level than this winner.

58 Aga Khan Studs National Stakes (Group 1), (7f) Curragh September 15 (Gd to Firm)

1 **Refuse To Bend** 9-0 — P J Smullen
2 **Van Nistelrooy** 9-0 — M J Kinane
3 **Dublin** 9-0 — L Dettori
7-1, 5-4f, 9-4. ¾l, nk. 7 ran. 1m 26.0 (b2.99)
Moyglare Stud Farm (D Weld, Ireland).

Though generally reckoned the pick of these on looks, it was asking a lot of Refuse To Bend to cope with this level of opposition after one maiden win. There was little sign of greenness, though, and Dermot Weld admitted afterwards that the Derby is in his thoughts.

59 Aga Khan Studs Blenheim Stakes (Listed), (6f) Curragh September 15 (Gd to Firm)

1 **Hurricane Alan** 8-11 — M J Kinane
2 **Mombassa** 8-11 — J P Murtagh
3 **Danaskaya** 8-8 — K J Manning
5-2, 9-2, 9-4f. 1½l, ¾l. 7 ran. 1m 10.9 (b5.19)
Mrs D M Wight (R Hannon, Marlborough).

Hurricane Alan hadn't tried to make all since his last success but a return to that tactic brought his fourth win. Though he was pressed two furlongs out, he galloped on strongly and won quite easily. Danaskaya paid a further compliment to Russian Rhythm.

60 Prix La Rochette Royal Thalasso Barriere (Group 3), (7f) Longchamp September 15 (Gd to Firm)

1 **Le Vie Dei Colori** 9-1 — T Thulliez
2 **Il Barone** 8-11 — T Jarnet
3 **Zanyboy** 8-11 — D Bonilla
2-1, 9-1, 9-1. nk, ½l. 6 ran. 1m 21.1 (a2.10)
Sc Archi Romani (R Brogi).

Italian raider Le Vie Dei Colori got a bit upset at the start but showed plenty of resolution in the race itself. Following the leader, he battled his way to the front a furlong out and held on under pressure. Added to a couple of successes over 6f at San Siro, this win makes him look useful.

61 Harry Rosebery Stakes (Listed), (5f) Ayr September 19 (Gd to Soft)

1 **Bella Tusa** 8-11 — S Sanders
2 **Membership** 8-11 — P Robinson
3 **Tilak** 9-0 — F Norton
4-1, 7-2, 14-1. 1½l, ¾l. 9 ran. 59.8 (b0.21)
Mr Ettore Landi (C Wall, Newmarket).

Suited by some cut, Bella Tusa landed her second Listed race over 5f (though her maiden win was over 6f). She quickened well off a strong pace and was a convincing winner. Trainer Chris Wall reported that she'd missed an intended target the previous week with a bruised foot.

62 Dubai Duty Free Mill Reef Stakes (Group 2), (6f8yds) Newbury September 20 (Gd to Firm)

1 **Zafeen** 8-12 — S Drowne
2 **Monsieur Bond** 8-12 — J P Spencer
3 **Cassis** 8-7 — Pat Eddery
8-11f, 5-1, 8-1. ¾l, ½l. 8 ran. 1m 12.9 (b4.11)
Mr Jaber Abdullah (M Channon, West Ilsley).

Runner-up to Elusive City in the Morny, Zafeen made that form look good with an authoritative success here, albeit one that was expected. Taking it up two out, he was always in control, though second and third look progressive.

63 Faucets First For Faucets Firth Of Clyde Fills' Listed Stks, (6f) Ayr September 21 (Gd)

1 **Airwave** 8-8 — C Rutter
2 **Irresistible** 8-8 — M Fenton
3 **Miss Takeortwo** 8-8 — P Hanagan
2-1f, 7-2, 50-1. 1½l, hd. 10 ran. 1m 13.1 (b0.86)
Henry Candy & Partners (H Candy, Wantage).

Airwave ended a decisive winner despite not getting a clear run. Last seen when fourth to Somnus (50), Henry Candy rates her the best two-year-old he's had.

64 Goffs Autumn Bonus Stakes, (7f) Cork September 21 (Gd to Firm)

1 **Blue Corrig** 8-12 P J Smullen
2 **Desert Glow** 8-7 J A Heffernan
3 **Boumoussa** 8-7 M C Hussey (5)
2-1, 5-4f, 16-1. 1l, 1l. 12 ran. 1m 26.5 (b3.82)
R Forristal (Miss F M Crowley, Ireland).

After four runs at a mile (three seconds and a dead-heat for first) Blue Corrig was trying 7f for the first time, and on fast ground, but a strong pace and blinkers helped him get there. Desert Glow had been third to Reach For The Moon in a big-field maiden on her debut.

65 Watership Down Stud Sales Race (Fillies), (6f110yds) Ascot September 27 (Gd to Firm)

1 **Sharplaw Venture** 8-11 R Hills
2 **Hector's Girl** 8-12 K Fallon
3 **Presto Vento** 8-11 Dane O'Neill
12-1, 6-1f, 10-1. hd, 1¼l. 25 ran. 1m 23.0 (b4.74)
Miss Tina Miller (W Haggas, Newmarket).

Hard to put much faith in this form when again the draw so obviously had a hand in the outcome, the first four running from stalls 25, 26, 20 and 23. The winner had looked both unexposed and progressive, so she merits respect but Presto Vento seemed on the decline.

66 Hackney Empire Royal Lodge Stakes (Group 2), (1m) Ascot September 28 (Gd to Firm)

1 **Al Jadeed** 8-11 R Hills
2 **Bahamian Dancer** 8-11 J P Spencer
3 **Van Nistelrooy** 9-0 M J Kinane
3-1, 16-1, 7-4f. hd, 1¼l. 9 ran. 1m 42.2 (b5.07)
Mr Hamdan Al Maktoum (J Gosden, Manton).

This was set up by Magistretti, who was sent to the front early and led at a strong pace, from which Al Jadeed got first run on the second. Van Nistelrooy didn't have an entirely clear run but also looked a bit one-paced.

67 Meon Valley Stud Fillies' Mile (Group 1), (1m) Ascot September 28 (Gd to Firm)

1 **Soviet Song** 8-10 O Urbina
2 **Casual Look** 8-10 Martin Dwyer
3 **Reach For The Moon** 8-10 M J Kinane
11-10f, 16-1, 9-1. 1¼l, 1¼l. 10 ran. 1m 42.3 (b4.96)
Elite Racing Club (J Fanshawe, Newmarket).

Three smooth wins from three for the winner, whose connections were purring about her Classic prospects afterwards. Though she was the best by a long way, **Oblige** stayed on stoutly in fifth and looks a three-year-old.

68 Somerville Tattersall Stakes (Group 3), (7f) Newmarket October 2 (Gd to Firm)

1 **Governor Brown** 8-9 T Quinn
2 **Muqbil** 8-12 R Hills
3 **Hurricane Alan** 8-12 Pat Eddery
6-1, 4-5f, 6-1. ½l, nk. 5 ran. 1m 25.9 (b5.34)
Mr Andy J Smith (P Cole, Whatcombe).

Governor Brown was the best on the day, but may not prove the best long-term prospect, since Muqbil ran green and seemed to lose his action in The Dip, something that will not necessarily be repeated once he's filled out a bit. Not form to rely on, due to the steady early pace.

69 Shadwell Stud Middle Park Stakes (Group 1), (6f) Newmarket October 3 (Gd to Firm)

1 **Oasis Dream** 8-11 J Fortune
2 **Tomahawk** 8-11 M J Kinane
3 **Elusive City** 8-11 K Fallon
6-1, 5-1, 6-4f. 1½l, nk. 10 ran. 1m 9.6 (b5.45)
Mr K Abdulla (J Gosden, Manton).

Advance rumours were strong for Oasis Dream, reckoned by Gosden to be the fastest juvenile in Europe over 6f. The first three were over three lengths clear and the form looks solid, though the winner seems unlikely to stay as far as a mile at three.

70 Betfair Cheveley Park Stakes (Group 1), (6f) Newmarket October 4 (Firm)

1 **Airwave** 8-11 C Rutter
2 **Russian Rhythm** 8-11 K Fallon
3 **Danaskaya** 8-11 K J Manning
11-2, 8-13f, 25-1. 1½l, ½l. 6 ran. 1m 10.7 (b4.34)
Henry Candy & Partners (H Candy, Wantage).

Russian Rhythm's first defeat, as she was unable to match the winner for speed – perversely, this doesn't harm her Guineas prospects, since she looks likely to need further than 6f, whereas Airwave seems an out-and-out sprinter. This is likely to prove excellent form.

71 C.L. Weld Park Stakes (Group 3), (7f) Curragh October 5 (Gd)

1 **Rag Top** 8-11 D O'Neill
2 **Feabhas** 8-11 K J Manning
3 **Finity** 8-11 J P Murtagh
9-4f, 9-1, 6-1. ½l, 2l. 14 ran. 1m 25.1 (b3.89)
Fergus Jones (R Hannon, Marlborough).

Rag Top was ridden to last home and settled well but may turn out to have more stamina than you'd expect of a Queen Mary third, since she ran right to the line for her second win in Ireland, and her fourth of the year.

72 Oh So Sharp Stakes (Listed), (7f) Newmarket October 5 (Firm)

1 **Khulood** 8-9   R Hills
2 **Soldera** 8-9   O Urbina
3 **Miss Assertive** 8-9   I Mongan
11-2, 11-10f, 16-1. 4l, 1¼l. 9 ran. 1m 23.0 (b8.19)
Mr Hamdan Al Maktoum (J Dunlop, Arundel).

The fast surface enabled Khulood to break an 11-year-old course record and turn this into a procession. On anything other than firm, she'd seem an unlikely stayer over a mile, though.

73 Betabet Two-Year-Old Trophy, (6f) Redcar October 5 (Firm)

1 **Somnus** 8-12   T E Durcan
2 **Tout Seul** 8-6   S Carson
3 **Monsieur Bond** 8-9   F Lynch
11-2, 7-2, 10-3f. hd, 1½l. 18 ran. 1m 10.5 (b3.30)
Legard Sidebottom & Sykes (T Easterby, Malton).

A fourth straight win for Somnus, three of which have been in fields of 18 or more, and he was defying what could have been a tough draw here, plus he's expected to prefer good going, so this was the end of a high-achieving season. However, even assuming he trains on, he'll be hard to place at three and is unlikely to be much of a price. Tout Seul was not at home on ground this fast, so deserves plenty of credit for going so close.

74 Prix Marcel Boussac Criterium Pouliches (Group 1), (1m) Longchamp October 6 (Gd to Soft)

1 **Six Perfections** 8-11   T Thulliez
2 **Etoile Montante** 8-11   R Hughes
3 **Luminata** 8-11   K J Manning
4-6f, 6-1, 16-1. 2l, 5l. 10 ran. 1m 37.9 (a2.90)
Niarchos Family (P Bary, France).

With the front pair finishing five lengths clear and some fillies with solid form in behind (**Pearl Dance** fourth, **Yesterday** sixth, **Cassis** ninth), this looked a good race, which Six Perfections won impressively. In four races, her only defeat was by less than a length on her debut, over a too-short 5f.

75 Gran Criterium-Lucien Barriere (Group 1), (7f) Longchamp October 6 (Gd to Soft)

1 **Hold That Tiger** 9-0   K Fallon
2 **Le Vie Dei Colori** 9-0   O Peslier
3 **Intercontinental** 8-10   C Soumillon
9-1, 15-2, 3-1f. ¾l, ¾l. 14 ran. 1m 20.1 (a1.10)
Mr M Tabor & Mrs John Magnier (A P O'Brien, Ireland).

On his first run since he was a highly disappointing favourite for the Phoenix Stakes (*31*), Hold That Tiger finished fast and late to beat a strong field. He was then sent to Chicago for the Breeders' Cup Juvenile in which he ran a similar race but couldn't get up, having been given plenty to do. His third of 13 there was a brilliant effort in the circumstances and he's an interesting prospect, though his three-year-old targets are opaque.

76 Danehill Dancer Tipperary Stakes (Listed), (5f) Tipperary October 6 (Gd to Firm)

1 **Shizao** 8-7   C O'Donoghue
2 **Miguel Cervantes** 8-10   P J Scallan
3 **Seattle Queen** 8-7   P Shanahan
6-1, 3-1j, 8-1. nk, ¾l. 9 ran. 57.3 (b2.32)
Ballylinch Stud (J Bolger, Ireland).

Just respectable for a Listed race, though they went a decent gallop. Shizao was sent to the front quickly and did it the hard way, though in the event it may have been the best tactic, since the others seemed short of acceleration. She showed gameness to hold on, though Miguel Cervantes was getting there with every stride.

77 Grey Breeders' Cup (Grade 2), (1m110yds) Woodbine October 6 (Gd)

1 **Wando** 8-3   R Migliore
2 **Gigawatt** 7-13   P Husbands
3 **Grand** 8-1   E Ramsammy
5-4f, 11-4, 9-1. 3¾l, 2l. 6 ran. 1m 45.1
G Schickedanz (M Keogh).

A good prep for a tilt at the Breeders' Cup as one of Canada's main hopes landed his second race at the track and his first over a mile. He got the run of the race, racing prominently and taking it up with a furlong to run before going clear, but he was only able to beat one home in the big one at Arlington.

78 Tom McGee Autumn Stakes (Listed), (1m) Ascot October 12 (Gd to Firm)

1 **Big Bad Bob** 8-11   Pat Eddery
2 **Rainwashed Gold** 8-11   T Quinn
3 **Choir Master** 8-11   J Fortune
3-1, 10-3, 8-1. 3½l, 1l. 6 ran. 1m 42.5 (b4.76)
Windflower Overseas Holdings Inc (J Dunlop, Arundel).

A step up in class for Big Bad Bob but he'd won his previous three and was clearly on the up and up. He did this convincingly enough and the race has produced some good sorts but it would be no surprise to see him go for some of the weaker Listed pots around Europe next year.

Sponsored by Stan James

79 Willmott Dixon Cornwallis Stakes (Group 3), (5f) Ascot October 12 (Gd to Firm)

1 **Peace Offering** 8-12 — K Darley
2 **Speed Cop** 8-7 — Martin Dwyer
3 **Revenue** 8-12 — J Murtagh
8-1, 4-1, 5-2f. ½l, 1l. 11 ran. 1m 2.2 (b2.81)
Mrs L M Askew (T Mills, Epsom).

Terry Mills had a tremendous relationship with this track in 2002 but even his most ardent supporters must have been a bit surprised to see him winning Group 3s for two-year-olds. Still, Peace Offering beat a handful of horses with solid form despite pulling hard early on. He showed a tendency to hang when beaten on his debut and did again here but looks a good sprinter in the making if he can get over that kink.

80 Newton Fund Managers Rockingham Stakes (Listed), (6f) York October 12 (Gd to Firm)

1 **Avonbridge** 8-11 — K Fallon
2 **Cumbrian Venture** 8-11 — R Winston
3 **Judhoor** 8-6 — W Supple
2-1f, 9-4, 7-1. ½l, 2½l. 7 ran. 1m 11.1 (b4.53)
Mr D J Deer (R Charlton, Beckhampton).

Avonbridge made it a hat-trick, following wins in a maiden and a nursery, and may yet have further progress to make, though this was his last outing as a juvenile. The form is nothing special but the front pair at least look useful sprinters for the future.

81 Juddmonte Beresford Stakes (Group 3), (1m) Curragh October 13 (Gd to Soft)

1 **Alamshar** 9-0 — J P Murtagh
2 **Brian Boru** 9-0 — M J Kinane
3 **Feabhas** 8-11 — K J Manning
7-1, 2-1f, 6-1. hd, 2l. 10 ran. 1m 44.9 (a0.35)
H H Aga Khan (J Oxx, Ireland).

Two from two as a juvenile for Alamshar, both over a mile, of which this was the second. Fourth with a furlong to go after a decent pace, he flew home. A performance like that at two years suggests he's going to find a mile on the short side next year. Brian Boru, the pick of O'Brien's four in the race, proved easily best of those and finished clear of the third.

82 Irish Breeders Foal Levy Stakes, (6f63yds) Curragh October 13 (Gd to Soft)

1 **Vettriano** 8-9 — F M Berry
2 **Miss Emma** 8-4 — T P O'Shea
3 **Ikan** 8-7 — I B Mongan
12-1, 20-1, 12-1. hd, nk. 14 ran. 1m 19.2 (b1.01)
Painestown Syndicate (C O'Brien, Ireland).

Vettriano had been tried at various trips during the season but seemed suited by this extended six. Ikan, a raider from Nick Littmoden's yard, looked unlucky, as she didn't get the gaps when they were most needed, and she was going on at the death.

83 £100000 Tattersalls Autumn Auction Stakes, (6f) Newmarket October 18 (Gd)

1 **Michelle Ma Belle** 7-12 — C Catlin
2 **Morning After** 7-12 — Martin Dwyer
3 **Ellamyte** 7-12 — D Kinsella
6-1, 9-4f, 20-1. 1l, shd. 30 ran. 1m 12.8 (b2.30)
Mr Bill Allan (S Kirk, Upper Lambourn).

With the first ten finishing within five lengths of each other and lightweights getting the upper hand, this looks form to ignore, though **One Last Time** put up a courageous effort to run a narrowly-beaten fifth under top weight.

84 Darley Dewhurst Stakes (Group 1), (7f) Newmarket October 19 (Gd)

1 **Tout Seul** 9-0 — S Carson
2 **Tomahawk** 9-0 — M J Kinane
3 **Trade Fair** 9-0 — R Hughes
25-1, 10-3, 11-4f. 1¼l, 1¼l. 16 ran. 1m 24.0 (b7.22)
Eden Racing (R Johnson Houghton, Didcot).

Stepped up to 7f for the first time, Tout Seul won this with unexpected reserves of stamina. **Great Pyramid**, one of four for O'Brien, set a strong pace up the centre that saw Tout Seul apparently struggling with a quarter of a mile to go, but he had the stands rail to himself and finished with a rattle as the prominent racers were dying on their feet. He should stay 1m at three and it's probably unfair that he was immediately dismissed as a Classic contender because of his unfashionable connections, but he's over-achieved so much at two that the suspicion must be his best form is already behind him. Trade Fair didn't cope well with the downhill stretch and still looks a good prospect for 2003.

85 Owen Brown Rockfel Stakes (Group 2 Fillies), (7f) Newmarket October 19 (Gd)

1 **Luvah Girl** 8-9 — K Darley
2 **Casual Look** 8-9 — Martin Dwyer
3 **Yesterday** 8-9 — M J Kinane
13-2, 4-1, 12-1. 1l, 1½l. 11 ran. 1m 25.0 (b6.23)
Team Valor (R Charlton, Beckhampton).

Luvah Girl had last been seen chasing home Russian Rhythm in Ascot's Princess Margaret. Fresh from three months on the sidelines, she made all at a steady pace and then had too much toe for those behind. Charlton was hoping to keep the filly through the winter for a crack at the 1,000 Guineas but she was packed off to America shortly afterwards to continue her career there.

86 Derrinstown Stud E.B.F Birdcatcher Premier Nursery Handicap, (6f) Naas October 20 (Soft)
1 **Roisin's Star** 8-1 S F Cleary (7)
2 **Miss Emma** 8-4 T P O'Shea (3)
3 **Kooyong** 8-2 F Norton
4 **Neeze** 8-1 T P Queally (3)
12-1, 7-1j, 10-1, 14-1. ½l, 3l, nk. 20 ran. 1m 14.2 (a1.53)
James Cummins (G Lyons, Ireland).

Another good juvenile winner for Ger Lyons, Roisin's Star had been runner-up in a nursery at Navan a fortnight before, the form for which held the key to this – the first three all made the first five here, with the extra furlong and a softer surface doing the trick for her.

87 Tote Bookmakers Silver Tankard Stakes (Listed), (1m4yds) Pontefract October 21 (Soft)
1 **Battle Chant** 8-11 S Sanders
2 **Inchberry** 8-6 K Fallon
3 **Black Belt Shopper** 8-7 M Hills
7-2, 7-4f, 12-1. 6l, 1¾l. 5 ran. 1m 47.1 (b1.95)
Cheveley Park Stud (E Dunlop, Newmarket).

Battle Chant had lost twice over 6f before getting off the mark when stepped up to 7f and a soft-ground 1m proved right up his street. He won this easily and showed little sign of fatigue as he beat four previous winners.

88 Prix des Reservoirs (Group 3), (1m) Deauville October 22 (Gd to Soft)
1 **High Praise** 8-9 D Boeuf
2 **Welcome Millenium** 8-9 I Mendizabal
3 **Mystic Melody** 8-9 O Plaais
3-1, 40-45f, 10-1. shd, 1½l. 8 ran. 1m 49.2 (a13.20)
K Abdullah (J Gosden, Manton).

An amazing way to win this from High Praise, who missed the kick completely but had already hit the front after a quarter-mile. She then came under strong pressure from Welcome Millenium, who went ahead inside the final furlong, but High Praise was able to battle back despite having set a good pace. Boeuf said that, although this was her third race, she was still immature and had a good look at her rival before responding to his urgings. He reckoned they'd have finished alone over a furlong further, though in the end it took the judge 20 minutes to split them. The runner-up's jockey felt he was beat for want of stamina.

Sponsored by Stan James

89 DBS October Yearling Stakes, (6f) Doncaster October 25 (Gd to Soft)
1 **Golden Nun** 8-6 T Quinn
2 **Cumbrian Venture** 9-0 R Winston
3 **Every Note Counts** 8-11 M Hills
4-1, 5-2f, 66-1. 6l, 3¼l. 21 ran. 1m 19.0 (a0.27)
Mr T G & Mrs M E Holdcroft (T Easterby, Malton).

Tim Easterby's pair dominated the betting (it was 10-1 bar) and came home one-two. Golden Nun probably had the best of the draw but she bounded clear in impressive fashion. She'd looked exposed before, though, so the form is probably not much.

90 Vodafone Horris Hill Stakes (Group 3), (7f) Newbury October 25 (Gd to Soft)
1 **Makhlab** 8-9 R Hills
2 **Zaide** 8-9 J Carroll
3 **Wizard of Noz** 8-9 S W Kelly
5-1, 8-1, 3-1f. 2½l. 10 ran. 1m 31.1 (a0.18)
Mr Hamdan Al Maktoum (B Hills, Lambourn).

Makhlab's only defeat in five starts at two was behind Rimrod at Goodwood, when he may not have taken to the track. He appreciated the ease in the going here.

91 Constant Security Doncaster Stakes (Listed), (6f) Doncaster October 26 (Soft)
1 **Miguel Cervantes** 8-9 K Darley
2 **Ikan** 8-4 I Mongan
3 **Michelle Ma Belle** 8-7 P Fitzsimons
9-2, 16-1, 12-1. 2½l, 2l. 9 ran. 1m 20.1 (a1.38)
Mrs John Magnier & Mr M Tabor (A P O'Brien, Ireland).

Hard to escape the feeling that this winner is a fair way down the pecking order at Ballydoyle but he did this convincingly and went clear in the final furlong, coping well with the surface. **Polar Force** was a disappointing favourite.

92 Racing Post Trophy (Group 1), (1m) Doncaster October 26 (Soft)
1 **Brian Boru** 9-0 K Darley
2 **Powerscourt** 9-0 G Duffield
3 **Illustrator** 9-0 Pat Eddery
11-8f, 6-1, 8-1. 1¼l, 1¾l. 9 ran. 1m 46.0 (b1.83)
Mrs John Magnier (A P O'Brien, Ireland).

'Derby' was on everyone's lips after this. The unexposed winner travelled well off a steady pace and overcame a certain amount of scrimmaging to win with a fair bit in hand, emulating High Chaparral, who'd won the race in similar style the year before. He's apparently lazy at home, but that was not evident here.

93 Gerrardstown House Stud Silken Gilder Stakes (Listed), (1m) Leopardstown October 26 (Gd to Soft)

1 **Miss Helga** 8-9 — J A Heffernan
2 **Feabhas** 8-9 — K J Manning
3 **Dixie Evans** 8-9 — P Shanahan
11-2, 11-4f, 10-1. 1½l, ½l. 12 ran. 0.0 (b1m46.36)
Mrs E M Stockwell (A P O'Brien, Ireland).

Miss Helga was a thrice-raced maiden before this, though two of those runs were in Group races and she was regarded as one of the best maidens in the yard. She appears to have the scope to make a three-year-old and looks progressive.

94 Reading Evening Post Radley Stakes (Fillies Listed), (7f) Newbury October 26 (Soft)

1 **Crystal Star** 8-8 — J Fortune
2 **Garmoucheh** 8-8 — S Sanders
3 **Al Ihtithar** 8-8 — R Hills
6-1, 11-1, 7-2. hd, nk. 11 ran. 1m 33.4 (a2.42)
Sir Evelyn De Rothschild (Sir M Stoute, Newmarket).

This winner looks promising. Nicely bred, she didn't get the best run but closed the leaders down very quickly once in the clear and was plainly best in the race. The first four pulled six lengths clear.

95 Killavullan Stakes (Group 3), (7f) Leopardstown October 28 (Soft)

1 **New South Wales** 8-10 — J P Murtagh
2 **Napper Tandy** 8-10 — K J Manning
3 **France** 8-10 — M J Kinane
11-4, 6-1, 5-1. hd, shd. 9 ran. 1m 29.1 (b3.82)
Sheikh Mohammed (J Oxx, Ireland)

New South Wales only made his debut earlier in the month, winning a Curragh maiden. He was against more experienced rivals here but showed professionalism to hold on in a tight finish, having led over a furlong out. He's bred to be decent at three.

96 Zetland Stakes (Listed), (1m2f) Newmarket November 2 (Gd to Soft)

1 **Forest Magic** 8-11 — J F Egan
2 **Allergy** 8-8 — R Hughes
3 **Wavertree Boy** 8-11 — Pat Eddery
5-2, 9-4f, 25-1. 1l, 6l. 10 ran. 2m 11.0 (b0.74)
Peter Gleeson & Julian Smith (P D'Arcy, Newmarket).

Though this was his fourth outing, Forest Magic ran very green. Having hit the front with two to go, he swerved right across the track to the stands rail. Once he was running straight again, he quickly made up the ground and he's probably value for a good bit more than this.

97 E.B.F. Christo Philipson Montrose Fillies' Stakes (Listed), (1m) Newmarket November 2 (Gd to Soft)

1 **Hanami** 8-8 — D Holland
2 **Avoidance** 8-8 — R Hughes
3 **Surval** 8-8 — S W Kelly
33-1, 11-2, 20-1. 2½l, 3½l. 7 ran. 1m 43.2 (b0.70)
G B Partnership (J Toller, Newmarket).

Hanami had shown little on her debut when seventh of nine to Khulood (72) but she seemed to relish this softer surface and ran away from her more fancied rivals. Fifth-placed favourite **Abundant** may have had excuses.

98 Criterium International Group 1, (1m) Saint-Cloud November 2 (Heavy)

1 **Dalakhani** 9-0 — C Soumillon
2 **Chevalier** 9-0 — M Kinane
3 **Governor Brown** 9-0 — D Boeuf
4-5f, 5-2, 17-2. nk, 5l. 5 ran. 1m 52.0 (a14.00)
HH Aga Khan (A Royer Dupre).

Good-looking form, especially with **Napper Tandy** well beaten in fourth. Dalakhani was three from three in good races at two and, being a half-brother to Daylami, is bred to keep on improving.

99 Blackthorn E.B.F. Premier Nursery Handicap, (7f) Leopardstown November 10 (Heavy)

1 **Bermaho** 8-7 — M J Kinane
2 **Woodstamp** 8-0 — A Nicholls (3)
3 **Blackhall Kestrel** 8-2 — J F Egan
4 **Akash** 9-4 — F M Berry
12-1, 25-1, 7-1, 11-1. ½l, hd, 1½l. 17 ran. 1m 36.9 (a3.98)
Third Avenue Syndicate (G Lyons, Ireland).

Another juvenile winner for the yard, though none of these look destined for anything better than handicap company. Mick Kinane rode a nice waiting race, producing the gelding inside the final furlong.

100 Eyrefield Stakes (Listed Race), (1m1f) Leopardstown November 10 (Heavy)

1 **Yesterday** 8-7 — M J Kinane
2 **Eklim** 8-10 — J P Murtagh
3 **Snippets** 8-7 — K J Manning
6-4f, 6-1, 13-2. 4l, 2l. 18 ran. 2m 1.2 (a2.31)
Mrs John Magnier (A P O'Brien, Ireland).

Just Yesterday's second win of a six-race campaign but it doesn't mean she's no good – she's a stayer (as her breeding suggests) and relished this first crack at 1m1f, particularly on heavy ground. It's by no means clear what she beat but she did it in style and looks a strong Oaks candidate.

Sponsored by Stan James

Two-year-old Index

All horses placed or commented on in our two-year-old review section, with race numbers

Abundant	97
Airwave	63, 70
Akanti	4
Akash	99
Alamshar	81
Al Ihtithar	94
Al Jadeed	66
Allergy	96
Almushahar	54
Approach	53
Arctic Burst	38
Arran Pilot	13
Avoidance	97
Avonbridge	80
Bahamian Dancer	66
Baron's Pit	8
Battle Chant	87
Bella Tusa	13, 61
Benicio	4, 17
Bermaho	99
Big Bad Bob	78
Black Belt Shopper	87
Blackhall Kestrel	99
Blue Corrig	64
Bond Becks	37
Boumoussa	64
Bourbonnais	26, 35
Brian Boru	81, 92
Bronntanas	11
Cassis	14, 62, 74
Casual Look	67, 85
Catcher In The Rye	4
Celtic Sapphire	7, 16
Chappel Cresent	23, 40
Checkit	19, 25
Chevalier	98
Choir Master	78
Cool Question	44
Cosmo	41
Country Reel	36
Court Masterpiece	38
Crimson Silk	50
Crystal Star	94
Cumbrian Venture	37, 80, 89
Daganya	18, 47
Dalakhani	98
Danaskaya	39, 59, 70
Danehill Stroller	55
Deportivo	19
Desert Glow	64
Devious Boy	29
Dhabyan	46
Dixie Evans	93
Dublin	26, 58
Duty Paid	10
Eklim	100
Ela Merici	24
Ellamyte	83
Elusive City	25, 42, 69
Etoile Montante	74
Etruscan King	23
Every Note Counts	89
Feabhas	71, 81, 93
Finity	71
Fleetwood Bay	55
Folio	27
Forest Magic	96
Foss Way	46
France	95
Garmoucheh	94
Geminiani	43
Gigawatt	77
Golden Nun	89
Go Tech	52
Governor Brown	38, 68, 98
Grand	77
Great Pyramid	84
Greek Revival	8, 19
Hanami	97
Harb	44
Hazelhatch	11
Hector's Girl	65
Helm Bank	7
Helms Deep	55
High Praise	88
Hold That Tiger	12, 31, 75
Huja	43
Hurricane Alan	4, 11, 49, 59, 68
Ikan	82, 91
Il Barone	60
Illustrator	92
Inchberry	87
Indy Groove	45
Intercontinental	75
Iron Lad	29
Irresistible	63
Judhoor	80
Kawagino	5
Khulood	72
Kooyong	86
La Mouline	33
Le Vie Dei Colori	60, 75
Loving Kindness	28, 42
Luminata	1, 2, 12, 18, 48, 74

Sponsored by Stan James

Name	Pages
Luvah Girl	10, 22, 85
Magistretti	16
Mail The Desert	10, 21, 43, 48
Makhlab	56, 90
Marino Marini	1, 8, 31
Membership	36, 49, 61
Michelle Ma Belle	83, 91
Miguel Cervantes	76, 91
Miss Assertive	30, 72
Miss Emma	82, 86
Miss Helga	93
Miss Houdini	45
Miss Takeortwo	63
Mister Links	15, 36, 50
Mombassa	47, 59
Monsieur Bond	62, 73
Monsieur Boulanger	3
Morning After	83
Muqbil	33, 68
Mysterinch	52
Mystic Melody	88
Naahy	56
Napper Tandy	95, 98
Nasij	22, 53
Neeze	86
Never A Doubt	6, 24
New Design	18
New South Wales	95
Newfoundland	12
Oasis Dream	69
Oblige	67
One Last Time	3, 9, 83
Ontario	9, 17, 31
Pakhoes	5, 12
Peace Offering	79
Pearl Dance	10, 14, 48, 74
Petite Histoire	1
Pinkerton	33
Pleasure Place	28, 51
Polar Force	31, 44, 91
Powerscourt	92
Presto Vento	20, 27, 65
Pure Speculation	52
Queen of Night	55
Queen's Victory	13
Rag Top	2, 6, 71
Rainbows For All	32
Rainwashed Gold	56, 78
Rapid Ransom	32
Reach For The Moon	67
Refuse To Bend	58
Revenue	9, 25, 57, 79
Ribbons And Bows	21
Rimrod	56
Roisin's Star	86
Romantic Liason	6, 39
Russian Rhythm	22, 39, 70
Salcombe	35
Santa Catarina	45
Sarayat	26
Seattle Queen	76
Sharplaw Venture	65
Shizao	76
Silca Boo	19
Sir Albert	9, 37
Sir Edwin Landseer	20, 27, 37, 49
Sister Bluebird	21
Six Perfections	74
Snippets	100
Soldera	72
Somnus	50, 73
Soviet Song	30, 67
Spartacus	5, 17, 31
Speed Cop	34, 57, 79
Spinola	14
Statue Of Liberty	5
St Pancras	46, 54
Summitville	30, 53
Surbiton	16
Surval	97
Sweet Return	46
Tacitus	15
The Bonus King	3, 6, 8, 15
Tilak	61
Tizzy May	15
Together	28
Tomahawk	7, 69, 84
Topkamp	34
Tout Seul	29, 41, 73, 84
Trade Fair	84
Traou Mad	51
Tusk	52
Tus Maith	2
Van Nistelrooy	23, 40, 58, 66
Vettriano	82
Wahsheeq	35
Walayef	47
Wando	77
Wavertree Boy	96
Weavers Pride	38
Welcome Millenium	88
Wilful	40
Wimple	34
Wizard of Noz	54, 90
Woodstamp	99
Wunders Dream	20, 27, 57
Yesterday	2, 32, 74, 85, 100
Zaby	41
Zafeen	42, 62
Zaide	90
Zanyboy	60
Zinziberine	24, 51

Sponsored by Stan James

Outlook

Time Test *with Ken Hussey*

Ken Hussey, for many years "Split Second" of *Raceform Update* and "Clockform" of the *Daily Star*, writes exclusively in the *Outlook*

The limits of technology

DURING SOME 50 years of devout clock-watching I've made occasional heartfelt pleas for electronic timing to be operational on all Flat racecourses, and not only on the original 16 Grade 1 tracks, catered for back in the late 1950s (or was it the early 1960s?).

At long last my wishes have been granted. Starting in March, every Flat track is to have state-of-the-art apparatus returning race times or, being a bit of a pessimist, so I am led to believe. You will all be fully aware that I am a great believer in the use of the clock as a means to gauge the merits or demerits of runners on our ancient and modern racetracks. So it goes without saying that I would also applaud sectional timing being operational on all courses.

Not so long ago, sectional timing – at no small cost – arrived at a Newmarket meeting. The hype that preceded its installation still colours the columns of those scribes who proclaim its inestimable value to all concerned with the sport.

This bubbling enthusiasm will doubtless continue unabated, but could this be yet another example of the Emperor's Clothes syndrome, the illusory malaise that has cloaked many a fatuous, superfluous, costly expedient that has pulled the wool over the eyes of the British public, particularly by politicians and most of the media in the past couple of decades?

I am not a fully paid-up member of the Luddite Society and welcome any technological advance that benefits backers, trainers, owners, jockeys, racing scribes and TV racing's Tellytubby clones, yet I fail to see how knowing that the

WELL SPREAD OUT: what could sectional timing tell us about a race like this one?

Sponsored by Stan James

second or third two-furlong section of, say, a 1m handicap was run in 25 seconds, will assist serious form students, or official handicappers for that matter, in their quest to accurately evaluate respective track performances.

Here I must stress that I believe this information will only be of academic interest, as there is a snag or two in blindly accepting the findings.

What consideration, for instance, is to be made of prevailing influences? Varying formative contours in each section may well necessitate individual standard times. And if furlong markers are to be sectional indicators, what guarantee have we that these are accurate to within a yard?

Take it from me, some so-called furlong posts were, in the past, measured by former colleague Dave Edwards (Topspeed of the *Racing Post*) to be anything from 190 yards to 240 yards apart!

And what about the persistent movement of plastic running rails, which can effect race distances? And finally, the state of the going in each section surely warrants serious consideration.

True, in most instances underfoot conditions can be replicated in each section, but occasionally the ground can vary to some degree, due mainly to the lie of the land when undulations will often cause discrepancies following rainfall . . . softer going in dips, for instance.

Don't get me wrong. Those responsible for putting the point of sectional timing across to the racecourse authorities are to be congratulated. But the now-promised electronic timing of all races from start to finish on every Flat track is the first priority. Sectionals, of which the uses, in my considered opinion, are conjectural, with the final tract being the most useful, come second.

Outlook

Ken Hussey's Masterlist for just £1.60 per week!

If you'd had Ken's Masterlist through the last year, you'd have backed . . .

Sarangani (right) **33-1**
Keltic Bard 33-1
The Last Fling 25-1
Quite Remarkable 25-1
Protectorate 25-1
Warden Warren 25-1
Tamarella 25-1
Moneytrain 25-1
Tuscan Flyer 25-1
Topton 25-1 & 16-1
Mary Jane 20-1

*and loads at good prices, all top or joint-top rated, plus tricasts and exactas including **994-1 tricast & 265-1 exacta (Curragh, July), 221-1 acca (Beverley, August), 483-1 tricast & 316-1 exacta (Lingfield, October), 124-1 exacta (York, July).***

We carry some of Ken's selections every week in the *Outlook* but, if you want his complete list of time figures for each horse every week, you have to subscribe. A year's supply costs just £80, or try a sample week for £2. Call 01635 578 080 to sign up, or send a cheque (pay 'Outlook Press') or postal order to RFO Time Figures, RFM House, High Street, Compton, Berks RG20 6NL.

Sponsored by Stan James

Ken's Top Two-year-olds of 2002

	Horse	Speed rating	Distance in furlongs	Going	Track	Date achieved
1	**Oasis Dream** (*above*)	**69**	**6**	**F**	**Newmarket**	**Oct 3**
2	Brian Boru	64	8	S	Doncaster	Oct 26
3	Russian Rhythm	63	6	GF	York	Aug 22
	Tomahawk		6	F	Newmarket	Oct 3
5	Elusive City	62	6	F	Newmarket	Oct 3
6	Zinziberine	61	6	S	M-Laffitte	Oct 28
7	Fiepes Shuffle	60	6	S	M-Laffitte	Oct 28
8	Powerscourt	59	8	S	Doncaster	Oct 26
	Tout Seul		7	F	Newmarket	Oct 19
10	Mister Links	58	6	VF	Doncaster	Sep 11
11	Romantic Liason	57	6	GF	York	Aug 22
	Six Perfections		7	Y	Deauville	Jul 11
	Wunders Dream		5	VF	Doncaster	Sep 14
14	Lateen Sails	56	8	F	Newmarket	Oct 2
15	Al Jadeed	55	8	GF	Ascot	Sep 28
	Bahamian Dancer		8	GF	Ascot	Sep 28
	Danaskaya		6	GF	York	Aug 22
	France		7	Y	Leopardstown	Oct 28
	Napper Tandy		7	Y	Leopardstown	Oct 28
	New South Wales		7	Y	Leopardstown	Oct 28
	Steelaninch		6	H	Newmarket	Oct 5
	Zafeen		6	G	Deauville	Aug 25

Going key: H = hard, VF = very firm, F = firm, GF = good to firm, G = good, Y = yielding, S = soft

Sponsored by Stan James

RACEFORM
FLAT ANNUAL FOR 2003

£26 (plus 95p p&p)

***Raceform Flat Annual 2003* is the British Horseracing Board's official record of the 2002 Flat season.**

- Race-by-race returns (as published weekly in Raceform)
- 2,208 pages with complete index including every race number
- Unique Note-Book comments pinpointing winners for 2003
- Adjusted Official Ratings, Raceform ratings, Speed ratings and every fact of form
- Includes major Irish and European races

Available from W H Smith and all good bookshops (ISBN 1-901100-74-X)

To order this book contact Raceform Ltd,
Compton, Newbury, Berkshire, RG20 6NL

CREDIT AND DEBIT CARD HOTLINE: 01635 578080 (24 hours)

Fax: 01635 578101 • email: rfsubscription@mgn.co.uk

Web: www.raceform.co.uk

Sponsored by Stan James

2003 Preview

Outlook Ante-Post
by Steffan Edwards

Get-out clause is a help

ANTE-POST betting has changed with the advent of betting exchanges. Any punter with access to the internet can now back a horse he likes at a fancy price with the hope of being able to lay off at a much shorter price a few weeks later, ensuring a profit whatever happens in the race – or even if the horse doesn't turn up.

The RFO's annual team can claim to have tipped some impressive shorteners in recent editions, most notably Asian Heights (50-1 into 6-1 for the 2001 Derby), King Of Happiness (33-1 into 11-2 for last year's 2,000 Guineas) and Hussard Collonges (66-1 into 10-1 for the 2003 Gold Cup). Anyone taking our advice would have been able to lay off well in advance of the race.

Of course, you may just prefer to let the bet run and see what happens, but you should at least be aware of the option, in case your nerve fails you nearer the day!

2,000 Guineas

SIR MICHAEL STOUTE, Aidan O'Brien and Saeed Bin Suroor have between them won each of the last seven renewals of the first colts Classic, and the ante-post list for this year's Guineas is dominated by colts trained by the last two named.

Favourite **Hold That Tiger** is a confusing animal. A half-brother to a Belmont Stakes winner, one could argue he will stay 1m4f, but as he's by Storm Cat I can't see him getting further than 1m2f. Following his amazing last-to-first victory in the Grand Criterium, owner Michael Tabor raised stamina doubts about him getting even 1m.

Tabor explained that the colt would be trained for the Guineas, with the option of dropping him back to sprinting later on. The colt, who has a dirt pedigree, then ran an excellent third in the Breeders' Cup Juvenile over 1m1f but, despite his seemingly obvious Kentucky Derby claims, Tabor has now been quoted as saying that the colt is to be aimed at the Epsom Derby! Whether he takes in the Guineas, in which he would hold strong claims, en route, is still up in the air.

Van Nistelrooy was a bit below the best of his generation on turf last year and his promising fifth in the Breeders' Cup Juvenile suggests an American dirt campaign could be on his agenda.

Tomahawk, runner-up in both the Middle Park and the Dewhurst, didn't seem to get home in the Juvenile and will appreciate the drop back to 1m, but it remains to be seen if the American adventure has left its mark on him or the other two.

Statue Of Liberty, the Coventry Stakes winner, missed the second half of the season, which coincided with the outbreak of coughing at the Ballydoyle stable. He looked more precocious than some of his stable companions and it's quite likely that there'll be others who will have overtaken him in terms of maturity by the time the Guineas comes round.

All in all, the O'Brien runners look difficult to weigh up.

Godolphin's best hope according to the bookmakers is **Almushahar**, and he would be entitled to serious consideration on the form he showed when an impressive winner of the Champagne Stakes at Doncaster. However, he subsequently knocked himself while cantering on the Newmarket Heath and reports coming out of Dubai suggest connections are doubtful he will be fit in time for the Guineas.

Country Reel and **Surbiton** ran their best races as juveniles with cut in the ground and may be inconvenienced by the faster surface one would normally expect at Newmarket in May, while **Dublin** looks short of top class.

Godolphin look to have a joker up their sleeve, though. **LATEEN SAILS** is a very interesting contender; a real good-looker who has a long stride on him, he was an impressive winner of a quality Newmarket maiden over the Guineas course and distance on his debut.

He recorded a time just under half a second outside the juvenile course record that day and, in beating the subsequent Racing Post Trophy runner-up by a cosy length and a quarter, he stamped himself a colt of enormous potential.

He's not really bred for dirt, so should not come into consideration by Godolphin for a raid on the American Triple Crown and, providing all goes well in the private trials, it would be no surprise to see him turn up at Newmarket as their number one hope.

Oasis Dream, the champion juvenile, shaped like a sprinter when winning the Middle Park, and his trainer has already suggested that the French Guineas, run over an easier mile, is the more likely target.

Refuse To Bend looks more of a Derby horse to me, while **Muqbil** is also bred to do better over further, and the fact that he got unbalanced running into The Dip on his last start suggests he will be seen to better effect on a flatter track. The owner's other main candidate,**Maghanim**, had been impressive when successful at Doncaster on his second start but disappointed when stepped up into Group company next time; he still has something to prove.

Dewhurst winner **Tout Seul** strikes me as one to take on. He looked a proper two-year-old and it will be a surprise if some of those he beat last year aren't able to progress past him at three.

TRADE FAIR is one who should find the necessary improvement.

Bred to do better this year and with the physical scope to progress, he will appreciate running over further than the 7f over which he competed at two. His impressive win in a maiden at Newbury, sealed with a terrific turn of foot, had class written all over it, and it just looked like inexperience that beat him at Newmarket. He deserves his place on the short-list.

Many of the also-rans in the Dewhurst litter the Guineas lists but in my opinion they will have it to do to reverse the form with Trade Fair.

Sagitta 2,000 Guineas
Newmarket, 3rd May 2003

	Bet365	C'mans	Coral	Hills	Lads	PPower	SJames	Tote
Hold That Tiger	8	8	10	8	10	8	10	5
Refuse To Bend	12	12	9	12	10	12	12	10
Trade Fair	12	12	14	12	14	10	14	10
Statue Of Liberty	12	16	12	14	10	14	12	10
Tomahawk	14	12	10	12	14	12	16	12
Tout Seul	16	16	16	14	14	16	14	16
Oasis Dream	16	20	12	12	16	16	20	20
Van Nistelrooy	16	33	25	16	16	20	20	16
Lateen Sails	20	20	33	25	20	20	25	33
Muqbil	20	20	25	20	25	25	33	16
Western Diplomat	25	33	33	25	33	25	33	25
Al Jadeed	25	33	25	25	33	33	33	-
Desert Star	25	33	33	25	33	25	33	-
Rimrod	25	-	33	33	33	33	33	33

each-way 1/4 odds, 1-2-3
Others on application, prices correct at time of going to press

Sponsored by Stan James

1,000 Guineas

LINES OF form involving Danaskya, Luminata **and** Huja **point to the form of Longchamp's Prix Marcel Boussac being much stronger than any of the other fillies' races run last season.**

Six Perfections, quite rightly recognised as the top-rated filly in the International Classifications, deserves to be favourite judged on that form. Her impressive success at Longchamp marked her down as a class act and the best of her generation. So why is she available at 7-1?

The answer is surely that she is most unlikely to travel over for the Guineas. Her trainer Pascal Bary rarely brings a horse over to Britain – he has had just three runners (no wins) here in the last five years, and connections are far more likely to take her back to Longchamp for the French version.

In contrast, Criquette Head-Maarek has won the race three times and her raiders are always worthy of consideration. **ETOILE MONTANTE** finished runner-up in the Boussac, five lengths clear of the third, and, should she take up her engagement at Newmarket rather than cross swords with Six Perfections again in France, she would deserve to be much shorter than her current price of 33-1.

In the last ten years, the going for the English 1,000 Guineas has been good six times and good to firm four times, while in France over the same period the going was also good six times but soft on the other four occasions. The greater likelihood of fast ground, coupled with a desire to avoid Six Perfections, could prompt Prince Khalid Abdullah, owner of Etoile Montante, to send his other high-class filly **INTERCONTINENTAL** over to Newmarket instead.

A full-sister to Banks Hill and Dansili, she's very well regarded by her trainer Andre Fabre. So much so, in fact, that he was confident enough to take on the colts with her in the Grand Criterium on only her third start. Sent off favourite for the race, she spoiled her chance by pulling too hard but still finished third.

Just like her brother and sister, she's thought to be at her best when her hooves are rattling and, given that Fabre is not averse to bringing one over for our Classics, one can imagine him being more than happy to aim his filly at, dare I say it, the easier Guineas.

In all honesty, I cannot imagine that both fillies will make the trip, as the sensible thing to do would be to keep them apart and give both a chance of winning a Guineas. However, I would also be surprised if neither challenged for the English version as, in the absence of Six Perfections, each would hold a major chance.

The best of the home brigade looks to

Sagitta 1,000 Guineas
Newmarket, 4th May 2003

	Bet365	VChand	C'mans	Coral	Lads	PPower	SJames	Tote
Soviet Song	5	9-2	5	4	4	4	5	4
Russian Rhythm	5	9-2	4	4	9-2	5	5	9-2
Six Perfections	5	9-2	6	7	5	5	5	5
Intercontinental	14	16	16	10	16	14	14	25
Khulood	20	20	20	-	20	16	20	20
Etoile Montante	16	33	20	25	16	20	20	16
Nayzak	20	25	25	25	33	25	-	25
Geminiani	25	33	25	25	33	25	28	16
Reach For The Moon	25	33	25	25	-	25	25	20
Hi Dubai	33	40	33	33	40	33	33	33
Cassis	40	40	33	33	40	33	33	-
Walayef	20	33	25	50	25	20	25	33
Camlet	33	40	33	33	50	33	33	33
Londonnetdotcom	40	40	50	40	50	-	33	33

each-way 1/4 odds, 1-2-3 (except Ladbrokes 1/5 odds, 1-2-3)
Others on application, prices correct at time of going to press

Sponsored by Stan James

be **Russian Rhythm**. She did little wrong at two, winning three times, including when impressive in the Lowther Stakes, and can be forgiven her defeat in the Cheveley Park as she was subsequently found to have been in season. She should get 1m on breeding without much trouble, too, but 5-1 is short enough at this stage.

Soviet Song is unbeaten in three starts and was a comfortable winner of the Fillies' Mile. The form of that race received a boost when the runner-up Casual Look went on to fill the same position in the Rockfel Stakes, but that contest was a slowly-run affair which favoured those who raced up with the pace, which is what Casual Look did. Sir Michael Stoute's Huja finished fourth, three lengths behind Soviet Song in the Fillies' Mile, and my impression is that an on-song Russian Rhythm would see off her inferior stable companion more easily than that.

Stamina doubts hang over **Khulood**, **Camlet** and **Walayef**. Khulood broke Dr Devious's 11-year-old course record when running away with a 7f Listed event at Newmarket in October, but this half-sister to Elnadim and Mehthaaf possesses so much toe that there has to be a doubt about her staying 1m.

Nayzak's maiden win, in which she beat the well-bred **Hi Dubai**, hasn't worked out at all, while **Ego** and **Reach For The Moon** are held by Russian Rhythm and Soviet Song respectively.

Geminiani's juvenile form, on a line through Huja, does not put her far behind Soviet Song and, given that the filly she defeated on her second start (Mail The Desert) went on to win a Group 1 in Ireland, she is worthy of consideration.

CRIQUETTE HEAD-MAAREK

One might think that now **Loving Kindness** has left Pascal Bary to join Godolphin, she has more of a chance of lining up for the English Guineas. However, that is not necessarily the case as, depending on how the private trials in Dubai go, she may well end up being campaigned in the US. In any case, she twice disappointed at the top level last year and has plenty of improvement to find.

Another Godolphin acquisition, **Echoes In Eternity**, would appeal more, but at present she's just a promising maiden winner who still has a lot to prove.

Oaks

THIS IS an open affair to judge by the betting but when you take out those unlikely to turn up and those who are doubtful stayers the list of possible winners becomes far more manageable.

Those with stamina questions against them include **Echoes In Eternity** and **Spanish Sun**, who are both by milers out of ten-furlong performers. **Reach The Moon** (a half-sister to Agnes Digital) is not sure to stay beyond 1m2f and neither is **Nayzak**, who beat **Hi Dubai** in what looked, at the time, a classy maiden at Newmarket last August – the form of the race hasn't worked out at all, though, with no subsequent winners (from 18 starts) emerging from those behind.

Hi Dubai, a full-sister to Fantastic Light who had her name changed from Joyous Greetings prior to her debut, is clearly well thought-of and remains an interesting prospect, however.

L'Ancresse should stay 1m4f alright, but the way she got unbalanced running into The Dip at Newmarket on her second start does not bode well for her ability to handle Epsom's undulations.

Similar comments apply to May Hill

Sponsored by Stan James

winner **Summitville**, whose long stride prompted her trainer to suggest they would go the France-Ireland route with her, rather than aim her at Epsom. **Casual Look** was also nominated for the Prix De Diane after her run in the Rockfel.

YESTERDAY looks sure to be a major player, being a full sister to last year's Oaks runner-up Quarter Moon. Having contested a couple of the top two-year-old events for fillies last season, she rounded off the year with a stylish victory on her first start over 1m1f.

Sure to improve at three, the only doubt about her is that she may develop temperament problems like her big sister, who did herself few favours by getting stewed up in the preliminaries before a number of big races.

Elasouna is a typically stoutly-bred filly owned by the Aga Khan. Impressive enough on her debut in a 7f maiden, she's guaranteed to stay and has every chance of developing into a leading candidate. **Al Ihtithar** has a good chance of staying on breeding but her trainer has yet to send out a winner of the Oaks or the Derby despite numerous attempts.

TIME HONOURED started out in the same maiden as Al Ihtithar and finished just over two lengths behind her, but she strikes me as more likely to develop into an Oaks filly. A full-sister to Time Allowed, who won the Princess Royal Stakes and Jockey Club Stakes, she's the last foal of Time Charter,

> *"Time Honoured, the last foal of 1982 Oaks winner Time Charter, has the right profile for this race, is sure to stay and could not be in better hands"*

who herself won the Oaks in 1982.

Despite still looking in need of the outing and running green, she wore down **Russian Society** (another likely to improve for middle distances this term) at Leicester on her second start. She has the right profile for the race, is sure to stay and could not be in better hands.

It would not surprise me at all to see her make her seasonal debut in the Musidora Stakes, like her owner's Pure Grain, who later went on to finish third to Moonshell in the Oaks. Her owner also won the key trial with Time Away in 2001 and is clearly keen on the race.

Time Honoured's stable companion **Rainbow City** is another bred to excel over middle distances, being a sister to Multi-coloured and half-sister to Gamut. It would not come as a shock to see her move up in the betting following the formality of a maiden win in the spring.

Vodafone Oaks
Epsom, 6th June 2003

	Bet365	VChand	C'mans	Coral	Hills	PPower	SJames	Tote
Yesterday	16	16	16	16	16	16	16	14
Echoes In Eternity	16	16	16	20	16	16	20	20
Casual Look	20	20	20	25	-	25	25	25
Time Honoured	25	25	33	33	25	25	25	25
Elasouna	33	33	33	33	25	25	25	25
L'Ancresse	33	33	33	33	25	33	33	25
Nayzak	33	25	33	25	20	33	25	25
Reach For The Moon	33	33	-	-	-	33	25	25
Hi Dubai	-	33	-	-	25	-	-	25
Al Ihtithar	33	33	40	-	-	33	33	33
Huja	33	33	40	33	-	33	33	40
Billbill	33	40	40	-	-	33	33	40
Summitville	40	40	33	33	-	-	33	40
Oblige	33	33	33	33	-	33	33	50

each-way 1/4 odds, 1-2-3 (except Hills, 1/4 odds 1,2,3,4 on their website)
Others on application, prices correct at time of going to press

Derby

THE IRISH went 15 years without a win in this between 1985 and 1999 but, in registering a victory in each of the last three renewals, they now appear to have the upper hand.

The key trials for the Derby are turning out to be the Ballysax Stakes and the Derrinstown Stud Derby Trial run at Leopardstown in the spring. Each of the last three Epsom heroes took in both races en route; Galileo and High Chaparral won both while Sinndar was narrowly denied in the Ballysax but went on to win the Derby Trial.

This year's ante-post list is dominated by Irish-trained runners and the prize once again looks destined to go to a challenger from across the Irish Sea.

Favourite **BRIAN BORU** holds similar credentials to last year's winner High Chaparral. Like his stablemate, he's a winner of a soft-ground Racing Post Trophy and bred to excel over middle distances. By Sadler's Wells out of a Park Hill winner, there can be little doubt that he will get 1m4f and, given that his trainer has won the last two renewals and that he's being aimed specifically at this one race, he must go on the short-list.

The horse generally second-favourite with most bookmakers, on the other hand, is definitely one to take on. **Dalakhani** certainly has the two-year-old form to entitle him to respect, having won the Criterium International over 1m in testing ground. He is also bred to stay 1m4f with no problems, as he is a half-brother to Daylami.

However, one cannot help but think that, as he's trained by Alain De Royer-Dupre, who has sent over just four runners to Britain in the last three years (with no wins), he's far more likely to turn out at Chantilly than at Epsom.

Prior to his success in the Racing Post Trophy, Brian Boru had suffered a narrow defeat in the Group 3 Beresford Stakes at The Curragh. The horse that beat him is currently trading at four times his price but has similar potential.

ALAMSHAR is trained by John Oxx, who won the Derby in 2000 with Sinndar. A son of Key Of Luck, who won the Dubai Duty Free in 1996 by 20 lengths and was fourth to Singspiel in the following year's Dubai World Cup, he's out of a Shahrastani mare who finished third in the 2m Irish November Handicap.

His trainer is only hopeful that he will get the Classic trip but I'm more positive. I think there's a very good chance he will stay and, having proven himself on firm and yielding ground, his chance should not be affected by the weather. He looks just the sort who could shorten dramatically in the betting if, as expected, he takes part and runs well in one or both of the key Irish trials.

Vodafone Derby

Epsom, 7th June 2003

	Bet365	VChand	C'mans	Coral	Hills	Lads	PPower	SJames
Brian Boru	8	6	5	6	6	8	7	13-2
Hold That Tiger	16	-	14	10	12	-	16	-
Dalakhani	16	14	14	20	14	14	16	16
New South Wales	16	16	20	20	16	20	16	25
Refuse To Bend	25	16	20	16	20	14	16	25
Chevalier	25	25	25	-	-	20	20	25
Alamshar	20	25	25	25	-	33	25	25
Statue Of Liberty	-	33	-	25	-	33	25	25
Maghanim	33	-	-	-	-	-	33	-
Muqbil	33	25	25	33	20	25	33	25
Powerscourt	25	33	33	-	25	33	33	33
Lateen Sails	20	33	25	33	-	40	25	25
Artistic Lad	25	-	-	33	-	40	-	-
Saturn	33	40	33	33	-	33	33	33

each-way 1/4 odds, 1-2-3
Others on application, prices correct at time of going to press

Sponsored by Stan James

The likely non-stayers include **Statue Of Liberty**, **Bourbonnais** and **Hold That Tiger** (who would have a much better chance in the Kentucky Derby). **Lateen Sails** is by the non-staying Derby third Elmaamul out of a Green Desert mare and appeals far more as a Guineas horse. **Chevalier** is by the sprinter Danehill, who has never sired a Derby runner, let alone winner. My suspicion is that each season his progeny have been exposed as non-stayers long before they get an opportunity to run at Epsom.

One whose pedigree gives him every chance of staying 1m4f is **Saturn**. He's from a lesser stable, though, so does not appeal ante-post, as he's likely to be underestimated in the market well up until the big day.

Refuse To Bend, a half-brother to Melbourne Cup winner Media Puzzle, should also stay the trip and deserves plenty of respect as a proven Group 1 winner. However, when his trainer had a similar type in Definite Article a few years back, he skipped Epsom in favour of the Irish Derby.

New South Wales appears to be Godolphin's main hope at this stage. The form of his Curragh maiden win could not have worked out any better, as the second, third and fourth all won next time out, and he followed up in good style in a Group 3 over a trip shorter than ideal. Bred to be a middle-distance horse, at first glance he looks to have plenty in his favour. However, all is not rosy.

For one thing, Dettori has already spoken in glowing terms about him (!) and in addition, depending on how the private trials go, he may end up running in America. It is also worth noting that he was withdrawn from his intended debut due to firm ground, so it would be a concern if the ground came up fast on Derby day, which it usually does. Last year was the first time in 19 years that the ground rode softer than good.

Alamshar

Recommended Bets

2,000 Guineas
2pts Lateen Sails 33-1
(Coral, Tote)
1pt Trade Fair 14-1
(Coral, Ladbrokes, Stan James)

1,000 Guineas
1pt Intercontinental 25-1
(Tote)
1pt Etoile Montante 33-1
(Victor Chandler)

Oaks
3pts Time Honoured 33-1
(Cashmans, Coral)
1pt Yesterday 16-1
(generally)

Derby
2pts Alamshar 33-1
(Ladbrokes)
1pt Brian Boru 8-1
(Bet 365, Ladbrokes)

All bets to win.
Prices correct at time of going to press.

Outlook

Morning Mole
by Steve Mellish

Flat racing's never dull

I LIKE both Flat and jumps racing but if I could only follow one it would have to be the Flat.

The main reason is the way it's set out. Besides the King George and a few big handicaps, in jump racing everything is about Cheltenham and, to a lesser extent, Liverpool. Wonderful though these two Festivals are, if a horse gets a slight injury in March and misses a few weeks, then the season is a let-down.

On the Flat it's so much better. After the Lincoln it gets into gear, with Classic trials from Newmarket and Newbury followed by the Guineas Meeting itself. Then there's the build up to the Derby and Oaks, with Chester, York and Goodwood holding important rehearsals.

After the two Classics, we have Royal Ascot, the July Meeting, Glorious Goodwood and York's Ebor meeting, followed by Doncaster's St Leger. Even when this is over, there are the big two-year-old events, the Autumn Double and races like the Ayr Gold Cup to look forward to.

On the International front, there's the Arc and then the Breeders' Cup bash. If a horse is forced to miss a few weeks at some point in the season, there's always something else to aim at when it returns.

So here are some performers, both human and equine, who can take advantage of these numerous opportunities in the upcoming season.

New trainer Andrew Balding (*see profile, page 6*) could have the first of many fine years. His father Ian always had good owners and they are reportedly staying on board, which should ensure a regular supply of well-bred horses.

Expect more winners in handicaps, as Andrew is more clued up in this field than his father; a spell with the Ramsdens obviously helped him there. With a virus-free year, Kingsclere should be a yard to follow.

My jockey to watch is attached to the Balding yard. He's the young claimer Liam Keniry, who has impressed over the last two seasons, both with his judgement of pace and strength in a finish. He's sensibly missed the All Weather campaign to preserve his claim and, sure to be given every opportunity by his trainer, could make a real stab at this year's apprentice championship. Now for the horses.

CORDIAL
3yo grey colt
Charnwood Forest – Moon Festival (Be My Guest)
Sir Mark Prescott

ONE of the joys of doing a list like this is trying to spot a Sir Mark Prescott three-year-old likely to leave their juvenile form behind when stepped up into handicap company; Cordial is my choice.

He had four runs, all over inadequate distances last year. Mole saw two of these – his second start at Lingfield and his final one at Brighton. Both times he took the eye in the paddock and both times he ran with promise, staying on in the closing stages under sympathetic riding.

He's from the family of those two top-notch performers, Moon Madness and Sheriff's Star. They both improved enormously from two to three and, with a step up in trip, Cordial looks sure to do the same. A strong, lengthy colt, he won't reach the heights of his illustrious relatives but should make up into a decent handicapper.

Sponsored by Stan James

BISHR
4yo bay colt
Royal Applause – Hawayah (Shareef Dancer)
Marcus Tregoning

BEAR this lightly raced four-year-old in mind for a good race this season.

Marcus Tregoning's colt has had just seven runs to date in his two seasons of racing and was really getting his act together last summer. He won a maiden in July and then a Mail On Sunday / Tote Mile Handicap qualifier in August. He really impressed me that day and I was looking forward to backing him in the final of that series but he wasn't seen out again.

I understand he didn't appreciate the cold autumn weather and connections decided to put him away. He's spent the winter sunning himself in Dubai (lucky git) and has apparently thrived. He's obviously a real fair-weather animal and the big summer handicaps such as the Royal Hunt Cup and William Hill Mile could be on the agenda.

FLASH OF GOLD
3yo bay filly
Darshaan – Trying For Gold (Northern Baby)
Sir Michael Stoute

THIS filly only had one start as a two-year-old in a 1m maiden at Newmarket's Cesarewitch meeting but she showed lots of promise there and could make up into a useful filly this season.

She was very green in the early stages at Newmarket and ran on nicely once she got the hang of things to finish seventh. I don't think any of the six who finished in front of her will beat her again. She's a lengthy, leggy filly who should thrive physically over the winter and I'm looking forward to seeing her when she reappears.

Group 1 performers Phantom Gold and Flight Of Fancy are among her relatives and, like them, Flash Of Gold is sure to prove best over middle distances.

JABAAR
5yo grey gelding
Silver Hawk – Sierra Madre (Baillamont)
David Nicholls

DESPITE a truncated first two seasons – he's only had six starts to date – this gelding has already shown himself to be a smart handicapper and, given a proper run at things, could land a big one.

Injury curtailed his first season, whilst sickness in Ed Dunlop's yard limited his opportunities last term. Sold in October he's now in the hands of Dandy Nicholls and this handler has few peers when it comes to training handicappers.

He starts the year off a mark of 97, which means he'll get in the bigger races. He's been entered for the Lincoln but whether he'll be ready in time I don't know and he may prove best over further anyway.

Whatever happens, his shrewd trainer is sure to place him to advantage.

NAYYIR
5yo chestnut gelding
Indian Ridge – Pearl Kite (Silver Hawk)
Gerard Butler

THIS gelding began the year with a maiden win on the polytrack at Lingfield and ended it with an easy success in a Group 2 race on Champions Day at Newmarket. This represents an improvement of at least 4st on my figures, which is truly phenomenal.

His last run earned him an invite for the very valuable Hong Kong Mile and it was a great shame that sickness forced him to miss the engagement. By all accounts it was a life-threatening illness and there's obviously a worry that he'll never return to his best.

He's worth chancing, though, because he's definitely Group 1 material.

NYSAEAN
4yo bay colt
Sadler's Wells – Irish Arms (Irish River)
Richard Hannon

BRITISH racegoers never saw the best of this colt. Fourth in the Irish Derby, where he didn't get the trip, and a facile success in a French Listed race were his best efforts. The French race was his penultimate start and the reason he was sent there was the ground; this beast must have a soft surface.

He got his going on his final start but once again the 1m4f trip found him out. Hacking all over his rivals two from home, his stride shortened and The Whistling Teal and Warrsan grabbed him late on.

Given soft ground and 1m2f, this horse has a good race in him. I wouldn't even rule him out of a race like the Eclipse on suitable going. A dry summer here would limit his chances and mean the passport

Nayyir

would have to come out with trips to Germany and Italy or even a return to France, whichever is the wettest.

OASIS DREAM
3yo bay colt
Green Desert – Hope (Dancing Brave)
John Gosden

THE sprint division was weak last season and the way is clear for a three-year-old to grab the crown – step forward Oasis Dream.

The colt had four runs as a youngster and improved each time, culminating with a win in the Group 1 Middle Park Stakes. The 6f at Newmarket that day on fast ground was a real speed test and Oasis Dream couldn't have been more impressive. The official handicappers thought that this was the best performance put up by a two-year-old in Europe last season.

Like many a Champion Sprinter before him, he'll start his three-year-old campaign chasing Classic glory; reportedly the French 2,000 Guineas is the aim. However, to me he looks a sprinter and I suspect we'll see him in races like the July Cup.

PERSIAN MAJESTY
3yo bay colt
Grand Lodge – Spa (Sadler's Wells)
Peter Harris

HALF an hour after Flash Of Gold took Mole's eye in the first division of a Newmarket maiden, Persian Majesty won the second division and the Furry One was most taken by the manner of his success. He looked booked for second place entering the final furlong but stayed on really strongly to win going away.

Unless I'm mistaken, this won't be the last time we see him in the winner's enclosure. From the family of Derby winner Slip Anchor, this horse has middle distances written all over him. It wouldn't surprise me to see him line up for one of the Derby trials and maybe even the greatest Classic itself.

RACING & FOOTBALL
Outlook

It doesn't have to be like this!

Call The Mole, one of the leading paddock judges in the country, and escape the bookie's clutches.

THE MOLE LINE
0906 911 0230
With Steve Mellish

Calls cost £1/min all times. Outlook Press, Raceform House, Compton, Berks RG20 6NL.

Outlook's Horses to Follow

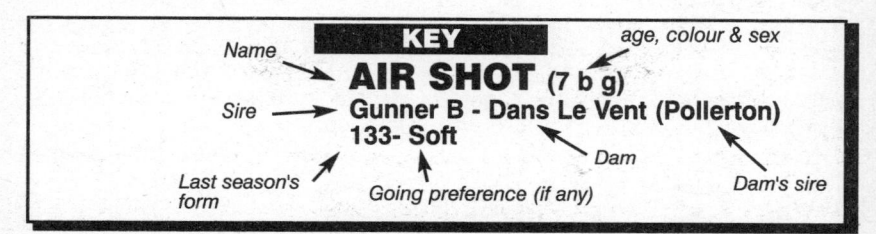

KEY

Name → **AIR SHOT** (7 b g) ← age, colour & sex
Sire → **Gunner B – Dans Le Vent (Pollerton)**
133- Soft
       ↑   ↑   ↖ Dam   ↖ Dam's sire
Last season's   Going preference (if any)
form

ADHAABA (3 b f)
Dayjur – Girchoop (Storm Cat)
4- Not soft

If this filly turns out anything like as good as her dad, she'll win her share. Her one outing was encouraging, at Newbury in a 6f maiden on good to soft. Although she finished over seven lengths behind the winner, she met trouble in running and appeared unsuited by the softish going. Like her sire she's not too big and, also like her sire, she may want firm ground. It's worth noting that her trainer won last year's King's Stand Stakes with a three-year-old filly.

Marcus Tregoning, Lambourn

ARTISTIC LAD (3 ch c)
Peintre Celebre – Maid For The Hills (Indian Ridge)
1-

Artistic Lad beat 12 others in his only race, a 7f Leicester maiden in early October. He pulled clear in the closing stages for a convincing two-length success over Fabulous Jet. Even though the ground was good to soft, the form of this maiden may stand up and the first five could all pay their way in the best company. That he was able to dominate speaks volumes for his potential. Sir Michael Stoute has been patient with this colt, who has a large frame still to fill. He is well-bred, is entered in the Derby and could be anything.

Sir Michael Stoute, Newmarket

BLACK SWAN (3 b g)
Nashwan – Sea Spray (Royal Academy)
9-

Here's the dark horse of the list. His only run was in the 7f Glorious Goodwood maiden for colts and geldings won by Ed Dunlop's Wahsheeq, in which subsequent Royal Lodge winner Al Jadeed was third. Black Swan was with them until the two-furlong marker and then faded into ninth of ten. We've heard, however, that he is well regarded. He's certainly well-bred, having been raised at the late Lord Weinstock's Ballymacoll Stud, the birthplace of so many choice horses. Do not let this one out of your sight.

Marcus Tregoning, Lambourn

Sponsored by Stan James

BOURBONNAIS (3 b c)
Singspiel – Rose Bourbon (Woodman)
121-

Is the first of two horses in this list to have been transferred from the unfortunate Mark Johnston to Saeed Bin Suroor, the other being Western Diplomat. Having won a small maiden at York, Bourbonnais then ran second to Dublin in the Champagne Stakes at Goodwood over 7f. Although he was entered for the Royal Lodge over 1m, Johnston dropped him back to 6f to win the Acomb Stakes at York. That was it for Bourbonnais and Godolphin have an exciting prospect. He should be Group standard at between 1m and 1m4f, since he was staying on at the end of all his races as a juvenile.

Saeed Bin Suroor, Newmarket

BRIAN BORU (3 b c)
Sadler's Wells – Eva Luna (Alleged)
121-

Won the Racing Post Trophy over 1m in the soft, the same race that stablemate High Chaparral won as a two-year-old. It wasn't the most eye-catching of displays because of the soft ground but Brian Boru is a grand stamp of a colt and his powerful action saw him home quite comfortably. He was beaten a head in the Group 3 Beresford Stakes at The Curragh the time before, when many of Aidan O'Brien's were below par. A son of Sadler's Wells, who has sired the last two Derby winners, he has been winter favourite for the Epsom Classic and we can think of no more likely winner.

Aidan O'Brien, Ireland

EXCELSIUS (3 ch g)
Dr Devious – Folgore (Irish River)
13-

With two races in Italy so far, British punters won't be too familiar with Excelsius – all the better, as we may get a price about him. He's talented all right. In his first run he hacked up by seven lengths in a colts and geldings maiden at San Siro. Next time, he was three lengths and a neck third to Spartacus and Checkit in the Group 1 Gran Criterium at the same course over 1m. He would have been closer if he hadn't been involved in some scrimmaging at the home turn where three horses were brought down. As a gelding, Excelsius can expect to be worked hard. There should be plenty of reward.

John Dunlop, Arundel

EYECATCHER (6 b g)
Green Desert – Reuval (Sharpen Up)
4/42122413-

This gelding has arrived late on the scene, with only one run prior to his 2002 campaign. He's making up for lost time, though, and there should be more to come in 2003. After winning a conditions event at Warwick, he was runner-up in two handicaps, the first at Haydock behind Bouncing Bowdler, the second at Newmarket behind Patavellian. If he can put the experience of three races on the All-Weather at Lingfield at the backend to good use, he could turn into a decent 7f handicapper.

James Fanshawe, Newmarket

Sponsored by Stan James

FALBRAV (5 b h)
Fairy King – Gift Of The Night (Slewpy)
2/231/111301- Good to firm, firm

The transfer of the Japan Cup winner Falbrav to Newmarket from Italy is great news for British racing and Luca Cumani. Falbrav is a top-class middle-distance colt who won two Group 1s in Italy. He wasn't all that far (less than six lengths) behind Marienbard in the Arc but it was in the Japan Cup, on his favoured firm ground, that he had his greatest moment. There he beat 15 of the world's best horses, Frankie Dettori getting him home in a three-way photo. Falbrav should be a contender this year in Japan. Before then, he can pick off such targets as Ascot's King George VI & Queen Elizabeth Diamond Stakes.

Luca Cumani, Newmarket

FLYING WANDA (3 b f)
Alzao – Royal York (Bustino)
21-

Made her debut in a Newmarket maiden in August, attempting to make all before being passed by the useful Saturn (later fifth in the Dewhurst). She then won a maiden at Yarmouth beating a David Loder two-year-old. Admittedly her form isn't world-beating but the point about this filly is her scope. She's a big, rangey, galloping sort who should make a three-year-old, especially over a trip. After the Yarmouth race Jeremy Noseda said: "She has got a great action and is still quite backward." She's not in the Oaks but we wouldn't rule her out of the St Leger.

Jeremy Noseda, Newmarket

JOHNSTON'S DIAMOND (5 b g)
Tagula – Toshair Flyer (Ballad Rock)
00225034-10 Not soft

The great thing about this gelding's All-Weather form over the winter is that it told us that he is talented without disturbing his turf handicap mark. On New Year's Day at Southwell, he won his first race at the 15th attempt. Ridden by Dean McKeown, he made all in a modest 6f handicap from an All-Weather mark of 53, prevailing by a short-head. His turf mark is the same so you don't have to have a degree in logic to work out that a sprint handicap is his for the taking. Throw in the fact that he's housed with Eric Alston (there's no better trainer of second-division sprint handicappers) and we have a horse to follow.

Eric Alston, Preston

LATEEN SAILS (3 ch c)
Elmaamul – Felucca (Green Desert)
1- Not firm

When Henry Cecil was told this one had been sold, he must have been devastated. As Lateen Sails powered home in a 1m maiden at Newmarket on October 2, he looked a smart prospect. He seemed nothing special in the parade ring, deep-girthed but not muscular. However, as Cecil said after the race: "He is backward and more of a three-year-old than a two-year-old." A high knee-action suggests that firm ground may not suit. Watch out for him at up to 1m2f because, in Cecil's words: "He might be all right one day."

Saeed Bin Suroor, Newmarket

LORD PROTECTOR (5 b g)
Nicolotte – Scared (Royal Academy)
47022035901- Not very soft

A slight drop in the ratings to 83 (he started the season on 87) looked like the reason for this gelding winning a 7f handicap at Newmarket on the last of his 11 runs. But there's probably more to it than that. This fellow requires covering up in mid-division and doesn't want to hit the front too soon. For that reason, he will be of interest in big fields, preferably with Richard Quinn on board – Quinn's three rides on him last season produced two seconds and a first. He has been entered for the Lincoln again (seventh last year) but he may be kept to 7f.

David Arbuthnot, Upper Lambourn

MAGHANIM (3 b c)
Nashwan – Azdihaar (Mr Prospector)
210- Good, good to firm

The Girton Maiden Stakes at Newmarket, in which Almushahar beat Maghanim and Trade Fair, may prove highly significant. With Almushahar on the sidelines, we include the second and third in this list of horses to follow. Maghanim is an attractive colt who wasn't as wound up as the winner. It was no surprise that he made amends next time, running away with a conditions stakes at Doncaster. He was comprehensively beaten in the Grand Criterium after that, but we can normally forgive a horse one bad run, especially when racing abroad.

John Dunlop, Arundel

MASAADER (3 b f)
Wild Again – Futuh (Diesis)
421-

Ed Dunlop had a great season with his three-year-old fillies in 2001 so let's hope he hasn't lost his touch. This one started off in a minor event at Yarmouth and had made considerable progress when she next appeared, running second of 18 in the Snailwell Maiden Stakes at Newmarket over 6f. She was the finished article when she next ran at Brighton, again over 6f, easily dismissing eight nothing-special maidens. On breeding, she's not sure to stay any trip beyond 6f.

Ed Dunlop, Newmarket

MOON BALLAD (4 ch c)
Singspiel – Velvet Moon (Shaadi)
2/1421312-

This genuine sort made steady progress last term and after four runs, including victory in the Dante Stakes at York, he earned Classic status with a third in the Derby. Although he was easily outclassed by High Chaparral and Hawk Wing, there was much to like about the way he set the pace and hung on for third. After the colt had run-up to Storming Home in the Champion Stakes, Simon Crisford said: "He will be a great horse for next year and could easily be a Dubai World Cup horse, as he goes on the sand." Marienbard and Grandera were the success stories for Godolphin's older brigade last season. Moon Ballad could be the one this season.

Saeed Bin Suroor, Newmarket

NEW SOUTH WALES (3 b c)
In the Wings – Temora (Ela-Mana-Mou)
11- Not firm

The 1m maiden, run at The Curragh on October 5, may provide a rich seam of form. The first two home, New South Wales and Chevalier, are Classic contenders. Chevalier won next time out while New South Wales went on to land a 7f Group 3 contest at Leopardstown a few weeks later. John Oxx, his former trainer, withdrew the colt from a Listowel race because of firm ground so the chances are this colt needs some cut. He has already been nibbled at in the Derby betting.

Saeed Bin Suroor, Newmarket

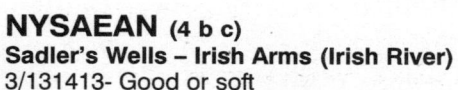

NYSAEAN (4 b c)
Sadler's Wells – Irish Arms (Irish River)
3/131413- Good or soft

The Windsor maiden last April in which Nysaean beat Burning Sun a neck (the pair 13 lengths clear) proved informative. Burning Sun went on to win at Royal Ascot and this fellow went on to win a 1m2f Listed event at Deauville by 5l. But he's probably better than Listed class, especially when there's some juice in the ground. After the French race there was talk of the Arc and, while that's overfacing him (he's yet to prove he stays 1m4f), a Group 2 over 1m2f is within his grasp. He's only run seven times to date.

Richard Hannon, Marlborough

ORIENTOR (5 b h)
Inchinor – Orient (Bay Express)
3640462- Good

It was a shame that Orientor couldn't get his head in front last term because he deserved at least one prize. What the form book won't tell you, however, is that Orientor had a foot problem. A large chunk of one of his feet disappeared after his second run and for the rest of the season he was running on three wheels. Jim Goldie reports that Orientor is fully restored now. He ran some cracking races in defeat, notably a length fourth to Invincible Spirit in the Duke Of York Stakes and a two-length fourth to the same horse in the Stanley Leisure Sprint Cup. His two-length sixth to Continent in the Group 1 Prix de l'Abbaye also makes good reading. He will start off in the Cammidge Trophy and we predict that he will win at least one Group race for his Scottish yard.

Jim Goldie, Uplawmoor

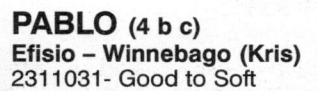

PABLO (4 b c)
Efisio – Winnebago (Kris)
2311031- Good to Soft

Two and a half lengths is quite a margin to win a Class C handicap especially when there are 24 runners and the race is at Newmarket. But that's what Pablo did in his final race of 2002, climaxing a season that only saw him out of the first three once. Unraced as a two-year-old, he won a maiden on his third start before taking the handicap route. There should be more handicaps waiting for him over 7f and 1m, especially on good to soft, the ground on which he had his two biggest wins. He can handle it good but is unproven on firm.

Barry Hills, Lambourn

Sponsored by Stan James

PERSIAN MAJESTY (3 b c)
Grand Lodge – Spa (Sadler's Wells)
1-

Was backed down to 8-1 for a 1m maiden at Newmarket's Cesarewitch meeting. He obliged in style, travelling just behind the leaders, making his challenge on the far rail and beating Henry Cecil's Regal Agenda by half a length. The time was fractionally faster than the other division of the race Persian Majesty, a Derby entry, is a wonderfully bred colt. He's the first foal of a dam who is a half-sister to Sandmason, Sardegna and Sardonic, all of whom were out of Sandy Island, a half-sister to Slip Anchor. It's a family with stamina aplenty and Persian Majesty should get at least 1m2f.

Peter Harris, Berkhamsted

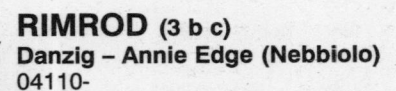

RIMROD (3 b c)
Danzig – Annie Edge (Nebbiolo)
04110-

The Dewhurst, in which Rimrod finished eighth of 16, was a confusing race won by Tout Seul at 25-1 in which several fancied types such as Al Jadeed (the Royal Lodge winner) ran poorly. It may be best to treat it with caution and concentrate on Rimrod's earlier form, such as the time that he trounced subsequent Middle Park winner Oasis Dream by three and a half lengths in a Sandown maiden in August. If you take that form literally, Rimrod was the best two-year-old of 2002 because Oasis Dream heads the International Classifications. That may be fanciful but this half-brother to champion miler Selkirk should be smart.

Andrew Balding, Kingsclere

SAFE FROM HARM (3 ch c)
Mt Livermore – Not So Careless (Desert Wine)
1-

Won a 7f Newmarket maiden with authority on his only start. The colt looked the part in the paddock, fit and well-grown. Pat Eddery set off to make all on him and, though he edged a bit to the right through greenness, he only had to be pushed out to prevail by a neck. The time of the race was slow but Safe From Harm gave a very classy impression and should develop. He cost $375,000 as a yearling and is a brother to the smart American Grade 1 winner Subordination.

Sir Michael Stoute, Newmarket

SCOTTY'S FUTURE (5 b g)
Namaqualand – Persian Empress (Persian Bold)
50106800000-

Anybody who saw the Victoria Cup demolition job put in by this fellow could be forgiven for thinking that they were watching a Group horse win a handicap. Well, they may be right. The handicapper raised Scotty's Future 9lb after Ascot but that wasn't the reason he did nothing of note in eight subsequent runs. The colt, as he was last season, was a beast to train. David Nicholls got his way during the winter and Scotty's Future was gelded. If the operation is a success we will see a different animal this term, one capable of Group brackets over 7f and 1m.

David Nicholls, Thirsk

Sponsored by Stan James

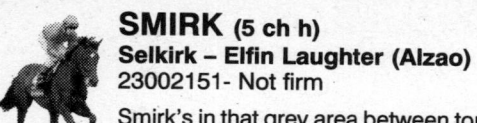

SMIRK (5 ch h)
Selkirk – Elfin Laughter (Alzao)
23002151- Not firm

Smirk's in that grey area between top handicapper and Listed class. His latest run in the Ben Marshall Stakes, however, in which he beat a Godolphin horse by 5l, suggested he could be Group class. So, though we may see Smirk in such races as the Royal Hunt Cup and the William Hill Mile at Goodwood (which he won last year), he could also be in Group 3 events. His trip is 1m and he acts on good to soft and good to firm. But fast ground doesn't suit.

Dominic Elsworth, Whitsbury

SPLENDID ERA (3 b c)
Green Desert – Valley Of Gold (Shirley Heights)
011-

Caught the eye in the Unfuwain Maiden Stakes won by Desert Star at Newmarket in October. He was held up at the back of the 26-runner field, made progress through tiring horses and was not given a hard time. So it came as no surprise that he collected a poor maiden at Lingfield on the All-Weather next time. He returned there in December for a novice event in which he tried to run out turning for home. The manoeuvre must have cost him between seven and ten lengths, yet he still got up on the line. Barry Hills is thinking in Listed terms for this son of an Italian Oaks winner.

Barry Hills, Lambourn

STATUE OF LIBERTY (3 b/br c)
Storm Cat – Charming Lassie (Seattle Slew)
11-

Won the Coventry Stakes at Royal Ascot, making it Aidan O'Brien's fourth win in the race in six years. Settled in midfield, he came with a strong run to take the lead inside the final furlong and, when challenged by Pakhoes, found more. It's often the mark of a top-class colt to quicken twice in a race and Statue Of Liberty impressed as a quality colt. That was the last we saw of him, possibly due to the coughing in O'Brien's yard. O'Brien has many other top-class colts to shuffle with but it would be no surprise to see him contest the 2,000 Guineas. As a $1,300,000 foal and a half-brother to The Lemon Drop Kid, he could be Classic standard.

Aidan O'Brien, Ireland

TRADE FAIR (3 b c)
Zafonic – Danefair (Danehill)
313- Good to firm

After sluicing up in a maiden at Newbury, Trade Fair had the professionals falling over themselves to back him for the 2,000 Guineas. Trade Fair arrived there following a third to Almushahar in a Newmarket maiden – another race that had the pros drooling. He quickened away without coming off the bridle at Newbury, bringing back memories of his sire Zafonic's two-year-old exploits. He ran third in the Dewhurst, hanging to the right in The Dip, a run which could be put down to inexperience. He should stay at least 1m2f and his supporters may yet collect in the 2,000 Guineas.

Roger Charlton, Marlborough

WESTERN DIPLOMAT (3 b c)
Gone West – Dabaweyaa (Shareef Dancer)
1-

Mark Johnston is at ease with the idea of starting off his best two-year-olds in small races at Scottish tracks. It gives them confidence and allows them to gallop without interference. This once-raced son of Gone West made his debut at Ayr in mid-July, contesting a six-runner 6f maiden. He stretched out in the final furlong, passing the post 7l clear. Gone West was the sire of Zafonic and Dabaweyaa was second in the 1,000 Guineas. Western Diplomat, who has now joined Godolphin, should prove useful at around 7f to 1m.

Saeed Bin Suroor, Newmarket

WIZARD OF NOZ (3 b c)
Inchinor – Winning Girl (Green Desert)
133- Fast

Having won a Haydock maiden, this colt was just under two lengths third to David Loder's best colt Almushahar in the Champagne Stakes at Doncaster. He might have been a little closer but for being short of room a furlong out. Arguably that form puts him right up there with the best and we can ignore his next run (third in the Horris Hill) because the ground was soft. Jeremy Noseda may start him off in the Free Handicap at Newmarket and insists that the horse wants fast ground. He should stay 1m.

Jeremy Noseda, Newmarket

YESTERDAY (3 b f)
Sadler's Wells – Jude (Darshaan)
012031- Soft

After this filly had won her final start, a Listed event at Leopardstown on heavy ground, Aidan O'Brien said: "She will be trained with the Oaks in mind." She looked one-paced in her two October races, the first of which was a sixth in the Prix Marcel Boussac, the other one being a third in the Rockfel. But O'Brien was unfazed and explained that these runs will have helped her "grow up". With such a decisive win on heavy under her belt, the balance of probability is that she may prefer some cut. She is a sister to Quarter Moon, who was second in the Oaks and the Irish Guineas.

Aidan O'Brien, Ireland

Outlook's 10 to follow

Artistic Lad	Persian Majesty
Brian Boru	Scotty's Future
Black Swan	Smirk
Lateen Sails	Trade Fair
Orientor	Yesterday

Sponsored by Stan James

Berkshire by Downsman

THE DAWN of another turf season is upon us and it's hard for Valleymen stout and true to be anything other than optimistic as we mass our forces for the arduous weeks ahead.

Whilst it is true to say that most trainers are positive at this time of year, there is good cause for the Lambourn area and its followers to be upbeat.

Just take a look at the final table for 2002 (*page 53*). No less than ten of our finest made the first 25 places in the Flat trainers' roll of honour, almost double the number of those based in Newmarket.

If you add to that the fact that we won all three juvenile Group 1 races at Newmarket with **Tout Seul** (Dewhurst), **Oasis Dream** (Middle Park) and the ultra-speedy **Airwave** (Cheveley Park), then there is firm evidence to suggest we can bag more than our fair share of the top races this year.

The victories of Tout Seul and Airwave gave this correspondent particular pleasure because they were engineered by two of our more senior and most respected figures, *FULKE JOHNSON HOUGHTON* and *HENRY CANDY*. Both have had their share of lows during long careers, but they prove time and again that, when the right material comes along, they make the very most of it.

Johnson Houghton will be keen to prove Tout Seul's win was no fluke and will also be looking to see off the mighty Ballydoyle and Godolphin camps in the Guineas trials, as both powerbases opted not to take up the option when this bonny colt was put on the market after his Newmarket success.

Airwave put a big dent in the reputation of Russian Rhythm with her win in the Cheveley Park, but Candy said immediately after that win that she was a sprinter through and through. It would be hard to see her stamina lasting out any further than 7f – however, we live in hope!

If the International Classifications are used as the guide, *JOHN GOSDEN* must take the top prize for supplying most high quality juveniles from the area. The Manton maestro has four entries in the top 40, spearheaded by top-ranked Oasis Dream, who earned his place at the head of the list with an impressive length-and-a-half win over Tomahawk in the Middle Park.

This well-related colt always looked top quality material from

LAMBOURN WINS AT NEWMARKET: our Fulke celebrates Tout Seul's Dewhurst triumph
Sponsored by Stan James

early on in his juvenile campaign – some of his work had to be seen to be believed – but it took him three outings before he managed the first of his two successes.

Connections were convinced he would get 7f, but he failed to last home on his only appearance over the distance at Sandown towards the end of August and it was interesting to hear Gosden doubt his colt's stamina for a tilt at the Guineas. First impressions are often best, so this correspondent will wait to see how things develop in his work before opting for a tickle in the ante-post market for the first Classic.

The sprinter/miler question apart, the word from the Wiltshire establishment is that he has done very well and all are looking forward to getting him back into the thick of the action.

Gosden's three other players in the top flight were **Foss Way**, **Summerland** and **Al Jadeed** and the pick of this trio was the last-named.

Like Oasis Dream, he took a run or two to find his feet, but ended the campaign with an ultra-game effort to land the Group 2 Royal Lodge Stakes. He could be anything when he is tried over middle distances this season, but a note of caution – he is at his most effective on fast ground.

Gosden is a very patient trainer who never rushes his horses and consequently has more untapped talent among his three-year-old counterparts. Among the wealth of unexposed talent, good things are predicted

Trade Fair

for **Calibre**. There was a huge message for this colt when he made his debut at one of Newmarket's backend meetings and he showed speed and tenacity to beat Lundy's Lane by a length and a half.

There was a lot to like about the way he rallied after being headed in the Dip, and it would come as no surprise to see this full-brother to Ryafan take high rank in the listings come season's end.

Blazing Thunder was another winner at HQ in the death throes of the campaign and there is no reason why **Mujarad**, who finished an eyecatching fourth in that race, should not progress through the ranks in his second season.

Make a note, also, of **Kingham**, a good-sized colt who handled the mud very well on his bow at Doncaster in October, and **Presenter**, who found only Kris Krin too good on his debut on Town Moor the previous month.

Gosden also has plenty of strength among the fairer sex and one of the more promising maidens is **Ocean Silk**, who looked a tad unlucky on her only start at Newmarket in November. Having lost several lengths at the start, she stuck on nicely in the closing stages despite running green to finish second to Goodness racious. Big improvement can be expected.

Gosden's next-door neighbour *ROGER CHARLTON* enjoyed a very fruitful season and his mid-term prediction concerning the presence of high quality among his juveniles proved right on the money.

Despite losing two of his very best prospects, Luvah Girl (America) and L'Ancresse (Ballydoyle) at season's end, he has a powerful team, with more than a fair shout of bagging a trial or two and maybe even one of the Classics.

All eyes will certainly be on **Trade Fair** when he steps out for the first time, possibly in the Greenham at Newbury in April. This most imposing colt was tipped for stardom even before his first appearance in a very hot maiden at Newmarket and he duly booked his place in the Dewhurst line-up with an easy win at Newbury on his next attempt.

There were high hopes that Trade Fair would win the juvenile setpiece but he ran far too freely in the early stages and was only able to stick on at the one pace when Tout Seul and Tomahawk swept past.

Sponsored by Stan James

> *'Tregoning reports Nayef is stronger and even more mature, which suggests he will improve on his 2002 exploits!'*

The Beckhampton team were quick to point out that Trade Fair would be a much stronger horse with the winter behind him and the word is they're delighted with the way he's progressed. But there is still a doubt within the camp that the colt's explosive speed may thwart his attempts to stay 1m.

Charlton unleashed a number of very promising colts in the closing weeks of the campaign and the one I liked most was **Midas Way**. A son of Halling out of a Darshaan mare, he looked a useful middle-distance performer in the making when he won a maiden at Newbury in October. Apparently, he has made more than average progress during the darker months and could pay his way at a high level.

Zabaglione should also continue the good work he produced at the backend and expect **Donizetti** to bounce back from what proved a very disappointing trip to Lingfield for a run-of-the-mill conditions event on the All-Weather. The son of Deputy Minister had hacked up in a maiden prior to that defeat and was always able to mix it with the very best Beckhampton juveniles on the Marlborough Downs.

Charlton also has a few very nice maidens primed, especially among the fillies. **Elegant Shadow** is one to spring immediately to mind after her promising second in a backend maiden and mention should also be made of **Innovation**. This one was very green and backward but still managed an eyecatching sixth to Goodness Gracious on her only attempt to date.

My pick of the distaff crop however, is **Chaffinch**. She was brought along very steadily last season and did well to sneak victory at York in October, even accepting the fact that the runner-up Rahaf appears to love finishing second.

Charlton always has a good team of older horses and **Frenchmans Bay** will be back once again. His 'gammy' knee has possibly stopped him becoming a real top-notch performer, but connections are more than hopeful he can build on the creditable third in the Group 2 Challenge Stakes on his final start.

On the sprinting front, the lightly-raced **Magic Glade** should pay her way in some of the top handicaps, though she may need a race or two to reach concert pitch.

Few trainers can boast a more powerful string of older horses than MARCUS TREGONING and the Kingwood trainer freely admits he will be relying quite heavily on the likes of **Nayef**, **Mubtaker** and **Bishr** until the two-year-olds begin to come out in force in the second half of the campaign.

Nayef was a revelation once again last season. He kicked his third campaign off in just the right way with his win in the valuable Sheema Classic, but it was not until the King George VI & Queen Elizabeth Stakes – and that brilliant but unsuccessful battle with Golan – that he showed he was an animal of the highest order.

Although his season came to a juddering halt after taking revenge on Sir Michael Stoute's charge in the Juddmonte International at York in August, he is back in top nick and busy preparing for a tilt at the Dubai World Cup.

Interestingly, Tregoning reports he is stronger and an even more mature individual now, which seems to suggest he will improve on his 2002 exploits!

Nayef

The lightly-raced **Mubtaker** is also in Dubai for the Sheema Classic and Tregoning will be hoping there is no repeat of 2002 when he had to miss his intended target at the World Cup fest because of lameness. He is another top quality performer and we may not have seen the best of him yet, despite the fact he is now a six-year-old.

Bishr, who has already enjoyed a successful winter campaign in Dubai, and King's Stand winner **Dominica** (may head for the Temple Stakes at Sandown in May) are back for more, along with two smart middle-distance four-year-olds **Bustan** and **Izdiham**.

Despite the fact that **Albareq** has already flown the Kingwood flag with honour in Dubai, Tregoning, with refreshing honesty, is not hugely optimistic about the prospects for his three-year-olds. The sickness that hit the yard in the second half of the last campaign affected them quite seriously and it remains to be seen if they can recover.

The star, if there is one, could be **Fatik**, who was strongly fancied to win the Richmond Stakes at Goodwood but ran no race at all. **Chin Chin** should also pay his way and a couple of unexposed ones to look out for are **Hashid**, a colt by Darshaan, and **Gold Bar**, a big scopey son of Barathea, who also boasts Oaks and St Leger heroine Sun Princess as a parent. He will be given a lot of time, but the wait could well be worthwhile.

BARRY HILLS (below, right) was once again far and away our most successful trainer of winners, a somewhat surprising statistic given that the Faringdon Place trainer was never happy with the health of his horses until the closing weeks of the season.

At this early stage, it is difficult to pick the plums from a number of potentially high-class three-year-olds but one to follow sooner rather than later would have to be **Grand Halo**, who could well head for one of Hills' favourite early-season races, the 1m2f maiden at Doncaster's Lincoln meeting. An Epsom Derby entry, it would surprise no-one at the Hills emporium if he made the line-up for the great race.

Private Charter and **Weavers Pride** are two more high-class maidens, primed for early forays. The latter was something of a talking horse last season but he was very much on the weak side and is much stronger now.

Gala Sunday ended his juvenile campaign with two fine seconds in hot company and is expected to do well around a mile, and two more for ten-furlong events are **Successor** and **Risk Taker**. Keep a particularly keen eye open for the last chap, as he has made more than average progress during the winter and has always showed a ton of potential in his homework.

Among the fairer sex, **Muwajaha** and **Introducing** are two names from the list of unproven individuals but if there is a real star filly at Faringdon it may well be **Geminiani**. She appeared to book her place for the Moyglare Stud Stakes after she followed up her debut win at Goodwood with a comfortable success over Mail The Desert in the Group 3 Prestige Stakes on the same course, but a setback ended her campaign soon after.

It was with decidedly mixed feelings that the Hills crew greeted Mail The Desert's success in the Group 1 prize, but at least they know Geminiani is right up with the very best of her generation.

Happily, she has fully recovered from the problem which sidelined her and there seems no reason why she shouldn't have a crack at one of the spring Classics.

Salcombe (has done well), **Flying Express** (should step up on his very useful juvenile form) and **Makhlab** are three destined for the colts trials in April, and a positive word should also be expressed for All-Weather wizard **Splendid Era**; he should also show his worth on the turf.

The mud-loving **Chancellor**, who will be hunting for that elusive Group 1 win when the clods are flying, heads up the older team, along with **Pablo** (another soft ground specialist) and Cambridgeshire runner-up **Far Lane**, who could well nab a Group 3 or Listed prize at some stage during the season.

Sponsored by Stan James

> *'It would surprise no-one at the Hills emporium if Grand Halo made the line-up for the Epsom Derby'*

Just over the Mandown Hill from the Hills team, *BRIAN MEEHAN* is planning a flying start to the campaign and, if his season on the All-Weather is anything to go by, he could well be one to follow in the opening exchanges.

He has a number of sharp juveniles and was not backward in coming forward with names. **Cape Fear**, a son of Cape Cross, has looked good in his early work and the very well-named Docksider colt **Stevedore** is one to keep on the right side.

The Newlands juveniles were quite a sickly bunch last spring from all accounts and a good number failed to show their true worth. But the classy **Hilbre Island** and **Chinkara** (in three-year-old handicaps) should pay their way, while the once-raced **Jubilee** is a maiden to note. She ran a pleasing race in a backend maiden at Newmarket, but Meehan is extremely hopeful she will make up into a very smart filly this spring.

Meehan has four-year-olds to follow at opposite ends of the distance spectrum with **Twilight Blues** and **Savannah Bay**. Twilight Blues enjoyed very little luck after his comeback win in the Free Handicap at Newmarket but there was plenty to suggest a big sprint could come his way, whilst Savannah Bay's win in the Group 3 at Longchamp leaves room for optimism he could make up into a Cup-class stayer this term.

Imoya never reached the heights hoped for last term but she seems back in very good form now and has a bit of class about her.

MICK CHANNON intimated quite early on last season that he did not think his juveniles were quite as good as in the immediate past, but it did not stop him bagging the Moyglare with **Mail The Desert**. There seems no reason why this daughter of Desert Prince should not continue to progress in her second season, despite the good number of miles she clocked up as a two-year-old, but one feels she may have to head to the continent to add to her Group 1 tally.

The former Southampton soccer ace is always a man to keep his feet firmly on the ground and he believes he has a number of three-year-olds who need to take that little jump in class if they are to succeed at the top level this year. **Zafeen**, who ran great races in both the Middle Park and the Dewhurst, is one who fits this category and the filly **Illustria** is another.

Londonnetdotcom looked a very exciting prospect when she scooted away with a Kempton maiden but she wasn't right on her final run of the campaign and should be up to winning at Group level after thriving during the winter.

The battle-hardened and ultra-tough **Checkit** should pay his way again and a decent 1m2f heat should come the way of **Roskilde**. If there is a really good maiden at West Ilsley, it just might be **Bravo Dancer**, who returned from a long break to finish fourth in a Listed race at Newmarket's Cambridgeshire meeting.

Just across the A34 from the Channon emporium lies *GERARD BUTLER*'s HQ, in the heart of the Churn Estate. The former assistant to John Dunlop took a further step up the ladder last season with a host of top class successes, most notably **Elusive City** in the Group 1 Prix Morny.

This colt has all the ability in the world but he has a star's attitude and the Butler team will be working hard to keep his mind on the job as they bid for top-class honours this season. I think they may find it increasingly difficult to do so but there is plenty of other three-year-old talent to look forward to.

I particularly like **Shield**, who followed up highly-talented stablemate Playapart's 2001 win in a maiden on Lingfield's polytrack towards the turn of the year. Playapart went on to land the Feilden Stakes at the Newmarket Craven meeting and it would come as no surprise to see Shield do as well come the trial season.

Berkshire's Best

Geminiani
Midas Way
Shield

Sponsored by Stan James

Newmarket by Aborigine

SIR MICHAEL STOUTE has been the top Newmarket trainer over the last couple of years and his quality fillies Islington **and** Russian Rhythm (pictured) **can help him retain that position this season.**

Islington won four of her first five starts last term, with her only disappointing run coming in the Oaks, when she could not handle the soft ground in finishing fifth to Kazzia.

Her true ability was shown in her Nassau Stakes and Yorkshire Oaks triumphs before a creditably close fifth to Marienbard in the Arc de Triomphe. Her busy season was showing when she rounded her campaign off with a financially-rewarding third to Starine and Banks Hill in the Breeders Cup Fillies And Mares Turf at Arlington Park.

This daughter of Sadler's Wells has made great progress during the winter and can reward the decision of Lord Weinstock's executors to keep her in training as a four-year-old.

Russian Rhythm goes into her three-year-old season looking a serious 1,000 Guineas challenger. She used a maiden win at Newmarket as a launching pad to scintillating performances both in the Princess Margaret at Ascot and York's Lowther before Airwave put paid to her unbeaten record in the Cheveley Park at Newmarket.

Time will show the winner to be exceptionally fast, so the defeat was no disgrace and stepping up to 1m in the fillies' Classic should see Russian Rhythm getting back into the winning groove, as her work at home suggests she could be one of the season's stars.

Among the up-and-coming Freemason Lodge three-year-olds, keep an eye out for progressive pair **Illustrator** and **Huja**, who are progressing well and are ready to make their mark at the highest level.

It is ironic that Sir Michael's former assistant *JAMES FANSHAWE* could be handling Russian Rhythm's main 1,000 Guineas rival, **Soviet Song**. From an early stage last year, she was catching my eye on the gallops and transferred her smart home work into winning racecourse form, completing a hat-trick with a sterling performance in the Meon Valley Fillies' Mile at Ascot.

She beat Casual Look by a length and a half, showing the acceleration that is the hallmark of a top-class filly. She was bred by and races in the colours of the Elite Racing Club. A Classic win would be a tremendous boost for racing's attraction, as it would show the smaller fish in racing's waters can occasionally defeat the big battalions like Coolmore and Godolphin.

There's no doubt she has strengthened up and I hope I'm not just speaking through the 33-1 Guineas voucher in my betting portfolio!

It was a bitter blow to Fanshawe when Godolphin headhunted **Grandera**, a colt he had nurtured at two and three years. This one won a major international race in Singapore for the "boys in blue", following up in the Prince Of Wales's Stakes and the Irish Champion Stakes.

Godolphin have decided to keep him in training this year and he should once again win his share of races round the world for *SAEED BIN SUROOR*.

DAVID LODER, who shocked the racing world by announcing that he will retire at the end of the season, prepared and passed on to Saeed Bin Suroor a couple of smart juveniles, in the shape of Gimcrack winner

Country Reel and Dublin. It is too early to assess Loder's juvenile prospects this year, but keep an eye open for one or two older horses he is training that were previously with Bin Suroor. These include **Parasol** and **King's Consul**, who originally cost $5.3 illion as a yearling in America.

HENRY CECIL has been soldiering on bravely over the last couple of seasons without the firepower he used to have during the lifetimes of Jim Joel and Lord Howard de Walden. That said, he still trains horses for another major owner-breeder in Khalid Abdullah, whose **Burning Sun** gave him his regular-as-clockwork Royal Ascot winner.

That was in the Listed 1m2f Hampton Court Stakes and this one went on to land the Group 2 Prix Eugene Adam at Maisons Lafitte. After that, a minor training problem held him up and he had not recaptured his sparkle when finishing last in the Dubai Champion Stakes.

In retrospect, Cecil feels the horse may also have been ill at ease on the fast ground and will be looking for him to re-establish himself in the top rank on more suitable ground. The Danzig colt has put on a lot of muscle during the winter months and stands out when Cecil's Warren Place string exercises on the heath.

JAMES TOLLER is a smaller trainer with a dream of Classic glory. Before **Hanami** won a Newmarket Listed race at 33-1, he told me she had a bright future. After that smoothly-gained success, she is understandably taking in one of the fillies' Classic trials to see if she justifies running in the Guineas itself.

Whatever the fate of this attractive Hernando filly early on in the season, he will be placing both her and his stalwart servant **Duck Row** to good advantage. Remember that, as his name suggests, Duck Row needs plenty of juice in the ground.

GILES BRAVERY may not have many horses in his Revida Place string but he obviously has an eye for a yearling, as he manages to come up with a top juvenile almost every year – remember his Cherry Hinton winner, Torgau. Last season, the bargain basement buy was **Striking Ambition**, who scored first time out at Nottingham. He was then unlucky in running in a valuable sales race before being despatched across the Channel to pick up a Listed race from some smart French two-year-olds at Saint Cloud.

He has developed into a fine, strong

HOW ABOUT A NICE GROUP RACE, EH? Henry Cecil and Burning Sun make their plans

Sponsored by Stan James

individual and his trainer tells me he will be sent to the continent again for the French 2,000 Guineas.

Bravery does not often get it wrong when going for a touch but **Kohima** let down her backers when well beaten in a three-year-old maiden on her debut at Lingfield. Former jockey Jason Weaver, Bravery's assistant trainer, says we should not desert her, as she gives him a great feel in her work at home.

He agrees with the trainer in putting up another as yet unnamed two-year-old for us to follow early on. This is a pint-sized but sharp Foxhound filly, who is out of the mare Sopran Marida, making her a half-sister to the stable's versatile Flat and jumps performer Lady Laureate.

NEVILLE CALLAGHAN will be hoping **St Pancras** puts him in the limelight after a quiet season in 2002. This is a lovely, big son of Danehill Dancer and he was in the frame in both the Solario and Doncaster's Champagne Stakes. Considering he was still growing at the time, his second to Almushahar in the last race was highly commendable.

St Pancras has been kept on the move during the winter months and is regularly ridden out by former lightweight jockey and trainer Colin Williams. Owned by Jockey Club steward Michael Hill, St Pancras could be the dark horse in the 2,000 Guineas.

SIR MARK PRESCOTT (below) has handled smart sprinter **Danehurst** brilliantly and it is through no fault of the bold baronet's that she has been so lightly raced during the last two seasons. The reason is that it is essential she has soft ground, as she cannot act on the usual midsummer conditions. Keeping her on the boil requires all his considerable skill and his softly-softly approach paid off with three Listed race wins in 2001.

Stepping up in class last season, she was placed in the Group 1 Golden Jubilee Stakes at Royal Ascot and the July Cup before landing the Flying Five at the Curragh. Revelling on the soft ground, she then won a couple of Group sprints in Europe to round her season off on a high note.

She always shows a real turn of foot on the gallops when there is enough give in the ground and there is definitely a Group 1 sprint to be won with her, granted the right going.

JEREMY NOSEDA makes no secret of his belief that **Wizard Of Noz** is destined to go to the top. Certainly, both his juvenile starts augured well for the future, as he followed up his three lengths Haydock debut win by running on into third to Almushahar in the Champagne Stakes at Doncaster.

As he was hampered a furlong out, he did well to finish so close and the plan is to try him in the European Free Handicap to see if the dream of a first Noseda Classic win

Sir Mark Prescott and brilliant sprinter Danehurst

> *'Wizard Of Noz did well to finish so close and the plan is to try him in the European Free Handicap to see if the dream of a first Noseda Classic win could be on the cards'*

could be on the cards in the 2,000 Guineas. The Jersey Stakes at Royal Ascot will be the target if it turns out he doesn't get 1m.

Stable companion **Bahamian Dancer** figures on a higher mark in the Free Handicap but, on all that they have shown me on the heath and the Al Bahathri, Wizard Of Noz is likely to make the greatest impact.

On the handicapping front, Noseda should be picking up his fair share of the races with the useful duo **Adiemus** and **Courageous Duke**.

Both were trained for dirt campaigns during the winter and should be adding to both their and their handler's reputations on grass, as they figure on handy marks.

MICHAEL JARVIS suffered a body blow last year when his Derby contender Coshocton broke a leg in the final furlong of the Derby and had to be put down on the course. This year, his improving Leicester winner **Sarayat** is a likely money-spinner and, along with **Soyuz** and **St Andrews**, makes up a strong task force which could afford him some measure of consolation.

PIP PAYNE had a quiet year after the headline-grabbing performances of his Wokingham Handicap winner Nice One Clare in 2001. We went for **Ezz Elkheil** as one for the notebook last spring but the move did not pay off, as he failed to fulfil the promise he showed as a two-year-old.

Payne says: "I think you must forgive him last year, as he was still backward and I think you will find he really comes into his own in staying races this year, as he is reasonably handicapped."

HUGH COLLINGRIDGE holds out high hopes for the grey **Stormont**, who contributed to his keep with a Lingfield win and several placings. " I had intended to aim him at a valuable All-Weather race in March, as he worked a treat on the surface, but sadly he suffered an injury and needed an operation. He's now back cantering.

"I would be disappointed if he did not win a couple of nice races later in the year and I hope he proves up to Pattern race class."

GEOFF WRAGG is the doyen of Newmarket trainers and his patience with **Asian Heights** could pay dividends this year. This one was strongly fancied to win the 2001 Derby but split a pastern as he was doing his final gallop on Racecourse Side before the Classic. He proved a model patient and made a complete recovery, winning on his reappearance at Windsor in the spring, before another minor injury sidelined him until his September Stakes win at Kempton four months later. It might have been aiming a little too high then to make a challenge for the Arc de Triomphe and, after a slow start, the horse finished way adrift after being eased down.

Though he could finish only 14th to Marienbard, this performance should be discounted, as both his previous public and home form indicates he is better than that.

LUCA CUMANI will miss his brilliant filly Gossamer this year but he has some potentially exciting material at his disposal at the Bedford House Stables. He will obviously be hoping to see her half-sister **Camlet** enhance the family's reputation.

She may not quite reach the same heights at Gossamer but, after winning on her debut at Yarmouth, was badly hampered when a close-enough eighth to Luvah Girl in the Rockfel at Newmarket. That and the way she is going at home indicate that there are more races to be won with her.

The Italian's globetrotting **Endless Hall** is again expected to pay his way and, among the older horses, there are handicaps to be won with **Sarin**, **Prado** and **Katmandu**.

NICK LITTMODEN hits the headlines mainly for his exploits as champion All-Weather trainer but he is steadily upgrading the quality of his turf team.

Originally, he thought the juvenile winner **Helen Bradley** would develop into a Pattern race filly. The expected progress did not materialise last year but everything she does at home suggests there are races to be won with her, as she has been plummeting down the handicap.

It should also pay to keep an eye open for **Iwo Jima**. This Desert King colt could prove a real bargain at the 20,000 guineas he cost as a yearling. He always looked the part in his work, though he did not make it to the racecourse until late in the year.

When he did make a belated first appearance in September, he was clearly a bit on the burly side in the paddock. Once his chance was gone, he was not knocked around in finishing mid-division to Jay Gee's Choice over 7f at Haydock.

The experience gained will stand him in good stead and it would come as an unwelcome surprise to all concerned if he failed to make up for lost time and pay his way this season.

Twelve months ago, *JAMES EUSTACE* was hoping that his first Group winner **Rapscallion** would hit the heights, but he had some niggling problems and was sent for a midsummer break at owner Jeff Smith's Littleton Stud in Hampshire. His enforced break did him a power of good and there are some decent races to be won with this one on his favoured soft ground.

Eustace has always held a high opinion of **Salute** and his charge, though he did not manage to win last year, put in some sound performances. He now figures on a handy mark and is the ideal type to win a big handicap and vindicate Eustace's insistence that the syndicate, which owns him, not send him to the sales.

Another syndicate horse, **Blue Patrick**, will provide not only fun but also a financial return for his owners, as he is very much on the upgrade.

Hot off the Heath
Ezz Elkheil
Salute
St Pancras

I know which one's fancied!

Tony Jakobson talks to HQ trainers on the gallops daily. Check in every day to hear which horses he's been told to back!

0906 911 0232

Calls cost £1/min all times. Outlook Press, Raceform House, Compton, Berks RG20 6NL.

Ireland
by Jerry M

AIDAN O'BRIEN **was, to no one's surprise, the top trainer last year, winning the £1.2million Epsom Derby with High Chaparral and saddling the runner-up Hawk Wing, having of course won it the previous year with Galileo. The Ballydoyle trainer is simply untouchable and one of the game's utmost gentlemen.**

Rock of Gibraltar was a great example of O'Brien's talent, soaring home in the English 2,000 Guineas on his way to winning seven consecutive Group 1 races, an unbelievable record, and surely he will go down in the history books as one of the best thoroughbreds ever to come out of Ireland.

O'Brien will, naturally, have as much ammunition this season to keep up his strike-rate.

Some pundits say it would be impossible for O'Brien to win three Epsom Derbys in a row but clearly the great man believes differently. **Brian Boru**, a classy two-year-old last year, when he won Doncaster's Racing Post Trophy, is ante-post favourite for this year's event – currently, 8-1 is on offer. This son of Sadler's Wells is held in very high regard and he will win major races this season. Obviously the Derby is the main target and he has the credentials to win it.

O'Brien has nursed along some lovely two-year-olds last season and they are ready to acquit themselves really well as three-year-olds. Firstly, one that has impressed me is the Mrs John Magnier-owned **Catcher In The Rye**. This horse will win nice races early in the season.

Hold That Tiger is a wonderful prospect owned by Michael Tabor and this one has the potential to go right to the top. This horse has Classics written all over him and Mick Kinane will enjoy riding this fellow.

Spartacus is yet another winner for the

Brian Boru

outstanding stallion Danehill and was unextended to win his maiden, beating Akanti by three lengths at Gowran Park. That form was boosted in later weeks when the second horse won two races on the trot.

Spartacus has the pedigree to figure prominently this season; he could be anything but is surely worth following, especially after winning the Group 1 Phoenix Stakes last August, trouncing a select field.

Van Nistelrooy, the world's most expensive yearling in 2001 at a cost of £4.4million, was disappointing last year but the son of Storm Cat will leave his mark this season and will reap great rewards.

Here's just a few of the rest of O'Brien's string to keep a close eye on. **Reach For The Moon** is one the stable think very highly of. She opened her account at Cork last year on her first ever run on a racecourse, trotting up by four lengths. Mick Kinane also rates her very highly indeed.

Kimberley Mine, **Yesterday**, **Tomahawk** and **In The Limelight** are other three-year-olds I have heard very good reports about.

Keep a close eye on the O'Brien two-year-olds. You can be sure there will be some nice types coming along and, especially early in the season, they are worthy of support, as most will be as fit as can be for their debuts.

KEVIN PRENDERGAST had another good season and has legitimate hopes of an even better 2003. His three-year-old crop are always worth consideration. **Before Dawn** ran some nice races last season and is top of my list for following. **Jakarta Jade** is a nice type and will win lots of races this term, while **Encircle** has lots of ability and will play a major part for the Prendergast stable – she'll be aimed at the highest level this season.

Evelyn One ran some fine races last year, most notably when going down to Brian Boru at the Curragh. The three-year-old by Alhaarth will progress and is a very classy type.

DERMOT WELD had another excellent year, capped when **Media Puzzle** (below, with stable staff) gave him his second Melbourne Cup, as tipped by yours truly a week in advance in the RFO. The six-year-old by Theatrical is a star and can go on in the same vein this season.

Revue didn't race at two but this lightly-raced four-year-old has a superb future and is maturing well. He is undoubtedly worth following. High on my list among Weld's younger brigade is **Peratus**, who looks more than average and is going the right way.

MICHAEL O'BRIEN had a good year and his **Flavian Dynasty** is a horse for my shortlist. This three-year-old by Titus Livius ran some very respectable races at two, most notably when third behind Chappel Crescent

MEDIA CIRCUS: Dermot Weld's stable staff with Media Puzzle and the Melbourne Cup

Sponsored by Stan James

Invincible Irish
Brian Boru Flavian Dynasty Revue

John Oxx

at Naas last June, when Aidan O'Brien's hotpot One Nice Cat was back in sixth place. This is solid form and the youngster will win his share of races this term.

JOHN OXX will enjoy his usual good season and was again well up with the top Irish trainers last year. He always seems to do well with his three-year-olds and I have listed a couple to keep a close eye on.

Firstly, **Szabo**, who ran in a Listed race on his debut behind Van Nistelrooy at the Curragh. This youngster is well regarded and will surely reap rewards. **Dabousiya** has potential and will make a mark in top class races at three. **Englishtown** could be a star for this stable this year – he is a lovely type and can only progress.

JIM BOLGER was another leading Irish trainer in 2002 and I fancy he'll play a major part with big successes this term. His three-year-old **Benicio** is a spectacular horse who will be aimed at Group races. He'll be off to a flying early start this season and Kevin Manning gets on particularly well with this horse – bear him in mind when this combination are put together.

Luminata is a firm contender for the big prizes this year. She started off her career in Listed races and progressed well, making the frame in two end-of-term Group 1s. She's definitely one to keep onside.

Tus Maith ran just behind her stablemate when third to Ragtop. The daughter of Entrepreneur is a certain future winner and this filly has a lovely action.

One four-year-old from the Bolger yard worth watching is **Twilight Breeze**, whose best run last year was when second to Vinthea in June. She is certainly on the up and ran some very decent races after that. She will be aimed at some top staying races in the months to come. If anything, we should have a better season than our last, with chances in all the major Group 1 races around the world.

Sponsored by Stan James

The North by Borderer

MARK JOHNSTON enjoyed another magical year and won over £2 million in prize-money whilst equalling Henry Cecil's record of nine consecutive centuries. The trainer and his wife Deirdre aim to repeat those feats and more this season.

She told me: "We won more Group races than anyone else in Britain last year and we want to win at least two Group 1 races this time."

Bandari bolted up by 13 lengths in the Lingfield Derby Trial, disappointed in the Epsom showpiece but rounded off with a fair effort behind Bollin Eric in the St Leger. The trainer's wife said: "Richard (Hills) didn't feel he stayed the trip at Doncaster, so we will be aiming him at all the major races over 1m4f."

His inability to maintain weight after each race was well documented but the problem seems to be cured. Deirdre added: "He's in fantastic form and put on over 40 kilos over the winter. We used to have a problem with him but we made a conscious effort to relax him and put on muscle as well as weight."

Zindabad enjoyed another outstanding season, winning the Group 3 John Porter Stakes and the Group 2 Yorkshire Cup and

TEAM JOHNSTON: Mark and Deirdre talk business during a raid on Sha Tin, Hong Kong

Sponsored by Stan James

> *'I've fallen in love with a horse called Love In Seattle . . . he is a huge horse with lots of scope'*

Hardwicke Stakes. He also put up a fine display in the Group 1 King George VI & Queen Elizabeth Diamond Stakes when third to Golan and Nayef but his season ended in anti-climax with a below-par effort in the Canadian International.

Deirdre stated: "He didn't sustain an injury but lost weight on the flight. He ran flat but is absolutely fine and in cracking order." The seven-year-old goes to Dubai for the Sheema Classic in March and will be a leading player in all the top middle-distance races in Britain.

Systematic won a Leicester handicap off 76 in April but progressed through the year. He won the Group 3 Cumberland Lodge Stakes at Ascot on his final start. Mrs Johnston told me: "He's a cracking horse and might stay a bit further than 1m4f. Let's hope we can find something suitable for him at Royal Ascot."

Sir George Turner had been bracketed with Johnston's top three-year-olds at the beginning of the season but didn't live up to his potential. His attitude was questioned by many experts but connections hope a recent gelding operation will bring significant improvement. Johnston added: "If he hadn't dropped himself out against Moon Ballad at Goodwood, he would have been very close.

"He wore cheekpieces that day but he might not need them now and he could be a serious horse."

She continued: "**Legal Approach** is a very progressive sort and we've realised he really needs a galloping track. His one bad race last year was at Windsor, where the track just didn't suit him at all. You'll see a lot of him this year."

Scott's View was another typical ohnston improver and would have run a big race in the Ebor had he not missed the cut by one. The trainer's wife revealed: "We certainly hope he can continue to progress but he has risen 40lb in the handicap. He needs to improve again to be Group class."

There is one horse that is undoubtedly the apple of her eye: "I have fallen in love with a horse called **Love In Seattle**. He is a son of Seattle Slew and the first horse to give me the same feeling as Fruits Of Love at the same stage.

"This is an unknown quantity, which makes him even more exciting. He is a huge horse with lots of scope and he floats up the gallop. He's doing road work at the moment and looking good."

There is another unraced three-year-old to watch closely called **Jebel Suraaj**. "He is a horse we like a lot. He was due to run at York but he sustained a stress fracture. He has lots of scope and went very well as a two-year-old at home."

BRYAN SMART wasted no time firing in the winners after moving into Hambleton House in Thirsk. The Yorkshireman returned to his roots in November, having left home aged 15. With huge financial backing from stable sponsor and principle owner Reg Bond, he is in a very strong position.

Bond Boy provided his trainer with the highlight of last season when winning the Stewards' Cup at Glorious Goodwood. Smart said: "He must have cut in the ground and looks great for the year ahead. The Stewards' Cup will be on the agenda again and we'll also look at the Great St Wilfrid at Ripon and probably the Ayr Gold Cup. He's as hard as old boots and I think he'll win a little Listed race abroad on soft ground."

Monsieur Bond had very good form throughout last season and will bid for a European Classic this time around. Smart told me: "He'll be entered in the Italian Guineas and he should get the trip, no problem. He was beaten three times by Somnus but we didn't have the run of the race in the sales event at Doncaster.

"I'm very excited about him and he looks marvellous."

Look out for a three-year-old filly called **Bond Stasia**. She finished third to Wunders Dream on her debut at Nottingham but didn't quite stay when stepped up to 6f on her next start at Hamilton. Smart said: "She looked all over the winner a furlong out but finished third to

Sponsored by Stan James

Steelaninch and Golden Nun. She wants a bit of cut in the ground and has a future."

Bond Becks won over the minimum trip at Beverley and Catterick but is expected to do much better over farther. The trainer stated: "He's not a 5f horse but finished fourth in the Flying Childers, despite Jimmy Fortune giving him a bit to do. He'll be a 7f horse but we've had to get him to settle. He's a lot more laid back now and I'm excited about him."

JAMES GIVEN's **Wunders Dream** won the Doncaster race but she will have her work cut out this season. Her trainer has been scanning old form books and revealed: "History says we'll have done better than average if we win another race with her.

"She'll have to take on older horses and carry a Group 2 penalty from the start of the campaign." However, she has guts and bucked a significant trend when comfortably carrying a Group 3 penalty to win the Flying Childers. Given added: "I hope we can go on to bigger and better sprinting races with her."

Hugs Dancer gave the Lincolnshire handler and Borderer readers the highlight of last season when winning the Ebor at 25-1. He will be back on the Knavesmire in August but Given revealed: "His first target is the Chester Cup. I don't think the tight course will be a problem, as he is a handy horse and holds his position without being intimidated.

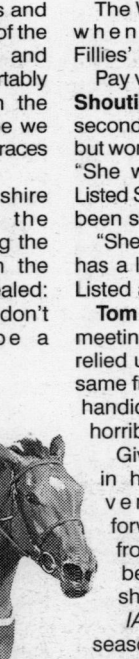

"It's a bit like the Ebor because you need to possess tactical speed and have the ability to jump from the gate."

Hugs Dancer also won the prestigious Goodwood Stakes for a second successive year in July, but a bid for the three-peat may be foiled by his inflated handicap mark, which could well stop him qualifying for the 0-95 race this time.

Given found one of the buys of the season when he paid just 7,000 guineas for star filly **Summitville**, who has the Epsom Oaks as her objective. The trainer told me: "She did very well through the winter and holds an entry in the Guineas but that will be a bit sharp for her and the Oaks will be more suitable."

The Willoughton yard was under a cloud when she disappointed in the Fillies' Mile at Ascot.

Pay very close attention to a horse called **Shouting The Odds**. She ran green when second at Musselburgh on her debut in July but won next time at Folkestone. Given said: "She was unlucky to finish fourth in the Listed St Hugh's Stakes at Newbury and had been slightly backward and weak all year.

"She's done really well over the winter and has a lot of scope. We hope to run her in Listed and Group races."

Tom Tun won at Doncaster's opening meeting last term and his trainer can be relied upon to have him cherry-ripe for the same fixture. He said: "He has gone up the handicap but is virtually unbeatable on horrible ground."

Given has always held **Branston Tiger** in high regard. He said: "He's done very well and I'm looking forward to running him again. He hails from a late-maturing family and will do better when he learns to settle. He shows plenty of dash."

IAN SEMPLE enjoyed a magnificent season and sent out the winners of 34 races. The Scot revealed: "**Chookie Heiton** is in good form at home and has done well over the winter. He's as big as a bull and really looks the part – he's got a backend on him like Hattie Jacques.

"I'm looking for him to stand up and be counted this year because I think he will be at his best. I hope he gets 7f but he has a lot of speed and won well over 6f for

Summitville

Frankie [Dettori] last year. I'm looking to get him started in a 7f Listed race at Haydock at the end of April and he'll also run over 6f at the Guineas meeting. "I'd be very disappointed if he doesn't win a Listed race and I really believe Newbury and other level tracks suit him perfectly. He finished third in the Wokingham last year but was a better horse a week afterwards, so I'll be aiming him at that race again. He isn't a sound horse, so I am only able to work him harder when he starts to move well but he's very good when he's right."

Kelburne has sustained a fracture to a cannon bone but will return after three months in his box. Semple said: "He's a real top-of-the-ground horse, so I'll get him ready for May. I'll run him a couple of times before Royal Ascot and let him take his chance in the Royal Hunt Cup again.

The Scotsman has a couple of dates for your diary. He revealed: "**Maktavish** is a good horse. We bought him out of Rod Millman's yard and he won for us on the sand but the handicapper raised him to a mark of 86. He's rated just 78 on turf, so I'm hoping to win the 0-100 handicap over 5f at Doncaster in March."

He continued: "**Tandava** beat Virgin Soldier at Pontefract last season and the owner would very much like to go for the Northumberland Plate on June 28."

Look out for a horse called **Millennium Hall**. Semple bought him out of Luca Cumani's yard and rates him highly. He said: "He has a future and I've always liked him. There are a couple of good races in him."

Sandgate Cygnet won at Hamilton last season and is expected to improve: "She only ran three times and we sent her home to strengthen up. She's a filly who should win for me this year."

And Semple gave us a horse for the notebook: "**Flight Commander** is the one to follow closely. He's by In The Wings and I bought him out of Marcus Tregoning's stable after his owner, Lord Weinstock, died. I have gelded him and he might be very good over 1m2f or 1m4f."

Northern rocks
Bond Becks Love In Seattle Shouting The Odds

KELBURNE: Ian Semple's tough handicapper takes a good prize at Sandown last June

Sponsored by Stan James

The West by Hastings

Captain Saif

RICHARD HANNON **continues to use his 30-plus years of experience in the game to remain one of the leading trainers in the land. With the help of his son Richard Jnr, he flew high during the last turf campaign to notch yet another century with an impressive total of 113 winners for the Wiltshire outfit.**

Having enjoyed a cracking campaign with his juvenile team last summer, he now has a wealth of second-season talent raring to go this spring and it's a short price he'll again reach the ton-up comfortably.

It's easy to see why the unbeaten **Captain Saif** ranks highly among the three-year-old brigade, having powered clear of Weavers Pride in a 7f conditions race at Ascot in September. The son of Compton Place possesses plenty of size and scope about him and, once filling his ample frame, he should make a big impact in Pattern company.

Although Classic ambitions are thin on the ground this time around, one to keep an eye on is **Rag Top**, being prepared for a possible tilt at the Irish 1,000 Guineas on May 25.

The chestnut daughter of Barathea bagged four races as a youngster, including a comfortable brush aside of Luminata (twice a winner since) in a Listed contest over 6f at Naas in June. Subsequent creditable efforts in Group company at Ascot and Deauville don't exactly blot the copybook.

Lesser horses would have cried enough for the gruelling campaign, so it was pleasing to see her sign off as a ready winner of a competitive Group 3 in the hands of stable jockey Dane O'Neill at The Curragh last backend. Her undoubted class and proven form on the track should see her give a good account in the Classic this spring.

The talented **Presto Vento** was one of a typically high number of precocious juveniles housed at East Everleigh last term. The Air Express filly completed an early season hat-

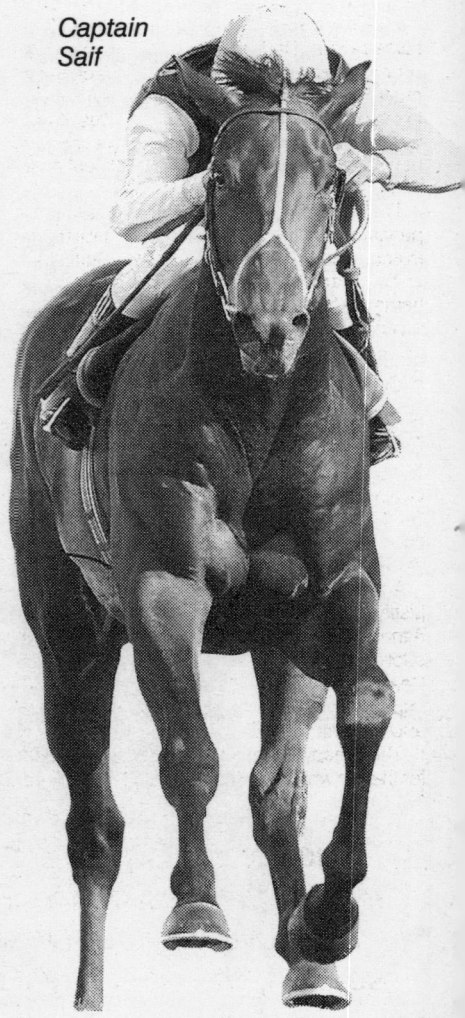

Sponsored by Stan James

trick when beating Arran Pilot for a Listed sprint prize at Sandown. She went on to rout 23 rivals in the valuable Weatherbys Super Sprint at Newbury and picked up more dough for connections when finishing a close third in a similar race at Ascot. Another money-spinning campaign is in the offing for the months ahead.

Mister Links came of age when leading home a memorable Hannon one-two in the July Stakes at Newmarket. The youngster showed pace and battling qualities in equal measure at Headquarters.

Subsequent seconds to Country Reel in the Gimcrack at York in August and Somnus in a sales race at Doncaster the following month prompted connections to have a crack at his elders in the Prix de l'Abbaye on the Arc card. In the circumstances, he acquitted himself very well to fill a midfield berth, just five lengths behind the vastly more experienced Continent, in the feature sprint at Longchamp.

His presence in the yard more than compensates for the loss of speedy stablemate Puma, who has been sold to race Stateside.

The yard's **Tacitus** did well to chase home the better-fancied Mister Links at HQ and, having mixed with some of the best as a juvenile, is sure to be pitched into similarly high-profile company on his second campaign.

The chestnut was unluckily impeded en route to claiming fourth behind Spartacus in an Italian Group 1 and got stuck in the mud when finishing tired in the Racing Post Trophy at Donny, an effort that's best overlooked. Described by Hannon Jnr as a 'baby' last season, it's safe to assume the best is yet to come with this one.

The nicely-bred **Al Turf** quickened to justify market confidence on his Newbury bow. Although the bubble was burst by a one-paced effort behind Elusive City in a Group 1 at Deauville in August, he's just the type to improve with age and is well worth giving another chance to.

The speedy **Hurricane Alan** looked destined for the top when blowing away Hazelhatch and company to land the Goffs Challenge over 6f at The Curragh. A return to trailblazing tactics resulted in another comfortable success when revisiting the Irish venue in September. He was ridden to get the 7f trip on his final start and any fears of him failing to get home were quashed when he stayed on into third behind the highly-touted Governor Brown at Newmarket that day.

A potent mix of stamina and speed provides connections with a plethora of opportunities in mapping out his upcoming campaign.

Although not quite in the same league, the following suggestions are sure to make a mark in lesser company for Hannon.

Looking Down clocked up plenty of miles on her juvenile campaign and showed toughness beyond her years to land a competitive Goodwood handicap in August. She showed no signs of burnout when plying her trade on Lingfield's polytrack last November, finishing behind Greek Revival and Boston Lodge on the artificial surface.

Another filly expected to land her share of handicaps is **Toy Show**. Although she didn't cut much ice over inadequate trips in maiden company, a hike up to 1m2f off a lowly 66 rating for her nursery bow resulted in a much more likeable display, when she took apart a competitive field at Nottingham.

Providing the ground rides on the fast side, she could easily pop up at a nice price in one of the more valuable middle-distance handicaps this summer.

Valuable purchase **Due Respect** looked overpriced on the strength of his first two modest displays, but showed more potential when getting off the mark at Chester in September. He's been likened in temperament to former stable star Tamburlaine and the world will be his oyster when he settles down to the job.

One Last Time ranks quite highly in the Hannon squad of handicap prospects. He did the business in style with an impressive debut success at Salisbury and gave connections a thrill when a battling second to Revenue in

> *'Tacitus got stuck in the mud when finishing tired in the Racing Post Trophy, an effort that's best overlooked. Described as a baby last season, the best is yet to come with this one'*

Sponsored by Stan James

the Windsor Castle at Royal Ascot.

Although originally thought best with juice in the ground, the formbook suggests a sound surface will play to his strengths this summer. Expect at least one big prize to go his way before the season is out.

I'm Magic is bred to improve with age and showed enough in a seven-race juvenile stint to suggest she's a certainty for an early-season maiden.

Avening had a busy time of things as a juvenile and was possibly feeling the effects in the latter stages. He showed a willing attitude to land a Goodwood sprint on his handicap bow and should pick up a few more when the emphasis is on speed.

The main hope among the older representatives at the Wiltshire outfit is the live Arc candidate **Nysaean**.

The valuable son of Sadler's Wells looked a bit special when sluicing through the mud to win by 5l in Listed company at Deauville and remains unexposed for his four-year-old campaign. He wasn't ready for a tilt at the Longchamp showpiece last backend and, having strengthened during the winter months, will now be better equipped to deal with the ravages of competing in Group company.

Big things are expected of this one and he's a worthy addition for anyone compiling a list of ten to follow.

The ultra-consistent **Umistim** possesses the heart of a lion and must be a treat to have in the yard. He gained compensation for being beaten a matter of inches in the Hungerford Stakes when nabbing the smart Blatant in a titanic three-pronged battle for a decent prize at The Curragh.

There's no substitute for courage in a racehorse and this one has it by the bucket-load. The veteran is sure to be plying his trade effectively in Listed/Group company throughout the year.

DAVID ELSWORTH didn't enjoy the best of times last turf season, finishing with a tally of just 18 winners and an equally disappointing strike-rate of 7%. The campaign highlights mainly surrounded the admirable pair **Persian Punch** (right) and **Smirk**, along with the classy youngster **Norse Dancer**.

The 'Punch' silenced any doubters calling for retirement following his Goodwood Cup flop, bouncing back with a win in a Salisbury conditions race. His old flair shone through in a subsequent second to Boreas in the Doncaster Cup and the old boy exacted revenge on that adversary when completing a brace of Jockey Club Cup victories in October.

His trademark never-say-die tactics have helped make him a firm favourite with the public and, at the grand old age of ten, he can once again show the youngsters the way home.

The chestnut Smirk also gives everything in his races and thoroughly deserves to add

UMISTIM: beating subsequent Guineas winner King's Best in the Craven Stakes of 2000

PERSIAN PUNCH: leads round first bend in Doncaster Cup

significantly to his four career wins when he returns to action in the spring. The Selkirk entire quashed his reputation of being a 'nearly horse' when pipping Atlantic Ace for the William Hill Mile at Glorious Goodwood, and again let off the fireworks when powering to a comprehensive Class A success at Newmarket on his final sighting.

He will come into his own as a five-year-old and is one to have on your side in the continuing battle with the bookies.

Regarding the younger team at the Whitsbury base, hopes are high for Norse Dancer making the grade this term. The colt did well to fill a fourth placing behind Dublin in the Vintage Stakes and Al Jadeed in the Royal Lodge. He can be forgiven for getting bogged down in the mud at Town Moor when managing only seventh behind Brian Boru in the Racing Post Trophy.

The faster conditions expected for the Derby at Epsom in June will suit his style of racing and, at lengthy odds, he might be worth a small wager for the prestigious Classic.

Devon-based handler *ROD MILLMAN* has a couple of useful recruits to look forward to in the form of **Coconut Penang** and **Fleetwood Bay**. The former is regarded as the flagbearer this summer and, having finished a cracking fourth from an awkward draw behind Statue Of Liberty in the Coventry last June, it's easy to see why. He showed signs of greenness as a youngster and wasn't overcooked in a relatively light campaign.

His connections' patience can be rewarded with some black-type success with this one as a three-year-old.

Tough cookie Fleetwood Bay provided one of the high points of last season when plundering the valuable St Leger Yearling Stakes at Doncaster in September. More can be expected on his second year in training.

Best of the West

Captain Saif
Nysaean
Rag Top

Sponsored by Stan James

The South by Southerner

TERRY MILLS has overcome enormous prejudice to establish himself as one of the top Flat trainers in the country.

Without the usual family connections in racing or a career as a jockey behind him, Terry was in his late forties when he decided to become a trainer after making a fortune from waste disposal. There were plenty in the sport ready to rubbish his ambitions in the early days but they seriously underestimated the hardworking Cockney whose multi-million bound business began with a single lorry in 1962.

An owner for many years, he purchased Loretta Lodge at Headley in 1988, appointed Epsom stalwart Wally Carter as trainer and became his assistant in order to gain the necessary experience to take out a licence himself. Terry took over the helm at Loretta Lodge in 1993 and Carter became his head lad.

Bobzao's victory in the Hardwicke Stakes at Royal Ascot in 1994 and a steady stream of high-profile successes since have forced the sceptics grudgingly to change their minds and horses trained by T Mills are now afforded the greatest respect.

Ascot has been a very lucky course for Terry and last year he saddled Norton to win the Royal Hunt Cup and **Peace Offering** to collect the Group 3 Willmott Dixon Cornwallis Stakes at the Berkshire track. However, there is no doubt stable star **Where Or When**'s demolition of the much-vaunted Hawk Wing in the Group 1 Netjets Queen Elizabeth II Stakes at Ascot in September was the victory that gave him the most satisfaction.

Afterwards he said: "Now I've won a Group 1 race, I can die a happy man."

Terry, who celebrates his 66th birthday this year, has announced that his son Robert will succeed him at the end of this season's Royal Ascot meeting. History and logic suggest that there's a good chance he will pass the reigns over in a blaze of glory.

Where Or When, who overcame being very nearly brought down to make an impressive winning debut at Ascot as a

HAPPY MEN: Terry Mills is congratulated by son and assistant trainer Robert after Where Or When's sensational QEII win

Sponsored by Stan James

> *'Muqbil looked something very special when producing a smart turn of foot on his debut at Newbury in August . . . by Swain, he's bred to improve with age and is an exciting prospect'*

juvenile, is likely to bid to enhance his course record in the Queen Anne Stakes at the Royal meeting, while the aforementioned Peace Offering is just the type for the King's Stand Stakes, a race Mills won with Mitcham in 1999. **Littleton Arwen**, **Ok Pal** and **Contractor** are a trio of other three-year-old Lorretta Lodge inmates to watch out for in the months to come.

The last-named showed promise in a couple of runs on turf last year and opened his account when staying on to beat subsequent scorer Wages by a comfortable three-parts of a length in a 7f maiden on the polytrack at Lingfield in December. The Spectrum colt has plenty of stamina in his pedigree and should make up into a very decent middle-distance performer this summer.

Ok Pal is going to be a sprinter, pure and simple. The Primo Dominie colt's dam, Sheila's Secret, was a real speedball who won six times, all over 5f, for the stable in the early nineties. Ok Pal powered home 3l clear of the useful Queen's Victory in a 5f Sandown maiden run on easy going in August on his second outing last year, after which his trainer said: "You will be hearing a lot more about this horse. He is at least as good as his mother, Sheila's Secret."

He lost his action and trailed home last of eight to Sir Edwin Landseer in the 6f Listed Sirenia Stakes at Kempton in September on his final appearance, when the ground was much too firm.

Littleton Arwen showed exceptional ability at home last year and the Mills team were surprised when she was only third on her debut in a 7f maiden run on lively ground at Leicester in October. It was only greenness that caused her defeat and she put the record straight when quickening in tremendous style to beat Heidelburg by three and a half lengths in a 7f maiden on the sand at Lingfield at the end of the same month.

Fillies hate cold weather and the Arctic blasts in January and early February interrupted her schedule but, provided she comes to hand in time, the daughter of Bahri will take her chance in the 1,000 Guineas and is sure to make her mark in the very best company eventually.

JOHN DUNLOP had a quiet season by his standards in 2002 but still managed to send out 79 winners and earn close to £1,500,000 in domestic prizemoney for his patrons. The master of Castle Stables, who was recovering from serious surgery last spring, has the usual wealth of talent at his disposal and, beneath the polite and laid-back, gentlemanly exterior, the coals of ambition burn as brightly as ever.

Muqbil (below) looked something very special when producing a smart turn of foot to beat Pinkerton by 5l on his debut in the Listed 7f Washington Singer Stakes at Newbury in August. It was disappointing when he failed by half a length to give Governor Brown 3lb in the 7f Group 3 Somerville Tattersalls

Muqbil

Stakes at Newmarket in early October on his only other start as a juvenile, but there were extenuating circumstances.

He became unbalanced racing into the dip and then met interference before running on strongly when meeting the rising ground inside the final furlong. By dual King George VI and Queen Elizabeth Diamond Stakes winner Swain, Muqbil is bred to improve with age and remains a very exciting prospect, despite his reverse at HQ.

Maghanim was pretty disappointing when only managing to beat one of his 13 rivals in the 7f Group 1 Grand Criterium at Longchamp on Arc day on his third and final outing last term but it wasn't as bad an effort as might first appear. In a strong-run affair, he expended too much energy trying to hold a handy position from the widest draw and, although dropping out of contention in the closing stages, he was eventually only beaten around 7l.

Previously, Maghanim trotted up in a good 7f conditions contest at Doncaster and he chased home subsequent Champagne Stakes victor Almushahar in a very hot 7f maiden at Newmarket on his introduction in August. The Nashwan colt will have no trouble staying 1m this year and the Group 2 Celebration Mile at Goodwood is one of his possible targets.

Big Bad Bob, who went from strength to strength last term, should enjoy a profitable campaign. The front-running colt opened his account at his third attempt in a 7f maiden at Newcastle in August and went on to complete a four-timer, culminating with a pillar-to-post victory in the Listed Tom McGee Stakes over 1m at Ascot in October.

Prince Tum Tum (below) was another to progress well as a juvenile and another who should continue to pay his followers. He did well to catch Rudood on the line in a 7f Warwick maiden after failing to get a clear run early in September, and the following month he readily beat some useful rivals to land a 7f conditions stakes at York.

Excelsius is an interesting individual who had both his races in Italy last year. He stormed home 7l clear of his rivals in a 7f

PRINCE TUM TUM: seen winning on the Knavesmire last season, there's more to come

Sponsored by Stan James

maiden at San Siro on his debut in September and in October was a fine third from a poor draw to Spartacus in the Group 1 Gran Criterium over 1m at the same track.

Khulood was the best juvenile filly at Castle Stables last season when she signed off with a 4l victory from Soldera in the 7f Listed Oh So Sharp Stakes at Newmarket in October. The American-bred made a winning start to her career in a 6f maiden at Ascot in July but was surprisingly only fifth in a 6f conditions event at Salisbury in September, when she refused to settle.

The highly-regarded **Blackwater Angel** is worth keeping an eye on. A well-made daughter of Kingmambo, she had four starts last season and won a 1m maiden at Haydock in September on the third of them. She was immature mentally last year and should be capable of winning in Listed company at least this time.

The Green Desert filly **Goodness Gracious**, who won a 7f Newmarket maiden in good style in November on the second of her two juvenile starts, should more than pay her way this year. As ever, there are a host of unexposed and late-developing types housed in darkest Sussex.

Pershaan and **Shujune** are two names to conjure with. The first-named, who had a couple of runs for experience last year, will come into her own when tackling distances around 1m4f this time.

Shujune reached the frame in all her three starts and improved steadily last year. The Imperial Ballet filly acts on all types of ground and will not test her handler's placing skills.

PETER HARRIS has a very nice bunch of three-year-olds and **Barrissimo** is one of those the Berkhamstead trainer is keen on. After being thrown in the deep end on his debut in the very competitive Betabet Two-Year-Old Trophy at Redcar on his debut, the Night Shift colt romped home by 10l in a 7f maiden at Doncaster in October.

Persian Majesty is no oil painting but he has a real engine. The Grand Lodge colt had been working well prior to winning a 1m maiden at Newmarket in October on his sole appearance last term. He should stay at least 1m4f this year.

Grooms Affection, **Rezzago**, **Serbelloni** and **Sophrano** are a quartet of lightly-raced but talented individuals who should all be capable of picking up decent prizes.

AMANDA PERRETT is set for another good season and, with over 100 horses in training at Coombelands, numbers are back to those of the days when her father, Guy Harwood, was in his pomp.

Orange Touch is expected to make a name for himself this season. The German-bred gamely accounted for Sir Michael Stoute's highly regarded Chief Yeoman on the second of his two starts last year in a 1m maiden at Sandown in September.

The well-named **Self Evident** (by Known Fact) should make up into a useful three-year-old. He also wound up with a victory in a 1m maiden last term, striding home three and a half lengths clear of Wozzeck at Bath in October.

The Grand Lodge colt **Revenante**, who landed a 1m maiden at Warwick in September on his sole start, has any amount of scope, while the fillies **Latest Edition** and **Amount** won their maidens nicely as juveniles and should prosper this year.

Fellow three-year-olds **Crown Counsel**, **Dance In The Sun** and **Island Rapture** have all shown above average ability and should be placed to advantage this time around.

> '*Blackwater Angel is worth keeping an eye on . . . the daughter of Kingmambo was immaculate mentally last year and should be capable of winning in Listed company at least this time*'

Southern stars

Muqbil
Peace Offering
Persian Majesty

Sponsored by Stan James

The Midlands by John Bull

BETTER known as a jumps trainer, *HEATHER DALTON* did well from the few runners she had on the Flat last year.

Magic Music came to her from Alan Bailey, having shown promise in a couple of maidens, but as a consequence of those efforts she suffered with her handicap mark of 75. It took a while for the assessor to relent but, once she was down to 57, she finally got off the mark at Nottingham. Upped 7lb, she looked to run a better race in defeat at Windsor when beaten less than a length by the useful Sir Desmond.

Six furlongs appears to be her best trip and, with her ability to handle most types of ground, she shouldn't be hard to place this year in low-grade handicaps.

Sienna Sunset, who carries the same colours as Magic Music, was another to run with plenty of credit from Norton House stables. After getting off the mark at Brighton, the filly was unlucky not to have won again, as she ruined her chance on more than one occasion by missing the break.

Time has been spent over the winter putting matters right and she can be found openings off her current mark. There is plenty of stamina on the dam's side and, even though she has only won over 1m, she should be at least as effective over further.

BRYAN MCMAHON can normally be relied upon to get the best out of his animals and he looks to have a very strong team of older horses this year.

Now Look Here will be trying to make up for lost time. The son of Reprimand only managed three runs at the end of last season, having suffered a setback. A classy performer on soft ground, it is somewhat surprising that he only has two successes

HEATHER DALTON: good Flat prospects

CLASSY: Now Look Here ploughs through the muck to win at Doncaster in March 2001 to his name but he starts this year on his lowest mark for nearly two seasons and, granted some give underfoot, he can start making up for lost time.

The stable star is **Needwood Blade**, who did nothing but progress through last season and ended up winning the Listed Bentinck Stakes at Newmarket. He had several high-class performers trailing in his wake that day, including a couple that have acquitted themselves well in Group 1 company.

Handicaps with him are out of the question now, but he gets into Group 3s without a penalty and should have no trouble winning one of those. Among likely early-season targets could be the Cammidge Trophy and possibly the Abernant Stakes. But if he continues to progress the way he did last season, he could well end up as one of the best sprinters around.

Another of McMahon's inmates to follow is the handicapper **Banjo Bay**, who struggled somewhat last year after a successful time as a three-year-old. By Common Grounds out of a Cadeaux Genereux mare, you would expect that he needs plenty of give underfoot but he is at least as effective on a faster surface, as he showed when beaten less than two lengths by the useful Sea Star at Newmarket last spring. While he stays 1m, he is just as happy at trips short of that, which gives his trainer plenty of options and he appeals as the sort who could win some nice handicaps this time round.

Ulundi was a great ambassador for PAUL WEBBER last year and, if he is over the problems that he encountered in the far east, he should again pay to follow this term.

Also now in the care of Webber, the enigmatic **Man O'Mystery** could benefit from the change of scenery. A high-class handicapper (rated 108 at his best), he often flattered only to deceive but there is no doubt he has plenty of ability, as he showed when just failing to give Foreign Affairs 18lb in the John Smith's Cup at York. He has schooled well over hurdles during the winter and appeals as the type of dual-purpose horse that his new trainer does well with.

After an unsuccessful attempt at hurdling, **Gingko** has been kept ticking over on the All-Weather. The winner of three races on the level between 1m and 1m2f, the most

> 'There is no doubt Man O'Mystery has plenty of ability . . . he appeals as the type of dual-purpose horse that his new trainer Paul Webber does well with'

significant thing with him is that he has only won when racing off a mark of 64 or lower. He starts this season off a lower mark and could be ready to strike early on.

IAN WILLIAMS has several decent handicappers in his care, including **Hirapour**, who made up into a fair stayer two years ago when in the care of Amanda Perrett. He was restricted to just four outings last term and finished off in the Tote Cesarewitch, where he was bang there until dropping away in the final quarter-mile.

It is to be hoped that the handicapper relents a little and, if given a chance by the assessor, he appeals as a stayer to follow, especially as he is tough and genuine and handles most types of ground.

Long gone are the days of housing a Classic winner at the Upper Longdon stables of REG HOLLINSHEAD but, as one of the elder statesman of the training ranks, he still churns out plenty of winners.

Royal Cavalier, who had done most of his racing at around 1m2f, found improvement for the step up in trip when landing the valuable November Handicap back in 2001. Campaigned mainly around that trip last year, picking up a couple of races along the way, he did shape quite well when tackling 1m6f for the first time at Haydock in September.

He is well worth another try at that trip and, with his ability to handle any going, he shouldn't be difficult to place again this term.

Royal Cavalier's half-brother **Prince Of Gold** has shaped with enough promise to suggest he can make his mark.

A big, weak two-year-old, he was always going to do better as he got older and stronger. He came back from his second at York, on fast ground, with sore shins and wasn't really right when he ran at Doncaster the following month. He has done well over the winter and should have no trouble winning his maiden, before making his mark in handicap company.

From the same family as the previous pair, **Goldeva**, unlike her half-brothers, is all speed. A useful two-year-old, she quickly made up into a decent class handicapper. She didn't disgrace herself in Listed company at the end of the year and, because the family get better as they get older, there is every reason to believe she could win in that grade this term.

MARK BRISBOURNE isn't a fashionable trainer but he certainly does well with the animals he has at his disposal and has turned out a steady stream of winners for the past three seasons. He no longer has his stable star Hannibal Lad, who was sold to race in the USA, so it is quantity rather than quality for the Shropshire trainer.

Summer Shades cost only 800 guineas at the Newmarket sales last year and it quickly proved to be money well spent, as she picked up three races. She has been kept busy through the winter, without much success, but she can bounce back on turf, granted her favoured fast ground.

The seven-year-old **Octane** was spoken of by his trainer as a possible for this year's Chester Cup, after his win at the Roodeye last year, although he would probably struggle to get into the handicap there at this time. He is unexposed as a stayer, though, and should be capable of picking up a race or two on fast ground.

Another money spinner for the yard over the past couple of years has been **Escalade**. Described by Brisbourne as "versatile", he is another who has been kept on the

Thihn

move throughout the winter, without quite hitting the target. Having been campaigned mainly at trips of around 1m, he was stepped up to middle distances at the turn of the year and showed enough to suggest that trip was within his compass, which gives his trainer far more options.

Without a win since last spring, where he won a 0-70 classified stakes race, his mark has slipped to 60, which his handler can be relied upon to exploit.

Better known for his exploits on the All-Weather, MARK POLGLASE has a decent sprinter in the making with **No Time**. He had a busy time of it as a two-year-old but held his form well, often when faced with difficult tasks. He didn't shape too badly when in need of the run behind the in-form Loyal Tycoon on the polytrack in January and could be ready to strike early on in the season.

Thihn has been the main flagbearer for JOHN SPEARING over the past couple of years but it is somewhat surprising that he has only managed to win four races along the way. A fair handicapper, he often ran his best races in defeat, as was the case in last years Lincoln, where he was beaten just over two lengths, off a mark of 90.

He showed a particular liking for straight courses such as Doncaster and Newmarket and again has the Lincoln as an early season target. If he is lucky in the draw, he should run a big race – a tough and genuine individual, well suited to strongly-run races, he will again give connections some fun throughout the coming season.

The Worcestershire handler also has charge of the frustrating mare **Skylark**, who finally got off the mark last season at the 32nd attempt. After racing mainly at sprint trips, she showed improvement for the step up to 7f when winning at Yarmouth. Rated 68 now, she could well add to her tally in 0-70 classified stakes races, where she can take advantage of her 5lb mares allowance.

Midlands magic

Banjo Bay
Needwood Blade
Thihn

Sponsored by Stan James

Outlook

Dave Nevison
Read Dave's diary every week in the Outlook

End of a golden age?

IT WOULD be cheering to kick off the start of the new season in an optimistic vein but for the first time in ages I feel there are dark skies ahead of us punters and there is a real danger that the golden years of punting are coming to an end.

If you had chalked up a race which involved the most ridiculous thing to happen in the last 12 months or so, what price would a bookmakers' strike be? It probably figures at about the same odds as Shergar winning the Grand National ridden by Lord Lucan. After all, didn't all our mothers warn us before we entered the world of gambling that "you never see a poor bookie." Indeed, my grandad used to tell me that every Rolls Royce we walked past on the way into York racecourse belonged to a bookmaker. So why are the bookies going on strike and how does the strike make things worse for us?

It would be nice to think the bookies are feeling sorry for us and that after years of collectively taking the punters' money, their

IS THAT ANOTHER BOOKIE? Probably not – most are down to their last Ford Fiesta

Sponsored by Stan James

consciences have woken up and they can no longer live with themselves.

I have often wondered how long it takes the bookies to practice that deadpan expression they put on when the unconsidered rag gets up to beat the favourite on the line. The face never moves despite the fact that the financial swing to the layer might be enormous and the temptation to smile must be overwhelming. After all, when the favourite gets up on the line to beat the no-hoper, punters leap up and down screaming, some almost wetting themselves with the excitement!

Alas, the bookmaker feeling sorry for the losing punters is another image that is hard to bring to mind but there is definitely something in this strike issue and if on-course bookies do become subject to a gross profits tax we could all be losers.

I've been on the track for about ten years now and, despite the fact that we are essentially on opposite sides of the fence, have generally got on very well with all the

HARD LIFE: a chill wind has been blowing through the wallets of on-course bookies

Sponsored by Stan James

bookies on the racecourse. In that ten years, I have rarely seen a bookie smile (except after a race, when he sees a queue of punters at the joint next door) but the general atmosphere in the ring has been jolly in a miserable sort of way.

Bookies have been getting enough out of the game to make a living but not enough to mean that they won't turn up for work the next day. Thus, we have had a perfect, self-perpetuating supply and demand system that ensures everyone is happy, just about, and also guarantees a reasonably competitive market for us punters to play in. We should treasure this situation–unfortunately, it looks like it will not last much longer.

Recently the atmosphere in the ring has been more miserable in a miserable sort of way and the bookies' cries of poverty are starting to ring true. There are certainly not too many of them turning up at the races in the Roller, indeed if you see a beat-up Volvo in the car park with about five people sat across the back seat you can almost bet odds-on it will belong to a bookie.

The bookies are leaving the races skint and the punters always leave the races skint, so who is getting the money?

The answer would appear to be the big off-course firms, who are recording record profits despite saying that we punters have never had it so good and that they can't afford to take the SP from the track any longer as it doesn't get them enough wedge.

We have a situation where the loveable rogue in the chequered suit will soon no longer be with us while the fat cat company director from the big off-course bookie will be smoking ever bigger cigars, their wealth coming courtesy of the fact that they can set prices to whatever suits the books.

The thought of the off-course firms setting their own prices has to send shivers down the backs of punters, as one thing is absolutely certain – it will not be a move that will favour us. Hopefully the support that is gathering for action against the imposition of a gross profits tax on-course will be strong enough to prevent it, but I am afraid I fear the worst this time.

When racing becomes a never-ending cycle of 0-65 handicaps interspersed with computer-generated carve-ups from Portman Park and the like, don't say you weren't warned. The only thing that prevents me from

Sponsored by Stan James

> *'Darmagi will get a modest rating after three promising but unrewarding efforts and will be closer to the judge this term'*

believing that the end is nigh is that it has been nigh for a number of seasons now and things still carry on and indeed have got better for the punter over the years. In the hope that sense prevails in the end, I have compiled a list of horses that will hopefully pay to follow over the next season.

Statue Of Liberty is the one I fancy for the 2,000 Guineas. **Soviet Song** is going straight for the 1,000, which I believe is the right move as the trials seem to cloud rather than clear the waters.

Brian Boru could hardly have been more impressive at Doncaster and is the Derby choice at this point.

Hopefully we should already have a few quid for the Classics after **Pablo** has won the Lincoln. There are rumours that the Barry Hills horse is not going to start at Doncaster but the race is worth so much that I feel sure he will be there.

Tante Rose will be a very good three-year-old filly for the same yard.

Terry Mills is a trainer I have a lot of respect for and his **High Reach** has impressed me greatly on the polytrack this winter, while **Incline** was a handicapper going the right way at the end of last season and both horses can be followed with confidence.

Gerard Butler does not just send his rubbish to Lingfield anymore and **Shield**, impressive on the All-Weather, can emulate Playapart from last season by showing up prominently in group events.

Pretence is one of the nicest-looking winners of a Lingfield maiden and I believe Jeremy Noseda will win plenty with him.

Amanda Perrett gave **Darmagi** three quick runs at the backend and this filly will get a modest rating after three promising but unrewarding efforts. She will be closer to the judge this term.

RACING & FOOTBALL
Outlook

ARE YOU PREPARED?

Get equipped with **Dave Nevison**, the shrewd pro-punter you must listen to!

0906 911 0234
From Ireland:1570 924351

CALLS COST £1/MIN.RACEFORM. RG20 6NL

Races and Racecourses

Fixtures

Key - **Flat**, *Flat evening*, Jumps, *Jumps evening*

March
- 20 Thursday...**Doncaster**, **Southwell**, Wincanton
- 21 Friday...**Doncaster**, Kelso, Newbury
- 22 Saturday.................Bangor, **Doncaster**, **Kempton**, Newbury, *Wolverhampton*
- 24 Monday...**Newcastle**, Taunton, **Wolverhampton**
- 25 Tuesday..Ascot, **Folkestone**, Sedgefield
- 26 Wednesday..**Catterick**, **Lingfield**, **Nottingham**
- 27 Thursday...Exeter, **Musselburgh**, **Leicester**
- 28 Friday...Carlisle, **Lingfield**, **Southwell**
- 29 Saturday...**Ascot**, Haydock, Hexham, Market Rasen
- 31 Monday..**Bath**, Plumpton, **Wolverhampton**

April
- 1 Tuesday..**Lingfield**, Newcastle, **Nottingham**
- 2 Wednesday..Ascot, Ludlow, **Ripon**
- 3 Thursday...**Leicester**, Aintree, Taunton
- 4 Friday...**Folkestone**, Aintree, **Southwell**
- 5 Saturday...Hereford, **Lingfield**, Aintree
- 7 Monday...Kelso, **Southwell**, **Windsor**
- 8 Tuesday..Exeter, **Pontefract**, Sedgefield
- 9 Wednesday..**Lingfield**, Uttoxeter, **Warwick**
- 10 Thursday...**Brighton**, **Musselburgh**, Ludlow
- 11 Friday...Ayr, **Newbury**, **Thirsk**
- 12 Saturday.................Ayr, Bangor, **Newbury**, Stratford, **Thirsk**, *Wolverhampton*
- 14 Monday...Hexham, **Pontefract**, Windsor
- 15 Tuesday..Exeter, **Folkestone**, **Newmarket**
- 16 Wednesday..**Beverley**, Cheltenham, **Newmarket**
- 17 Thursday..Cheltenham, **Newmarket**, **Ripon**
- 19 Saturday...Carlisle, **Haydock**, **Kempton**, Newton Abbot, Plumpton, Towcester
- 21 Monday.................Carlisle, Fakenham, Hereford, Huntingdon, **Kempton**,
  ....Market Rasen, **Newcastle**, **Nottingham**, Plumpton, Towcester,
  ....Uttoxeter, **Warwick**, Wetherby, Wincanton, **Yarmouth**
- 22 Tuesday...Chepstow, **Newcastle**, **Southwell**
- 23 Wednesday..**Catterick**, **Epsom**, Perth
- 24 Thursday...**Beverley**, Fontwell, Perth
- 25 Friday...Perth, Sandown, **Wolverhampton**
- 26 Saturday.................**Leicester**, Market Rasen, **Ripon**, Sandown, Sedgefield
- 28 Monday...............**Hamilton**, *Newcastle*, Towcester, **Windsor**, **Wolverhampton**
- 29 Tuesday..**Bath**, Newton Abbot, **Nottingham**
- 30 Wednesday.........................**Ascot**, *Cheltenham*, Exeter, *Kelso*, **Pontefract**

May
- 1 Thursday...Hereford, **Redcar**, **Southwell**
- 2 Friday.................*Bangor*, **Musselburgh**, **Newmarket**, *Sedgefield*, Worcester
- 3 Saturday.............**Brighton**, Haydock, Hexham, **Newmarket**, **Thirsk**, Uttoxeter
- 4 Sunday...**Hamilton**, **Newmarket**, **Salisbury**

Sponsored by Stan James

5	Monday	**Doncaster**, Fontwell, **Kempton**, Ludlow, **Newcastle**, Towcester, **Warwick**
6	Tuesday	**Bath, Chester**
7	Wednesday	Chepstow, **Chester**, *Fakenham*, Kelso, *Wetherby*
8	Thursday	**Chester**, Folkestone, **Southwell**
9	Friday	**Carlisle**, *Hamilton*, Lingfield, **Nottingham**, *Wincanton*
10	Saturday	**Beverley**, Hexham, *Huntingdon*, **Lingfield**, ***Thirsk***, *Warwick*, Worcester
12	Monday	**Redcar**, *Towcester*, **Windsor, Wolverhampton**
13	Tuesday	Hereford, **York**
14	Wednesday	**Brighton**, Exeter, **Newcastle**, *Perth*, **York**
15	Thursday	*Ludlow*, Perth, **Salisbury**, *Wincanton*, **York**
16	Friday	**Hamilton**, *Aintree*, **Newbury**, **Nottingham**, *Stratford*, **Yarmouth**
17	Saturday	Bangor, **Hamilton**, *Lingfield*, **Newbury**, **Nottingham**, *Sedgefield*, **Thirsk**
18	Sunday	Fakenham, **Ripon**, Southwell
19	Monday	**Bath**, *Musselburgh*, **Windsor, Wolverhampton**
20	Tuesday	**Beverley**, Goodwood
21	Wednesday	*Folkestone*, **Goodwood**, Kelso, *Uttoxeter*, Worcester
22	Thursday	*Bangor*, **Goodwood**, *Kelso*, **Newcastle**, Wetherby
23	Friday	**Brighton, Haydock**, *Pontefract*, Towcester, **Wolverhampton**
24	Saturday	Cartmel, **Doncaster, Haydock**, Hexham, **Kempton**, *Lingfield*, Market Rasen, **Newmarket**
26	Monday	Cartmel, **Chepstow**, Fontwell, Hereford, Huntingdon, **Leicester, Redcar, Sandown**, Uttoxeter
27	Tuesday	Hexham, **Leicester, Redcar, Sandown**
28	Wednesday	Cartmel, **Lingfield, Newbury, Ripon**, Yarmouth
29	Thursday	**Ayr, Goodwood**, *Huntingdon*, Newton Abbot, *Wetherby*
30	Friday	**Ayr**, *Bath*, **Brighton**, Catterick, **Newmarket**, *Stratford*
31	Saturday	**Catterick, Musselburgh, Newmarket**, Stratford, **Windsor**

June

1	Sunday	**Pontefract, Windsor**, Worcester
2	Monday	**Carlisle, Leicester**, *Thirsk*, **Windsor**
3	Tuesday	**Lingfield**, Newton Abbot
4	Wednesday	**Bath**, *Beverley*, **Chester**, *Kempton*, Newcastle, **Nottingham**
5	Thursday	**Chepstow, Haydock**, Perth, *Sandown*, *Uttoxeter*
6	Friday	**Catterick**, *Epsom*, **Goodwood, Haydock**, *Perth*, **Wolverhampton**
7	Saturday	**Doncaster, Epsom, Haydock**, Worcester
9	Monday	Newton Abbot, **Pontefract, Southwell, Windsor**
10	Tuesday	**Redcar, Salisbury**
11	Wednesday	**Beverley**, *Hamilton*, Hereford, Market Rasen, **Newbury**
12	Thursday	*Brighton*, **Hamilton, Newbury**, Uttoxeter, **Yarmouth**
13	Friday	**Chepstow, Goodwood**, Newton Abbot, **Sandown, Wolverhampton, York**
14	Saturday	**Bath**, Hexham, **Nottingham, Sandown, York**
15	Sunday	**Carlisle, Leicester, Salisbury**
16	Monday	**Brighton, Musselburgh**, *Warwick*, **Windsor**
17	Tuesday	**Ascot, Thirsk**
18	Wednesday	**Ascot, Hamilton**, *Ripon*, Southwell, *Worcester*
19	Thursday	**Ascot**, *Ayr*, **Beverley**, Ripon, **Southwell**
20	Friday	**Ascot, Ayr**, *Goodwood*, Hexham, **Newmarket**, Redcar

Sponsored by Stan James

21	Saturday	**Ascot, Ayr,** *Lingfield*, Market Rasen, Newton Abbot, **Redcar,** *Warwick,* **Wolverhampton**
22	Sunday	Perth, **Pontefract,** Warwick
23	Monday	*Chepstow,* **Musselburgh, Nottingham,** *Windsor*
24	Tuesday	**Beverley, Brighton**
25	Wednesday	*Bath,* **Carlisle,** *Kempton,* **Salisbury, Southwell**
26	Thursday	**Carlisle,** *Hamilton,* **Leicester,** **Salisbury, Thirsk**
27	Friday	**Folkestone,** *Goodwood,* **Newcastle,** **Newmarket,** *Stratford,* **Wolverhampton**
28	Saturday	**Chester, Doncaster,** *Lingfield,* **Newcastle,** **Newmarket,** *Newton Abbot,* **Worcester**
29	Sunday	**Doncaster, Goodwood,** Uttoxeter
30	Monday	*Musselburgh,* **Pontefract,** *Windsor,* **Wolverhampton**

July

1	Tuesday	**Brighton, Hamilton**
2	Wednesday	**Catterick,** *Kempton,* **Lingfield,** Perth, *Yarmouth*
3	Thursday	*Epsom,* **Haydock,** *Newbury,* Perth, *Yarmouth*
4	Friday	*Beverley, Haydock, Salisbury,* **Sandown,** Southwell, **Warwick**
5	Saturday	**Beverley, Chepstow, Haydock, Leicester, Sandown**
6	Sunday	**Brighton,** Market Rasen, **Redcar**
7	Monday	**Bath, Musselburgh,** *Ripon, Windsor*
8	Tuesday	**Newmarket, Pontefract**
9	Wednesday	**Catterick,** *Kempton,* **Lingfield, Newmarket,** *Worcester*
10	Thursday	*Doncaster, Epsom,* **Folkestone, Newmarket, Warwick**
11	Friday	**Ascot,** *Chepstow,* **Chester,** *Hamilton,* **Wolverhampton, York**
12	Saturday	**Ascot, Chester, Nottingham, Salisbury, York**
13	Sunday	**Bath, Haydock,** Stratford
14	Monday	**Ayr,** Newton Abbot, *Windsor,* **Wolverhampton**
15	Tuesday	**Beverley, Brighton**
16	Wednesday	**Catterick,** *Kempton,* **Lingfield,** Uttoxeter, *Worcester*
17	Thursday	Cartmel, *Doncaster, Epsom,* **Hamilton, Leicester**
18	Friday	**Carlisle,** *Hamilton,* Newbury, *Newmarket, Pontefract,* Southwell
19	Saturday	*Haydock, Lingfield,* Market Rasen, **Newbury,** **Newmarket,** Ripon, Warwick, **Wolverhampton**
21	Monday	**Ayr,** *Beverley,* **Brighton,** *Windsor*
22	Tuesday	**Ayr,** Sedgefield
23	Wednesday	**Catterick,** *Leicester,* **Lingfield,** *Sandown,* Worcester
24	Thursday	**Bath,** *Doncaster,* **Hamilton, Sandown, Yarmouth**
25	Friday	**Ascot,** *Chepstow,* **Newmarket,** *Salisbury,* Thirsk, **Wolverhampton**
26	Saturday	**Ascot, Newcastle, Nottingham, Redcar,** Stratford
27	Sunday	**Ascot, Newmarket,** Newton Abbot
28	Monday	**Folkestone,** Sedgefield, *Windsor, Yarmouth*
29	Tuesday	**Beverley, Goodwood**
30	Wednesday	**Carlisle, Goodwood,** *Kempton,* **Leicester,** Newton Abbot
31	Thursday	*Musselburgh, Epsom,* Goodwood, **Newcastle,** Stratford

August

1	Friday	*Ayr,* Bangor, **Goodwood,** *Newmarket, Nottingham,* Thirsk
2	Saturday	**Doncaster, Goodwood, Newmarket, Thirsk,** Worcester
3	Sunday	**Chester,** Market Rasen, **Newbury**
4	Monday	*Carlisle,* Newton Abbot, **Ripon,** *Windsor*

5	Tuesday	**Bath, Catterick**
6	Wednesday	**Brighton,** *Kempton*, **Newcastle, Pontefract,** *Yarmouth*
7	Thursday	**Brighton, Chepstow, Haydock,** *Uttoxeter*, **Wolverhampton**
8	Friday	*Haydock*, **Lingfield,** *Newmarket*, Sedgefield, **Wolverhampton,** *Worcester*
9	Saturday	**Ascot, Haydock, Newmarket, Redcar,** Stratford
10	Sunday	**Leicester, Redcar, Windsor**
11	Monday	**Folkestone,** Southwell, *Thirsk*, **Windsor**
12	Tuesday	**Brighton,** Newton Abbot
13	Wednesday	**Beverley,** *Hamilton*, **Salisbury,** *Sandown*, **Yarmouth**
14	Thursday	**Beverley,** *Chepstow*, **Haydock,** **Salisbury, Sandown**
15	Friday	*Catterick*, **Newbury, Newcastle,** *Newmarket*, **Wolverhampton**
16	Saturday	Bangor, **Newbury, Newmarket,** Perth, **Ripon**
17	Sunday	**Bath, Kempton, Pontefract**
18	Monday	**Brighton,** *Fontwell*, **Nottingham,** *Windsor*
19	Tuesday	**Hamilton, York**
20	Wednesday	**Carlisle,** *Kempton*, **Lingfield,** *Nottingham*, **York**
21	Thursday	**Musselburgh, Folkestone,** York
22	Friday	*Bath*, Fontwell, *Newcastle*, **Newmarket, Thirsk**
23	Saturday	**Beverley,** Cartmel, **Goodwood, Newmarket,** **Redcar,** *Windsor*, **Worcester**
24	Sunday	**Beverley, Goodwood, Yarmouth**
25	Monday	Cartmel, **Chepstow, Epsom, Folkestone,** Fontwell, Huntingdon, **Newcastle,** Newton Abbot, **Ripon,** Southwell, **Warwick**
26	Tuesday	**Ripon, Yarmouth**
27	Wednesday	**Ascot, Brighton, Catterick**
28	Thursday	**Chester, Lingfield, Salisbury**
29	Friday	**Ayr, Chester, Sandown**
30	Saturday	**Chester,** Market Rasen, **Ripon, Sandown**

September

1	Monday	**Folkestone, Hamilton, Leicester**
2	Tuesday	**Brighton, Southwell, Yarmouth**
3	Wednesday	**Lingfield,** Newton Abbot, **York**
4	Thursday	**Carlisle, Redcar, Salisbury**
5	Friday	**Haydock, Kempton,** Sedgefield
6	Saturday	**Haydock, Kempton,** Stratford, **Thirsk,** *Wolverhampton*
7	Sunday	Uttoxeter, Worcester, **York**
8	Monday	**Bath, Newcastle, Warwick**
9	Tuesday	**Catterick, Leicester, Lingfield**
10	Wednesday	**Doncaster, Epsom,** Hereford
11	Thursday	**Chepstow, Doncaster, Epsom**
12	Friday	**Doncaster, Goodwood,** Southwell
13	Saturday	Bangor, **Doncaster, Musselburgh, Goodwood,** Worcester
14	Sunday	Hexham, **Sandown,** Worcester
15	Monday	**Bath, Musselburgh, Redcar**
16	Tuesday	**Salisbury, Thirsk, Yarmouth**
17	Wednesday	**Beverley, Sandown, Yarmouth**
18	Thursday	**Ayr, Pontefract, Yarmouth**
19	Friday	**Ayr, Newbury, Nottingham**
20	Saturday	**Ayr, Catterick, Newbury, Warwick,** *Wolverhampton*
22	Monday	**Chepstow, Kempton, Leicester**

Sponsored by Stan James

23	Tuesday	**Beverley**, Fontwell, **Newmarket**
24	Wednesday	**Chester**, **Goodwood**, Perth
25	Thursday	**Goodwood**, Perth, **Pontefract**
26	Friday	**Ascot**, **Haydock**, **Southwell**
27	Saturday	**Ascot**, **Haydock**, Market Rasen, Plumpton, **Ripon**
28	Sunday	**Ascot**, **Musselburgh**, Huntingdon
29	Monday	**Bath**, **Hamilton**, **Windsor**
30	Tuesday	Exeter, **Nottingham**, Sedgefield

October

1	Wednesday	**Newcastle**, **Nottingham**, **Salisbury**
2	Thursday	**Brighton**, Hereford, **Newmarket**
3	Friday	Hexham, **Lingfield**, **Newmarket**
4	Saturday	Chepstow, **Epsom**, **Newmarket**, Redcar, Uttoxeter, **Wolverhampton**
5	Sunday	Fontwell, Kelso, Market Rasen
6	Monday	Plumpton, **Pontefract**, **Windsor**
7	Tuesday	**Catterick**, **Southwell**, Stratford
8	Wednesday	Exeter, **Lingfield**, Towcester
9	Thursday	Ludlow, Wincanton, **York**
10	Friday	Carlisle, Huntingdon, **York**
11	Saturday	**Ascot**, Bangor, Hexham, Southwell, **York**
12	Sunday	**Bath**, **Goodwood**, Newcastle
13	Monday	**Ayr**, **Leicester**, **Windsor**
14	Tuesday	**Ayr**, **Leicester**, Sedgefield
15	Wednesday	**Lingfield**, Uttoxeter, Wetherby
16	Thursday	**Newmarket**, **Southwell**, Taunton
17	Friday	**Brighton**, **Newmarket**, **Redcar**
18	Saturday	**Catterick**, Kelso, Market Rasen, **Newmarket**, Stratford
20	Monday	Plumpton, **Pontefract**, **Wolverhampton**
21	Tuesday	Exeter, **Southwell**, **Yarmouth**
22	Wednesday	Chepstow, **Newcastle**, **Nottingham**
23	Thursday	**Brighton**, Haydock, Ludlow
24	Friday	**Doncaster**, Fakenham, **Newbury**
25	Saturday	Carlisle, **Doncaster**, **Musselburgh**, Kempton, **Newbury**
26	Sunday	Aintree, Towcester, Wincanton
27	Monday	Bangor, **Leicester**, **Lingfield**
28	Tuesday	Cheltenham, **Nottingham**, **Redcar**
29	Wednesday	Cheltenham, Sedgefield, **Yarmouth**
30	Thursday	**Lingfield**, Stratford, Taunton
31	Friday	**Brighton**, **Newmarket**, Wetherby

November

1	Saturday	Ascot, Kelso, **Newmarket**, Wetherby, *Wolverhampton*
2	Sunday	Carlisle, Huntingdon, **Lingfield**
3	Monday	Plumpton, **Redcar**, Warwick
4	Tuesday	**Catterick**, Exeter, Folkestone
5	Wednesday	**Musselburgh**, Kempton, Newton Abbot
6	Thursday	Haydock, **Nottingham**, Towcester
7	Friday	**Doncaster**, Hexham, Uttoxeter
8	Saturday	Chepstow, **Doncaster**, Sandown, Wincanton
9	Sunday	Southwell, Worcester

10	Monday	Carlisle, Fontwell, **Wolverhampton**
11	Tuesday	Huntingdon, Lingfield, Sedgefield
12	Wednesday	Kelso, **Lingfield**, Newbury
13	Thursday	**Lingfield**, Ludlow, Taunton
14	Friday	Cheltenham, Newcastle, **Wolverhampton**
15	Saturday	Ayr, Cheltenham, Uttoxeter, Wetherby, **Wolverhampton**
16	Sunday	Ayr, Cheltenham, Haydock
17	Monday	Folkestone, Leicester, **Wolverhampton**
18	Tuesday	**Lingfield**, Newton Abbot, Towcester
19	Wednesday	Hexham, Kempton, **Southwell**
20	Thursday	Hereford, Market Rasen, Wincanton
21	Friday	Ascot, Exeter, **Wolverhampton**
22	Saturday	Ascot, Catterick, Huntingdon, **Lingfield**, Aintree
23	Sunday	Fakenham, Aintree, Plumpton
24	Monday	Ludlow, Newcastle, **Southwell**
25	Tuesday	Sedgefield, **Southwell**, Warwick
26	Wednesday	Chepstow, **Lingfield**, Wetherby
27	Thursday	Carlisle, Taunton, Uttoxeter
28	Friday	Bangor, Musselburgh, **Wolverhampton**
29	Saturday	Haydock, **Lingfield**, Newbury, Newcastle, Towcester, **Wolverhampton**
30	Sunday	Doncaster, Newbury

December

1	Monday	Folkestone, Kelso, **Wolverhampton**
2	Tuesday	Hereford, **Lingfield**, Newton Abbot
3	Wednesday	Catterick, Plumpton, **Southwell**
4	Thursday	Leicester, Market Rasen, Wincanton
5	Friday	Exeter, Sandown, Southwell
6	Saturday	Chepstow, **Lingfield**, Sandown, Warwick, Wetherby, **Wolverhampton**
8	Monday	Ayr, Newcastle, **Wolverhampton**
9	Tuesday	Fontwell, Sedgefield, **Southwell**
10	Wednesday	Leicester, **Lingfield**, Newbury
11	Thursday	Huntingdon, Ludlow, Taunton
12	Friday	Cheltenham, Doncaster, **Wolverhampton**
13	Saturday	Cheltenham, Doncaster, Haydock, Lingfield, **Southwell**, **Wolverhampton**
15	Monday	Plumpton, Towcester, **Wolverhampton**
16	Tuesday	Musselburgh, Folkestone, **Southwell**
17	Wednesday	Bangor, Hexham, **Lingfield**
18	Thursday	Catterick, Exeter, Ludlow
19	Friday	Ascot, Uttoxeter, **Wolverhampton**
20	Saturday	Ascot, Hereford, **Lingfield**, Newcastle, Warwick
22	Monday	Fakenham, Fontwell, **Wolverhampton**
26	Friday	Ayr, Huntingdon, Kempton, Market Rasen, Sedgefield, Towcester, Uttoxeter, Wetherby, Wincanton, **Wolverhampton**
27	Saturday	Chepstow, Kempton, Leicester, **Southwell**, Wetherby
29	Monday	Haydock, **Lingfield**, Newbury, Taunton
30	Tuesday	Musselburgh, **Lingfield**, Southwell, Stratford
31	Wednesday	Catterick, Cheltenham, Fontwell, Warwick, **Wolverhampton**

Sponsored by Stan James

Big-race Dates

March
22 Sat Doncaster ....Freephone Stanley Lincoln Handicap (1m)

April
12 Sat Newbury...John Porter Stakes (1m4f)
12   Newbury...Lane's End Greenham Stakes (7f)
12   Newbury..Dubai Duty Free Fred Darling Stakes (7f)
15 Tue Newmarket...Shadwell Stud Nell Gwyn Stakes (7f)
16 Wed Newmarket..............................Weatherbys Earl Of Sefton Stakes (1m1f)
16   Newmarket........................Victor Chandler European Free Handicap (7f)
17 Thu Newmarket............................Macau Jockey Club Craven Stakes (1m)
25 Fri   Sandown ....Masai Mile (1m)
25   Sandown ....cantorindex.com Classic Trial (1m2f)
26 Sat Sandown ....Heathorns Bookmakers Gordon Richards Stakes (1m2f)
30 Wed Ascot..Bovis Homes Sagaro Stakes (2m)
30   Ascot..Sony Victoria Cup (Handicap) (7f)

May
2   Fri   Newmarket..Sagitta Jockey Club Stakes (1m4f)
3   Sat Newmarket..Sagitta 2,000 Guineas Stakes (1m)
3   Newmarket................................Victor Chandler Palace House Stakes (5f)
4   Sun Newmarket...Sagitta 1,000 Guineas Stakes (1m)
4   Newmarket...............................R. L. Davison Pretty Polly Stakes (1m2f)
6   Tue Chester..........................Victor Chandler Chester Vase (1m4f 66yds)
7   Wed Chester ....Tote Chester Cup (Handicap) (2m 2f 117yds)
7   Chester ....Shadwell Stud Cheshire Oaks (1m3f 79yds)
8   Thu Chester ....Ormonde Stakes (1m5f 89yds)
8   Chester ....Philip Leverhulme Dee Stakes (1m2f 75yds)
10 Sat Lingfield ....Arena Racing Derby Trial Stakes (1m3f 106yds)
10   Lingfield ....Arena Oaks Trial Stakes (1m3f 106yds)
13 Tue York ....Tattersalls Musidora Stakes (1m2f)
14 Wed York..................Convergent Communications Dante Stakes (1m2f)
15 Thu York ....Merewood Homes Yorkshire Cup (1m5f 194yds)
15   York ....Duke Of York Victor Chandler Stakes (6f)
16 Fri   Newbury.....................................Cantor Index Fillies' Trial Stakes (1m2f)
17 Sat Newbury.....................................Juddmonte Lockinge Stakes (1m)
17   Newbury.....................Grundon Recycle Aston Park Stakes (1m5f 61yds)
20 Tue Goodwood ....Predominate Stakes (1m2f)
21 Wed Goodwood ....Victor Chandler Lupe Stakes (1m2f)
24 Sat Haydock ....Tote Credit Club Silver Bowl (Handicap) (1m)
24   Haydock ....Sandy Lane Rated Stakes (6f)
26 Mon Sandown ....Bonusprint Henry II Stakes (2m)
26   Redcar........Stanley Racing Zetland Gold Cup Stakes (Handicap) (1m2f)
26   Sandown ....Tripleprint Temple Stakes (5f)
27 Tue Sandown ....Credit Suisse First Boston Brigadier Gerard Stakes (1m2f)

June
6   Fri   Epsom ....Vodafone Oaks (1m4f 10yds)

6		Epsom	Vodafone Coronation Cup (1m4f 10yds)
7	Sat	Epsom	Vodafone Derby (1m4f 10yds)
7		Epsom	Vodafone Diomed Stakes (1m114yds)
7		Haydock	bet365.com John Of Gaunt Stakes (7f 30yds)
12	Thu	Newbury	Ballymacoll Stud Stakes (1m2f)
14	Sat	York	William Hill Trophy (6f)
17	Tue	Royal Ascot	St James's Palace Stakes (1m)
17		Royal Ascot	Queen Anne Stakes (1m)
17		Royal Ascot	Coventry Stakes (6f)
17		Royal Ascot	Queen's Vase (2m 45yds)
18	Wed	Royal Ascot	Prince Of Wales's Stakes (1m2f)
18		Royal Ascot	Royal Hunt Cup (Handicap) (1m)
18		Royal Ascot	Jersey Stakes (7f)
18		Royal Ascot	Chesham Stakes (6f)
18		Royal Ascot	Queen Mary Stakes (5f)
19	Thu	Royal Ascot	Gold Cup (2m 4f)
19		Royal Ascot	Ribblesdale Stakes (1m4f)
19		Royal Ascot	Cork And Orrery Stakes (6f)
19		Royal Ascot	Norfolk Stakes (5f)
20	Fri	Royal Ascot	Hardwicke Stakes (1m4f)
20		Royal Ascot	Coronation Stakes (1m)
20		Royal Ascot	King Edward VII Stakes (1m4f)
28	Sat	Newcastle	Foster's Lager Northumberland Plate (Handicap) (2m 19yds)
28		Newmarket	Hitchins Criterion Stakes (7f)
28		Newmarket	Ladbrokes Fred Archer Stakes (1m4f)

July

5	Sat	Haydock	Halliwell Landau Lancashire Oaks Stakes (1m4f)
5		Haydock	Tote Old Newton Cup (Handicap) (1m4f)
5		Sandown	Coral Eurobet Eclipse Stakes (1m2f)
8	Tue	Newmarket	Princess of Wales's Pearl & Coutts Stakes (1m4f)
8		Newmarket	Cherry Hinton Stakes (6f)
9	Wed	Newmarket	Falmouth Stakes (1m)
9		Newmarket	TNT July Stakes (6f)
10	Thu	Newmarket	Darley July Cup (6f)
10		Newmarket	Ladbroke Bunbury Cup (Handicap) (7f)
12	Sat	York	John Smith's Cup (Handicap) (1m2f 85yds)
12		York	Foster's Silver Cup Rated Stakes (1m5f 194yds)
14	Mon	Ayr	Sodexho Prestige Scottish Classic (1m2f)
18	Fri	Newbury	Rose Bowl Stakes (6f)
19	Sat	Newbury	Weatherbys Super Sprint (5f 34yds)
26	Sat	Ascot	King George VI and The Queen Elizabeth Diamond Stakes (1m4f)
26		Ascot	Princess Margaret Stakes (6f)
29	Tue	Goodwood	Peugot Gordon Stakes (1m2f)
29		Goodwood	Oak Tree Stakes (6f)
30	Wed	Goodwood	Champagne Lanson Sussex Stakes (1m)
30		Goodwood	Tote Gold Trophy (Handicap) (1m4f)
30		Goodwood	Champagne Lanson Vintage Stakes (7f)
31	Thu	Goodwood	William Hill Mile (Handicap) (1m)
31		Goodwood	cantorsport.co.uk Molecomb Stakes (5f)
31		Goodwood	J. P. Morgan Private Bank Goodwood Cup (2m)

Sponsored by Stan James

August

1	Fri	Goodwood	Lady O Memorial Glorious Rated Stakes (1m4f)
2	Sat	Goodwood	Vodafone Stewards' Cup (Handicap) (6f)
2		Goodwood	Vodafone Nassau Stakes (1m2f)
9	Sat	Newmarket	Milcars Sweet Solera Stakes (7f)
9		Haydock	Petros Rose Of Lancaster Stakes (1m2f 120yds)
15	Fri	Newbury	Washington Singer Stakes (7f)
15		Newbury	St Hugh's Stakes (5f)
16	Sat	Newbury	Hungerford Stakes (7f 64yds)
16		Newbury	Geoffrey Freer Stakes (1m5f 61yds)
16		Ripon	William Hill Great St Wilfrid Handicap Stakes (6f)
19	Tue	York	Juddmonte International Stakes (1m2f 85yds)
19		York	Great Voltigeur Stakes (1m4f)
19		York	Weatherbys Insurance Lonsdale Stakes (2m)
20	Wed	York	Aston Upthorpe Yorkshire Oaks (1m4f)
20		York	Scottish Equitable Gimcrack Stakes (6f)
20		York	Tote Ebor (Handicap) (1m6f)
21	Thu	York	Peugot Lowther Stakes (6f)
21		York	Victor Chandler Nunthorpe Stakes (5f)
21		York	European Breeders Fund Galtres Stakes (1m4f)
23	Sat	Goodwood	Celebration Mile (1m)
23		Goodwood	San Migel March Stakes (1m6f)
24	Sun	Goodwood	Touchdown in Malaysia Prestige Stakes (7f)
25	Mon	Ripon	Ripon Champion Two Years Old Trophy (6f)
30	Sat	Sandown	Ford Solario Stakes (7f)

September

5	Fri	Kempton	Sirenia Stakes (6f)
6	Sat	Kempton	Milcars September Stakes (1m3f)
10	Wed	Doncaster	Rothmans Royals Park Hill Stakes (1m6f 132yds)
10		Doncaster	£200,000 St Leger Yearling Stakes (6f)
10		Doncaster	Tote Trifecta Portland Handicap Stakes (1m)
10		Doncaster	Great North Eastern Railway Doncaster Cup (2m 2f)
11	Thu	Doncaster	Kyoto Scarbrough Stakes (5f)
11		Doncaster	G.N.E.R White Rose Park Stakes (1m)
11		Doncaster	Rothmans Royals May Hill Stakes (1m)
12	Fri	Doncaster	Champagne Stakes (7f)
12		Doncaster	DBS St Leger Yearling Stakes (1m6f 132yds)
12		Goodwood	Select Stakes (1m2f)
13	Sat	Doncaster	Polypipe Flying Childers Stakes (5f)
13		Doncaster	Rothmans Royals St Leger Stakes
19	Fri	Newbury	Dubai Duty Free Cup (7f)
19		Newbury	Dubai Duty Free Mill Reef Stakes (6f)
20	Sat	Newbury	Dubai Airport World Trophy (5f 34yds)
20		Newbury	Dubai Arc Trial (1m3f 5yds)
20		Ayr	Tote Ayr Gold Cup (Handicap) (6f)
20		Ayr	Doonside Cup (1m2f 192yds)
25	Thu	Goodwood	Charlton Hunt Supreme Stakes (7f)
27	Sat	Ascot	Queen Elizabeth II Stakes (1m)
27		Ascot	Meon Valley Stud Fillies' Mile (1m)
27		Ascot	Hackney Empire Royal Lodge Stakes (1m4f)

Sponsored by Stan James

27	Ascot	Tote Trifecta Handicap Stakes (7f)
27	Ascot	Diadem Stakes (6f)
28 Sun	Ascot	Old Vic Cumberland Lodge Stakes (1m)
28	Ascot	Mail On Sunday Mile Final (Handicap) (1m)

October

3 Fri	Newmarket	Shadwell Stud Middle Park Stakes (6f)
4 Sat	Newmarket	Cheveley Park Stakes (6f)
4	Newmarket	Tote Cambridgeshire Handicap Stakes (1m1f)
4	Newmarket	Peugot Sun Chariot Stakes (1m2f)
4	Redcar	Betabet Two-Year-Old Trophy (7f)
11 Sat	Ascot	Willmott Dixon Princess Royal Stakes (1m4f)
11	Ascot	Willmott Dixon Cornwallis Stakes (5f)
18 Sat	Newmarket	Dubai Champion Stakes (1m2f)
18	Newmarket	Tote Cesarewitch (Handicap) (2m 2f)
18	Newmarket	Victor Chandler Challenge Stakes (1m)
18	Newmarket	Darley Dewhurst Stakes (6f)
18	Newmarket	Owen Brown Rockfel Stakes (7f)
18	Newmarket	Jockey Club Cup
24 Fri	Doncaster	Vodafone Horris Hill Stakes (7f)
25 Sat	Doncaster	Racing Post Trophy (1m)
25	Newbury	St Simon Stakes (1m4f)

November

1 Sat	Newmarket	Autumn Handicap Stakes (1m)
8 Sat	Doncaster	Tote Scoop6 November Handicap Stakes (1m4f)

Ireland

May	24 Sat	Curragh	Entenmann's Irish 2,000 Guineas (1m)
	25 Sun	Curragh	Entenmann's Irish 1,000 Guineas (1m)
June	29 Sun	Curragh	Budweiser Irish Derby (1m 4f)
July	13 Sun	Curragh	Darley Irish Oaks (1m 4f)
August	11 Sun	Curragh	Waterford Wedgewood Phoenix Park Stakes (6f)
	31 Sun	Curragh	Moyglare Stud Stakes (7f)
		Curragh	Flying Five Stakes (5f)
September	6 Sat	Leopardstown	Irish Champion Stakes (1m 2f)
	13 Sat	Curragh	Irish St Leger (1m 6f)
	14 Sun	Curragh	National Stakes (7f)

Overseas

March	29 Sat	Nad Al Sheba, UAE	Dubai World Cup
May	3 Sat	Churchill Downs, USA	Kentucky Derby
	11 Sun	Longchamp, France	Poule d'Essai des Poulains
		Longchamp, France	Poule d'Essai des Pouliches
	17 Sat	Pimlico, USA	Preakness Stakes
June	1 Sun	Chantilly, France	Prix du Jockey Club
	7 Sat	Belmont Park, USA	Belmont Stakes
	8 Sun	Chantilly, France	Prix de Diane
October	5 Sun	Longchamp, France	Prix de l'Arc de Triomphe
	25 Sat	Santa Anita, USA	Breeders Cup
November	4 Tue	Flemington, Australia	Melbourne Cup
	23 Sun	Nakayama, Japan	Japan Cup

Sponsored by Stan James

KNOW YOUR BETS

David Bennett
£5.95 (plus 50p p&p)

Latest edition of this popular, fact-filled A-Z guide to the principles and practice of betting. Over 240 entries from 'Abbreviations to Yankee', covering

- Popular bets
- Betting terminology
- Betting arithmetic
- Hot to settle singles, accumulators and multiple bets
- Odds, percentages and probability
- Stakes and staking plans
- Value
- Tote betting
- Bookmakers' rules and how to avoid disputes
- The evolution and practice of bookmaking

CREDIT AND DEBIT CARD HOTLINE: 01635 578080 (24 hours)

To order the book contact Raceform Ltd, Compton, Newbury, Berkshire, RG20 6NL

Fax: 01635 578101 • email: rfsubscription@mgn.co.uk

Web: www.raceform.co.uk

Sponsored by Stan James

Outlook
Big Race Records

Lincoln Handicap (1m) Doncaster

Year	Winner	Trainer	Jockey	SP	Draw/ran
1993	High Premium 5-8-8	J. Ramsden	K. Fallon	(16-1)	5/24
1994	Our Rita 5-8-5	Dr. J. Scargill	D. Holland	(16-1)	6/24
1995	Roving Minstrel 4-8-3	B. McMahon	K. Darley	(33-1)	11/23
1996	Stone Ridge 4-8-7	R. Hannon	D. O'Neill	(33-1)	6/24
1997	Kuala Lipis 4-8-6	P. Cole	T. Quinn	(11-1)	21/24
1998	Hunters Of Brora 8-9-0	J. Bethell	J. Weaver	(16-1)	23/23
1999	Right Wing 5-9-5	J. Dunlop	T. Quinn	(9-2)	8/24
2000	John Ferneley 5-8-10	P. Cole	J. Fortune	(7-1)	1/24
2001	Nimello 5-8-9	P. Cole	J. Fortune	(9-2)	1/23
2002	Zucchero 6-8-13	D. Arbuthnot	S. Whitworth	(33-1)	7/23

BET ANTE-POST or, better still, take a morning price but, whatever you do, don't bet at SP. The perennial question is what effect the draw will have. The best thing is to watch the Spring Mile run a day earlier. 1998 winner, Hunters Of Brora, was the exception, she was the oldest winner since 1963, the first to carry 9st or more to victory since 1985 and was winning for the first time in three years. Form on a straight course over a stiff 1m or further is ideal, as is experience of the hurly burly of a big race - both applied to the 1999 winner, Right Wing hence his 9-2 starting price. The vast majority of both winners and runners were having their first outings of the season. Northern-based trainers no longer seem to dominate and Paul Cole has done particularly well in the last six years. Both his last two winners had won a 1m Class B handicap run at Wolverhampton on the All-Weather a fortnight earlier.

1,000 Guineas (1m) Newmarket

1993	Sayyedati	C. Brittain	W. Swinburn	(4-1)	4/12
1994	Las Meninas	T. Stack	J. Reid	(12-1)	1/15
1995	Harayir	W. Hern	R. Hills	(5-1)	2/14
1996	Bosra Sham	H. Cecil	Pat Eddery	(10-11)	11/13
1997	Sleepytime	H. Cecil	K. Fallon	(5-1)	3/15
1998	Cape Verdi	S. bin Suroor	L. Dettori	(10-3)	7/16
1999	Wince	H. Cecil	K. Fallon	(4-1)	19/22 (July course)
2000	Lahan	J. Gosden	R. Hills	(14-1)	10/18
2001	Ameerat	M. Jarvis	P. Robinson	(11-1)	10/18
2002	Kazzia	S. bin Suroor	L. Dettori	(9-2)	12/17

FIRST RUN in 1814, since 1995 it has been run on a Sunday. A high place in the International Classifications has been critical – very few winners register less than 112. Ameerat (106) and Cape Verdi (109) bucked this trend but the latter was campaigned at distances short of her best at two. The Marcel Boussac and the Cheveley Park are the races to study from the previous year. Two key trials are Newbury's Fred Darling and Newmarket's Nell Gwyn, but don't necessarily be put off by horses beaten in those.

Sponsored by Stan James

2,000 Guineas (1m) Newmarket

Year	Horse	Trainer	Jockey	Odds	
1993	Zafonic	A. Fabre	Pat Eddery	(5-6)	10/14
1994	Mister Baileys	M. Johnston	J. Weaver	(16-1)	21/23
1995	Pennekamp	A. Fabre	T. Jarnet	(9-2)	11/11
1996	Mark Of Esteem	S. bin Suroor	L. Dettori	(8-1)	2/13
1997	Entrepreneur	Sir M. Stoute	M. Kinane	(11-2)	4/16
1998	King Of Kings	A. O'Brien	M. Kinane	(7-2)	17/18
1999	Island Sands	S. bin Suroor	L. Dettori	(10-1)	3/16 (July course)
2000	King's Best	Sir M. Stoute	K. Fallon	(13-2)	12/27
2001	Golan	Sir M. Stoute	K. Fallon	(11-1)	19/18
2002	Rock Of Gibraltar	A. O'Brien	J. Murtagh	(9-1)	22/22

THE FIRST colts' Classic was first run in 1809 and is usually held on the first Saturday in May. It's often a specialist miler's race. Like the 1,000 Guineas, you don't get many winners who haven't earned themselves a high place in the International Classifications, although Island Sands bucked the trend. King Of Kings was rated 111 and was already a Group 1 winner at two, as was Rock Of Gibraltar, who had won the Dewhurst, which has proved the best of the two-year-old trials. The race currently known as the Racing Post Trophy has produced only one winner, High Top. The Craven Stakes has proved a far better guide than the Greenham in recent years. It appears that horses having their seasonal debut in the race are not disadvantaged

The Derby (1m4f) Epsom

Year	Horse	Trainer	Jockey	Odds	
1993	Commander In Chief	H. Cecil	M. Kinane	(15-2)	6/16
1994	Erhaab	J. Dunlop	W. Carson	(7-2)	15/25
1995	Lammtarra	S. bin Suroor	W. Swinburn	(14-1)	7/15
1996	Shaamit	W. Haggas	M. Hills	(12-1)	9/20
1997	Benny The Dip	J. Gosden	W. Ryan	(11-1)	8/13
1998	High-Rise	L. Cumani	O. Peslier	(20-1)	14/15
1999	Oath	H. Cecil	K. Fallon	(13-2)	1/16
2000	Sinndar	J. Oxx	J. Murtagh	(7-1)	15/15
2001	Galileo	A. O'Brien	M. Kinane	(11-4)	10/12
2002	High Chaparral	A. O'Brien	J. Murtagh	(7-2)	9/12

IN AN effort to re-establish the Derby's popularity, the BHB moved it to a Saturday from its traditional Wednesday in 1995. Many high-class colts fail due to lack of stamina. It's vital to have a top-class sire (Sadler's Wells has produced the last two winners) and a staying pedigree on the dam's side. Since the golden years of Nijinsky and Mill Reef (1970 and 1971) only one horse, Nashwan, has won both the 2,000 Guineas and Derby, although Dancing Brave should have done. The Guineas is still a key race and others include the Dante Stakes and the Lingfield Derby Trial. Oath departed from the norm, winning a Listed race at Chester. Generally this is a race for fancied runners in the first four in the betting – 20-1 winner High-Rise was the biggest priced winner for 25 years. In the last three years, Leopardstown's Derby Trial has been the key pointer.

The Oaks (1m4f) Epsom

Year	Horse	Trainer	Jockey	Odds	
1993	Intrepidity	A. Fabre	M. Roberts	(5-1)	9/14
1994	Balanchine	H. Ibrahim	L. Dettori	(6-1)	9/10
1995	Moonshell	S. bin Suroor	L. Dettori	(3-1)	9/10
1996	Lady Carla	H. Cecil	Pat Eddery	(100-30)	9/11
1997	Reams Of Verse	H. Cecil	K. Fallon	(5-6)	6/12
1998	Shahtoush	A. O'Brien	M. Kinane	(12-1)	5/8
1999	Ramruma	H. Cecil	K. Fallon	(3-1)	5/10
2000	Love Divine	H. Cecil	T. Quinn	(9-4)	3/16
2001	Imagine	A. O'Brien	M. Kinane	(3-1)	10/14
2002	Kazzia	S. bin Suroor	L. Dettori	(100-30)	13/14

Sponsored by Stan James

FIRST RUN in 1779, the Oaks is one year older then the Derby. In 1995, it was moved from its traditional Saturday spot to the Friday of the meeting. Breeding is just as important as in the Derby and not many three-year-old fillies stay so far at this time of the year. The 1,000 Guineas provides the best guide, followed by the Musidora at York. In 1998, Shahtoush kept up the good record of 1,000 Guineas runners – she had finished second in the first fillies' Classic, while Kazzia provided a further boost last year by winning both. Ramruma won the Lingfield Oaks Trial. Imagine was the first filly to do the Irish Guineas/Oaks double since 1966.

Queen Anne Stakes (1m) Royal Ascot

Year	Horse	Trainer	Jockey	SP	
1993	Alflora 4-9-2	C. Brittain	M. Kinane	(20-1)	6/9
1994	Barathea 4-9-8	L. Cumani	M. Kinane	(3-1)	1/10
1995	Nicolotte 4-9-2	G. Wragg	M. Hills	(16-1)	2/7
1996	Charnwood Forest 4-9-2	S. bin Suroor	M. Kinane	(10-11)	6/9
1997	Allied Forces 4-9-5	S. bin Suroor	L. Dettori	(10-1)	11/11
1998	Intikhab 4-9-2	S. bin Suroor	L. Dettori	(9-4)	6/9
1999	Cape Cross 5-9-7	S. bin Suroor	G. Stevens	(7-1)	2/8
2000	Kalanisi 4-9-2	Sir M. Stoute	K. Fallon	(11-2)	11/11
2001	Medicean 4-9-7	Sir M. Stoute	K. Fallon	(11-2)	8/10
2002	No Excuse Needed 4-9-2	Sir M. Stoute	J. Murtagh	(13-2)	11/12

THE FIRST race of the Royal Ascot meeting, usually run at a furious pace, was upgraded from a Group 3 to a Group 2 in 1985. Four-year-olds who were once considered Classic contenders fit the bill and the age group has taken nine of the last ten runnings. Three-year-olds have a dreadful record. Godolphin won the race four times in a row before Kalanisi's success in 2000, since when Sir Michael Stoute has taken over as the race's dominant force. The Lockinge Stakes (Newbury, May, a Group 1 for the first time in 1996) is a key race; Medicean won both races, while No Excuse Needed ran a feeble race behind Keltos in the Lockinge before landing this.

Prince Of Wales's Stakes (1m2f) Royal Ascot

Year	Horse	Trainer	Jockey	SP	
1993	Placerville 3-8-4	H. Cecil	Pat Eddery	(11-2)	1/11
1994	Muhtarram 5-9-7	J. Gosden	W. Carson	(3-1)	8/10
1995	Muhtarram 6-9-8	J. Gosden	W. Carson	(5-1)	5/6
1996	First Island 4-9-3	G. Wragg	M. Hills	(9-1)	3/12
1997	Bosra Sham 4-9-5	H. Cecil	K. Fallon	(4-11)	1/6
1998	Faithful Son 4-9-3	S. bin Suroor	J. Reid	(11-2)	7/8
1999	Lear Spear 4-9-3	D. Elsworth	M. Kinane	(20-1)	5/8
2000	Dubai Millennium 4-9-0	S. bin Suroor	J. Bailey	(5-4)	7/6
2001	Fantastic Light 5-9-0	S. bin Suroor	L. Dettori	(100-30)	8/8
2002	Grandera 4-9-0	S. bin Suroor	L. Dettori	(4-1)	3/12

FIRST RUN in 1968 and now one of the races of the week. Four-year-olds have mostly proved successful in recent years. Three-year-olds have won only twice since the inception of the race, while three horses have doubled up – Muhtarram, Mtoto and Connaught. For the above reason, a key race is the previous year's running. The Brigadier Gerard Stakes, won four years ago by Bosra Sham, the Gordon Richards Stakes and the Tattersalls Gold Cup (won by Fantastic Light in 2001) are others. Grandera came into the race from a spring international campaign taking in Dubai, Hong Kong and Singapore.

St James's Palace Stakes (1m) Royal Ascot

Year	Horse	Trainer	Jockey	SP	
1993	Kingmambo	F. Boutin	C. Asmussen	(2-5)	4/4
1994	Grand Lodge	W. Jarvis	M. Kinane	(6-1)	3/9
1995	Bahri	J. Dunlop	W. Carson	(11-4)	7/9
1996	Bijou D'Inde	M. Johnston	J. Weaver	(9-1)	7/9
1997	Starborough	D. Loder	L. Dettori	(11-2)	5/8

Sponsored by Stan James

1998	Dr Fong	H. Cecil	K. Fallon	(4-1)	4/8
1999	Sendawar	A. Royer Dupre	G. Mosse	(2-1)	11/11
2000	Giant's Causeway	A. O'Brien	M. Kinane	(7-2)	3/11
2001	Black Minnaloushe	A. O'Brien	J. Murtagh	(8-1)	1/11
2002	Rock Of Gibraltar	A. O'Brien	M. Kinane	(4-5)	4/9

FIRST RUN in 1925, is restricted to three-year-olds and has Group 1 status. Winners and also-rans from the Irish, French and English Guineas often line up for this valuable prize. Black Minnaloushe (winner) and Giant's Causeway (second) ran in the Irish Guineas. Five of the last seven winners made the frame in the English version. Less exposed types such as Persian Heights and Shavian can make a breakthrough. Derby runners have a mixed record. Marju was second in the Derby and won, but Rodrigo De Triano flopped in both.

Coronation Stakes (1m) Royal Ascot

1993	Gold Splash	Mrs C. Head	G. Mosse	(100-30)	2/5
1994	Kissing Cousin	H. Cecil	M. Kinane	(13-2)	2/10
1995	Ridgewood Pearl	J. Oxx	J. Murtagh	(9-2)	8/10
1996	Shake The Yoke	E. Lellouche	O. Peslier	(Evens)	4/7
1997	Rebecca Sharp	G. Wragg	M. Hills	(25-1)	3/6
1998	Exclusive	Sir M. Stoute	W. Swinburn	(5-1)	10/9
1999	Balisada	G. Wragg	M. Roberts	(16-1)	8/9
2000	Crimplene	C. Brittain	P. Robinson	(4-1)	6/9
2001	Banks Hill	A. Fabre	O. Peslier	(4-1)	4/13
2002	Sophisticat	A. O'Brien	M. Kinane	(11-2)	3/11

A CHAMPIONSHIP race for three-year-old fillies, first run in 1870. Winners and runners from all the Guineas races fare well (Exclusive was third in English version, while last year was a triumph for the form of the French Guineas), but Irish 1,000 Guineas winners have the best record through Ridgewood Pearl, Kooyonga and Crimplene. English 1,000 Guinness winners are worth opposing – failures include Harayir, Las Meninas, Shadayid and Sleepytime.

Royal Hunt Cup Handicap (1m) Royal Ascot

1993	Imperial Ballet 4-8-12	H. Cecil	Pat Eddery	(20-1)	19/30
1994	Face North 6-8-3	R. Akehurst	A. Munro	(25-1)	30/32
1995	Realities 5-9-0	G. Harwood	M. Kinane	(11-1)	30/32
1996	Yeast 4-8-6	W. Haggas	K. Fallon	(8-1)	3/31
1997	Red Robbo 4-8-6	R. Akehurst	O. Peslier	(16-1)	17/32
1998	Refuse To Lose 4-7-11	J. Eustace	J. Tate	(20-1)	6/32
1999	Showboat 5-8-6	B. Hills	N. Pollard	(14-1)	30/32
2000	Caribbean Monarch 5-8-10	Sir M. Stoute	K. Fallon	(11-2)	28/32
2001	Surprise Encounter 5-8-9	E. Dunlop	L. Dettori	(8-1)	29/30
2002	Norton 5-8-9	T. Mills	J. Fortune	(25-1)	10/30

A GREAT betting race in which the draw can play a crucial part, especially if the ground is soft – no less than five of the last ten winners have run from stall 28 or higher. There are few pointers and plots are thick on the ground, so most winners are a working man's price. Watch the Victoria Cup at Ascot in May.

Gold Cup (2m4f) Royal Ascot

1993	Drum Taps 7-9-2	Lord Huntingdon	L. Dettori	(13-2)	6/10
1994	Arcadian Heights 6-9-2	G. Wragg	M. Hills	(20-1)	5/9
1995	Double Trigger 4-9-0	M. Johnston	J. Weaver	(9-4)	6/7
1996	Classic Cliche 4-9-0	S. bin Suroor	M. Kinane	(3-1)	7/7
1997	Celeric 5-9-2	D. Morley	Pat Eddery	(11-2)	2/13
1998	Kayf Tara 4-9-0	S. bin Suroor	L. Dettori	(11-1)	17/16

1999	**Enzeli** 4-9-0	J. Oxx	J. Murtagh	(20-1)	16/17
2000	**Kayf Tara** 6-9-2	S. bin Suroor	M. Kinane	(11-8)	6/11
2001	**Royal Rebel** 5-9-2	M. Johnston	J. Murtagh	(8-1)	10/12
2002	**Royal Rebel** 6-9-2	M. Johnston	J. Murtagh	(16-1)	8/15

THIS IS the only British Group 1 race run over 2m4f. Many winners, including most recently Royal Rebel, have followed up from the year before, probably because winners have to possess a blend of speed and stamina that is very rare in modern racing stock. Apart from the winner of the previous year's heat, the key races are the St Leger and Sandown's Henry II Stakes.

Wokingham Handicap (6f) Royal Ascot

1993	**Nagida** 4-8-7	J. Toller	J. Weaver	(11-1)	4/30
1994	**Venture Capitalist** 5-8-12	R. Hannon	J. Reid	(20-1)	30/30
1995	**Astrac** 4-8-7	R. Akehurst	S. Sanders	(14-1)	16/30
1996	**Emerging Market** 4-8-13	J. Dunlop	K. Darley	(33-1)	7/29
1997	**Selhurstpark Flyer** 6-8-9	J. Berry	P. Roberts	(25-1)	5/30
1998	**Selhurstpark Flyer** 7-9-7	J. Berry	C. Lowther	(16-1)	20/29
1999	**Deep Space** 4-8-7	E. Dunlop	G. Carter	(14-1)	3/30
2000	**Harmonic Way** 5-9-6	R. Charlton	R. Hughes	(12-1)	28/29
2001	**Nice One Clare** 5-9-3	J. Payne	J. Murtagh	(7-1)	4/30
2002	**Capricho** 5-8-11	J. Akehurst	T. Quinn	(20-1)	21/28

WAS FIRST run in 1896 and is a tough race in which to find a winner, though the *Outlook* tipped Nice One Clare on the front page ahead of the 2001 race. Winners are often long-priced and low-weighted. A key race is the Victoria Cup (Ascot, May). Winners tend to be aged four to six, with only two winners having been older. Favourites have a dismal record.

Eclipse (1m2f) Sandown

1993	**Opera House** 5-9-7	Sir M. Stoute	M. Kinane	(9-2)	2/8
1994	**Ezzoud** 5-9-7	Sir M. Stoute	W. Swinburn	(5-1)	6/8
1995	**Halling** 4-9-7	S. bin Suroor	W. Swinburn	(7-1)	3/8
1996	**Halling** 5-9-7	S. bin Suroor	J. Reid	(100-30)	1/7
1997	**Pilsudski** 5-9-7	Sir M. Stoute	M. Kinane	(11-2)	1/5
1998	**Daylami** 4-9-7	S. bin Suroor	L. Dettori	(6-4)	5/7
1999	**Compton Admiral** 3-8-10	G. Butler	D. Holland	(20-1)	7/8
2000	**Giant's Causeway** 3-8-10	A. O'Brien	G. Duffield	(8-1)	4/8
2001	**Medicean** 4-9-7	Sir M. Stoute	K. Fallon	(7-2)	7/8
2002	**Hawk Wing** 3-8-10	A. O'Brien	M. Kinane	(8-15)	6/5

CHANGES IN the weight-for-age scale meant that from 1990 onwards three-year-olds became 2lb worse off with their elders, but that didn't stop Environment Friend, Compton Admiral, Giant's Causeway or Hawk Wing. Pebbles was the first filly to succeed this century. Derby winners and fillies have a poor record. Proven Group 1 form is a major asset. Daylami, beaten half a length in the Prince of Wales's Stakes, kept up the good record of runners from that race and Royal Ascot form in general is a key to this race; Giant's Causeway won the St James's Palace and Medicean won the Queen Anne.

July Cup (6f) Newmarket

1993	**Hamas** 4-9-6	P. Walwyn	W. Carson	(33-1)	9/12
1994	**Owington** 3-8-13	G. Wragg	Paul Eddery	(3-1)	1/9
1995	**Lake Coniston** 4-9-6	G. Lewis	Paul Eddery	(13-8)	9/9
1996	**Anabaa** 4-9-5	Mme C. Head	F. Head	(11-4)	2/10
1997	**Compton Place** 3-8-13	J. Toller	S. Sanders	(50-1)	1/9
1998	**Elnadim** 4-9-5	J. Dunlop	R. Hills	(3-1)	18/17

Sponsored by Stan James

1999	**Stravinsky** 3-8-13	A. O'Brien	M. Kinane	(8-1)	6/17
2000	**Agnes World** 5-9-5	H. Mori	Y. Take	(4-1)	6/10
2001	**Mozart** 3-8-13	A. O'Brien	M. Kinane	(4-1)	19/18
2002	**Continent** 5-9-5	D. Nicholls	D. Holland	(12-1)	2/14

THE BLUE RIBAND event of Newmarket's July meeting and first run in 1876. Horses dropping down in distance succeeded in 1987, 1988, 1999 and 2001. Mozart had won the 7f Jersey Stakes and finished second in the Irish Guineas. However, in the main over the last 10 years it is specialist sprinters who have been doing well in this race. The Cork and Orrery (Royal Ascot, June), the King's Stand (also Royal Ascot), the Duke of York (York, May), the 2,000 Guineas (Newmarket, May) and the 1,000 Guineas (also Newmarket, May) give the most helpful clues.

King George VI and Queen Elizabeth Diamond Stakes (1m4f) Ascot

1993	**Opera House** 5-9-7	Sir M. Stoute	M. Roberts	(8-1)	2/10
1994	**King's Theatre** 3-8-9	H. Cecil	M. Kinane	(12-1)	7/12
1995	**Lammtarra** 3-8-9	S. bin Suroor	L. Dettori	(9-4)	3/7
1996	**Pentire** 4-9-7	G. Wragg	M. Hills	(100-30)	7/8
1997	**Swain** 5-9-7	S. bin Suroor	J. Reid	(16-1)	5/8
1998	**Swain** 6-9-7	S. bin Suroor	L. Dettori	(11-2)	5/8
1999	**Daylami** 5-9-7	S. bin Suroor	L. Dettori	(3-1)	8/8
2000	**Montjeu** 4-9-7	J. Hammond	M. Kinane	(1-3)	5/7
2001	**Galileo** 3-8-9	A. O'Brien	M. Kinane	(1-2)	7/12
2002	**Golan** 4-9-7	Sir M. Stoute	K. Fallon	(11-2)	8/9

ALTHOUGH IT has less prestige than the Arc, the King George is always won by a top-class horse. It was first run in 1951. There are two Derby winners in the above list and two Derby runners-up. Although a top-class older horse, trained by an established handler, best fits the bill, (1999, 2000, 2002), Galileo bucked the trend and took full advantage of his weight-for-age allowance. A seriously good Derby winner is almost given a head-start by the weight-for-age scale. The Eclipse is also a big influence on the race. For the older horses, the Coronation Cup is a good pointer. Golan was the first horse ever to win this on his seasonal debut, though few serious contenders will have attempted such a feat.

Stewards' Cup Handicap (5f) Goodwood

1993	**King's Signet** 4-9-10	J. Gosden	W. Carson	(16-1)	21/29
1994	**For The Present** 4-8-3	T. Barron	J. Fortune	(16-1)	16/26
1995	**Shikari's Son** 8-8-13	J. White	R. Hughes	(40-1)	30/27
1996	**Coastal Bluff** 4-8-5	T. Barron	J. Fortune	(10-1)	29/30
1997	**Danetime** 3-8-10	N. Callaghan	Pat Eddery	(5-1)	5/30
1998	**Superior Premium** 4-8-12	R. Fahey	R. Winston	(14-1)	28/29
1999	**Harmonic Way** 4-8-6	R. Charlton	R. Hughes	(12-1)	8/30
2000	**Tayseer** 6-8-11	D. Nicholls	R. Hughes	(13-2)	28/30
2001	**Guinea Hunter** 5-9-0	T. Easterby	J. Spencer	(33-1)	19/30
2002	**Bond Boy** 5-8-2	B. Smart	C. Catlin	(14-1)	29/28

INAUGURATED IN 1840, this is a major betting heat with a strong ante-post market. However, the race has been altered in recent seasons by the opening up of a fresh strip of ground on the far rail which has given high numbers a huge advantage, to the detriment of the ante-post market. A high draw is now thought essential and even a casual glance at the results above will tell you why. In 1998, winner Superior Premium was drawn 28 of 29, the second 25 and the third 29 and though in 1999 it was more even, in 2000 Tayseer (28) won from Bon Ami (24). Bond Boy (29) won from horses drawn 9, 22, 16, 7, 25, 30 and 28 last year. Do not bet ante-post in this race. The Wokingham Handicap has the most bearing; Knight Of Mercy pulled off the double, Danetime was an unlucky second in the Ascot race.

Sponsored by Stan James

Juddmonte International Stakes (1m2f85yds) York

Year	Horse	Trainer	Jockey	SP	
1993	Ezzoud 4-9-6	Sir M. Stoute	W. Swinburn	(28-1)	3/11
1994	Ezzoud 5-9-6	Sir M. Stoute	W. Swinburn	(4-1)	4/8
1995	Halling 4-8-12	S. bin Suroor	W. Swinburn	(9-4)	2/6
1996	Halling 5-9-5	S. bin Suroor	L. Dettori	(6-4)	1/6
1997	Singspiel 5-9-5	Sir M. Stoute	L. Dettori	(4-1)	2/4
1998	One So Wonderful 4-9-2	L. Cumani	Pat Eddery	(6-1)	5/8
1999	Royal Anthem 4-9-5	H. Cecil	G. Stevens	(3-1)	9/12
2000	Giant's Causeway 3-8-11	A. O'Brien	M. Kinane	(10-11)	5/6
2001	Sakhee 4-9-5	S. bin Suroor	L. Dettori	(7-4)	5/8
2002	Nayef 4-9-5	M. Tregoning	R. Hills	(6-4)	5/7

FAMOUS FOR its many upsets since its first running in 1972 when Roberto beat Grundy. Bosra Sham six years ago was one of many hot favourites to be beaten in this race. Older horses, especially lightly-raced ones (e.g. Sakhee) have mostly kept on top of the three-year-olds, though Giant's Causeway bucked the trend in 2000. Note the previous year's running and the Eclipse.

Ebor Handicap (1m6f) York

Year	Horse	Trainer	Jockey	SP	
1993	Sarawat 5-8-2	R. Akehurst	T. Quinn	(14-1)	9/21
1994	Hasten To Add 4-9-3	Sir M. Prescott	G. Duffield	(13-2)	9/21
1995	Sanmartino 3-7-11	B. Hills	W. Carson	(8-1)	21/21
1996	Clerkenwell 3-7-11	Sir M. Stoute	F. Lynch	(17-2)	2/21
1997	Far Ahead 5-8-0	J. Eyre	T. Williams	(33-1)	10/21
1998	Tuning 3-8-7	H. Cecil	K. Fallon	(9-2)	1/21
1999	Vicious Circle 5-8-4	L. Cumani	K. Darley	(11-1)	7/21
2000	Give The Slip 3-8-8	Mrs A. Perrett	Pat Eddery	(8-1)	16/22
2001	Mediterranean 3-8-4	A. O'Brien	M. Kinane	(16-1)	20/22
2002	Hugs Dancer 5-8-5	J. Given	D. McKeown	(25-1)	20/22

IS ONE of the oldest and most famous handicaps, first run in 1847, with a strong ante-post market. Sea Pigeon brought the house down when humping top-weight home in 1979. Stamina is a premium (as Sea Pigeon showed) and many Ebor winners, such as Further Flight, go on to be top stayers. Unexposed three-year-olds have come to the fore in recent years. Watch the Northumberland Plate (Newcastle, June) and the Duke Of Edinburgh Handicap (Royal Ascot, June).

St. Leger (1m6f127yds) Doncaster

Year	Horse	Trainer	Jockey	SP	
1993	Bob's Return	M. Tompkins	P. Robinson	(3-1)	9/9
1994	Moonax	B. Hills	Pat Eddery	(40-1)	3/8
1995	Classic Cliche	S. bin Suroor	L. Dettori	(100-30)	7/10
1996	Shantou	J. Gosden	L. Dettori	(8-1)	10/11
1997	Silver Patriarch	J. Dunlop	Pat Eddery	(5-4)	9/10
1998	Nedawi	S. bin Suroor	J. Reid	(5-2)	1/9
1999	Mutafaweq	S. bin Suroor	R. Hills	(11-2)	6/9
2000	Millenary	J. Dunlop	T. Quinn	(11-4)	5/11
2001	Milan	A. O'Brien	M. Kinane	(13-8)	7/10
2002	Bollin Eric	T. Easterby	K. Darley	(7-1)	3/8

THE OLDEST of the five Classics, first run in 1776, and the last to be staged each year. You don't have to have a Classic profile to win and you don't necessarily have to be a stayer. Horses such as Bob's Return and Commanche Run returned to shorter distances, while others such as Le Moss went on to be Cup horses. Two of the last eight winners were placed in the Epsom Derby and Mutafaweq was fifth in the Irish version. Important races are the Great Voltigeur at York in August (won by Milan in 2001, the first three went on to finish 3-2-1 in the Leger in 2002); the Derby and the Oaks (both Epsom, June).

Sponsored by Stan James

Ayr Gold Cup Handicap (6f) Ayr

1993	Hard To Figure 7-9-6	R. Hodges	R. Cochrane	(12-1)	8/29
1994	Daring Destiny 3-8-0	K. Burke	J. Tate	(18-1)	29/29
1995	Royale Figurine 4-8-9	M. F'-Godley	D. Holland	(8-1)	27/29
1996	Coastal Bluff 4-9-10	T. Barron	J. Fortune	(3-1)	28/28
1997	Wildwood Flower 4-9-3	R. Hannon	D. O'Neill	(14-1)	24/29
1998	Always Alight 4-8-7	K. Burke	J. Egan	(16-1)	8/29
1999	Grangeville 4-9-0	I. Balding	K. Fallon	(11-1)	17/28
2000	Bahamian Pirate 5-8-0	D. Nicholls	A. Nicholls	(33-1)	7/28
2001	Continent 4-8-10	D. Nicholls	D. Holland	(10-1)	22/28
2002	Funfair Wane 3-9-3	D. Nicholls	A. Nicholls	(16-1)	16/28

A HISTORIC race first run in 1804, for which there is a lively ante-post book. The effect of the draw can be gleaned from the Ayr Silver Cup, run the day before. A horse with good recent form who can settle in large fields and who can come from off the pace is required. Key races are; the Wokingham Handicap (Royal Ascot, June), the Tote Portland Handicap (Doncaster, September) and the Stewards' Cup (Goodwood, August).

Cambridgeshire Handicap (1m1f) Newmarket

1993	Penny Drops 4-7-13	Lord Huntingdon	D. Harrison	(7-1)	18/33
1994	Halling 3-8-8	J. Gosden	L. Dettori	(8-1)	24/30
1995	Cap Juluca 3-9-10	R. Charlton	R. Hughes	(11-1)	26/39
1996	Clifton Fox 4-8-2	J. Glover	N. Day	(14-1)	17/38
1997	Pasternak 4-9-1	Sir M. Prescott	G. Duffield	(4-1)	17/36
1998	Lear Spear 3-7-13	D. Elsworth	N. Pollard	(20-1)	33/35
1999	She's Our Mare 6-7-12	A. Martin	F. Norton	(11-1)	14/33 (July course)
2000	Katy Nowaitee 4-8-8	P. Harris	J. Reid	(6-1)	34/35
2001	I Cried For You 6-8-6	J. Given	M. Fenton	(33-1)	11/35
2002	Beauchamp Pilot 4-9-5	G. Butler	E. Ahern	(9-1)	26/30

THE FIRST leg of the Autumn Double, dating back to 1839. Because of its unusual distance and its straight course, the Cambridgeshire has thrown up a number of specialists. Apart from perennials, look for a late-maturing three-year-old bred to find improvement over longer trips which are not attempted until after the weights are set. Two races at Doncaster on St Leger day, a 0-105 handicap over the straight 1m and a 0-95 over an extended 1m2f should provide clues. Longer-priced horses often do well.

Prix De L' Arc De Triomphe (1m4f) Longchamp

1993	Urban Sea 4-9-1	J. Lesbordes	E. St Martin	(37-1)	9/23
1994	Carnegie 3-8-11	A. Fabre	T. Jarnet	(3-1)	2/20
1995	Lammtarra 3-8-11	S. bin Suroor	L. Dettori	(21-10)	7/16
1996	Helissio 3-8-11	E. Lellouche	O. Peslier	(18-10)	5/16
1997	Peintre Celebre 3-8-11	A. Fabre	O. Peslier	(22-10)	2/18
1998	Sagamix 3-8-11	A. Fabre	O. Peslier	(25-10)	7/14
1999	Montjeu 3-8-11	J. Hammond	M. Kinane	(6-4)	4/14
2000	Sinndar 3-8-11	J. Oxx	J. Murtagh	(6-4)	7/10
2001	Sakhee 4-9-5	S. bin Suroor	L. Dettori	(22-10)	15/17
2002	Marienbard 5-9-5	S. bin Suroor	L. Dettori	(158-10)	3/16

RESULTS HAVE been more reliable over the last decade or so but this is a reflection of the fact that winners have been trained specifically for the race. Three-year-olds have dominated and, though four-year-old Sakhee succeeded in 2001, he was lightly-raced. Andre Fabre has trained four of the last 11 winners. There are three key trials for the Arc at Longchamp, three weeks prior to the race; the Prix Vermeille, for three-year-old fillies, the Prix Niel, for three-year-old colts, and the Prix Foy. The Derbys all have a major bearing. Marienbard was something of an aberration, being prepared with two races in Germany.

Dubai Champion Stakes (1m2f) Newmarket

1993	**Hatoof** 4-9-0	Mrs C. Head	W. Swinburn	(5-2)		1/12
1994	**Dernier Empereur** 4-9-4	A. Fabre	S. Guillot	(8-1)		2/8
1995	**Spectrum** 3-8-10	P. Chapple-Hyam	J. Reid	(5-1)		1/8
1996	**Bosra Sham** 3-8-8	H. Cecil	Pat Eddery	(9-4)		4/6
1997	**Pilsudski** 5-9-2	Sir M. Stoute	M. Kinane	(Evens)		1/7
1998	**Alborada** 3-8-8	Sir M. Prescott	G. Duffield	(6-1)		5/10
1999	**Alborada** 4-8-13	Sir M. Prescott	G. Duffield	(5-1)	10/13 (July course)	
2000	**Kalanisi** 4-9-2	Sir M. Stoute	J. Murtagh	(5-1)		3/15
2001	**Nayef** 3-8-11	M. Tregoning	R. Hills	(3-1)		1/12
2002	**Storming Home** 4-9-2	B. Hills	M. Hills	(8-1)		4/11

FRENCH CONTENDERS and fillies have an excellent record in the last 10 years and more. Guineas winners of the same year or the year before have a good record. The overseas races with influence are the Irish Champion Stakes, the Arc de Triomphe and the Coupe de Maisons-Laffitte, which was won by Hatoof and Dernier Empereur.

Cesarewitch Handicap (2m2f) Newmarket

1993	**Aahsaylad** 7-8-12	J. White	J. Williams	(12-1)		21/31
1994	**Captain's Guest** 4-9-9	G. Harwood	A. Clark	(25-1)		28/32
1995	**Old Red** 5-7-11	Mrs M. Reveley	L. Charnock	(11-1)		18/21
1996	**Inchcailloch** 7-7-3	J. King	R. Ffrench	(20-1)		15/26
1997	**Turnpole** 6-7-10	Mrs M. Reveley	L. Charnock	(16-1)		6/30
1998	**Spirit Of Love** 3-8-8	M. Johnston	O. Peslier	(11-1)		19/29
1999	**Top Cees** 9-8-10	I. Balding	K. Fallon	(7-1)	17/32 (July course)	
2000	**Heros Fatal** 6-8-1	M. Pipe	G. Carter	(11-1)		18/33
2001	**Distant Prospect** 4-8-8	I. Balding	M. Dwyer	(14-1)		32/31
2002	**Miss Fara** 7-8-0	M. Pipe	R. Moore	(12-1)		36/36

THE SECOND leg of the Autumn Double. Normally a race won by five-year-olds and above, Spirit Of Love being a rare three-year-old winner. Fresh horses at the lower end of the weights have a good record. The Tote Ebor and previous runnings of this race itself have the most influence. Go for horses who have shown good autumn form in the past.

November Handicap (1m4f) Doncaster

1993	**Quick Ransom** 5-8-10	M. Johnston	J. Weaver	(6-1)	9/25
1994	**Saxon Maid** 3-8-9	L. Cumani	J. Weaver	(16-1)	20/24
1995	**Snow Princess** 3-8-2	Lord Huntingdon	R. Hills	(5-1)	10/18
1996	**Clifton Fox** 4-8-10	J. Glover	N. Day	(9-1)	14/22
1997	**Sabadilla** 3-7-8	J. Gosden	R. Ffrench	(10-1)	22/24
1998	**Yavana's Pace** 6-9-10	M. Johnston	D. Holland	(8-1)	12/23
1999	**Flossy** 3-7-7	C. Thornton	A. Beech	(5-1)	10/16
2000	**Batswing** 5-8-8	B. Ellison	R. Winston	(14-1)	14/20
2001	**Royal Cavalier** 4-7-10	R. Hollinshead	P. Quinn	(50-1)	5/14
2002	**Red Wine** 3-8-1	J. Osborne	M. Dwyer	(16-1)	20/23

THE LAST big ante-post race of the season traces back to 1876. Three-year-olds, lightly raced, progressive and with stout pedigrees, are most likely to succeed. The 1m4f Ladbroke Handicap run over course and distance at the previous meeting is worth studying.

Sponsored by Stan James

Outlook By The Numbers

by Chris Cook

Numbers lead to profits

BY THE NUMBERS is a new feature in *Racing & Football Outlook*. Having made its debut in December, tipping one horse for the big handicap each week, the concept quickly showed its worth by putting up a 9-1 winner at the third time of asking.

But it's not just about tipping – we hope the format also provides you with plenty of raw data that you'll find helpful in sorting out some of the year's trickiest races. We don't necessarily have space for By The Numbers every week in the RFO but we've made space here so that you have some time to ponder our stats.

Over the next ten pages, we've produced statistical breakdowns of the top betting races of the Flat season, as judged by turnover levels with Ladbrokes last year. They're listed in order of popularity.

The idea here is to provide you with as much information as we think will be relevant to analysis of the big race and let you get on with it.

The following ten races are some of the highlights of any punter's Flat racing season. They're all the kind of race you find yourself betting in every year, even though you may not be able to recall the last time you had the winner. We'll be covering these races in the RFO, space permitting, in the week each one takes place. When we do so, our analysis will take in ten years of data.

Rather than anticipate that coverage now, we're providing a complementary service. For the purposes of this annual, we're confining the data in our stats boxes to the last five years, in the hope of identifying the most current trends.

Each race is analysed under six headings; age of the runners, the weight they carried, the Official Ratings they were assigned at the time of running, their SPs, their draws and their genders.

Under each heading, all the runners in the race over the last five years are sorted into their appropriate categories. In each case, we tell you how many times horses that fit that category won the race in the last five years, how many runners there were from that category, their strike-rate, the outcome if you had backed them all to a £1 stake and the percentage return on your total stakes represented by that outcome.

For example, let's take five-year-olds in the Lincoln, for which our stats are on the facing page. You'll see that five-year-olds have won three of the last five Lincolns, dominating horses of other ages.

But that bare result is put in context by the fact that there were 36 five-year-old runners in the race over the last five years, so they're only winning at a strike-rate of 8%. If you'd had £1 on each of them, you'd have made a net loss of £17, which is 47% of your total stakes – in other words, you'd have made a net loss of about half the money you risked.

Leafing through these stats, it seems a common theme is that the category which produces most winners is not necessarily the category that offers the best return.

Hopefully, our data will lead you to profitable conclusions. Just look at those draw stats for the John Smith's Cup and tell me you can't use this feature to make money.

Lincoln
Doncaster, March 22, 1m

Age

Age	Wins/runs	%	£+-	% of stakes
4	0/40	0	-£40.00	-100
5	3/36	8	-£17.00	-47
6	1/29	3	+£5.00	+17
7	0/10	0	-£10.00	-100
8+	1/2	50	+£15.00	+750

Weight

Weight	Wins/runs	%	£+-	% of stakes
Under 8-00	0/4	0	-£4.00	-100
8-00 to 8-06	0/34	0	-£34.00	-100
8-07 to 8-13	3/50	6	-£2.50	-5
9-00 to 9-05	2/13	15	+£9.50	+73
9-06+	0/16	0	-£16.00	-100

Official Ratings

OR	Wins/runs	%	£+-	% of stakes
Under 85	0/22	0	-£22.00	-100
85-89	1/41	2	-£35.50	-87
90-94	3/27	11	+£32.00	+119
95-99	0/15	0	-£15.00	-100
100+	1/12	8	-£6.50	-54

Starting Prices

SP	Wins/runs	%	£+-	% of stakes
Under 3-1	0/1	0	-£1.00	-100
3-1 to 11-2	2/3	67	+£8.00	+267
6-1 to 8-1	1/7	14	+£1.00	+14
9-1 to 11-1	0/10	0	-£10.00	-100
12-1 to 14-1	0/15	0	-£15.00	-100
16-1 to 20-1	1/24	4	-£7.00	-29
22-1 to 28-1	0/18	0	-£18.00	-100
33-1 to 40-1	1/28	4	+£6.00	+21
50-1+	0/11	0	-£11.00	-100

Draw

Draw	Wins/runs	%	£+-	% of stakes
0-8	4/39	10	+£14.00	+36
9-16	0/39	0	-£39.00	-100
17-24	1/39	3	-£22.00	-56

Sex

Sex	Wins/runs	%	£+-	% of stakes
Colt/horse	1/33	3	-£27.50	-83
Filly/mare	1/3	33	+£14.00	+467
Gelding	3/81	4	-£33.50	-41

	Winner	Age	Weight	OR	SP	Sex	Draw
2002	Zucchero	6	8-13	91	33-1	G	7
2001	Nimello	5	8-09	89	9-2	G	1
2000	John Ferneley	5	8-10	90	7-1	G	1
1999	Right Wing	5	9-05	100	9-2	H	8
1998	Hunters Of Brora	8	9-00	90	16-1	M	23
1997	Kuala Lipis	4	8-06	86	11-1	H	21
1996	Stone Ridge	4	8-07	87	33-1	G	6
1995	Roving Minstrel	4	8-03	82	33-1	H	11
1994	Our Rita	5	8-05	76	16-1	M	6
1993	High Premium	5	8-08	80	16-1	H	5

Sponsored by Stan James

Ayr Gold Cup
Ayr, September 20, 6f

Age

Age	Wins/runs	%	£+-	% of stakes
3	1/37	3	-£20.00	-54
4	3/39	8	+£1.00	+3
5	1/22	5	+£12.00	+56
6	0/22	0	-£22.00	-100
7	0/13	0	-£13.00	-100
8+	0/8	0	-£8.00	-100

Weight

Weight	Wins/runs	%	£+-	% of stakes
Under 8-00	0/4	0	-£4.00	-100
8-00 to 8-06	1/39	3	-£5.00	-13
8-07 to 8-13	2/50	4	-£22.00	-44
9-00 to 9-05	2/26	8	+£3.00	+12
9-06+	0/22	0	-£22.00	-100

Official Ratings

OR	Wins/runs	%	£+-	% of stakes
Under 90	2/35	6	+£16.00	+46
90-94	1/45	2	-£34.00	-76
95-99	1/24	4	-£12.00	-50
100-104	1/18	6	-£1.00	-6
105+	0/19	0	-£19.00	-100

Starting Prices

SP	Wins/runs	%	£+-	% of stakes
Under 3-1	No runners			
3-1 to 11-2	0/1	0	-£1.00	-100
6-1 to 8-1	0/5	0	-£5.00	-100
9-1 to 11-1	2/10	20	+£13.00	+130
12-1 to 14-1	0/21	0	-£21.00	-100
16-1 to 20-1	2/21	10	+£13.00	+61
22-1 to 28-1	0/24	0	-£24.00	-100
33-1 to 40-1	1/32	3	+£2.00	+6
50-1+	0/27	0	-£27.00	-100

Draw

Draw	Wins/runs	%	£+-	% of stakes
0-8	2/40	5	+£11.00	+28
9-16	1/40	3	-£23.00	-58
17-24	2/38	5	-£15.00	-39
25+	0/23	0	-£23.00	-100

Sex

Sex	Wins/runs	%	£+-	% of stakes
Colt/horse	0/22	0	-£22.00	-100
Filly/mare	0/24	0	-£24.00	-100
Gelding	5/95	5	-£4.00	-4

Winners

Year	Winner	Age	Weight	OR	SP	Sex	Draw
2002	Funfair Wane	3	9-03	100	16-1	G	16
2001	Continent	4	8-10	92	10-1	G	22
2000	Bahamian Pirate	5	8-00	86	33-1	G	7
1999	Grangeville	4	9-00	98	11-1	G	17
1998	Always Alight	4	8-07	89	16-1	G	8
1997	Wildwood Flower	4	9-03	97	14-1	M	24
1996	Coastal Bluff	4	9-10	104	3-1	G	28
1995	Royale Figurine	4	8-09	95	8-1	M	27
1994	Daring Destiny	3	8-00	89	18-1	M	29
1993	Hard To Figure	7	9-06	101	12-1	G	8

Sponsored by Stan James

Cambridgeshire N'market, October 4, 1m 1f

Age

Age	Wins/runs	%	£+-	% of stakes
3	1/48	2	-£27.00	-56
4	3/55	6	-£33.00	-60
5	0/29	0	-£29.00	-100
6	1/20	5	+£14.00	+70
7	0/12	0	-£12.00	-100
8+	0/7	0	-£7.00	-100

Weight

Weight	Wins/runs	%	£+-	% of stakes
Under 8-00	1/29	3	-£8.00	-28
8-00 to 8-06	1/50	2	-£16.00	-32
8-07 to 8-13	1/57	2	-£50.00	-88
9-00 to 9-05	2/20	10	-£5.00	-25
9-06 to 9-10	0/15	0	-£15.00	-100

OR

OR	Wins/runs	%	£+-	% of stakes
Under 80	0/11	0	-£11.00	-100
80-84	0/28	0	-£28.00	-100
85-89	1/45	2	-£11.00	-24
90-94	3/37	8	-£4.00	-11
95-99	1/28	4	-£18.00	-64
100-104	0/12	0	-£12.00	-100
105+	0/10	0	-£10.00	-100

Starting Prices

SP	Wins/runs	%	£+-	% of stakes
Under 3-1	No runners			
3-1 to 11-2	1/5	20	Level	Level
6-1 to 8-1	1/7	14	Level	Level
9-1 to 11-1	1/6	17	+£4.00	+67
12-1 to 14-1	0/15	0	-£15.00	-100
16-1 to 20-1	1/25	4	-£4.00	-16
22-1 to 28-1	0/21	0	-£21.00	-100
33-1 to 40-1	1/48	2	-£14.00	-29
50-1+	0/44	0	-£44.00	-100

Draw

Draw	Wins/runs	%	£+-	% of stakes
0-8	0/39	0	-£39.00	-100
9-16	1/38	3	-£4.00	-11
17-24	1/38	3	-£33.00	-87
25-32	1/40	3	-£30.00	-75
33+	2/16	13	+£12.00	+75

Sex

Sex	Wins/runs	%	£+-	% of stakes
Colt/horse	2/45	4	-£19.00	-42
Filly/mare	1/23	4	-£16.00	-70
Gelding	2/103	2	-£59.00	-57

Winners

	Winner	Age	Weight	OR	SP	Sex	Draw
2002	Beauchamp Pilot	4	9-05	99	9-1	G	26
2001	I Cried For You	6	8-06	88	33-1	G	11
2000	Katy Nowaitee	4	8-08	92	6-1	M	34
1999	She's Our Mare	6	7-12	78	11-1	M	14
1998	Lear Spear	3	7-13	90	20-1	C	33
1997	Pasternak	4	9-01	91	4-1	H	17
1996	Clifton Fox	4	8-02	85	14-1	G	17
1995	Cap Juluca	3	9-10	107	11-1	G	26
1994	Halling	3	8-08	93	8-1	C	24
1993	Penny Drops	4	7-13	84	7-1	M	18

Sponsored by Stan James

Steward's Cup
Goodwood, August 2, 6f

Age
Age	Wins/runs	%	£+-	% of stakes
3	0/22	0	-£22.00	-100
4	2/45	4	-£17.00	-38
5	2/34	6	+£15.00	+44
6	1/23	4	-£15.50	-67
7	0/15	0	-£15.00	-100
8+	0/8	0	-£8.00	-100

Official Ratings
OR	Wins/runs	%	£+-	% of stakes
Under 80	0/6	0	-£6.00	-100
80-84	1/21	5	-£6.00	-29
85-89	0/34	0	-£34.00	-100
90-94	2/35	6	-£14.50	-41
95-99	2/25	8	+£24.00	+96
100-104	0/12	0	-£12.00	-100
105+	0/14	0	-£14.00	-100

Draw
Draw	Wins/runs	%	£+-	% of stakes
0-8	1/40	3	-£27.00	-68
9-16	0/39	0	-£39.00	-100
17-24	1/39	3	-£5.00	-13
25+	3/29	10	+£8.50	+29

Starting Prices
SP	Wins/runs	%	£+-	% of stakes
Under 3-1	0			
3-1 to 11-2	0/4	0	-£4.00	-100
6-1 to 8-1	1/8	13	-£0.50	-6
9-1 to 11-1	0/5	0	-£5.00	-100
12-1 to 14-1	3/20	15	+£23.00	+115
16-1 to 20-1	0/19	0	-£19.00	-100
22-1 to 28-1	0/23	0	-£23.00	-100
33-1 to 40-1	1/42	2	-£8.00	-19
50-1+	0/26	0	-£26.00	-100

Weight
Weight	Wins/runs	%	£+-	% of stakes
Under 8-00	0/27	0	-£27.00	-100
8-00 to 8-06	2/51	4	-£23.00	-45
8-07 to 8-13	2/37	5	-£14.50	-39
9-00 to 9-05	1/17	6	+£17.00	+100
9-06+	0/15	0	-£15.00	-100

Sex
Sex	Wins/runs	%	£+-	% of stakes
Colt/horse	2/23	9	+£5.00	+22
Filly/mare	0/13	0	-£13.00	-100
Gelding	3/111	3	-£54.50	-49

Year	Winner	Age	Weight	OR	SP	Sex	Draw
2002	Bond Boy	5	8-02	83	14-1	G	29
2001	Guinea Hunter	5	9-00	98	33-1	G	19
2000	Tayseer	6	8-11	93	13-2	G	28
1999	Harmonic Way	4	8-06	92	12-1	H	8
1998	Superior Premium	4	8-12	99	14-1	H	28
1997	Danetime	3	8-10	100	5-1	C	5
1996	Coastal Bluff	4	8-05	91	10-1	G	29
1995	Shikari's Son	8	8-13	92	40-1	G	30
1994	For The Present	4	8-03	81	16-1	G	16
1993	King's Signet	4	9-10	98	16-1	H	21

Sponsored by Stan James

John Smith's Cup
York, July 12, 1m2f

Age

Age	Wins/runs	%	£+-	% of stakes
3	3/19	16	+£12.50	+66
4	1/28	4	-£2.00	-7
5	1/26	4	-£5.00	-19
6	0/12	0	-£12.00	-100
7	0/7	0	-£7.00	-100
8+	0/4	0	-£4.00	-100

Weight

Weight	Wins/runs	%	£+-	% of stakes
Under 8-00	0/17	0	-£17.00	-100
8-00 to 8-06	2/27	7	-£16.50	-61
8-07 to 8-13	2/23	9	+£24.00	+104
9-00 to 9-05	0/16	0	-£16.00	-100
9-06+	1/13	8	+£8.00	+62

OR

OR	Wins/runs	%	£+-	% of stakes
Under 80	0/13	0	-£13.00	-100
80-84	0/13	0	-£13.00	-100
85-89	0/22	0	-£22.00	-100
90-94	2/15	13	+£18.00	+120
95-99	1/17	6	-£13.50	-79
100+	2/16	13	+£26.00	+163

Starting Prices

SP	Wins/runs	%	£+-	% of stakes
Under 3-1	1/4	25	-£0.50	-13
3-1 to 11-2	0/4	0	-£4.00	-100
6-1 to 8-1	1/10	10	-£3.00	-30
9-1 to 11-1	0/6	0	-£6.00	-100
12-1 to 14-1	0/14	0	-£14.00	-100
16-1 to 20-1	2/18	11	+£24.00	+133
22-1 to 28-1	1/12	8	+£14.00	+117
33-1 to 40-1	0/15	0	-£15.00	-100
50-1+	0/13	0	-£13.00	-100

Draw

Draw	Wins/runs	%	£+-	% of stakes
0-7	2/32	6	+£1.00	+3
8-14	3/33	9	+£12.50	+38
15+	0/31	0	-£31.00	-100

Sex

Sex	Wins/runs	%	£+-	% of stakes
Colt/horse	2/23	9	-£12.50	-54
Filly/mare	0/10	0	-£10.00	-100
Gelding	3/63	5	+£5.00	+87

Winners

	Winner	Age	Weight	OR	SP	Sex	Draw
2002	Vintage Premium	5	9-09	101	20-1	G	9
2001	Foreign Affairs	3	8-06	97	5-2	H	8
2000	Sobriety	3	8-08	100	20-1	G	8
1999	Achilles	4	8-11	90	25-1	G	6
1998	Porto Foricos	3	8-03	90	6-1	H	7
1997	Pasternak	4	8-03	85	13-2	H	1
1996	Wilcuma	5	9-02	89	10-1	G	2
1995	Naked Welcome	3	8-04	90	6-1	G	9
1994	Cezanne	5	9-12	105	9-2	G	3
1993	Baron Ferdinand	3	8-09	92	4-1	G	1

Sponsored by Stan James

Cesarewitch — Newmarket, October 18, 2m2f

Age

Age	Wins/runs	%	£+-	% of stakes
3	1/15	7	-£3.00	-20
4	1/55	2	-£40.00	-73
5	0/35	0	-£35.00	-100
6	2/24	8	+£5.00	+21
7	1/21	5	-£8.00	-38
8+	0/10	0	-£10.00	-100

Official Ratings

OR	Wins/runs	%	£+-	% of stakes
Under 75	1/17	6	Level	Level
75-79	0/37	0	-£37.00	-100
80-84	1/37	3	-£25.00	-68
85-89	2/27	7	+£1.00	+4
90-94	0/20	0	-£20.00	-100
95-99	1/13	8	-£1.00	-8
100+	0/9	0	-£9.00	-100

Draw

Draw	Wins/runs	%	£+-	% of stakes
0-8	1/39	3	-£22.00	-56
9-16	0/39	0	-£39.00	-100
17-24	2/39	5	-£15.00	-38
25-32	1/37	3	-£22.00	-59
33+	1/6	17	+£7.00	+117

Starting Prices

SP	Wins/runs	%	£+-	% of stakes
Under 3-1	No runners			
3-1 to 11-2	0/5	0	-£5.00	-100
6-1 to 8-1	0/9	0	-£9.00	-100
9-1 to 11-1	2/7	29	+£17.00	+243
12-1 to 14-1	2/15	13	+£13.00	+87
16-1 to 20-1	1/23	4	-£6.00	-26
22-1 to 28-1	0/14	0	-£14.00	-100
33-1 to 40-1	0/23	0	-£23.00	-100
50-1+	0/64	0	-£64.00	-100

Weight

Weight	Wins/runs	%	£+-	% of stakes
Under 7-07	0/18	0	-£18.00	-100
7-08 to 7-13	1/53	2	-£36.00	-68
8-00 to 8-06	2/41	5	-£16.00	-39
8-07 to 8-13	2/26	8	+£1.00	+4
9-00 to 9-05	0/15	0	-£15.00	-100
9-06+	0/7	0	-£7.00	-100

Sex

Sex	Wins/runs	%	£+-	% of stakes
Colt/horse	0/13	0	-£13.00	-100
Filly/mare	1/25	4	-£12.00	-48
Gelding	4/122	3	-£66.00	-54

Winners

Year	Winner	Age	Weight	OR	SP	Sex	Draw
2002	Miss Fara	7	8-00	85	12-1	M	36
2001	Distant Prospect	4	8-08	88	14-1	G	32
2000	Heros Fatal	6	8-01	84	11-1	G	18
1999	Top Cees	9	8-10	95	7-1	G	17
1998	Spirit Of Love	3	8-08	95	11-1	G	19
1997	Turnpole	6	7-10	74	16-1	G	6
1996	Inchcailloch	7	7-03	70	20-1	G	15
1995	Old Red	5	7-11	66	11-1	G	18
1994	Captain's Guest	4	9-09	92	25-1	G	28
1993	Aahsaylad	7	8-12	81	12-1	H	21

Sponsored by Stan James

Northumberland Plate
Newcastle, June 28, 2m

Age

Age	Wins/runs	%	£+-	% of stakes
3	1/3	33	+£10.00	+333
4	2/44	5	-£25.50	-58
5	0/18	0	-£18.00	-100
6	1/12	8	-£3.00	-25
7	0/9	0	-£9.00	-100
8+	1/6	17	+£2.00	+33

Official Ratings

OR	Wins/runs	%	£+-	% of stakes
Under 80	0/10	0	-£10.00	-100
80-84	0/21	0	-£21.00	-100
85-89	2/18	11	+£0.50	+3
90-94	1/17	6	-£9.00	-53
95-99	1/7	14	+£2.00	+29
100+	1/19	5	-£6.00	-32

Starting Prices

SP	Wins/runs	%	£+-	% of stakes
Under 3-1	0/1	0	-£1.00	-100
3-1 to 11-2	1/9	11	-£3.50	-39
6-1 to 8-1	2/10	20	+£7.00	+70
9-1 to 11-1	0/8	0	-£8.00	-100
12-1 to 14-1	2/11	18	+£15.00	+136
16-1 to 20-1	0/22	0	-£22.00	-100
22-1 to 25-1	0/12	0	-£12.00	-100
33-1 to 40-1	0/12	0	-£12.00	-100
50-1+	0/7	0	-£7.00	-100

Weight

Weight	Wins/runs	%	£+-	% of stakes
Under 8-00	1/31	3	-£18.00	-58
8-00 to 8-06	2/14	14	+£7.00	+50
8-07 to 8-13	1/18	6	-£12.50	-69
9-00 to 9-05	1/18	6	-£9.00	-50
9-06+	0/11	0	-£11.00	-100

Draw

Draw	Wins/runs	%	£+-	% of stakes
0-7	3/33	9	-£6.50	-20
8-14	1/34	3	-£25.00	-74
15+	1/25	4	-£12.00	-48

Sex

Sex	Wins/runs	%	£+-	% of stakes
Colt/horse	0/14	0	-£14.00	-100
Filly/mare	0/8	0	-£8.00	-100
Gelding	5/70	7	-£21.50	-31

	Winner	Age	Weight	OR	SP	Sex	Draw
2002	Bangalore	6	9-05	99	8-1	G	9
2001	Archduke Ferdinand	3	8-04	100	12-1	G	17
2000	Bay Of Islands	8	8-04	90	7-1	G	4
1999	Far Cry	4	8-10	89	9-2	G	6
1998	Cyrian	4	7-13	85	12-1	G	2
1997	Windsor Castle	3	8-10	104	10-1	H	20
1996	Celeric	4	9-04	96	2-1	G	7
1995	Bold Gait	4	9-10	105	12-1	G	5
1994	Quick Ransom	6	8-08	95	25-1	G	4
1993	Highflying	7	7-11	73	7-1	G	20

Sponsored by Stan James

Tote International
Ascot, July 26, 7f

Age

Age	Wins/runs	%	£+-	% of stakes
3	0/28	0	-£28.00	-100
4	3/44	7	-£6.00	-14
5	1/31	3	-£16.00	-52
6	1/16	6	-£6.00	-38
7	0/9	0	-£9.00	-100
8+	0/4	0	-£4.00	-100

Weight

Weight	Wins/runs	%	£+-	% of stakes
Under 8-00	0/50	0	-£50.00	-100
8-00 to 8-06	3/40	8	+£2.00	5
8-07 to 8-13	1/25	4	-£14.00	-56
9-00 to 9-05	0/11	0	-£11.00	-100
9-06+	1/6	17	+£4.00	+67

Official Ratings

OR	Wins/runs	%	£+-	% of stakes
Under 95	2/49	4	-£22.00	-45
95-99	1/28	4	-£13.00	-46
100-104	1/29	3	-£18.00	-62
105-109	0/16	0	-£16.00	-100
110+	1/10	10	Level	Level

Starting Prices

SP	Wins/runs	%	£+-	% of stakes
Under 3-1	No runners			
3-1 to 11-2	0/3	0	-£3.00	-100
6-1 to 8-1	0/8	0	-£8.00	-100
9-1 to 11-1	3/16	19	+£17.00	+106
12-1 to 14-1	2/18	11	+£12.00	+67
16-1 to 20-1	0/19	0	-£19.00	-100
22-1 to 28-1	0/13	0	-£13.00	-100
33-1 to 40-1	0/31	0	-£31.00	-100
50-1+	0/24	0	-£24.00	-100

Draw

Draw	Wins/runs	%	£+-	% of stakes
0-8	1/40	3	-£29.00	-73
9-16	3/40	8	+£2.00	5
17-24	0/38	0	-£38.00	-100
25+	1/14	7	-£4.00	-29

Sex

Sex	Wins/runs	%	£+-	% of stakes
Colt/horse	3/62	5	-£29.00	-47
Filly/mare	0/9	0	-£9.00	-100
Gelding	2/61	3	-£31.00	-51

	Winner	Age	Weight	OR	SP	Sex	Draw
2002	Crystal Castle	4	8-00	94	14-1	G	13
2001	Atavus	4	8-01	93	11-1	H	9
2000	Tillerman	4	8-10	103	10-1	H	2
1999	Russian Revival	6	9-07	114	9-1	H	25
1998	Jo Mell	5	8-04	98	14-1	G	10

This race was inaugurated in 1998

Why is Dave Nevison feeling a bit gloomy? See page 127

Sponsored by Stan James

Wokingham
Royal Ascot, June 20, 6f

Age

Age	Wins/runs	%	£+-	% of stakes
3	0/9	0	-£9.00	-100
4	1/48	2	-£33.00	-69
5	3/37	8	+£5.00	+14
6	0/22	0	-£22.00	-100
7	1/19	5	-£2.00	-11
8+	0/11	0	-£11.00	-100

Weight

Weight	Wins/runs	%	£+-	% of stakes
Under 8-07	0/17	0	-£17.00	-100
8-07 to 8-13	2/67	3	-£31.00	-46
9-00 to 9-05	1/38	3	-£30.00	-79
9-06+	2/24	8	+£6.00	+25

Official Ratings

OR	Wins/runs	%	£+-	% of stakes
Under 90	2/40	5	-£4.00	-10
90-94	0/43	0	-£43.00	-100
95-99	1/38	3	-£30.00	-79
100-104	2/16	13	+£14.00	+88
105+	0/9	0	-£9.00	-100

Starting Prices

SP	Wins/runs	%	£+-	% of stakes
Under 3-1	No runners			
3-1 to 11-2	0/2	0	-£2.00	-100
6-1 to 8-1	1/5	20	+£3.00	+60
9-1 to 11-1	0/11	0	-£11.00	-100
12-1 to 14-1	2/14	14	+£14.00	+100
16-1 to 20-1	2/26	8	+£12.00	+46
22-1 to 28-1	0/21	0	-£21.00	-100
33-1 to 40-1	0/48	0	-£48.00	-100
50-1+	0/19	0	-£19.00	-100

Draw

Draw	Wins/runs	%	£+-	% of stakes
0-8	2/39	5	-£16.00	-41
9-16	0/38	0	-£38.00	-100
17-24	2/39	5	-£1.00	-3
25+	1/30	3	-£17.00	-57

Sex

Sex	Wins/runs	%	£+-	% of stakes
Colt/horse	1/25	4	-£12.00	-48
Filly/mare	1/16	6	-£8.00	-50
Gelding	3/105	3	-£52.00	-50

Year	Winner	Age	Weight	OR	SP	Sex	Draw
2002	Capricho	5	8-11	87	20-1	G	21
2001	Nice One Clare	5	9-03	98	7-1	M	4
2000	Harmonic Way	5	9-06	102	12-1	H	28
1999	Deep Space	4	8-07	88	14-1	G	3
1998	Selhurstpark Flyer	7	9-07	100	16-1	G	20
1997	Selhurstpark Flyer	6	8-09	94	25-1	G	5
1996	Emerging Market	4	8-13	95	33-1	G	7
1995	Astrac	4	8-07	89	14-1	G	16
1994	Venture Capitalist	5	8-12	91	20-1	G	30
1993	Nagida	4	8-07	84	11-1	M	4

Sponsored by Stan James

Royal Hunt Cup — Royal Ascot, June 18, 1m

Age

Age	Wins/runs	%	£+-	% of stakes
4	1/77	1	-£56.00	-73
5	4/43	9	+£13.50	31
6	0/23	0	-£23.00	-100
7	0/9	0	-£9.00	-100
8+	0/4	0	-£4.00	-100

Weight

Weight	Wins/runs	%	£+-	% of stakes
Under 8-00	1/18	6	+£3.00	+17
8-00 to 8-06	1/55	2	-£40.00	-73
8-07 to 8-13	3/46	7	-£4.50	-10
9-00 to 9-05	0/19	0	-£19.00	-100
9-06+	0/18	0	-£18.00	-100

Official Ratings

OR	Wins/runs	%	£+-	% of stakes
Under 85	1/16	6	+£5.00	+31
85-89	0/39	0	-£39.00	-100
90-94	2/39	5	+£2.00	+5
95-99	2/26	8	-£10.50	-40
100-104	0/21	0	-£21.00	-100
105+	0/15	0	-£15.00	-100

Starting Prices

SP	Wins/runs	%	£+-	% of stakes
Under 3-1	No runners			
3-1 to 11-2	1/3	33	+£3.50	+117
6-1 to 8-1	1/6	17	+£3.00	+50
9-1 to 11-1	0/7	0	-£7.00	-100
12-1 to 14-1	1/15	7	Level	Level
16-1 to 20-1	1/27	4	-£6.00	-22
22-1 to 28-1	1/28	4	-£2.00	-7
33-1 to 40-1	0/43	0	-£43.00	-100
50-1+	0/27	0	-£27.00	-100

Draw

Draw	Wins/runs	%	£+-	% of stakes
0-8	1/39	3	-£18.00	-46
9-16	1/38	3	-£12.00	-32
17-24	0/39	0	-£39.00	-100
25+	3/40	8	-£9.50	-24

Sex

Sex	Wins/runs	%	£+-	% of stakes
Colt/horse	2/64	3	-£28.00	-44
Filly/mare	0/9	0	-£9.00	-100
Gelding	3/83	4	-£41.50	-50

Winners

Year	Winner	Age	Weight	OR	SP	Sex	Draw
2002	Norton	5	8-09	91	25-1	G	10
2001	Surprise Encounter	5	8-09	95	8-1	G	29
2000	Caribbean Monarch	5	8-10	96	11-2	G	28
1999	Showboat	5	8-06	92	14-1	H	30
1998	Refuse To Lose	4	7-11	83	20-1	H	6
1997	Red Robbo	4	8-06	88	16-1	H	17
1996	Yeast	4	8-06	87	8-1	G	3
1995	Realities	5	9-00	99	11-1	H	30
1994	Face North	6	8-03	83	25-1	G	30
1993	Imperial Ballet	4	8-12	98	20-1	H	19

Sponsored by Stan James

RACING & FOOTBALL

Outlook HOTLINE

PRICK UP YOUR EARS

WE'VE GOT WINNERS WORTH BRAYING ABOUT!

0906 911 0231

on line 9pm evening before racing Calls cost £1/min . Outlook Press, Compton. RG20 7NL

Sponsored by Stan James

Hamilton
Musselburgh
Ayr
Newcastle
Carlisle
Redcar
Catterick
Thirsk
York
Ripon
Beverley
Pontefract
Doncaster
Haydock
Chester
Southwell
Nottingham
Wolverhampton
Yarmouth
Leicester
Warwick
Newmarket
Chepstow
Windsor
Kempton
Bath
Newbury
Ascot
Epsom
Sandown
Lingfield
Goodwood
Folkestone
Salisbury
Brighton

Track Facts

FOR THE first time, we bring you three-dimensional maps of all Britain's Flat tracks, allowing you to see at a glance the extent of any undulations likely to affect the race you're weighing up. The maps come to you courtesy of the Racing Post's website (www.racingpost.co.uk).

Graham Wheldon, whose Sprintline column is a popular feature of RFO during the Flat season, has chipped in with his views on the draw at every course. As his analysis has repeatedly shown, most tracks feature a bias of some kind, so check whether your fancy's running on the right side before you bet.

We've listed the top dozen trainers and jockeys at each course, ranked by strike-rate, with a breakdown of their relevant statistics from 1st January 1998 to 31st December 2002. The record of favourites is here as well – Thirsk (35%) has seen the best strike-rate for jollies, while Ascot (25%) has produced the worst. Note that market leaders generated a profit (to level stakes of £1) at only two of the 36 tracks, underlining a basic fact of racing; as a general rule, favourites offer little in the way of value.

Finally, we've included addresses, phone numbers, directions and fixture lists for each track, together with Ken Hussey's standard times for all you clock-watchers.

ASCOT	188	MUSSELBURGH	208
AYR	189	NEWBURY	209
BATH	190	NEWCASTLE	210
BEVERLEY	191	NEWMARKET (ROWLEY)	211
BRIGHTON	192	NEWMARKET (JULY)	212
CARLISLE	193	NOTTINGHAM	213
CATTERICK	194	PONTEFRACT	214
CHEPSTOW	195	REDCAR	215
CHESTER	196	RIPON	216
DONCASTER	197	SALISBURY	217
EPSOM	198	SANDOWN	218
FOLKESTONE	199	SOUTHWELL	219
GOODWOOD	200	THIRSK	220
HAMILTON	201	WARWICK	221
HAYDOCK	202	WINDSOR	222
KEMPTON	204	WOLVERHAMPTON	223
LEICESTER	205	YARMOUTH	224
LINGFIELD (TURF)	206	YORK	225
LINGFIELD (SAND)	207		

Sponsored by Stan James

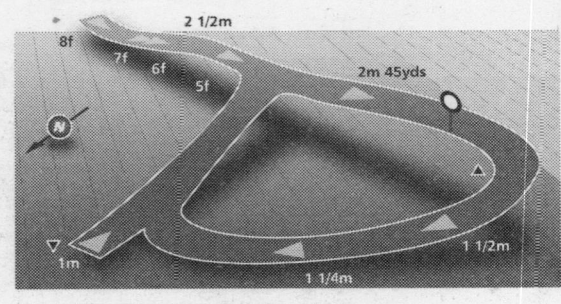

ASCOT

Ascot, Berks, SL5 7JN.
Tel. 01344 22211

How to get there – Road: M4 Jct 6, M3 Jct 6, M25 Jct 13. Rail: Ascot from London Waterloo
Features: Stiff, galloping RH 1m6f circuit
2003 Flat fixtures: Mar 29, Apr 30, Jun 17, 18, 19, 20, 21, Jul 11, 12, 25, 26, 27, Aug 9, 27, Sep 26, 27, 28, Oct 11.
Draw: Before 2000, low numbers were thought to have an edge on the straight course in big fields, but no longer. At the 2001 Royal Meeting, high numbers had an edge, while last season there wasn't much in it. The one factor that does lead to one flank dominating is heavy ground, in which case the nearer the far rail (high) the better. High numbers also do best in the 2m4f Ascot Stakes, with runners drawn low often forced to use early energy to gain a position.

Ken Hussey's standard times

5f	59.4	1m2f	2min3.4
6f	1min13	1m4f	2min27.3
6f110yds	1min19.5	2m45yds	3min25.3
7f	1min26	2m4f	4min18
1m (str)	1min38.7	2m6f34yds	4min48
1m (rnd)	1min39.4		

Favourites

2-y-o	36%	+£2.27
3-y-o+	22%	-£64.50
Overall	25%	-£62.25

Trainers	Wins-Runs	%	2yo	3yo+	£1 level stks
J E Hammond	4-11	36.4	0-0	4-11	+26.33
D Loder	7-20	35.0	5-13	2-7	+4.68
J Oxx	3-12	25.0	0-1	3-11	+35.00
W Brisbourne	3-13	23.1	0-1	3-12	+20.50
W Musson	4-18	22.2	0-0	4-18	+22.50
M Tregoning	8-36	22.2	3-10	5-26	+18.11
M Johnston	37-182	20.3	10-33	27-149	+132.62
S Bin Suroor	18-100	18.0	1-2	17-98	+22.03
A Stewart	6-34	17.6	0-1	6-33	-11.00
J Eustace	4-23	17.4	2-3	2-20	+24.00
A P O'Brien	17-101	16.8	9-39	8-62	+4.47
Sir M Stoute	26-158	16.5	3-26	23-132	+1.25

Jockeys	Wins-Rides	%	£1 level stks	Best Trainer	W-R
K Dalgleish	7-25	28	+53.50	M Johnston	5-17
J Murtagh	24-106	23	+118.16	Sir M Stoute	7-22
P Fitzsimons	3-15	20	+22.00	J J Quinn	1-1
L Dettori	42-228	18	+19.13	S Bin Suroor	13-57
J Tate	4-26	15	+21.00	J Eustace	4-18
K Darley	25-168	15	+33.60	M Johnston	10-32
K Fallon	37-259	14	-37.55	Sir M Stoute	10-45
M Kinane	27-200	14	-40.33	A P O'Brien	13-74
D O'Neill	15-138	11	+29.63	R Hannon	14-81
R Hills	21-193	11	-62.66	E Dunlop	4-17
T Quinn	23-211	11	-8.25	M Channon	3-17
S Carson	3-28	11	+6.00	E Wheeler	2-12

Sponsored by Stan James

AYR

Whitletts Road Ayr KA8 0JE
Tel: 01292 264179

How to get there – Road: south from Glasgow on A77 or A75, A70, A76. Rail: Ayr, bus service from station on big race days

Features: LH 1m4f oval, easy turns, generally flat, suits galloping types

2003 Flat fixtures: May 29, 30, Jun 19, 20, 21, Jul 14, 21, 22, Aug 1, 29, Sep 18, 19, 20, Oct 13, 14.

Draw: Between 1995 and 1997 and particularly in the last two of those years, a high draw proved crucial in both the Gold and Silver Cups on fast ground, but since then the bias has become less accentuated. Prior to 1995, runners drawn between 5 and 15 had the best of it on soft ground, and that's probably about true again now. On the round course, low numbers enjoy a decent advantage when the fields are big.

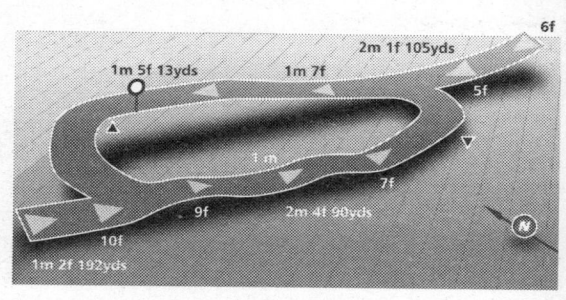

Ken Hussey's standard times

5f	57.7	1m2f	2min4.4
6f	1min9.7	1m2f192yds	2min14.3
7f	1min25	1m5f13yds	2min45.4
7f50yds	1min28	1m7f	3min13.2
1m	1min37.7	2m1f105yds	3min46
1m1f20yds	1min50	2m4f90yds	4min25

Favourites

2-y-o	34.1%	-£21.06
3-y-o+	29.2%	-£27.88
Overall	30.6%	-£48.94

Trainers	Wins-Runs	%	2yo	3yo+	£1 level stks
W Jarvis	4-9	44.4	1-2	3-7	+14.00
M Tregoning	3-7	42.9	2-5	1-2	-0.87
G Wragg	3-9	33.3	0-0	3-9	+3.80
W Haggas	9-27	33.3	0-8	9-19	+11.58
Miss J Camacho	3-10	30.0	0-0	3-10	+5.33
L Cumani	3-10	30.0	0-2	3-8	+6.37
C Wall	3-10	30.0	1-4	2-6	+0.95
B McMahon	4-14	28.6	1-1	3-13	+31.00
M Bell	10-36	27.8	5-12	5-24	+3.53
B Hills	26-95	27.4	15-37	11-58	+3.00
W Storey	5-19	26.3	0-1	5-18	+13.75
M Brittain	6-24	25.0	2-4	4-20	+41.00

Jockeys	Wins-Rides	%	£1 level stks	Best Trainer	W-R
L Dettori	8-17	47.1	+6.84	J Gosden	3-7
R Hughes	10-26	38.5	+34.61	B Hills	7-10
K Fallon	15-54	27.8	+36.18	R Fahey	2-2
R Hills	3-11	27.3	-3.27	M Tregoning	2-3
S Sanders	15-57	26.3	+60.16	M Tompkins	2-7
P Goode	3-15	20.0	+4.50	P Haslam	2-4
D Sweeney	4-20	20.0	+11.00	D Ivory	1-1
M Hills	5-30	16.7	-4.86	B Hills	4-22
J Egan	9-55	16.4	+24.13	J Goldie	2-10
T E Durcan	10-64	15.6	-13.84	M Tompkins	6-31
D Holland	19-125	15.2	-22.88	M Johnston	5-43
K Darley	29-191	15.2	-19.55	M Johnston	8-26

Sponsored by Stan James

BATH

Lansdown, Bath,
Gloucestershire BA1 9BU.
Tel 01295 688 030

How to get there – Road: M4, Jctn 18, then A46 south.
Rail: Bath Spa, special bus service to course on race-days
Features: LH oval, uphill straight of 4f.
2003 Flat fixtures: Mar 31, Apr 29, May 6, 19, 30, Jun 4, 14, 25, Jul 7, 13, 24, Aug 5, 17, 22, Sep 8, 15, 29, Oct 12.
Draw: It used to thought that low numbers were favoured in races of up to 1m, as the course turns left most of the way. However, results in recent times suggest that high numbers often do best in big-field sprints, the logic being that those drawn low tend to go too fast early in order to hold a position, and duck away when the rail kinks left about a furlong out, allowing high numbers to fly past.

Ken Hussey's standard times

5f11yds	1min0.5	1m3f144yds	2min26
5f161yds	1min9	1m5f22yds	2min47.3
1m5yds	1min38	2m1f34yds	3min44
1m2f46yds	2min6.2		

Favourites

2-y-o	33.1%	-£25.01
3-y-o+	31.7%	-£3.34
Overall	32.0%	-£28.35

Trainers	Wins-Runs	%	2yo	3yo+	£1 level stks
G Bravery	4-11	36.4	3-3	1-8	+26.13
T Mills	4-14	28.6	0-2	4-12	+7.08
L Cumani	8-28	28.6	0-4	8-24	-6.63
H Cecil	4-15	26.7	0-0	4-15	-6.05
Sir M Stoute	9-37	24.3	0-0	9-37	-0.77
Sir M Prescott	3-13	23.1	0-5	3-8	-1.00
Mrs A Perrett	13-59	22.0	4-13	9-46	+23.38
G A Butler	9-42	21.4	2-17	7-25	-9.08
W Haggas	3-15	20.0	0-2	3-13	-2.08
P Makin	7-35	20.0	2-11	5-24	+34.50
P Cole	9-45	20.0	2-11	7-34	-10.07
M Pipe	6-31	19.4	0-2	6-29	-11.01

Jockeys	Wins-Rides	%	£1 level stks	Best Trainer	W-R
K Fallon	23-85	27.1	-5.69	G A Butler	4-6
J Fanning	3-12	25.0	+1.75	M Johnston	2-5
L Dettori	7-30	23.3	-0.75	G A Butler	2-3
D McGaffin	4-20	20.0	+13.50	B Palling	2-11
P Dobbs	7-35	20.0	+33.25	R Hannon	3-15
R Hughes	31-167	18.6	+10.36	R Hannon	10-40
J P Spencer	7-38	18.4	-15.96	Sir M Stoute	2-2
B Doyle	4-23	17.4	+3.66	B Meehan	3-8
R Hills	7-42	16.7	-13.29	B Hills	3-10
Pat Eddery	18-111	16.2	-27.83	Mrs A Perrett	4-9
T Quinn	22-136	16.2	-29.04	M Channon	7-31
M Hills	14-88	15.9	+7.45	B Hills	6-38

Sponsored by Stan James

BEVERLEY

York Road, Beverley, E Yorkshire,
HU17 8QZ. Tel 01482 867 488

How to get there – Road: Course is signposted from the M62.
Rail: Beverley, bus service to course on race-days
Features: RH, uphill finish
2003 Flat fixtures: Apr 16, 24, May 10, 20, Jun 4, 11, 19, 24, Jul 4, 5, 15, 21, 29, Aug 13, 14, 23, 24, Sep 17, 23
Draw: A high draw is essential on good or faster over the round course up to 1m100yds. In sprints, it's very hard for those drawn low to get over to the favoured rail. When it's soft, there's a strip of ground by the stands' rail (low) that is fastest. The course tried moving the stalls to the stands' side over 5f last season, which caused a major bias in favour of those drawn low. This was due to a strip of ground compressed by vehicles. They plan to continue the trial, after doing work to even out the surface.

Ken Hussey's standard times

5f	1min0.5	1m3f216yds	2min30.6
7f100yds	1min29.5	1m4f16yds	2min32
1m100yds	1min42.4	2m35yds	3min29.5
1m1f207yds	2min0	2m3f100yds	4min16.7

Favourites

2-y-o	43.0%	-£3.57
3-y-o+	29.6%	-£47.20
Overall	33.0%	-£50.77

Trainers	Wins-Runs	%	2yo	3yo+	£1 level stks
L Cumani	8-21	38.1	2-5	6-16	+7.19
Sir M Prescott	13-38	34.2	8-23	5-15	+5.48
W Jarvis	4-12	33.3	1-4	3-8	+37.25
J Dunlop	14-47	29.8	2-15	12-32	+2.69
W Haggas	7-25	28.0	3-7	4-18	-3.21
M Tregoning	5-18	27.8	1-5	4-13	-6.55
H Cecil	4-15	26.7	2-3	2-12	-7.55
P Hiatt	3-12	25.0	0-0	3-12	+15.33
E Dunlop	10-40	25.0	4-17	6-23	-1.78
M Jarvis	5-21	23.8	2-5	3-16	-1.11
N Callaghan	5-22	22.7	3-7	2-15	-1.90
Sir M Stoute	7-32	21.9	1-12	6-20	-7.81

Jockeys	Wins-Rides	%	£1 level stks	Best Trainer	W-R
L Dettori	5-15	33.3	-0.11	L Cumani	2-3
M Hills	6-18	33.3	+9.54	B Hills	3-11
Pat Eddery	7-22	31.8	+17.70	J Dunlop	2-4
K Fallon	21-75	28.0	-12.47	Sir M Stoute	2-3
O Urbina	3-12	25.0	+2.75	J Fanshawe	2-5
J P Spencer	7-32	21.9	-4.48	L Cumani	2-6
T Quinn	5-23	21.7	+9.88	H Cecil	2-4
M Henry	4-19	21.1	+11.50	C Brittain	2-3
R Ffrench	6-29	20.7	+2.75	R Fahey	2-2
J Fortune	9-46	19.6	+9.54	Mrs J Ramsden	4-6
D O'Donohoe	3-17	17.6	-1.50	J Fanshawe	1-1
D Holland	12-69	17.4	+3.23	M Johnston	6-19

Sponsored by Stan James

BRIGHTON

Freshfield Road, Brighton,
E Sussex BN2 2XZ.
Tel 01273 603 580

How to get there – Road: Signposted from A23 London Road and A27.
Rail: Brighton, bus to course on race-days
Features: LH, sharp and undulating, mainly downhill for last 7f, suitable for handy, speedy types
2003 Flat fixtures: Apr 10, May 3, 14, 23, 30, Jun 12, 16, 24, Jul 1, 6, 15, 21, Aug 6, 7, 12, 18, 27, Sep 2, Oct 2, 17, 23, 31
Draw: When the ground is soft or heavy, runners invariably tack across to the stands' rail in the straight, under which conditions high numbers enjoy a slight edge, but results are not conclusive enough to be bullish about them. On fast ground, low-drawn prominent-racers are best in sprints.

Ken Hussey's standard times

5f59yds	59.5	7f214yds	1min32
5f213yds	1min7.5	1m1f209yds	1min57.5
6f209yds	1min19.6	1m3f196yds	2min26

Favourites

2-y-o	41.9%	+£9.42
3-y-o+	27.9%	-£86.45
Overall	30.9%	-£77.04

Trainers	Wins-Runs	%	2yo	3yo+	£1 level stks
P Cundell	3-4	75.0	2-2	1-2	+10.73
H Cecil	6-14	42.9	1-1	5-13	+2.43
M Wigham	5-12	41.7	0-0	5-12	+23.25
B Curley	3-8	37.5	0-0	3-8	+8.25
J Noseda	10-29	34.5	4-7	6-22	-1.65
Sir M Stoute	5-18	27.8	3-4	2-14	-4.17
Sir M Prescott	13-47	27.7	5-24	8-23	-6.39
R Charlton	3-11	27.3	0-1	3-10	+13.00
A Stewart	5-21	23.8	1-5	4-16	+0.90
L Cottrell	4-17	23.5	0-0	4-17	+35.00
L Cumani	9-39	23.1	1-11	8-28	-1.81
J Hills	7-31	22.6	2-7	5-24	+12.77

Jockeys	Wins-Rides	%	£1 level stks	Best Trainer	W-R
R FitzPatrick	5-8	62.5	+14.83	R Wilman	4-4
M Hills	9-23	39.1	+2.77	B Hills	5-9
Claire Stretton	4-15	26.7	+54.00	R Spicer	2-2
R Hills	6-24	25.0	-1.12	E Dunlop	2-5
T Quinn	47-207	22.7	-10.49	M Channon	10-43
Hayley Turner	3-14	21.4	+27.50	K Bell	1-1
E Ahern	6-30	20.0	+60.50	G A Butler	2-8
S Sanders	43-226	19.0	+55.70	Sir M Prescott	8-21
R Smith	6-32	18.8	+6.00	R Hannon	4-16
D O'Donohoe	4-22	18.2	+12.50	S Dow	1-1
J P Spencer	12-71	16.9	+6.53	L Cumani	3-19
L Dettori	3-18	16.7	+5.00	A Newcombe	1-1

Sponsored by Stan James

CARLISLE

Blackwell, Carlisle, Cumbria, CA2 4TS. Tel: 01228 22973.

How to get there – Road: M6 Jctn 42, follow signs on Dalston Road.
Rail: Carlisle, 66 bus to course on race-days
Features: RH, undulating, uphill finish
2003 Flat fixtures: May 9, Jun 2, 15, 25, 26, Jul 18, 30, Aug 4, 20, Sep 4.
Draw: It has been considered that high numbers do best in sprints. That was true in the early part of last season, apparently because those nearest the inside rail were on virgin ground uncovered by the removal of hurdle wings, while those wider were on the surface used in hurdle races. This advantage disappeared later in the campaign and a watching brief is advised this time. When it's soft, low numbers, who race widest, enjoy a definite advantage and soft ground was often in evidence during the wet summer last year.

Ken Hussey's standard times

5f	59.6	1m1f61yds	1min55
5f193yds	1min11.8	1m3f206yds	2min28.7
6f192yds	1min24.7	1m6f32yds	2min59.2
7f200yds	1min37.6	2m1f52yds	3min42

Favourites

2-y-o	37.8%	-£6.86
3-y-o+	27.6%	-£22.20
Overall	29.2%	-£29.06

Trainers	Wins-Runs	%	2yo	3yo+	£1 level stks
R Wilman	3-4	75.0	0-0	3-4	+42.00
R Guest	3-8	37.5	0-0	3-8	-1.06
K Burke	6-22	27.3	2-2	4-20	+4.36
Sir M Prescott	5-20	25.0	1-5	4-15	-4.68
E Weymes	3-14	21.4	1-3	2-11	+1.50
J M Bradley	4-24	16.7	0-0	4-24	+14.50
Mrs J Ramsden	3-19	15.8	2-3	1-16	-10.63
Mrs M Reveley	5-34	14.7	0-1	5-33	-4.40
M Tompkins	6-41	14.6	1-8	5-33	+4.75
J J Quinn	3-21	14.3	1-3	2-18	-1.00
M Johnston	7-54	13.0	1-13	6-41	-5.00
E Alston	8-64	12.5	0-6	8-58	+8.00

Jockeys	Wins-Rides	%	£1 level stks	Best Trainer	W-R
N Callan	3-11	27.3	-0.89	K Burke	3-5
J Fortune	7-32	21.9	+4.23	T Easterby	2-5
K Fallon	3-14	21.4	+6.25	Jonjo O'Neill	1-1
K Darley	18-94	19.1	-21.39	G M Moore	2-2
P Robinson	4-22	18.2	-5.92	M Jarvis	2-9
A Nicholls	5-28	17.9	+12.25	M Tompkins	3-8
K Dalgleish	3-19	15.8	+3.37	J J Quinn	1-1
F Norton	5-33	15.2	+10.00	Mrs G Rees	2-2
P Goode	3-20	15.0	+7.00	F Watson	1-3
W Supple	10-69	14.5	+21.50	E Alston	5-30
D Holland	3-21	14.3	-9.25	J Noseda	1-1
J Carroll	16-129	12.4	-33.56	J Berry	4-21

Sponsored by Stan James

CATTERICK

Catterick Bridge, Richmond,
N Yorkshire, DL10 7PE.
Tel: 01748 811478

How to get there – Road: A1, exit 5m south of Scotch Corner.
Rail: Darlington or Northallerton and bus.
Features: LH, undulating, tight turns, lends itself to course specialists
2003 Flat fixtures: Mar 26, Apr 23, May 30, 31, Jun 6, Jul 2, 9, 16, 23, Aug 5, 15, 27, Sep 9, 20, Oct 7, 18, Nov 4
Draw: When it's testing, the stands' rail (high) is the place to be in 5f races. When it's good or firmer, horses drawn on the far side (low) usually hold the edge. Low numbers are marginally preferred in races run on the round course on faster surfaces, particularly over 5f212yds as runners have to take a left-hand bend into the straight. When it's soft, however, horses switched to race on the stands' rail are benefited.

Ken Hussey's standard times

5f	57.5	1m3f214yds	2min31
5f212yds	1min10.5	1m5f175yds	2min55.3
7f	1min23.2	1m7f177yds	3min21.2

Favourites

2-y-o	31.5%	-£32.62
3-y-o+	31.4%	-£30.93
Overall	31.4%	-£63.55

Trainers	Wins-Runs	%	2yo	3yo+	£1 level stks
W Jarvis	4-7	57.1	2-2	2-5	+5.23
Sir M Stoute	6-14	42.9	2-4	4-10	+3.92
P Cole	10-24	41.7	7-17	3-7	+11.14
E Dunlop	5-13	38.5	3-5	2-8	+0.35
J Pearce	4-14	28.6	0-2	4-12	+10.50
S C Williams	4-16	25.0	2-4	2-12	+9.50
I A Wood	4-17	23.5	2-4	2-13	+45.00
A Turnell	4-17	23.5	0-2	4-15	+3.25
W Haggas	4-18	22.2	2-6	2-12	-3.53
B Hills	8-40	20.0	2-11	6-29	-0.63
S Kettlewell	5-26	19.2	1-7	4-19	+13.13
B Smart	3-16	18.8	2-9	1-7	-6.45

Jockeys	Wins-Rides	%	£1 level stks	Best Trainer	W-R
J F McDonald	3-7	42.9	+14.75	I A Wood	2-4
D McGaffin	3-9	33.3	+12.00	J Hetherton	2-3
I Mongan	3-10	30.0	+1.00	M Jarvis	1-1
D Holland	13-46	28.3	-0.19	M Johnston	5-10
J Fortune	11-40	27.5	+32.04	S Kettlewell	3-3
K Fallon	9-35	25.7	+12.82	D Nicholls	2-5
G Carter	5-21	23.8	+7.00	A Berry	2-7
S Sanders	8-37	21.6	-5.91	Sir M Prescott	4-14
Alex Greaves	9-43	20.9	+9.58	D Nicholls	9-42
F Lynch	25-134	18.7	+19.85	K Ryan	7-30
K Darley	26-165	15.8	-46.80	J Berry	4-11
T Hamilton	3-21	14.3	-2.50	D Nicholls	3-13

Sponsored by Stan James

Chepstow, Gwent, NP6 5YH.
Tel: 01291 622260.

CHEPSTOW

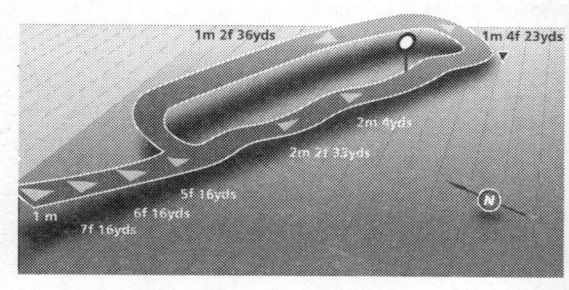

How to get there – Road: M4 Jct 22 on west side of Severn Bridge, A48 north, then A446 Monmouth Rd. Rail: Chepstow, bus to course on race-days

Features: LH, undulating

2003 Flat fixtures: May 26, Jun 5, 13, 23, Jul 5, 11, 25, Aug 7, 14, 25, Sep 11, 22

Draw: High numbers enjoyed a massive advantage in straight-course races (up to 1m14yds) two years ago, but the strip of ground responsible was broken up by machine in the winter of 2001-02 and last season there was little, if anything, in the draw.

Ken Hussey's standard times

5f16yds	57	1m4f23yds	2min31.3
6f16yds	1min8.8	2m49yds	3min28
7f16yds	1min20.5	2m1f40yds	3min41
1m14yds	1min32.6	2m2f	3min52
1m2f36yds	2min4.2		

Favourites

2-y-o	36.6%	-£0.15
3-y-o+	24.5%	-£80.53
Overall	27.4%	-£80.67

Trainers	Wins-Runs	%	2yo	3yo+	£1 level stks
D Loder	3-4	75.0	2-3	1-1	+6.08
A Stewart	3-5	60.0	1-2	2-3	+3.42
E Dunlop	7-19	36.8	3-6	4-13	+8.60
Sir M Stoute	10-28	35.7	4-8	6-20	-5.46
Sir M Prescott	8-26	30.8	2-10	6-16	-3.58
R Charlton	6-23	26.1	1-5	5-18	+11.73
M Tregoning	3-12	25.0	0-7	3-5	+7.60
M Johnston	4-16	25.0	0-1	4-15	-0.12
G A Butler	5-20	25.0	3-6	2-14	+11.29
S C Williams	3-13	23.1	0-1	3-12	+16.00
J King	4-18	22.2	0-0	4-18	+28.13
M Pipe	7-34	20.6	0-3	7-31	+13.50

Jockeys	Wins-Rides	%	£1 level stks	Best Trainer	W-R
P Robinson	3-8	37.5	+6.33	C Brittain	2-4
Pat Eddery	7-20	35.0	+8.82	B Meehan	3-4
G Duffield	7-25	28.0	+1.88	Sir M Prescott	5-12
K Fallon	7-26	26.9	+5.30	Sir M Stoute	2-2
R Hughes	8-37	21.6	-4.61	R Hannon	3-15
S Sanders	18-91	19.8	+23.13	Sir M Prescott	3-13
G Carter	7-37	18.9	-5.03	E Dunlop	3-5
L Newman	7-38	18.4	-8.00	T McGovern	1-1
J P Spencer	7-39	17.9	-1.35	L Cumani	2-10
T McLaughlin	3-18	16.7	0.00	M Saunders	2-3
B Doyle	4-25	16.0	+2.50	B Meehan	3-10
D O'Neill	12-77	15.6	+29.78	R Hannon	6-42

Sponsored by Stan James

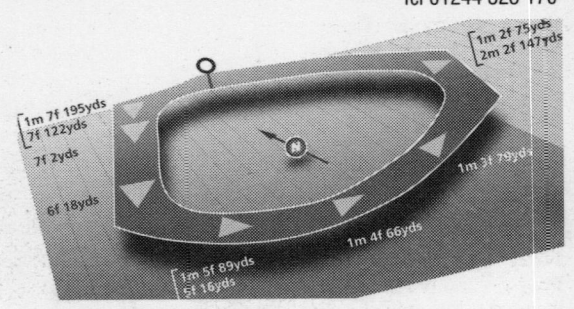

CHESTER

Steam Mill Street, Chester,
CH3 5AN.
Tel 01244 323 170

How to get there – Road: Join Inner Ring Road and A458 Queensferry Road. Rail: Chester General, bus to city centre
Features: LH, flat, almost circular
2003 Flat fixtures: May 6, 7, 8, Jun 4, 28, Jul 11, 12, Aug 3, 28, 29, 30, Sep 24
Draw: Low numbers have the advantage, especially in races at up to 7f122yds, and a slow start from a high draw can be virtually impossible to overcome, given the constantly turning nature of the course. Soft ground seems to accentuate the advantage enjoyed by those drawn low, until it has been raced on a few times, when a higher draw becomes less of a disadvantage as the ground on the inside becomes chewed up.

Ken Hussey's standard times

5f16yds	59.8	1m3f79yds	2min22.7
6f18yds	1min13	1m4f66yds	2min35
7f2yds	1min24.7	1m5f89yds	2min48.6
7f122yds	1min31.2	1m7f195yds	3min22
1m1f70yds	1min55	2m2f147yds	4min1
1m2f75yds	2min8		

Favourites

2-y-o	47.9%	+£15.62
3-y-o+	29.2%	-£28.67
Overall	34.1%	-£13.05

Trainers	Wins-Runs	%	2yo	3yo+	£1 level stks
J Noseda	5-12	41.7	3-7	2-5	+4.92
G Wragg	8-24	33.3	1-1	7-23	-2.74
J Dunlop	13-39	33.3	3-7	10-32	+10.22
W Jarvis	3-10	30.0	1-4	2-6	+4.50
J Goldie	3-11	27.3	0-0	3-11	+6.50
J Gosden	6-22	27.3	1-3	5-19	+11.44
W G M Turner	4-15	26.7	4-9	0-6	+14.63
G A Butler	5-19	26.3	0-2	5-17	+4.75
Sir M Prescott	6-23	26.1	2-10	4-13	-6.75
P Cole	14-56	25.0	3-10	11-46	+10.69
Sir M Stoute	12-51	23.5	2-7	10-44	-7.47
M W Easterby	10-46	21.7	0-3	10-43	+15.75

Jockeys	Wins-Rides	%	£1 level stks	Best Trainer	W-R
R Hills	10-32	31.3	+3.03	J Dunlop	4-7
P Dobbs	3-12	25.0	+2.50	R Hannon	2-4
K Fallon	28-118	23.7	+14.53	Sir M Stoute	6-23
D Holland	24-107	22.4	-3.91	B Hills	4-9
S Sanders	8-37	21.6	+1.25	Sir M Prescott	5-7
J Fanning	5-26	19.2	+22.00	C Fairhurst	1-1
G Bardwell	3-16	18.8	+16.50	Mrs A Perrett	1-1
R Hughes	14-76	18.4	-1.58	R Hannon	6-24
M Hills	13-72	18.1	+10.05	B Hills	11-58
A Culhane	6-36	16.7	+7.83	S Woods	1-1
Pat Eddery	10-65	15.4	+19.25	J Dunlop	5-17
P Robinson	4-28	14.3	+13.50	M Jarvis	2-11

Sponsored by Stan James

DONCASTER

Leger Way, Doncaster, DN2 6BB.
Tel: 01302 320 066 / 067.

How to get there – Road: M18, Jncts 3 or 4
Rail: Doncaster, bus to course
Features: LH, flat, easy turns, suits galloping type
2003 Flat fixtures: Mar 20, 21, 22, May 5, 24, Jun 7, 28, 29, Jul 10, 17, 24, Aug 2, Sep 10, 11, 12, 13, Oct 24, 25, Nov 7, 8
Draw: High numbers are best in sprints, a bias accentuated by softer ground. Low numbers take over on the straight mile, as long as there are enough runners for a split (12+), while 7f seems to be the cut-off point, when both rails are favoured over the centre. Low numbers are best in big fields on the round course.

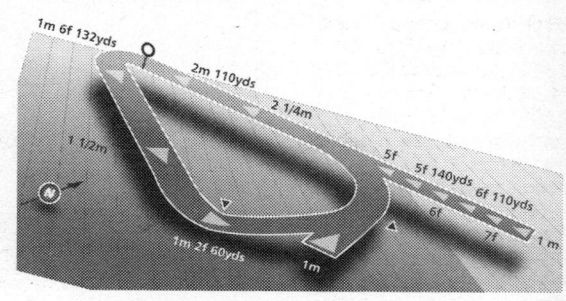

Ken Hussey's standard times

5f	58.7	1m(round)	1min37.2
5f140yds	1min7.4	1m2f60yds	2min6
6f	1min11.5	1m4f	2min30
6f110yds	1min18	1m6f132yds	3min3
7f	1min24.3	2m110yds	3min32
1m(str)	1min36.8	2m2f	3min53

Favourites

2-y-o	39.0%	+£24.67
3-y-o+	28.8%	-£17.29
Overall	31.8%	+£7.38

Trainers	Wins-Runs	%	2yo	3yo+	£1 level stks
S Bin Suroor	16-36	44.4	1-2	15-34	+12.59
D Loder	8-26	30.8	8-25	0-1	-6.60
John Berry	3-12	25.0	0-3	3-9	+10.25
J O'Keeffe	3-13	23.1	0-0	3-13	+23.50
W G M Turner	4-19	21.1	2-16	2-3	+22.50
H Cecil	20-104	19.2	5-26	15-78	+1.49
J Gosden	24-125	19.2	10-53	14-72	+1.98
A P O'Brien	5-27	18.5	4-21	1-6	0.00
Sir M Stoute	17-92	18.5	8-35	9-57	+5.61
B Hills	52-290	17.9	25-128	27-162	+23.33
J Dunlop	27-160	16.9	11-67	16-93	-44.36
J Fanshawe	9-56	16.1	0-9	9-47	-18.66

Jockeys	Wins-Rides	%	£1 level stks	Best Trainer	W-R
R Price	3-12	25.0	+20.75	K Wingrove	1-1
L Dettori	30-126	23.8	-9.00	D Loder	8-16
K Fallon	22-122	18.0	-17.95	H Cecil	4-15
D Holland	28-161	17.4	-17.39	M Johnston	8-47
J Murtagh	7-41	17.1	+3.00	Sir M Stoute	2-4
M Hills	31-186	16.7	-18.18	B Hills	29-135
G Hind	5-31	16.1	-0.50	J Gosden	3-9
R Hills	13-81	16.0	-29.37	J Dunlop	4-18
T Quinn	27-169	16.0	+8.25	J Dunlop	7-15
A Beech	5-34	14.7	+3.00	P Harris	2-4
G Faulkner	4-28	14.3	+16.00	M Ryan	1-1
S Sanders	12-90	13.3	+25.33	Sir M Prescott	5-9

Sponsored by Stan James

EPSOM

Epsom Downs, Surrey,
KT18 5LQ.
Tel 01372 726 311

How to get there – Road: M25 Jctn 8 (A217) or 9 (A24) 2m south of Epsom on B290
Rail: Epsom & raceday bus, Epsom Downs or Tattenham Corner
Features: LH, undulating, downhill 5f is fastest in the world
2003 Flat fixtures: Apr 23, Jun 6, 7, Jul 3, 10, 17, 31, Aug 25, Sep 10, 11, Oct 4
Draw: On soft, jockeys tack over to the stands' side for the better ground, as the course cambers downhill from the stands' rail towards the far side. In 5f races, the stalls are placed on the stands' side, so when it's soft most runners are on the best ground from the go. Prominent-racers drawn low in round-course races can take the shortest route for home and on faster ground have a decisive edge over 6f-7f and 1m114yds. Over 5f, high numbers used to hold an advantage but the bias is not so great these days.

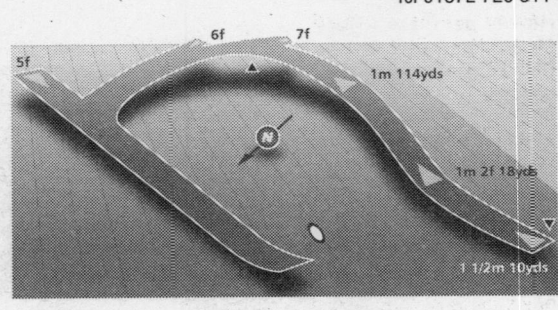

Ken Hussey's standard times

5f	53.8	1m114yds		1min41.6
6f	1min8	1m2f18yds		2min3.5
7f	1min20.2	1m4f10yds		2min33.6

Favourites

2-y-o	37.7%	-£8.70
3-y-o+	25.5%	-£37.84
Overall	27.5%	-£46.54

Trainers	Wins-Runs	%	2yo	3yo+	£1 level stks
Mrs J Ramsden	3-5	60.0	0-0	3-5	+10.50
H Morrison	3-8	37.5	0-1	3-7	+5.60
L Cumani	3-12	25.0	0-1	3-11	+15.62
G Balding	4-16	25.0	0-0	4-16	+24.00
A P O'Brien	4-17	23.5	0-0	4-17	+8.25
S C Williams	3-14	21.4	0-1	3-13	+10.50
S Bin Suroor	8-39	20.5	0-0	8-39	-10.74
Mrs A Perrett	3-15	20.0	1-2	2-13	+2.41
J Dunlop	8-41	19.5	0-9	8-32	-16.25
E Dunlop	8-44	18.2	1-6	7-38	+0.83
H Cecil	5-28	17.9	0-0	5-28	-6.25
I A Wood	3-17	17.6	0-1	3-16	+8.50

Jockeys	Wins-Rides	%	£1 level stks	Best Trainer	W-R
A Beech	6-19	31.6	+20.00	J Spearing	2-3
L Dettori	21-74	28.4	+6.63	S Bin Suroor	8-23
O Urbina	3-14	21.4	+8.75	J Fanshawe	2-4
K Fallon	22-109	20.2	-25.76	J Dunlop	3-4
Alex Greaves	3-15	20.0	+1.00	D Nicholls	3-15
M Kinane	6-31	19.4	+15.25	A P O'Brien	3-9
J Fanning	5-26	19.2	+12.00	M Johnston	3-12
C Catlin	10-57	17.5	+60.00	S Dow	4-11
R Hills	8-46	17.4	+15.73	J Hills	3-11
A Daly	5-30	16.7	+18.00	G Balding	3-6
G Carter	5-30	16.7	-3.87	E Dunlop	2-6
J Fortune	10-61	16.4	-3.17	P Cole	3-16

Sponsored by Stan James

FOLKESTONE

Westenhanger, Hythe, Kent.
Tel: 01303 266407.

How to get there – Road: M20 Jctn 11, A20 south. Rail: Westenhanger from Charing Cross or Victoria
Features: RH, sharp turns
2003 Flat fixtures: Mar 25, Apr 4, 15, May 8, Jun 27, Jul 10, 28, Aug 11, 21, 25, Sep 1
Draw: Prior to 1998, Folkestone was never thought of as having much of a bias, but nowadays it is common to see fields split into two groups in straight-course races, with runners rarely taken down the centre. The far rail usually rides faster than the stands' rail, particularly on soft ground, favouring horses drawn high, and front-runners drawn on that side are always worth consideration.

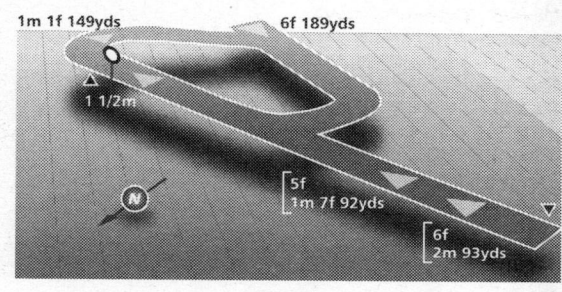

Ken Hussey's standard times

5f	58.6	1m1f149yds	2min0.2
6f	1min11	1m4f	2min33.6
6f189yds (Rnd)	1min21.8	1m7f92yds	3min19.4
7f(str)	1min24	2m93yds	3min32.7

Favourites

2-y-o	31.0%	-£23.67
3-y-o+	30.9%	-£22.28
Overall	30.9%	-£45.95

Trainers	Wins-Runs	%	2yo	3yo+	£1 level stks
H Cecil	3-6	50.0	0-1	3-5	+6.75
A Stewart	3-9	33.3	0-3	3-6	+14.60
Sir M Prescott	7-22	31.8	4-11	3-11	+30.57
J W Payne	6-19	31.6	1-6	5-13	+25.63
J Toller	5-17	29.4	0-1	5-16	+38.75
H Candy	3-11	27.3	1-4	2-7	+0.23
D Arbuthnot	6-22	27.3	1-4	5-18	+8.88
R Charlton	4-15	26.7	2-5	2-10	-7.08
Mrs A Perrett	7-31	22.6	2-10	5-21	-11.28
J Fanshawe	4-18	22.2	1-6	3-12	+10.37
N Callaghan	6-27	22.2	2-11	4-16	+6.17
T Mills	4-19	21.1	2-5	2-14	-3.22

Jockeys	Wins-Rides	%	£1 level stks	Best Trainer	W-R
M Hills	6-13	46.2	+23.68	B Hills	3-7
R L Moore	3-8	37.5	+6.00	I A Wood	2-2
B Doyle	3-9	33.3	+10.25	John Berry	1-2
G Duffield	6-20	30.0	+18.25	Sir M Prescott	3-7
A McCarthy	4-15	26.7	+14.24	D Nicholls	1-1
J Fortune	5-19	26.3	+9.75	P Cole	3-6
G Carter	9-40	22.5	+6.08	E Dunlop	3-5
Pat Eddery	11-51	21.6	+3.86	B Meehan	3-8
P Dobbs	6-31	19.4	-7.90	P Cole	2-4
J P Spencer	3-16	18.8	-0.75	S Gollings	1-1
K Fallon	5-27	18.5	-8.96	J W Payne	1-1
S Sanders	13-76	17.1	+3.15	Sir M Prescott	2-6

Sponsored by Stan James

GOODWOOD

Chichester, W Sussex,
PO18 0PS. Tel 01243 755 022

How to get there – Road: signposted from A27 south and A285 north
Rail: Chichester, bus to course on race-days
Features: RH, undulating
2003 Flat fixtures: May 20, 21, 22, 29, Jun 6, 13, 20, 27, 29, Jul 29, 30, 31, Aug 1, 2, 23, 24, Sep 12, 13, 24, 25, Oct 12
Draw: High numbers are favoured on the round course, particularly over 7f and 1m, except on soft when jockeys tack over to the stands' side in the straight. The edge enjoyed by high draws in the Stewards' Cup has returned, having disappeared in 1999 after work to break up the surface by machine on that side, but those on the stands' side have finished closer than they used to. In sprints of 12-20 runners, high numbers have enjoyed a definite edge lately.

Ken Hussey's standard times

5f	56.4	1m3f	2min20
6f	1min10	1m4f	2min32.7
7f	1min24.4	1m6f	2min59
1m	1min36.8	2m	3min22
1m1f	1min52	2m4f	4min13
1m1f192yds	2min2.2	2m5f	4min27.3

Favourites

2-y-o	36.9%	-£13.21
3-y-o+	28.8%	-£41.46
Overall	30.7%	-£54.67

Trainers	Wins-Runs	%	2yo	3yo+	£1 level stks
D Loder	3-7	42.9	3-7	0-0	+15.11
S Bin Suroor	23-59	39.0	1-2	22-57	+25.61
J Cullinan	3-9	33.3	0-2	3-7	+30.91
J Given	3-10	30.0	1-3	2-7	+15.50
M Tregoning	16-62	25.8	6-26	10-36	+17.06
A P O'Brien	5-22	22.7	1-4	4-18	-1.25
J Gosden	40-176	22.7	9-43	31-133	+36.55
J Fanshawe	10-46	21.7	2-5	8-41	+23.10
A Bailey	3-14	21.4	0-2	3-12	+28.50
Sir M Stoute	22-107	20.6	3-11	19-96	-14.12
M Johnston	27-144	18.8	7-27	20-117	+49.05
H Cecil	14-75	18.7	3-10	11-65	-26.58

Jockeys	Wins-Rides	%	£1 level stks	Best Trainer	W-R
L Dettori	39-160	24.4	+0.51	S Bin Suroor	17-39
R Miles	3-14	21.4	+2.25	T Mills	3-10
O Peslier	6-28	21.4	+32.00	M Johnston	2-4
M Kinane	12-57	21.1	+4.69	A P O'Brien	5-15
Alex Greaves	5-25	20.0	+13.50	D Nicholls	5-25
R Hills	38-205	18.5	-17.68	M Tregoning	9-27
K Fallon	44-242	18.2	-6.91	H Cecil	7-28
J P Spencer	20-120	16.7	+43.50	L Cumani	4-19
D Holland	22-132	16.7	+45.63	M Johnston	5-29
J Mackay	8-49	16.3	+60.00	M Wigham	1-1
R Havlin	5-33	15.2	+32.03	J Gosden	4-12
L Newman	6-41	14.6	-9.33	R Hannon	3-14

Sponsored by Stan James

Bothwell Road, Hamilton, Lanarkshire
WA12 0HQ. Tel 01698 283 806

HAMILTON

How to get there – Road: M74 Jctn 5, off the A74
Rail: Hamilton West
Features: RH, undulating, dip can become testing in wet weather
2003 Flat fixtures: Apr 28, May 4, 9, 16, 17, Jun 11, 12, 18, 26, Jul 1, 11, 17, 18, 24, Aug 13, 19, Sep 1, 29

Draw: It's helpful to be drawn high in sprints if the ground is good to soft or softer, particularly early in the season, and last year it looked a case of the nearer the fence the better (due to the wet summer in Scotland, the ground was often soft). A high draw is a definite advantage in races over 1m65yds, as there is a tight right-hand loop into the home straight. It is not uncommon for the ground to become too bad for the use of stalls here.

Ken Hussey's standard times

5f4yds	58.2	1m1f36yds	1min54.3
5f200yds	1min9.2	1m3f16yds	2min19.2
6f5yds	1min10	1m4f17yds	2min32.2
1m65yds	1min43.5	1m5f9yds	2min45.4

Favourites

2-y-o	44.8%	+£5.86
3-y-o+	29.4%	-£25.41
Overall	32.6%	-£19.55

Trainers	Wins-Runs	%	2yo	3yo+	£1 level stks
D Cantillon	4-5	80.0	0-0	4-5	+7.08
Lady Herries	3-4	75.0	0-0	3-4	+9.58
Sir M Stoute	5-8	62.5	0-1	5-7	+3.49
J Dunlop	3-6	50.0	2-3	1-3	-0.56
M Ryan	3-7	42.9	0-0	3-7	+10.50
Sir M Prescott	12-28	42.9	4-9	8-19	+10.96
G A Butler	4-10	40.0	2-3	2-7	+7.75
R Guest	3-8	37.5	0-1	3-7	+8.00
P Cole	4-12	33.3	2-3	2-9	-4.26
M Channon	18-55	32.7	11-21	7-34	+18.00
J G FitzGerald	3-11	27.3	0-0	3-11	+0.08
T Etherington	4-15	26.7	0-0	4-15	+25.00

Jockeys	Wins-Rides	%	£1 level stks	Best Trainer	W-R
C Catlin	3-5	60.0	+11.40	M Channon	2-3
Helen Cuthbert	3-5	60.0	+10.75	T Cuthbert	3-4
T Quinn	3-7	42.9	-1.20	M Channon	3-3
Emma Ramsden	3-8	37.5	+3.75	J J Quinn	1-1
R Clark	4-11	36.4	+13.75	D Chapman	4-9
J Mackay	4-12	33.3	+15.25	Miss L Perratt	2-5
G Carter	5-15	33.3	+0.07	J Dunlop	3-6
Darren Williams	5-17	29.4	+5.66	P Cole	2-4
R Ffrench	7-24	29.2	+16.51	J Noseda	2-3
D Holland	11-39	28.2	+5.68	M Johnston	7-16
T E Durcan	12-46	26.1	+35.50	M Tompkins	6-22
J D Smith	3-12	25.0	+2.41	C Dwyer	1-1

Sponsored by Stan James

HAYDOCK

Newton-Le-Willows, Lancashire, WA12 0HQ. Tel: 01942 725 963

How to get there – Road: M6 Jctn 23, A49 to Wigan
Rail: Wigan & 320 bus or Newton-le-Willows
Features: LH flat track, easy turns, suits the galloping type
2003 Flat fixtures: Apr 19, May 3 (mixed), 23, 24, Jun 5, 6, 7, Jul 3, 4, 5, 13, 19, Aug 7, 8, 9, 14, Sep 5, 6, 26, 27
Draw: High numbers used to be favoured in sprints when the ground was good or softer, but now there's rarely a great deal in it.

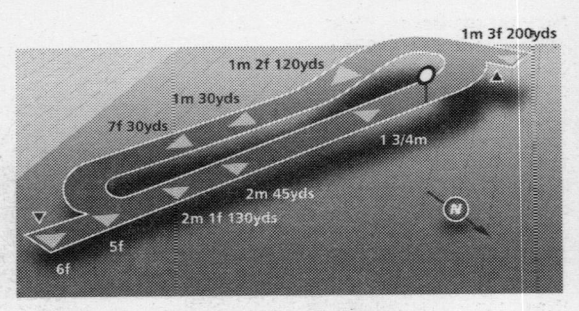

Ken Hussey's standard times

5f	59	1m3f200yds	2min28
6f	1min11.3	1m6f	2min54
7f30yds	1min27.4	2m45yds	3min28
1m30yds	1min40.2	2m1f130yds	3min47
1m2f120yds	2min10	2m3f	4min7

Favourites

2-y-o	31.0%	-£25.79
3-y-o+	31.0%	-£30.49
Overall	31.0%	-£56.28

Trainers	Wins-Runs	%	2yo	3yo+	£1 level stks
H Cecil	19-48	39.6	1-1	18-47	+19.79
S Bin Suroor	5-13	38.5	0-0	5-13	-3.00
M Jarvis	24-77	31.2	3-19	21-58	+49.90
J Pearce	3-11	27.3	0-0	3-11	+66.00
M Ryan	7-27	25.9	0-2	7-25	+5.75
M Tompkins	6-24	25.0	2-7	4-17	+22.00
M Tregoning	6-24	25.0	1-2	5-22	-1.00
J Dunlop	30-121	24.8	11-26	19-95	+48.53
Sir M Stoute	18-73	24.7	4-12	14-61	-3.81
W Haggas	10-41	24.4	4-8	6-33	+15.03
Sir M Prescott	7-33	21.2	1-14	6-19	-2.10
P Makin	4-19	21.1	3-5	1-14	+1.12

Jockeys	Wins-Rides	%	£1 level stks	Best Trainer	W-R
B Doyle	4-12	33.3	+6.12	H Morrison	1-1
O Urbina	5-17	29.4	+34.58	J Fanshawe	3-9
D McGaffin	4-14	28.6	+26.50	I Semple	2-2
L Dettori	14-51	27.5	+4.03	J Gosden	3-10
K Fallon	27-99	27.3	+0.05	Sir M Stoute	7-15
G Faulkner	3-12	25.0	+23.33	M Ryan	2-2
M Henry	5-21	23.8	+19.25	J Unett	2-2
Darren Williams	4-19	21.1	+20.50	J J Quinn	2-3
D Kinsella	4-19	21.1	+8.75	Miss L Siddall	1-1
P Goode	4-20	20.0	+19.00	G Woodward	1-1
Pat Eddery	26-137	19.0	-22.93	J Dunlop	7-26
I Mongan	3-16	18.8	+14.00	E L James	1-1

Sponsored by Stan James

Sunbury-On-Thames, Middlesex, TW16 5AQ. Tel: 01932 782292.

KEMPTON

How to get there – Road: M3 Jctn 1, A308 towards Kingston-on-Thames
Rail: Kempton Park from Waterloo
Features: RH, flat, sharp turn into straight
2003 Flat fixtures: Mar 22, Apr 19, 21, May 5, 24, Jun 4, 25, Jul 2, 9, 16, 30, Aug 6, 17, 20, Sep 5, 6, 22,
Draw: On the separate sprint track, when the stalls are on the far side and the ground is on the soft side, a high draw is an advantage. When the stalls are placed on the stands' side, low numbers are clearly favoured, and when the runners stretch right across the track, low numbers now comfortably hold the edge (which was not the case prior to 2000). The advantages become less defined on faster ground.

Ken Hussey's standard times

5f	58.2	1m1f	1min50
6f	1min10.3	1m2f	2min2
7f(round)	1min24.6	1m3f30yds	2min17.4
7f(Jubilee)	1min24	1m4f	2min30.3
1m(round)	1min37.4	1m6f92yds	3min2
1m(Jubilee)	1min36.6	2m	3min25.5

Favourites

2-y-o	40.0%	+£6.22
3-y-o+	27.4%	-£26.77
Overall	30.2%	-£20.55

Trainers	Wins-Runs	%	2yo	3yo+	£1 level stks
S Bin Suroor	4-11	36.4	0-1	4-10	+7.36
M Pipe	5-16	31.3	0-0	5-16	+9.75
R Phillips	3-10	30.0	0-0	3-10	+17.33
A Stewart	9-30	30.0	0-5	9-25	+22.67
M Tregoning	9-35	25.7	3-10	6-25	-4.67
J King	3-12	25.0	0-0	3-12	+9.00
H Cecil	11-44	25.0	2-3	9-41	-5.60
Mrs A Perrett	14-62	22.6	1-13	13-49	+57.08
J Fanshawe	14-63	22.2	2-8	12-55	+36.58
J Noseda	7-37	18.9	3-9	4-28	+0.09
P Makin	5-28	17.9	2-5	3-23	+35.33
J Gosden	10-57	17.5	4-22	6-35	-12.54

Jockeys	Wins-Rides	%	£1 level stks	Best Trainer	W-R
R L Moore	5-19	26.3	+22.50	R Hannon	2-6
G Sparkes	3-13	23.1	+30.83	R Phillips	1-1
R Hills	29-132	22.0	+24.06	M Tregoning	8-17
L Dettori	14-67	20.9	-15.50	S Bin Suroor	3-5
D Kinsella	7-34	20.6	+21.00	J W Payne	1-1
Pat Eddery	37-207	17.9	+3.65	J Dunlop	13-36
K Fallon	34-205	16.6	-40.18	H Cecil	4-16
J Mackay	4-25	16.0	+7.75	M Pipe	2-3
M Hills	15-96	15.6	+8.76	J Fanshawe	3-4
T Quinn	25-169	14.8	-14.61	H Cecil	4-17
O Urbina	6-41	14.6	+8.00	J Fanshawe	4-21
J Fortune	16-122	13.1	-35.60	P Cole	4-23

Sponsored by Stan James

OUT OF LUCK: even in the middle of Leicester's broad home straight, a jockey can find himself suddenly running out of room when it matters

London Road, Leicester, LE2 4AL.
Tel: 0116 271 6515

LEICESTER

How to get there – Road: M1 Jctn 21, A6, 2m south of city
Rail: Leicester, bus
Features: RH, straight mile is downhill for first 4f, then uphill to finish
2003 Flat fixtures: Mar 27, Apr 3, 26, May 26, 27, Jun 2, 15, 26, Jul 5, 17, 23, 30, Aug 10, Sep 1, 9, 22, Oct 13, 14, 27
Draw: It used to be considered that low numbers had an advantage on the straight course, particularly on soft ground, but in recent seasons the bias has turned full circle, and high numbers (who usually race towards the centre) are now almost always favoured.

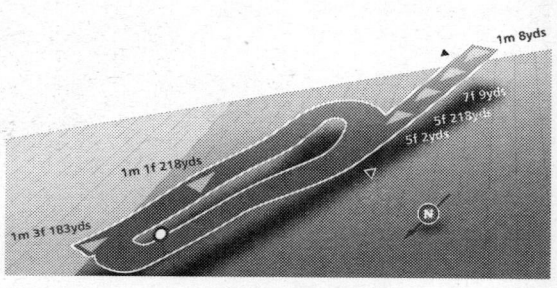

Ken Hussey's standard times

5f2yds	58.3	1m (rnd)	1min39.7
5f218yds	1min10.2	1m1f218yds	2min2.7
7f9yds	1min22.3	1m3f183yds	2min28.6
1m8yds	1min38.7		

Favourites

2-y-o	36.2%	-£22.06
3-y-o+	28.1%	-£63.02
Overall	30.3%	-£85.08

Trainers	Wins-Runs	%	2yo	3yo+	£1 level stks
D Loder	9-15	60.0	8-14	1-1	+5.34
P D'Arcy	4-12	33.3	0-1	4-11	+24.00
Sir M Stoute	23-80	28.8	14-52	9-28	+20.06
J Fanshawe	12-45	26.7	1-9	11-36	+25.68
J Gosden	14-53	26.4	5-30	9-23	+2.97
Mrs J Ramsden	3-12	25.0	1-6	2-6	+0.83
M Tregoning	5-23	21.7	2-9	3-14	+11.71
Mrs A Perrett	9-42	21.4	5-20	4-22	+4.71
G L Moore	4-21	19.0	0-2	4-19	+5.00
R Cowell	3-16	18.8	1-3	2-13	+10.50
J W Payne	3-17	17.6	0-2	3-15	+32.88
Dr J Scargill	3-17	17.6	0-1	3-16	+22.44

Jockeys	Wins-Rides	%	£1 level stks	Best Trainer	W-R
L Dettori	18-64	28.1	-11.17	D Loder	6-10
J Fortune	17-76	22.4	+4.39	P Cole	5-18
K Fallon	23-117	19.7	-2.05	Sir M Stoute	8-22
J P Spencer	12-65	18.5	+10.68	W Haggas	2-2
T Quinn	23-124	18.5	+15.75	J Dunlop	6-16
K Darley	11-60	18.3	-8.66	M Johnston	4-8
D Holland	17-102	16.7	+40.46	M Johnston	3-15
W Ryan	16-97	16.5	+0.28	Sir M Stoute	2-4
L Keniry	3-19	15.8	-0.50	D Haydn Jones	1-1
S W Kelly	4-26	15.4	+5.70	J A Osborne	2-13
P Hanagan	5-34	14.7	+31.50	R Fahey	3-10
P Dobbs	4-28	14.3	-3.00	R Hannon	2-10

Sponsored by Stan James

LINGFIELD Turf

Racecourse Road,
Lingfield,
Surrey, RH7 6PQ.
Tel: 01342 834300

How to get there – Road: M25 Jctn 6, south on A22, then B2029.
Rail: Lingfield from London Bridge or Victoria
Features: LH, undulating, straight runs downhill
2003 Flat fixtures: May 9, 10, 17, 28, Jun 3, 21, 28, Jul 2, 9, 16, 19, 23, Aug 8, 20, 28, Sep 3, 9, Oct 3, 8, 15, 30

Draw: Only the occasional meeting seems affected, in favour of high numbers. Heavy rainfall onto previously firm ground can have a massive effect, though - it seems to make the middle and far side of the straight course ride a lot slower. In these conditions, runners drawn right up against the stands' rail, often only the top three or four stalls, have a big edge. That edge doesn't seem anything like as great over sprint distances as it is over 7f and 7f140yds.

Ken Hussey's standard times

5f	56.3	1m2f	2min5.4
6f	1min9	1m3f106yds	2min24.4
7f	1min20.7	1m6f	2min58.6
7f140yds	1min28.2	2m	3min24.6
1m1f	1min52.5		

Favourites

2-y-o	39.9%	-£2.10
3-y-o+	30.8%	-£26.33
Overall	33.8%	-£28.43

Trainers	Wins-Runs	%	2yo	3yo+	£1 level stks
Sheena West	3-6	50.0	0-0	3-6	+58.00
S Bin Suroor	7-14	50.0	1-1	6-13	+6.20
D Nicholls	6-17	35.3	0-0	6-17	+13.41
H Cecil	12-36	33.3	3-7	9-29	-5.94
J Noseda	9-33	27.3	4-12	5-21	+18.81
Sir M Stoute	11-43	25.6	5-23	6-20	-6.95
B Hills	13-56	23.2	4-15	9-41	+4.73
R Brotherton	3-13	23.1	0-3	3-10	+12.50
M Tregoning	8-35	22.9	2-12	6-23	-5.01
J Fanshawe	9-45	20.0	3-19	6-26	+15.00
R Charlton	9-45	20.0	2-15	7-30	+27.62
B Hanbury	6-32	18.8	1-8	5-24	+17.33

Jockeys	Wins-Rides	%	£1 level stks	Best Trainer	W-R
K Fallon	28-96	29.2	-4.25	Sir M Stoute	5-12
P Bradley	4-18	22.2	+7.25	A Berry	2-6
Pat Eddery	23-105	21.9	-7.75	J Dunlop	8-25
L Keniry	3-14	21.4	+12.50	S Kirk	1-1
P M Quinn	3-15	20.0	+11.50	B J Llewellyn	1-1
R Hills	11-56	19.6	-13.92	B Hills	2-3
T E Durcan	6-34	17.6	+12.00	M Tompkins	2-12
L Dettori	4-26	15.4	-1.88	R Whitaker	1-1
D Holland	14-94	14.9	-30.85	G Wragg	3-12
T Quinn	16-111	14.4	-39.93	H Cecil	3-13
J P Spencer	6-43	14.0	-11.49	S Bin Suroor	2-4
P Fitzsimons	5-36	13.9	-8.00	J M Bradley	3-15

Sponsored by Stan James

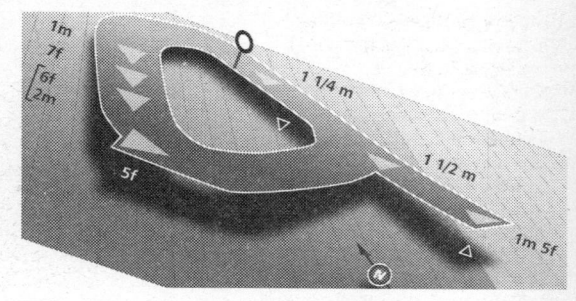

LINGFIELD Sand

Features: LH, polytrack, tight

2003 Flat fixtures: Mar 26, 28, Apr 1, 5, 9, May 24, Oct 27, Nov 2, 12, 13, 18, 22, 26, 29, Dec 2, 6, 10, 17, 20, 29, 30

Draw: Since the Polytrack was laid, horses have been able to win from just about anywhere. Front-runners do well over the shorter trips, especially 6f, but over any distance beyond 1m they have a desperate time.

Ken Hussey's standard times

5f	58	1m2f	2min3
6f	1min11	1m4f	2min29.6
7f	1min23.2	1m5f	2min43
1m	1min36.6	2m	3min21.5

Favourites

2-y-o	34.4%	-£22.96
3-y-o+	31.0%	-£158.67
Overall	31.4%	-£181.63

Trainers

Trainers	Wins-Runs	%	2yo	3yo+	£1 level stks
D Loder	7-16	43.8	1-2	6-14	+0.25
J Ffitch-Heyes	3-8	37.5	0-0	3-8	+18.00
Ron Thompson	3-9	33.3	0-1	3-8	+21.25
J Noseda	24-84	28.6	3-16	21-68	+3.05
A Turnell	3-11	27.3	0-3	3-8	+14.00
G A Butler	47-179	26.3	13-45	34-134	+31.76
P Eccles	3-12	25.0	0-1	3-11	+10.00
C Thornton	4-17	23.5	0-1	4-16	+0.25
D Barker	3-13	23.1	0-0	3-13	+1.00
D Chapman	26-123	21.1	0-1	26-122	+8.40
T Mills	25-122	20.5	4-19	21-103	+3.47
C Wall	9-46	19.6	0-4	9-42	-9.10

Jockeys

Jockeys	Wins-Rides	%	£1 level stks	Best Trainer	W-R
Kimberley Hart	7-17	41.2	+45.29	T Barron	6-9
Alex Greaves	3-12	25.0	-2.87	D Nicholls	3-12
I Mongan	4-16	25.0	-0.09	G L Moore	4-12
L Dettori	7-28	25.0	-6.71	D Loder	2-3
E Ahern	28-116	24.1	+66.29	G A Butler	21-65
M Hills	22-97	22.7	+9.14	C Cyzer	5-10
Lisa Jones	3-14	21.4	+11.75	W Musson	3-10
L Carter	9-42	21.4	-1.76	T Mills	9-42
J-P Guillambert	4-19	21.1	+11.50	N Littmoden	3-13
Jane Moore	3-15	20.0	+3.00	G L Moore	3-14
A Quinn	6-30	20.0	+8.75	G Enright	2-4
K Fallon	24-124	19.4	-28.66	D Loder	4-8

Sponsored by Stan James

MUSSELBURGH

Linkfield Road,
Musselburgh,
E Lothian EH21 7RE
Tel: 01316 652859

How to get there – Road: M8 Jctn 2, A8 east, follow Ring Road, A1 east.
Rail: Musselburgh from Edinburgh Waverley
Features: RH, flat, tight
2003 Flat fixtures: Mar 27, Apr 10, May 2, 19, 31, Jun 16, 23, 30, Jul 7, 31, Aug 21, Sep 13, 15, 28, Oct 25, Nov 5
Draw: High numbers are slightly favoured over 7f and 1m. Over 5f, low numbers have a considerable advantage on soft ground, irrespective of the size of the field, but high numbers do best in big fields on very firm going. The one place usually not to be is down the centre.

Course diagram distances: 5f, 1m 7f 16yds, 7f 15yds, 1m 16yds, 1m 4f 131yds, 1m 3f 32yds

Ken Hussey's standard times

5f	57.6	1m4f	2min32.4
7f15yds	1min26.3	1m5f	2min45.3
1m	1min38.3	1m6f	2min58.4
1m1f	1min50.7	1m7f16yds	3min11.3
1m3f32yds	2min20	2m	3min25

Favourites

2-y-o	33.1%	-£29.34
3-y-o+	27.0%	-£47.53
Overall	28.5%	-£76.87

Trainers	Wins-Runs	%	2yo	3yo+	£1 level stks
Sir M Stoute	4-7	57.1	1-1	3-6	+3.75
M Jarvis	4-9	44.4	0-3	4-6	+1.53
Sir M Prescott	12-29	41.4	2-13	10-16	+22.19
M Bell	12-29	41.4	1-5	11-24	+33.08
P Harris	5-15	33.3	5-8	0-7	+6.70
G A Butler	6-18	33.3	3-7	3-11	+1.37
L Cumani	4-15	26.7	2-6	2-9	-6.00
H Morrison	3-12	25.0	1-1	2-11	+20.50
W Haggas	4-17	23.5	1-7	3-10	-8.40
John Berry	5-23	21.7	0-3	5-20	-5.27
R Whitaker	7-33	21.2	2-13	5-20	+61.00
M Johnston	26-124	21.0	7-35	19-89	-4.79

Jockeys	Wins-Rides	%	£1 level stks	Best Trainer	W-R
S Drowne	5-13	38.5	+22.10	M Channon	3-6
E Ahern	3-11	27.3	+2.00	G A Butler	3-5
T Lucas	7-26	26.9	+28.13	M W Easterby	7-22
R Ffrench	3-12	25.0	+3.07	J Noseda	1-1
P Robinson	5-20	25.0	+1.53	M Jarvis	4-7
G Carter	6-26	23.1	+6.00	J Berry	2-7
T E Durcan	8-37	21.6	-2.24	A Berry	5-15
D Holland	10-48	20.8	-3.23	M Johnston	6-15
F Norton	14-72	19.4	-7.72	A Berry	9-23
Joanna Badger	3-16	18.8	+12.33	Miss A Stokell	1-1
K Fallon	6-35	17.1	-7.00	L Cumani	1-1
M Fenton	11-73	15.1	+10.58	M Bell	5-12

Sponsored by Stan James

Newbury, Berkshire, RG14 7NZ.
Tel: 01635 40015 or 41485.

NEWBURY

How to get there – Road: M4 Jctn 13 and A34 south
Rail: Newbury racecourse
Features: LH, wide, flat
2003 Flat fixtures: Apr 11, 12, May 16, 17, 28, Jun 11, 12, Jul 3, 18, 19, Aug 3, 15, 16, Sep 19, 20, Oct 24, 25

Draw: On soft, runners sometimes go wide down the back straight and along the side of the course in 1m3f56yds to 2m races, so a high draw is a huge advantage. A low draw can be an advantage in big-field races over the round 7f64yds and 1m7yds courses, as there's a sharpish left-hand bend into the straight soon after the starts, but not on soft; the ground on the rail becomes chewed up and horses drawn high race on the better ground. On the straight course, a high draw is always an advantage.

Ken Hussey's standard times

5f34yds	1min0	1m1f	1min49.7
6f8yds	1min11.2	1m2f6yds	2min2
7f	1min23	1m3f5yds	2min15.8
7f64yds(round)	1min26.4	1m4f4yds	2min29.3
1m(str)	1min36	1m5f61yds	2min45.8
1m7yds(round)	1min35.3	2m	3min23

Favourites

2-y-o	35.2%	-£7.25
3-y-o+	24.8%	-£79.06
Overall	27.7%	-£86.32

Trainers	Wins-Runs	%	2yo	3yo+	£1 level stks
N Henderson	4-7	57.1	0-0	4-7	+41.75
P Hedger	3-7	42.9	1-1	2-6	+36.00
S Bin Suroor	8-25	32.0	0-1	8-24	+25.51
D Loder	4-16	25.0	4-14	0-2	-5.06
M Johnston	19-76	25.0	3-14	16-62	+43.19
W Haggas	6-25	24.0	1-4	5-21	+9.50
H Cecil	19-87	21.8	2-7	17-80	+23.58
M Tregoning	13-60	21.7	7-27	6-33	+13.71
B Hanbury	8-41	19.5	3-8	5-33	+16.00
N Callaghan	4-21	19.0	1-6	3-15	+2.50
T Easterby	3-16	18.8	2-12	1-4	+0.20
J Gosden	27-157	17.2	8-42	19-115	-16.82

Jockeys	Wins-Rides	%	£1 level stks	Best Trainer	W-R
K Dalgleish	4-19	21.1	+1.25	M Johnston	3-13
L Dettori	24-130	18.5	-27.90	S Bin Suroor	5-10
M Kinane	6-35	17.1	-10.29	P Harris	1-1
R Hills	32-188	17.0	-6.06	M Tregoning	7-25
T Quinn	39-241	16.2	+5.00	H Cecil	9-40
Pat Eddery	46-290	15.9	+5.44	J Dunlop	15-63
O Peslier	4-26	15.4	+0.25	C Laffon-Parias	1-1
K Fallon	32-227	14.1	-81.42	H Cecil	7-25
J Fortune	26-197	13.2	-29.44	J Gosden	10-46
W Supple	6-47	12.8	+15.25	S Bin Suroor	1-1
E Ahern	4-32	12.5	+3.00	T Easterby	1-1
O Urbina	4-32	12.5	+0.50	R Charlton	1-1

Sponsored by Stan James

NEWCASTLE

High Gosforth Park,
Newcastle-Upon-Tyne NE3 5HP.
Tel: 01912 362020.

How to get there – Road: Signposted from A1
Rail: Newcastle Central, metro to Regent Centre or Four Lane End & bus
Features: LH, 1m6f round, galloping, half-mile straight is all uphill
2003 Flat fixtures: Mar 24, Apr 21, 22, May 5, 14, 22, Jun 4, 27, 28, Jul 26, 31, Aug 6, 15, 22, 25, Sep 8, Oct 1, 12, 22
Draw: On the straight course, it used to be a case of high numbers being favoured when the ground was good or firmer, and low numbers having an advantage when the ground rode good to soft or softer. However, these days the far side (low) seems best whatever the going.

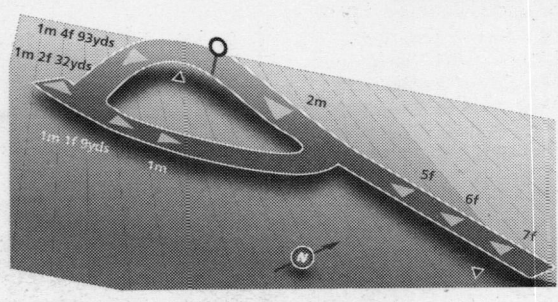

Ken Hussey's standard times

5f	59	1m1f9yds	1min52.5
6f	1min11.8	1m2f32yds	2min6.7
7f	1min24.2	1m4f93yds	2min37
1m(round)	1min39.7	1m6f97yds	3min2
1m3yds(str)	1min37.2	2m19yds	3min23.7

Favourites

2-y-o	31.9%	-£35.09
3-y-o+	29.1%	-£47.69
Overall	29.8%	-£82.78

Trainers	Wins-Runs	%	2yo	3yo+	£1 level stks
H Cecil	11-20	55.0	0-2	11-18	+22.00
D Morris	3-6	50.0	0-0	3-6	+11.00
W G M Turner	3-8	37.5	3-6	0-2	+3.75
W Haggas	11-30	36.7	2-6	9-24	+18.52
M Jarvis	3-10	30.0	0-1	3-9	-1.56
J Dunlop	18-65	27.7	6-13	12-52	-10.84
P Harris	6-22	27.3	3-7	3-15	+10.69
Sir M Stoute	14-52	26.9	4-11	10-41	-8.37
J Noseda	6-24	25.0	2-9	4-15	-4.30
M Bell	13-53	24.5	4-16	9-37	+49.69
Sir M Prescott	10-41	24.4	4-21	6-20	+6.19
M Channon	10-48	20.8	5-19	5-29	-3.72

Jockeys	Wins-Rides	%	£1 level stks	Best Trainer	W-R
I Mongan	3-8	37.5	+32.80	N Littmoden	3-4
L Dettori	6-19	31.6	+5.07	D Eddy	1-1
R Hills	7-23	30.4	+20.13	B Hanbury	2-3
W Ryan	3-11	27.3	+0.67	H Cecil	2-3
K Fallon	27-105	25.7	-9.11	T Easterby	4-5
M Hills	9-36	25.0	+8.24	B Hills	5-21
A Beech	4-17	23.5	+34.87	G Margarson	1-1
T Quinn	7-33	21.2	+6.29	P Harris	2-3
S W Kelly	5-24	20.8	-4.14	J Weymes	1-1
R Ffrench	4-21	19.0	+10.67	T Etherington	1-1
D Holland	23-127	18.1	-3.50	M Johnston	10-48
K Darley	49-275	17.8	-45.43	M Johnston	5-35

Sponsored by Stan James

Westfield House, The Links, Newmarket, Suffolk, CB8 0TG.
Tel 01638 663 482

NEWMARKET

Rowley Mile Course

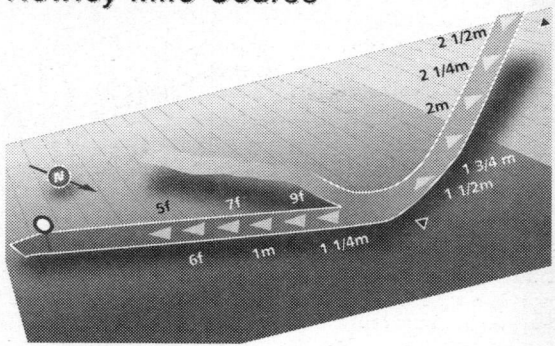

How to get there – Road: from south M11 Jctn 9, then A11, from east or west A45, from north A1 or A45
Rail: Newmarket

Features: RH, wide, galloping, uphill finish

2003 Flat fixtures: Apr 15, 16, 17, May 2, 3, 4, 24, 30, 31, Sep 23, Oct 2, 3, 4, 16, 17, 18, 31, Nov 1

Draw: The far rail has definitely ridden faster than the centre of the course since racing resumed here in 2000, favouring high numbers in big fields. When the going is soft, runners right up against the far rail (high) have always held sway as long as nothing switches up the stands' side (in which case, those that switch are favoured) but soft ground is not a common occurrence here. In late season, it has been known for the stands' rail to be moved to unveil virgin ground up against the stands' side. In these circumstances, runners drawn low can have a big advantage.

Favourites

2-y-o	35.5%	-£30.57	3-y-o+	25.3% -£134.74
			Overall	28.2% -£165.30

Ken Hussey's standard times

5f	57.5	1m2f	2min1.4
6f	1min10.5	1m4f	2min27.7
7f	1min22.7	1m6f	2min54.4
1m	1min35.7	2m	3min20.3
1m1f	1min48.6	2m2f	3min48

Trainer stats below apply for both Newmarket courses. See over page for jockey stats.

Trainers	Wins-Runs	%	2yo	3yo+	£1 level stks
Mrs A L King	4-13	30.8	0-0	4-13	+12.50
D Loder	24-82	29.3	20-74	4-8	-3.21
E Wheeler	4-16	25.0	0-0	4-16	+38.00
Sir M Prescott	10-44	22.7	3-12	7-32	+2.08
P Felgate	4-22	18.2	0-0	4-22	+16.50
J Gosden	60-337	17.8	20-123	40-214	+28.71
J Akehurst	4-25	16.0	0-1	4-24	+19.50
H Cecil	47-302	15.6	9-41	38-261	-95.46
A P O'Brien	14-91	15.4	8-51	6-40	-35.61
M Tregoning	15-98	15.3	3-35	12-63	-11.29
S Bin Suroor	16-107	15.0	3-4	13-103	-37.22
Bob Jones	3-21	14.3	0-2	3-19	+6.00
N Tinkler	3-21	14.3	0-3	3-18	+11.50
J Fanshawe	33-233	14.2	6-31	27-202	-42.22
D Elsworth	26-191	13.6	5-45	21-146	+53.46
M Johnston	32-244	13.1	6-54	26-190	-13.92
P Cole	25-196	12.8	13-58	12-138	-23.96
J Dunlop	61-485	12.6	22-190	39-295	-35.24
J Glover	4-32	12.5	0-6	4-26	+9.50
J Given	5-41	12.2	2-16	3-25	+28.13

Sponsored by Stan James

NEWMARKET ctd

How to get there: see previous page
Features: RH, wide, galloping, uphill finish
2003 Flat fixtures: Jun 20, 27, 28, Jul 8, 9, 10, 18, 19, 25, 27, Aug 1, 2, 8, 9, 15, 16, 22, 23
Draw: The draw often plays a part here, although it varies with some regularity. Here are few rules of thumb. When they're racing on the stands' side half of the track, high numbers are best when the ground is good to firm or faster; there's not much in it on good; on slower, runners racing away from the stands' rail (low) are best. When they race on the far-side half of the track, runners racing nearest the far rail (low) are best on soft ground.

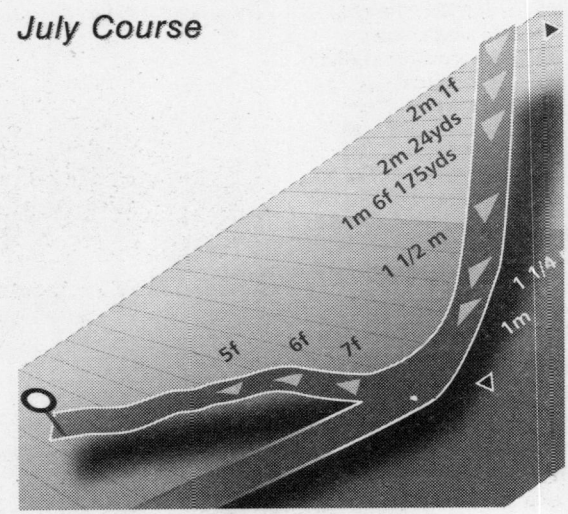

July Course

Ken Hussey's standard times

5f	57.7	1m2f	2min1
6f	1min10	1m4f	2min26.7
7f	1min22.8	1m6f175yds	3min3
1m	1min35.7	2m24yds	3min21.2
1m110yds	1min42	2m1f65yds	3min36

Jockey stats apply for both Newmarket courses. See previous page for trainer & favourite stats.

Jockeys	Wins-Rides	%	£1 level stks	Best Trainer	W-R
Carol A Williams	3-12	25.0	+8.50	Mrs A L King	2-3
G Mosse	5-22	22.7	+25.17	L Cumani	2-7
L Dettori	85-475	17.9	-83.09	J Gosden	20-87
K Fallon	88-508	17.3	-14.94	H Cecil	17-68
R Hills	79-492	16.1	-33.24	J Dunlop	18-90
M Kinane	27-182	14.8	+14.23	A P O'Brien	13-53
L Keniry	3-22	13.6	+11.00	I A Wood	1-1
T Quinn	71-582	12.2	-75.71	H Cecil	22-134
R Hughes	43-384	11.2	-106.04	R Hannon	20-167
M Hills	57-507	11.2	-26.24	B Hills	32-280
S W Kelly	7-63	11.1	+21.00	J Noseda	2-6
O Urbina	13-120	10.8	-43.51	J Fanshawe	10-52
Pat Eddery	61-588	10.4	-171.11	J Dunlop	22-159
J Fortune	43-426	10.1	-98.94	J Gosden	13-77
D McGaffin	4-40	10.0	+16.00	P Mitchell	1-1
J Fanning	3-31	9.7	+1.00	K Ryan	1-1
D Holland	32-335	9.6	-20.75	M Johnston	5-41

Sponsored by Stan James

NOTTINGHAM

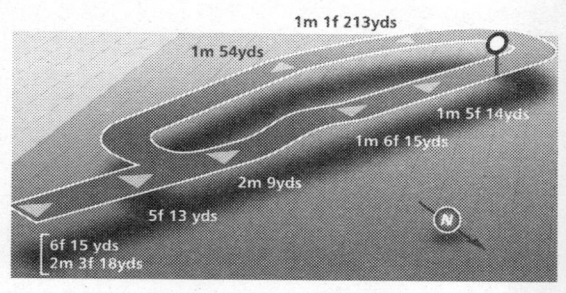

Colwick Park, Colwick Road,
Nottingham, NG2 4BE.
Tel 01159 580 620

How to get there – Road: M1 Jctn 25, A52 east to B686, signs for Trent Bridge, then Colwick Park
Rail: Nottingham

Features: LH, flat, easy turns

2003 Flat fixtures: Mar 26, Apr 1, 21, 29, May 9, 16, 17, Jun 4, 14, 23, Jul 12, 26, Aug 1, 18, 20, Sep 19, 30 Oct 1, 22, 28, Nov 6

Draw: On the straight course, it used to be a case of low numbers being favoured when the stalls were on the far rail and high numbers when they were on the stands' rail, but these days the advantage does not seem to be that great. The occasional meeting will pop up where one side or the other has the edge, normally in early season.

Ken Hussey's standard times

5f13yds	58.7	1m6f15yds	2min58.5
6f15yds	1min11.3	2m9yds	3min24.3
1m54yds	1min40.3	2m2f18yds	3min52.3
1m1f213yds	2min2.4		

Favourites

2-y-o	44.3%	-£5.31
3-y-o+	24.8%	-£117.02
Overall	29.4%	-£122.33

Trainers	Wins-Runs	%	2yo	3yo+	£1 level stks
S Bin Suroor	4-6	66.7	1-1	3-5	+1.07
R Charlton	14-41	34.1	6-9	8-32	+27.38
D Loder	4-12	33.3	4-12	0-0	+13.01
G L Moore	5-18	27.8	0-2	5-16	+15.33
P Cundell	3-12	25.0	0-0	3-12	+16.00
H Cecil	13-52	25.0	6-18	7-34	-14.04
A Stewart	9-37	24.3	2-9	7-28	-4.95
J Gosden	15-62	24.2	4-18	11-44	+10.40
J W Payne	3-13	23.1	2-7	1-6	-5.20
Sir M Prescott	10-47	21.3	2-17	8-30	+9.33
H Candy	8-39	20.5	1-8	7-31	+1.08
J Dunlop	30-149	20.1	8-54	22-95	-33.50

Jockeys	Wins-Rides	%	£1 level stks	Best Trainer	W-R
L Dettori	13-55	23.6	-0.15	D Loder	2-6
Pat Eddery	27-128	21.1	-20.65	J Dunlop	10-29
R Hughes	14-69	20.3	-10.00	R Charlton	4-7
R Hills	12-60	20.0	-24.10	A Stewart	3-5
K Fallon	30-152	19.7	-36.70	H Cecil	5-14
D Holland	23-127	18.1	+58.25	G Wragg	4-22
P Goode	3-18	16.7	-2.25	F Murphy	1-1
D O'Donohoe	4-24	16.7	-10.24	S Bin Suroor	2-3
P Fessey	7-42	16.7	+59.40	K Ryan	2-2
J P Spencer	13-78	16.7	+29.52	P D Evans	2-3
W Ryan	15-93	16.1	-7.96	E Dunlop	3-5
J Fortune	16-100	16.0	-35.24	J Gosden	7-16

Sponsored by Stan James

PONTEFRACT

33 Ropergate, Pontefract,
WF8 1LE. Tel 01977 703 224

How to get there – Road: M62 Jctn 32, then A539
Rail: Pontefract Monkhill or Pontefract Baghill from Leeds

Features: LH, undulating, sharp home turn, last half-mile is all uphill

2003 Flat fixtures: Apr 8, 14, 30, May 23, Jun 1, 9, 22, 30, Jul 8, 18, Aug 6, 17, Sep 18, 25, Oct 6, 20

Draw: Low numbers are considered best here for the same reason as at Chester, in that the course has several distinct left-hand turns with a short home straight, but the advantage is not great. A high draw can be a setback on fast ground, as it forces runners to race wide or drop in behind and onto the rail. The ground can be so bad that the stalls are moved to the outside, or dispensed with, but high numbers racing wide haven't enjoyed an edge on bad going since drainage work was carried out.

Ken Hussey's standard times

5f	1min1.3	1m4f8yds	2min34.5
6f	1min14.2	2m1f22yds	3min42.2
1m4yds	1min41.8	2m1f216yds	3min52
1m2f6yds	2min7.2	2m5f122yds	4min48

Favourites

2-y-o	40.5%	+£1.45
3-y-o+	23.4%	-£89.06
Overall	27.1%	-£87.61

Trainers	Wins-Runs	%	2yo	3yo+	£1 level stks
R Charlton	4-7	57.1	1-2	3-5	+10.54
Miss G Kelleway	3-7	42.9	0-1	3-6	+17.00
J Noseda	7-18	38.9	3-7	4-11	+6.57
Mrs A Perrett	4-12	33.3	1-2	3-10	-1.90
M Jarvis	8-29	27.6	2-6	6-23	+14.63
A Stewart	9-33	27.3	1-3	8-30	-1.51
P Cole	7-27	25.9	5-15	2-12	-11.21
Sir M Stoute	11-43	25.6	1-5	10-38	-0.12
H Cecil	6-25	24.0	0-1	6-24	+13.25
J Dunlop	12-50	24.0	3-9	9-41	-9.69
G Bravery	3-13	23.1	1-3	2-10	+5.50
L Cumani	6-26	23.1	0-3	6-23	-0.63

Jockeys	Wins-Rides	%	£1 level stks	Best Trainer	W-R
T Quinn	12-49	24.5	+24.74	P Cole	2-3
Pat Eddery	14-59	23.7	-3.43	J Noseda	4-5
P Robinson	12-53	22.6	+35.13	M Jarvis	7-19
K Fallon	27-121	22.3	+4.84	Sir M Stoute	3-11
L Dettori	3-15	20.0	-7.26	D Loder	2-3
J P Spencer	8-42	19.0	+9.61	A Scott	1-1
R Hills	6-33	18.2	-17.16	Sir M Stoute	1-1
K Darley	43-251	17.1	+33.17	T Easterby	6-35
A Daly	3-18	16.7	-2.37	C Egerton	1-1
A Clark	6-36	16.7	+26.00	M Dods	3-15
T E Durcan	12-73	16.4	+39.60	M Tompkins	3-20
J Fortune	13-81	16.0	-10.46	Mrs J Ramsden	3-14

Sponsored by Stan James

REDCAR

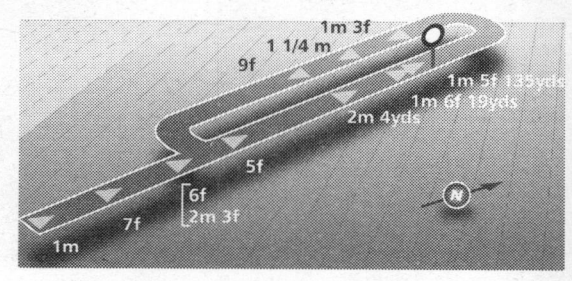

Redcar, Cleveland, TS10 2BY.
Tel 01642 484 068

How to get there – Road: A1, A168, A19, then A174
Rail: Redcar Central from Darlington
Features: LH, flat, galloping
2003 Flat fixtures: May 1, 12, 26, 27, Jun 10, 20, 21, Jul 6, 26, Aug 9, 10, 23, Sep 4, 15, Oct 4, 17, 28, Nov 3
Draw: It is not unusual to see fields verging on 30 in straight-course races several times throughout a season but there is rarely much in the draw.

Ken Hussey's standard times

5f	56.7	1m3f	2min17
6f	1min9.4	1m4f	2min30
7f	1min22	1m5f135yds	2min54.7
1m	1min34.7	1m6f19yds	3min0
1m1f	1min49.3	2m4yds	3min25
1m2f	2min2.6	2m3f	4min5.3

Favourites

2-y-o	32.6%	-£40.36
3-y-o+	26.9%	-£69.14
Overall	28.3%	-£109.49

Trainers	Wins-Runs	%	2yo	3yo+	£1 level stks
T Mills	3-6	50.0	2-2	1-4	+37.25
J Noseda	11-29	37.9	2-8	9-21	+20.61
M Tregoning	3-8	37.5	2-3	1-5	+6.58
J Gosden	12-33	36.4	6-15	6-18	+25.90
H Cecil	5-14	35.7	3-4	2-10	-0.57
D Loder	3-9	33.3	2-8	1-1	-5.18
B Smart	3-10	30.0	0-4	3-6	+11.13
G A Butler	5-17	29.4	4-10	1-7	+9.40
J Fanshawe	7-24	29.2	2-9	5-15	-0.65
John Berry	3-11	27.3	0-0	3-11	+13.75
C Dwyer	6-22	27.3	0-4	6-18	+10.25
J Hills	6-23	26.1	1-6	5-17	+5.25

Jockeys	Wins-Rides	%	£1 level stks	Best Trainer	W-R
Emma Ramsden	3-6	50.0	+4.25	Mrs J Ramsden	2-2
J Mackay	4-11	36.4	+6.63	M Bell	3-3
D Corby	3-10	30.0	+10.25	M Channon	2-2
G Faulkner	5-21	23.8	+27.50	T Barron	4-8
D Sweeney	3-13	23.1	+6.25	N Littmoden	2-2
K Darley	44-209	21.1	-6.97	T Easterby	5-22
G Carter	11-54	20.4	-7.82	J Berry	3-9
J P Spencer	3-15	20.0	-0.30	D Loder	1-1
W Ryan	3-17	17.6	+5.58	H Cecil	2-5
G Hind	4-23	17.4	+16.50	J Gosden	3-5
S Drowne	5-29	17.2	-11.42	R Charlton	2-3
M Henry	3-18	16.7	-5.38	C Dwyer	1-1

Sponsored by Stan James

RIPON

77 North Street, Ripon, N Yorkshire HG44 1DS.
Tel 01765 602 156

How to get there – Road: A1, then B6265
Rail: Harrogate, bus to Ripon centre, 1m walk
Features: RH, sharp
2003 Flat fixtures: Apr 2, 17, 26, May 18, 28 Jun 18, 19, Jul 7, 19, Aug 4, 16, 25, 26, 30, Sep 27
Draw: High numbers are favoured on the round course, especially over 1m. However, the draw has a massive effect in sprint races, where any runner drawn in the centre stalls can be completely ignored. The optimum conditions for low numbers seem to be when the ground is good or faster and there are 12 runners or fewer. When the stalls stretch far enough across the course, there is a fast strip of ground towards the far rail that horses drawn high can use.

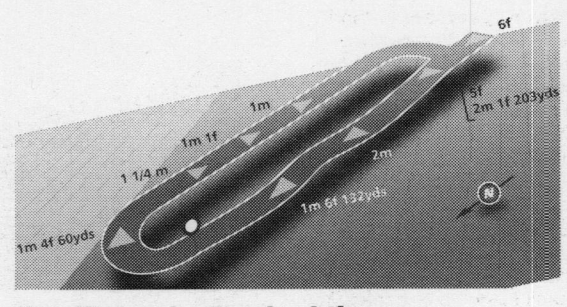

Ken Hussey's standard times

5f	57.8	1m2f	2min3.3
6f	1min10.6	1m4f60yds	2min34
1m	1min37.8	2m	3min27
1m1f	1min50.8	2m1f203yds	3min52

Favourites

2-y-o	40.6%	-£10.36
3-y-o+	33.2%	-£18.96
Overall	34.8%	-£29.32

Trainers	Wins-Runs	%	2yo	3yo+	£1 level stks
H Cecil	10-16	62.5	0-0	10-16	+11.92
Sir M Prescott	4-8	50.0	3-4	1-4	+2.84
M Tregoning	4-10	40.0	1-1	3-9	+3.26
B Hanbury	3-9	33.3	0-0	3-9	+12.75
C Brittain	6-19	31.6	0-3	6-16	+17.37
W Haggas	6-23	26.1	2-5	4-18	+4.38
M Jarvis	3-12	25.0	1-1	2-11	-4.07
A Stewart	4-16	25.0	0-0	4-16	+1.25
J Dunlop	17-70	24.3	4-7	13-63	-16.98
B Hills	17-72	23.6	3-7	14-65	-9.78
J Fanshawe	6-26	23.1	1-5	5-21	-1.88
B McMahon	8-44	18.2	3-12	5-32	+25.63

Jockeys	Wins-Rides	%	£1 level stks	Best Trainer	W-R
L Dettori	4-6	66.7	+8.45	C Brittain	1-1
S Drowne	4-9	44.4	+41.00	M Tompkins	2-2
T Quinn	9-29	31.0	+16.08	H Cecil	5-6
P Robinson	6-22	27.3	+12.63	C Brittain	3-5
K Fallon	12-44	27.3	-7.83	W Haggas	2-3
G Hind	5-21	23.8	-1.25	C Dwyer	1-1
J P Spencer	5-24	20.8	+9.02	L Cumani	2-4
R Ffrench	11-53	20.8	+25.07	A Stewart	3-5
T Hamilton	3-16	18.8	+32.00	J G FitzGerald	1-1
R Hills	4-22	18.2	+0.75	A Stewart	1-1
G Carter	9-52	17.3	-10.56	J Berry	2-7
J Fortune	12-71	16.9	-10.09	J Gosden	2-3

Sponsored by Stan James

SALISBURY

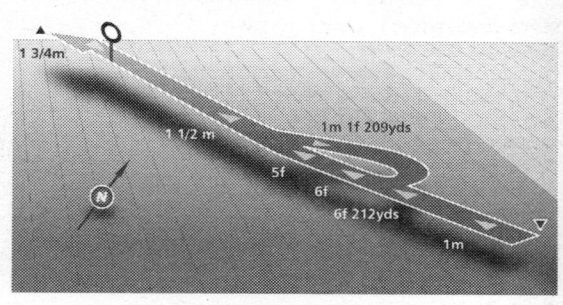

Netherhampton, Salisbury, Wilts, SP2 8PN. Tel 01722 326 461

How to get there – Road: 2m west of Salisbury on A3094
Rail: Salisbury, bus
Features: RH, uphill finish
2003 Flat fixtures: May 4, 15, Jun 10, 15, 25, 26, Jul 4, 12, 25, Aug 13, 14, 28, Sep 4, 16, Oct 1
Draw: High numbers are best on the straight course on good or faster ground, particularly so last season after a temporary rail was taken down in midsummer. Low numbers take over on good to soft or slower.

Ken Hussey's standard times

5f	59.6	1m1f209yds	2min5
6f	1min12	1m4f	2min32
6f212yds	1min25.2	1m6f15yds	2min58.3
1m	1min39.2		

Favourites

2-y-o	39.4%	-£0.92
3-y-o+	28.8%	-£23.30
Overall	31.7%	-£24.23

Trainers	Wins-Runs	%	2yo	3yo+	£1 level stks
D Loder	4-7	57.1	3-6	1-1	+2.83
P L Gilligan	3-6	50.0	0-0	3-6	+30.50
G Wragg	5-13	38.5	0-0	5-13	+8.87
W Haggas	5-15	33.3	1-2	4-13	+15.71
H Cecil	8-31	25.8	1-4	7-27	-8.26
J Gosden	20-82	24.4	9-30	11-52	-3.26
C Brittain	4-17	23.5	2-4	2-13	-1.25
J Fanshawe	8-36	22.2	1-8	7-28	+7.75
G L Moore	11-58	19.0	0-5	11-53	+27.75
A Reid	3-16	18.8	0-4	3-12	+3.75
R Brotherton	3-16	18.8	0-3	3-13	+5.33
R Charlton	13-70	18.6	2-15	11-55	-22.31

Jockeys	Wins-Rides	%	£1 level stks	Best Trainer	W-R
L Dettori	13-48	27.1	+1.53	D Loder	3-5
R Hughes	43-186	23.1	+40.34	R Hannon	15-78
K Fallon	17-77	22.1	+1.94	H Cecil	3-7
B Doyle	5-25	20.0	+29.25	B Meehan	2-10
T Quinn	23-120	19.2	-28.51	J Dunlop	6-15
R Hills	12-64	18.8	-10.35	J Dunlop	5-16
D Holland	5-27	18.5	+2.00	G Wragg	3-4
W Ryan	14-81	17.3	+4.11	Sir M Stoute	4-6
P Robinson	4-24	16.7	+28.50	G Margarson	3-5
G Duffield	5-32	15.6	-2.45	S Woods	2-8
D O'Neill	25-178	14.0	+1.22	R Hannon	18-109
J Fortune	14-101	13.9	-27.26	J Gosden	7-19

Sponsored by Stan James

SANDOWN

Esher, Surrey, KT10 9AJ.
Tel: 01372 463 072 or 464 348.

How to get there – Road: M25 Jctn 10 then A3
Rail: Esher from Waterloo
Features: RH, last 7f uphill
2003 Flat fixtures: Apr 26 (mixed), May 26, 27, Jun 5, 13, 14, Jul 4, 5, 23, 24, Aug 13, 14, 29, 30, Sep 14, 17
Draw: High numbers have an edge in big fields over 7f16yds and 1m. On the sprint track, the advantage is even greater; when it's soft and the stalls are on the far side, high numbers have a massive advantage. When the stalls are on the stands' side of the sprint track, low numbers enjoy a slight edge when all the runners stay towards the stands' rail, but when a few go far side high numbers hold the upper hand again. The far rail is much faster than the stands' rail, which in turn is much faster than the centre of the course over 5f. The softer it is, the greater the advantage.

Ken Hussey's standard times

5f6yds	59.2	1m2f7yds	2min5
7f16yds	1min27	1m3f91yds	2min21.7
1m14yds	1min40	1m6f	2min57
1m1f	1min52	2m78yds	3min30.4

Favourites

2-y-o	33.3%	-£19.40
3-y-o+	25.8%	-£74.62
Overall	27.6%	-£94.02

Trainers	Wins-Runs	%	2yo	3yo+	£1 level stks
J J Quinn	4-5	80.0	1-1	3-4	+16.88
J L Harris	3-6	50.0	0-0	3-6	+29.00
D Loder	7-18	38.9	7-15	0-3	+1.10
A Stewart	10-35	28.6	0-1	10-34	+32.67
G Wragg	7-27	25.9	0-1	7-26	+8.58
Sir M Stoute	29-118	24.6	7-19	22-99	+26.91
P Cole	16-66	24.2	4-19	12-47	+49.12
S C Williams	5-21	23.8	0-0	5-21	+41.75
J R Poulton	7-31	22.6	0-0	7-31	+62.25
N Callaghan	4-18	22.2	2-3	2-15	-3.00
L Montague Hall	3-14	21.4	0-2	3-12	+17.00
T Easterby	3-14	21.4	0-2	3-12	+5.75

Jockeys	Wins-Rides	%	£1 level stks	Best Trainer	W-R
R Thomas	3-13	23.1	+13.00	R J Price	2-3
Alex Greaves	3-13	23.1	+26.00	D Nicholls	3-13
W Supple	8-37	21.6	+42.75	J Balding	1-1
J P Spencer	8-38	21.1	+17.25	L Cumani	2-5
L Dettori	33-158	20.9	-17.87	D Loder	6-15
E Ahern	5-26	19.2	+17.00	G A Butler	3-12
M Kinane	5-26	19.2	+0.28	Mrs A Perrett	2-3
D Holland	13-69	18.8	+33.00	G Wragg	4-11
B Doyle	3-17	17.6	+15.00	L Cottrell	1-1
K Darley	12-72	16.7	-5.67	M Johnston	3-19
K Fallon	33-199	16.6	-55.09	Sir M Stoute	9-30
R Hills	16-99	16.2	-1.65	M Tregoning	3-13

Sponsored by Stan James

SOUTHWELL

Rolleston, Nr. Newark,
Notts, NG25 0TS.
Tel: 01636 814481.

How to get there – Road: A1 to Newark, then A617 or M1 to Nottingham then A612
Rail: Rolleston
Features: LH fibresand, sharp
2003 Flat fixtures: Mar 20, 28 (turf), Apr 4, 7, 22 (turf), May 1, 8 (turf), Jun 9, 19, 25, Sep 2, 26, Oct 7, 16, 21, Nov 19, 24, 25, Dec 3, 9, 13, 16, 27

Draw: A low draw is a major advantage over the straight 5f. Horses can win from most positions from 6f to 1m, though a very wide draw is an inconvenience. For some reason, horses drawn low have a spectacular record over 1m4f, while front-runners do very well at trips of up to 7f.

NB: Due to the shortage of meetings on the turf course, our trainer, jockey and favourite stats relate to AW racing only.

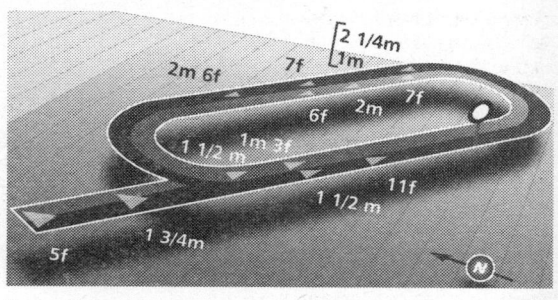

Ken Hussey's standard times

5f	57.7	1m4f	2min34
6f	1min13.5	1m5f	2min47.4
7f	1min27	1m6f	3min1.7
1m	1min40	2m	3min30
1m3f	2min21.6	2m2f	3min58

Favourites

2-y-o	35.4%	-£13.36
3-y-o+	29.9%	-£188.73
Overall	30.6%	-£202.09

Trainers

Trainers	Wins-Runs	%	2yo	3yo+	£1 level stks
H Morrison	12-36	33.3	2-3	10-33	+56.93
Sir M Prescott	40-125	32.0	8-44	32-81	-25.46
A Kelleway	7-22	31.8	0-3	7-19	+33.50
J A Gilbert	4-14	28.6	0-2	4-12	+41.33
P Cole	13-53	24.5	4-15	9-38	+8.54
C Wall	4-17	23.5	1-1	3-16	-9.57
M Bell	12-51	23.5	3-9	9-42	-1.77
B Meehan	17-75	22.7	14-40	3-35	-5.28
P Makin	14-62	22.6	1-4	13-58	+53.87
Miss S Hall	5-23	21.7	2-3	3-20	+40.50
C Egerton	5-23	21.7	0-4	5-19	+9.98
M Jarvis	6-28	21.4	3-6	3-22	+2.37

Jockeys

Jockeys	Wins-Rides	%	£1 level stks	Best Trainer	W-R
L Dettori	4-9	44.4	+8.36	J Jenkins	2-3
M Hills	7-16	43.8	+4.97	B Hills	2-4
I Mongan	4-13	30.8	+0.25	Sir M Prescott	3-3
S Walker	4-14	28.6	+14.25	J L Harris	3-9
L Vickers	3-11	27.3	+1.75	D Shaw	2-3
K Fallon	19-82	23.2	+19.41	J Eyre	3-4
B Reilly	3-16	18.8	+13.33	J A Gilbert	3-6
D Holland	22-119	18.5	+8.06	M Johnston	5-17
G Duffield	47-261	18.0	-66.52	Sir M Prescott	17-55
R Hughes	4-23	17.4	+4.50	H Morrison	2-3
P Dobbs	9-56	16.1	+9.38	J Balding	3-15
W Ryan	10-63	15.9	+5.28	Lord Huntingdon	5-7

Sponsored by Stan James

THIRSK

Station Road, Thirsk, N Yorkshire,
Y07 1QL. Tel 01845 522 276

How to get there – Road: A61 from A1 in the west or A19 in the east
Rail: Thirsk, 10 min walk
Features: LH, sharp, tight turns, drains well
2003 Flat fixtures: Apr 11, 12, May 3, 10, 17, Jun 2, 17, 26, Jul 25, Aug 1, 2, 11, 22, Sep 6, 16
Draw: In sprints, high numbers are definitely favoured when the ground is genuinely firm. However, on good to firm ground and softer the bias does not seem as great as it used to be, and last year the far side (low) often proved best, thanks to selective watering. When the going is on the soft side, low numbers always have the advantage, as the far rail becomes the place to be. Low numbers are also favoured over 7f and 1m.

Ken Hussey's standard times

5f	57.4	1m	1min35.8
6f	1min9.5	1m4f	2min30
7f	1min23	2m	3min22.6

Favourites

2-y-o	37.0%	-£5.57
3-y-o+	34.9%	+£10.20
Overall	35.4%	+£4.63

Trainers

	Wins-Runs	%	2yo	3yo+	£1 level stks
M Tregoning	7-14	50.0	1-1	6-13	+2.81
M Jarvis	4-9	44.4	1-1	3-8	+12.25
G Margarson	3-7	42.9	0-0	3-7	+1.86
J Dunlop	15-35	42.9	0-7	15-28	+15.59
H Cecil	7-18	38.9	0-0	7-18	-2.37
J Toller	3-8	37.5	0-0	3-8	+8.50
G Wragg	3-8	37.5	0-0	3-8	+0.88
E Dunlop	7-19	36.8	1-5	6-14	+12.34
Sir M Prescott	5-15	33.3	3-5	2-10	+4.46
B Hills	8-25	32.0	1-4	7-21	+0.44
Sir M Stoute	10-32	31.3	0-3	10-29	+12.57
J Fanshawe	8-29	27.6	1-4	7-25	+7.31

Jockeys

	Wins-Rides	%	£1 level stks	Best Trainer	W-R
B Doyle	3-4	75.0	+8.63	G A Swinbank	1-1
Emma Ramsden	3-5	60.0	+16.00	M Dods	1-1
T Quinn	3-8	37.5	-1.12	H Cecil	2-2
S Whitworth	4-11	36.4	+5.25	J Toller	2-4
R Hills	3-10	30.0	+8.50	M Tregoning	1-1
A Mackay	3-12	25.0	+21.00	M Channon	2-4
M Henry	4-16	25.0	-5.20	J Dunlop	3-3
K Darley	31-142	21.8	-31.01	T Easterby	6-26
G Baker	3-15	20.0	+7.38	M Usher	1-1
D Holland	9-47	19.1	-9.21	M Johnston	4-13
D Sweeney	6-33	18.2	+33.18	P Cole	2-3
S Sanders	10-56	17.9	-8.10	D Nicholls	2-3

Sponsored by Stan James

Hampton Street, Warwick
CV34 6HN. Tel 01926 491 553

WARWICK

How to get there – Road: M40 Jctn 14, A429
Rail: Warwick
Features: LH, sharp turns
2003 Flat fixtures: Apr 9, 21, May 5, Jun 16, 21, 22, Jul 4, 10, 19, Aug 25, Sep 8, 20
Draw: Low numbers are slightly favoured on fast ground, only because the course turns left-handed at some point over all distances. However, when the ground is genuinely soft, high numbers have the edge, as the outside rail rides much faster.

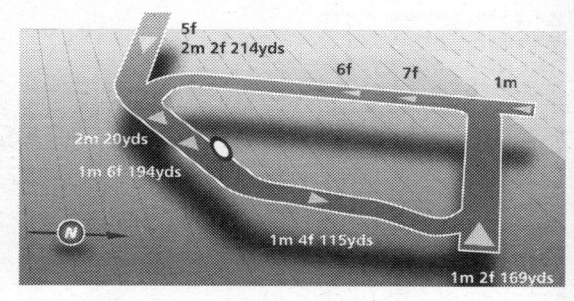

Ken Hussey's standard times

5f	58	1m4f115yds	2min34.6
5f110yds	1min4	1m6f194yds	3min6
6f	1min10.6	2m20yds	3min24
7f	1min22.2	2m2f214yds	3min58
1m	1min35.3	2m3f13yds	4min0
1m2f169yds	2min12		

Favourites

2-y-o	44.6%	+£11.85
3-y-o+	29.6%	-£29.98
Overall	33.0%	-£18.13

Trainers	Wins-Runs	%	2yo	3yo+	£1 level stks
Sir M Stoute	9-23	39.1	3-8	6-15	+17.80
H Cecil	3-9	33.3	1-2	2-7	-1.81
M Johnston	9-27	33.3	2-7	7-20	+12.42
J Dunlop	10-32	31.3	2-12	8-20	+2.25
J Fanshawe	14-45	31.1	5-15	9-30	+14.71
M Pipe	7-25	28.0	0-4	7-21	+6.77
Lady Herries	3-11	27.3	0-0	3-11	+13.50
N Callaghan	3-13	23.1	2-5	1-8	+11.50
J Eustace	3-13	23.1	2-4	1-9	+20.00
H Morrison	4-18	22.2	0-3	4-15	+18.12
B Hills	14-69	20.3	3-20	11-49	-1.60
W Haggas	5-25	20.0	0-9	5-16	-9.25

Jockeys	Wins-Rides	%	£1 level stks	Best Trainer	W-R
T Quinn	14-49	28.6	+4.27	D Elsworth	2-2
M Hills	17-63	27.0	+19.39	B Hills	8-29
J Fortune	8-30	26.7	+19.41	P Cole	3-8
Pat Eddery	11-44	25.0	+15.39	B Meehan	3-9
J D Smith	4-18	22.2	+39.83	P Felgate	1-1
G Carter	12-58	20.7	+4.53	A Berry	3-6
J Fanning	4-22	18.2	+0.50	M Johnston	2-8
W Supple	7-39	17.9	-7.63	D Coakley	1-1
P Dobbs	4-23	17.4	+2.83	J Toller	1-1
K Darley	8-46	17.4	-13.54	M Johnston	2-2
R Hughes	7-41	17.1	+6.42	R Hannon	2-18
R Winston	4-24	16.7	+56.50	A Hales	1-1

Sponsored by Stan James

WINDSOR

Maidenhead Road, Windsor,
Berkshire SL4 5JJ.
Tel 01753 864 726

How to get there – Road: M4 Jctn 6, A355, A308
Rail: Windsor Central from Paddington or Windsor Riverside from Waterloo
Features: Figure of eight, flat, easy turns, straight almost 5f long
2003 Flat fixtures: Apr 7, 14, 28, May 12, 19, 31, Jun 1, 2, 9, 16, 23, 30, Jul 7, 14, 21, 28, Aug 4, 10, 11, 18, 23, Sep 29, Oct 6, 13

Draw: It's common to see large fields in the summer, particularly in sprints and 1m67yds events. Over the latter trip, runners drawn high enjoy the edge since the start is on a chute and the course follows a tight right-handed loop to the point where it joins the sprint track. In sprints, high numbers hold a definite advantage when the ground is good or faster, and a very low draw can be tough to overcome in big fields. Soft ground swings the bias to the opposite, good to soft levels things out.

Ken Hussey's standard times

5f10yds	59	1m2f7yds	2min3.6
5f217yds	1min10.2	1m3f135yds	2min22.6
1m67yds	1min41.6		

Favourites

2-y-o	31.3%	-£27.22
3-y-o+	26.3%	-£68.85
Overall	27.6%	-£96.07

Trainers	Wins-Runs	%	2yo	3yo+	£1 level stks
S Bin Suroor	4-8	50.0	0-0	4-8	+0.50
J Noseda	10-34	29.4	4-9	6-25	-0.66
M Johnston	8-28	28.6	1-3	7-25	+33.83
Sir M Stoute	28-103	27.2	0-8	28-95	-0.27
Miss D McHale	4-20	20.0	0-0	4-20	+20.50
J Gosden	13-68	19.1	0-2	13-66	-34.51
R Brotherton	3-16	18.8	0-1	3-15	+11.00
I A Wood	7-38	18.4	0-6	7-32	+33.75
D Cosgrove	4-23	17.4	1-6	3-17	+11.00
Sir M Prescott	4-26	15.4	1-17	3-9	-12.45
G Wragg	4-29	13.8	1-1	3-28	-14.67
R J Price	3-22	13.6	0-1	3-21	+10.00

Jockeys	Wins-Rides	%	£1 level stks	Best Trainer	W-R
R Winston	3-4	75.0	+14.00	R Beckett	1-1
J Fanning	4-16	25.0	+8.75	M Johnston	2-6
L Dettori	23-110	20.9	-27.77	J Gosden	9-27
G Gibbons	3-16	18.8	+19.00	J R Best	1-1
K Darley	6-35	17.1	-8.43	I Balding	2-5
R Hughes	40-242	16.5	-28.08	R Hannon	18-107
K Fallon	28-177	15.8	-50.15	Sir M Stoute	6-31
R Hills	12-80	15.0	+59.47	J Hills	3-20
A Beech	4-27	14.8	+8.50	P Mitchell	1-1
Pat Eddery	41-294	13.9	-137.30	B Meehan	11-69
N Callan	11-80	13.8	+88.50	K Burke	4-23
T Quinn	30-220	13.6	-37.63	J Dunlop	4-19

Sponsored by Stan James

WOLVES

Gorsebrook Road, Wolverhampton,
West Midlands BV6 0PE.
Tel 01902 24481

How to get there – Road: of A449, close to M6, M42 and M54
Rail: Wolverhampton, bus
Features: LH, fibresand, very sharp

2003 Flat fixtures: Mar 22, 24, 31, Apr 12, 25, 28, May 12, 19, 23, Jun 6, 13, 21, 27, 30, Jul 11, 14, 19, 25, Aug 7, 8, 15, Sep 6, 20, Oct 4, 20, Nov 1, 10, 14, 15, 17, 21, 28, 29, Dec 1, 6, 8, 12, 13, 15, 19, 22, 26, 31

Draw: There is little in the draw over 5f but from 6f to 1m4f low numbers are at a disadvantage at most meetings, as the inside of the track rides slower than elsewhere. This can be reversed, however, by the track being prepared differently following very wet or very cold weather.

Ken Hussey's standard times

5f	1min0.3	1m1f79yds	1min57.6
6f	1min13.2	1m4f	2min35.3
7f	1min27	1m6f166yds	3min11.7
1m100yds	1min46.8	2m46yds	3min36.7

Favourites

2-y-o	30.8%	-£63.63
3-y-o+	31.0%	-£170.20
Overall	30.9%	-£233.82

Trainers

Trainers	Wins-Runs	%	2yo	3yo+	£1 level stks
D Loder	5-9	55.6	1-2	4-7	+0.66
J Fanshawe	7-20	35.0	1-3	6-17	-2.28
M Tregoning	3-9	33.3	1-1	2-8	+1.63
J Noseda	10-30	33.3	0-3	10-27	+10.21
Sir M Prescott	49-169	29.0	18-67	31-102	-29.20
M Jarvis	16-56	28.6	2-12	14-44	+22.20
Sir M Stoute	6-22	27.3	1-6	5-16	-5.07
W Jarvis	14-54	25.9	3-16	11-38	+24.24
Paul Johnson	4-16	25.0	0-0	4-16	+10.33
T Mills	17-69	24.6	0-5	17-64	+48.86
M Chapman	4-17	23.5	2-3	2-14	+9.25
P Hedger	3-13	23.1	0-1	3-12	-3.59

Jockeys

Jockeys	Wins-Rides	%	£1 level stks	Best Trainer	W-R
C Hannaford	6-13	46.2	+45.58	A Newcombe	6-12
Clare Roche	3-12	25.0	+18.75	D Nicholls	2-7
M Hills	6-24	25.0	-2.75	B Hills	2-7
S Sanders	41-171	24.0	+72.66	Sir M Prescott	12-35
A Beech	4-18	22.2	+2.57	B Hills	1-1
D Holland	29-131	22.1	+6.83	M Johnston	7-13
Carol A Williams	3-14	21.4	+16.25	D Barker	1-1
Lynsey Hanna	7-34	20.6	+14.25	T Barron	6-25
Sarah Bosley	3-15	20.0	+29.00	D Shaw	2-3
K Fallon	17-86	19.8	-19.87	E Alston	3-10
P Robinson	5-26	19.2	-7.46	M Jarvis	4-11
R Smith	10-52	19.2	+38.80	R Hannon	6-18

Sponsored by Stan James

YARMOUTH

Jellicoe Road, Great Yarmouth,
Norfolk NR30 4AU.
Tel 01493 842 527

How to get there – Road: A47 to end, A1064
Rail: Great Yarmouth, bus
Features: LH, flat, drains well
2003 Flat fixtures: Apr 21, May 16, 28, Jun 12, Jul 2, 3, 24, 28, Aug 6, 13, 24, 26, Sep 2, 16, 17, 18, Oct 21, 29
Draw: High numbers enjoy a definite advantage when the ground is firm and fields are large, but nothing like as much as they had in 1996/97. The offshore breeze, which blows away from the stands' rail, can make it difficult for the watering to be even.

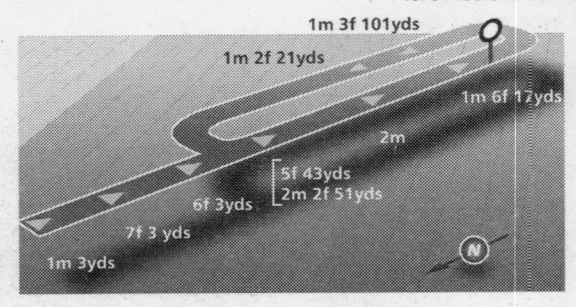

Ken Hussey's standard times

5f43yds	1min0.4	1m3f101yds	2min23
6f3yds	1min10.7	1m6f17yds	2min58
7f3yds	1min23	2m	3min25
1m3yds	1min35.5	2m1f170yds	3min48
1m2f21yds	2min3.3	2m2f51yds	3min54

Favourites

2-y-o	40.4%	-£11.93
3-y-o+	30.8%	-£62.13
Overall	33.5%	-£74.06

Trainers	Wins-Runs	%	2yo	3yo+	£1 level stks
P R Webber	5-8	62.5	0-0	5-8	+26.25
D Loder	8-15	53.3	8-14	0-1	+13.12
H Cecil	21-55	38.2	6-15	15-40	-6.01
D Cantillon	4-14	28.6	0-0	4-14	+24.00
Mrs A Perrett	6-21	28.6	0-2	6-19	-0.95
Sir M Prescott	14-56	25.0	6-36	8-20	+19.36
J Dunlop	13-54	24.1	5-9	8-45	-11.71
L Cumani	9-39	23.1	3-12	6-27	+6.45
Miss J Feilden	3-14	21.4	0-3	3-11	+20.80
Sir M Stoute	15-70	21.4	5-36	10-34	-22.45
J Gosden	17-81	21.0	6-30	11-51	-9.26
D Nicholls	6-29	20.7	0-1	6-28	-0.88

Jockeys	Wins-Rides	%	£1 level stks	Best Trainer	W-R
Emma Ramsden	3-5	60.0	+11.50	P R Webber	1-1
L Dettori	24-76	31.6	-8.13	D Loder	7-11
T Quinn	30-107	28.0	+27.54	H Cecil	10-23
L Newman	8-31	25.8	+43.50	N Callaghan	2-4
N Mackay	4-17	23.5	+40.75	Miss J Feilden	2-2
J P Spencer	17-79	21.5	+26.55	L Cumani	6-15
R Hills	21-101	20.8	-2.70	J Dunlop	5-8
K Fallon	24-116	20.7	-48.88	H Cecil	6-13
R Hughes	14-76	18.4	+5.28	S Woods	2-3
J Fortune	11-64	17.2	+6.13	J Gosden	4-21
Pat Eddery	13-78	16.7	-27.11	J Dunlop	3-6
D McGaffin	4-25	16.0	+17.50	D Morris	3-12

YORK

York, YO2 1EX.
Tel 01904 620 911

How to get there – Road: Course south of city on Knavesmire Road. From north, A1, A59 to York, northern bypass from A19 to A64. Otherwise, A64
Rail: York, bus
Features: LH, flat
2003 Flat fixtures: May 13, 14, 15, Jun 13, 14, Jul 11, 12, Aug 19, 20, 21, Sep 3, 7, Oct 9, 10, 11
Draw: The draw here is not as unpredictable in sprints as some would believe, and runners who race just to the far side of centre (low) are usually favoured. This changes on soft/heavy ground, though, when the stands' rail (high) definitely rides best.

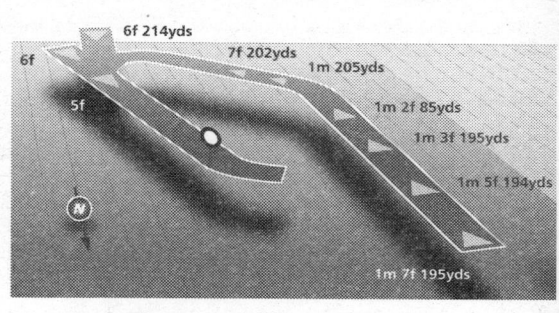

Ken Hussey's standard times

5f	56.6	1m2f85yds	2min7
6f	1min9.2	1m3f195yds	2min26.4
6f214yds	1min21.7	1m5f194yds	2min53
7f202yds	1min35.4	2m7f195yds	3min20
1m205yds	1min48		

Favourites

2-y-o	37.2%	-£2.41
3-y-o+	26.1%	-£13.23
Overall	28.9%	-£15.64

Trainers	Wins-Runs	%	2yo	3yo+	£1 level stks
D Loder	5-14	35.7	3-12	2-2	-1.96
M Tregoning	4-13	30.8	3-4	1-9	+7.62
S Bin Suroor	11-36	30.6	0-0	11-36	+2.31
Mrs A Perrett	4-16	25.0	0-1	4-15	+18.33
A P O'Brien	10-42	23.8	4-13	6-29	-0.76
P Makin	3-14	21.4	1-1	2-13	-3.80
H Cecil	13-62	21.0	1-3	12-59	-14.57
S Dow	3-15	20.0	0-2	3-13	+13.50
W Storey	3-15	20.0	0-0	3-15	+9.00
Sir M Stoute	25-130	19.2	5-18	20-112	-30.92
L Cumani	10-54	18.5	1-6	9-48	-2.59
J Dunlop	17-104	16.3	7-20	10-84	-17.40

Jockeys	Wins-Rides	%	£1 level stks	Best Trainer	W-R
R L Moore	3-9	33.3	+18.75	S Dow	1-1
J Murtagh	5-17	29.4	+9.00	Sir M Stoute	3-6
M Kinane	21-112	18.8	-2.01	A P O'Brien	10-33
L Dettori	25-147	17.0	-22.79	S Bin Suroor	8-25
A Beech	4-26	15.4	+11.63	D Eddy	1-1
K Fallon	37-259	14.3	-60.79	Sir M Stoute	8-43
J P Spencer	9-64	14.1	+17.44	L Cumani	3-18
R Hills	17-122	13.9	+0.18	J Dunlop	3-19
T Quinn	25-181	13.8	-34.38	P Cole	5-22
Pat Eddery	27-200	13.5	-27.60	J Dunlop	7-48
P Doe	3-23	13.0	+27.00	R J Price	1-1
K Darley	37-287	12.9	+10.79	M Johnston	12-61

Sponsored by Stan James

BETTING CHART

ON	ODDS	AGAINST
50	Evens	50
52.4	11-10	47.6
54.5	6-5	45.5
55.6	5-4	44.4
58	11-8	42
60	6-4	40
62	13-8	38
63.6	7-43	6.4
65.3	15-8	34.7
66.7	2-13	3.3
68	85-40	32
69.2	9-4	30.8
71.4	5-2	28.6
73.4	11-4	26.6
75	3-1	25
76.9	100-30	23.1
77.8	7-2	22.2
80	4-1	20
82	9-2	18
83.3	5-1	16.7
84.6	11-2	15.4
85.7	6-2	14.3
86.7	13-2	13.3
87.5	7-1	12.5
88.2	15-2	11.8
89	8-1	11
89.35	100-12	10.65
89.4	17-2	10.6
90	9-1	10
91	10-1	9
91.8	11-1	8.2
92.6	12-1	7.4
93.5	14-1	6.5
94.4	16-1	5.6
94.7	18-1	5.3
95.2	20-1	4.8
95.7	22-1	4.3
96.2	25-1	3.8
97.2	33-1	2.8
97.6	40-1	2.4
98.1	50-1	1.9
98.5	66-1	1.3
99.0	100-1	.99

The table above (often known as the 'Field Money Table') shows both bookmakers' margins and how much a backer needs to invest to win £100. To calculate a bookmaker's margin, simply add up the percentages of all the odds on offer. The difference between the total and 100% gives the 'over-round' on the book. To determine what stake is required to win £100 (includes returned stake) at a particular price, just look at the relevant row, either odds-against or odds-on.

Sponsored by Stan James

RULE 4 DEDUCTIONS

When a horse is withdrawn before coming under starter's orders, but after a market has been formed, bookmakers are entitled to make the following deductions from win and place returns (excluding stakes) in accordance with Tattersalls' Rule 4(c).

Odds of withdrawn horse	Deduction from winnings
(1) 3-10 or shorter	75p in the £
(2) 2-5 to 1-3	70p in the £
(3) 8-15 to 4-9	65p in the £
(4) 8-13 to 4-7	60p in the £
(5) 4-5 to 4-6	55p in the £
(6) 20-21 to 5-6	50p in the £
(7) Evens to 6-5	45p in the £
(8) 5-4 to 6-4	40p in the £
(9) 13-8 to 7-4	35p in the £
(10) 15-8 to 9-4	30p in the £
(11) 5-2 to 3-1	25p in the £
(12) 100-30 to 4-1	20p in the £
(13) 9-2 to 11-2	15p in the £
(14) 6-1 to 9-1	10p in the £
(15) 10-1 to 14-1	5p in the £
(16) longer than 14-1	no deductions

(17) When more than one horse is withdrawn without coming under starter's orders, total deductions shall not exceed 75p in the £.

*Starting-price bets are affected only when there was insufficient time to form a new market.

Feedback!

If you have any comments or critiscism about this book, or suggestions for future editions, please tell us.

Write Chris Cook,
2003 Flat Annual
Racing & Football Outlook
Floor 23,
1 Canada Square,
London E14 5AP

email c.cook@mgn.co.uk

Fax FAO Chris Cook, 0207 293 3758

WIN!
.... a half-year's supply of RFO – FREE!

Instead of testing your patience with one of those smart-alecy quizzes, this year's annual competition asks you to do something more creative. Imagine a race over 1m4f at Epsom in which the only runners are the last ten winners of the Derby. What's the finishing order?

Just write each horse's finishing position in your Derby of Derbys in the box next to its name and return the list to us, together with your details in the entry form below. Entries to:

Chris Cook, Flat Annual Competition, Racing & Football Outlook, Floor 23, 1 Canada Square, London, E14 5AP.

Entries must reach us no later than first post on Monday May 26. The winner and their finishing order will be printed in the RFO's Derby edition, June 3.

☐ Commander In Chief	☐ Benny The Dip	☐ Galileo
☐ Erhaab	☐ High-Rise	☐ High Chaparral
☐ Lammtarra	☐ Oath	
☐ Shaamit	☐ Sinndar	

Name

Address

Town

Postcode

The winner will be the entry most closely corresponding to the Editor's finishing order. In the event of more than one correct entry, the winner will be drawn at random from the correct entries. The Editor's decision is final and no correspondence will be entered into.

Sponsored by Stan James

Horse index

All horses mentioned, with page numbers, except for references in the Group 1 and two-year-old reviews, for which there are seperate indexes following those sections

Adhaaba	91
Adiemus	107
Airwave	99
Al Ihtithar	84
Al Jadeed	77, 81, 100
Al Turf	117
Alamshar	85, 86
Albareq	102
Almushahar	80
Amount	123
Arctic Desert	8
Artistic Lad	85, 91
Asian Heights	107
Avening	118
Bahamian Dancer	77, 107
Bandari	112
Banjo Bay	125
Barrissimo	123, 129
Before Dawn	110
Benicio	111
Big Bad Bob	122
Billbill	84
Bishr	88, 101
Black Swan	91
Blackwater Angel	123
Blazing Thunder	100
Blue Patrick	108
Bluegrass Beau	12
Bond Becks	114
Bond Boy	113
Bond Stasia	113
Border Arrow	9
Bourbonnais	86, 92
Bourgainville	9
Branston Tiger	114
Bravo Dancer	103
Brian Boru	77, 85, 86, 92, 109, 129
Burning Sun	105
Bustan	102
Calibre	100
Camlet	82, 83, 107
Cape Fear	103
Captain Saif	116
Cassis	82
Casual Look	8, 84
Catcher In The Rye	109
Chaffinch	101
Chancellor	102
Checkit	103
Chevalier	85, 86
Chin Chin	102
Chinkara	103
Chookie Heiton	114
ClannA Cougar	12
Coconut Penang	119
Contractor	121
Country Reel	81
Courageous Duke	107
Cordial	87
Crown Counsel	123
Dabousiya	111
Dalakhani	85
Danaskaya	77, 82
Dance In The Sun	123
Dandy Jim	9
Danehurst	106
Darmagi	129
Debbie	13
Desert Star	81
Distant Prospect	9
Dominica	102
Donizetti	101
Dublin	81
Duck Row	105
Due Respect	117
Dumaran	8
Eastborough	13
Echoes In Eternity	83, 84
Ego	83
Elasouna	84
Elegant Shadow	101
Elusive City	77, 103
Encircle	110
Endless Hall	107
Englishtown	111
Escalade	126
Etoile Montante	82, 86
Evelyn One	110
Excelsius	92, 122
Eyecatcher	92
Ezz Elkheil	107
Falbrav	93
Far Lane	102
Fatik	102
Fiepes Shuffle	77
Flash Of Gold	88
Flavian Dynasty	110
Fleetwood Bay	119
Flight Commander	115
Flying Express	102
Flying Wanda	93
Foss Way	100
France	77
Frenchman's Bay	101
Gala Sunday	102
Geminiani	82, 83, 102
Gingko	125
Gold Bar	102
Golden Chalice	8
Goldeva	126
Goodness Gracious	123
Grand Halo	102
Grandera	104
Grooms Affection	123
Hanami	105
Hashid	102
Helen Bradley	107
Hi Dubai	82, 83, 84
High Reach	129
Hilbre Island	103
Hirapour	125
Hold That Tiger	80, 85, 86, 109
Hugs Dancer	114
Huja	82, 84, 104
Hurricane Alan	117
Illustria	103
Illustrator	104
I'm Magic	118
Imoya	103
In The Limelight	110
Innovation	101
Intercontinental	82, 86
Introducing	102
Island Rapture	123
Iwo Jima	108
Izdiham	102
Jabaar	88
Jakarta Jade	110
Jebel Suraaj	113
Johnston's Diamond	93
Jonny Ebeneezer	12
Jubilee	103
Katmandu	107
Kelburne	115
Khulood	82, 83, 123
Kimberley Mine	110
Kingham	100
King's Consul	105

Sponsored by Stan James

Name	Page(s)
Kohima	106
L'Ancresse	83, 84
Lateen Sails	77, 81, 85, 86, 93
Latest Edition	123
Legal Approach	113
Littleton Arwen	121
Londonnetdotcom	82, 103
Lochridge	9
Look First	13
Looking Down	117
Lord Protector	94
Love In Seattle	113
Loving Kindness	83
Luminata	82, 111
Maghanim	81, 85, 94, 122
Magic Glade	101
Magic Music	124
Mail The Desert	103
Makhlab	102
Maktavish	115
Man O'Mystery	125
Masaader	94
Media Puzzle	110
Midas Way	101
Millennium Hall	115
Mister Links	77, 117
Monsieur Bond	113
Moon Ballad	94
Most-Saucy	12
Mubtaker	101
Mujarad	100
Muqbil	81, 85, 121
Muwajaha	102
Napper Tandy	77
Nayef	101
Nayyir	88
Nayzak	82, 83, 84
Needwood Blade	125
New Foundation	12
New South Wales	77, 85, 86, 95
No Time	126
Norse Dancer	118
Now Look Here	124
Nysaean	88, 95, 118
Oasis Dream	77, 81, 88, 99
Oblige	8, 84
Ocean Silk	100
Octane	126
Ok Pal	121
One Last Time	117
Opera Glass	8
Orange Touch	123
Orientor	95
Pablo	95, 102, 129
Parasol	105
Passing Glance	9
Pay The Silver	13
Peace Offering	120
Pentecost	9
Peratus	110
Pershaan	123
Persian Majesty	88, 96, 123
Persian Punch	118
Phoenix Reach	8
Polka Princess	12
Powerscourt	77, 85
Prado	107
Presenter	100
Presto Vento	116
Pretence	129
Prince Of Gold	125
Prince Tum Tum	122
Private Charter	102
Protectorate	13
Rag Top	116
Rainbow City	84
Rapscallion	108
Reach For The Moon	82, 83, 84, 110
Refuse To Bend	81, 85, 86
Revenante	123
Revue	110
Rezzago	123
Rimrod	8, 81, 96
Risk Taker	102
Riva Royale	12
Romantic Liason	77
Roskilde	103
Royal Cavalier	125
Russian Rhythm	77, 82, 83, 104
Russian Society	84
Safe From Harm	96
Salcombe	102
Salute	108
Sandgate Cygnet	115
Sarayat	107
Sarin	107
Saturn	85, 86
Savannah Bay	103
Scott's View	113
Scotty's Future	96
Self Evident	23
Serbelloni	23
Shield	103, 129
Shouting The Odds	114
Shujune	123
Sienna Sunset	124
Sir George Turner	113
Six Perfections	77, 82
Skylark	126
Smirk	97, 118
Sophrano	123
Soviet Song	82, 83, 104, 129
Soyuz	107
Spanish Sun	83
Spartacus	109
Special Ellie	12
Speed Cop	8
Splendid Era	97, 102
St Andrews	107
St Pancras	106
Statue Of Liberty	80, 85, 86, 97, 129
Steelaninch	77
Stevedore	103
Stormont	107
Striking Ambition	105
Successor	102
Summer Shades	126
Summerland	100
Summitville	84, 114
Surbiton	81
Systematic	113
Szabo	111
Tacitus	117
Tandava	115
Tante Rose	129
Telori	13
Thesaurus	13
Thihn	126
Time Honoured	84, 86
Tom Tun	114
Tomahawk	77, 80, 110
Tout Seul	77, 81, 99
Toy Show	117
Trade Fair	81, 86, 97, 100
Tus Maith	111
Twilight Blues	103
Twilight Breeze	111
Ulundi	125
Umistim	118
Vanderlin	9
Van Nistelrooy	80, 110
Walayef	82, 83
Weavers Pride	102
Western Diplomat	81, 98
Where Or When	120
White Ledger	13
Wizard Of Noz	98, 106
Wunders Dream	77, 114
Yesterday	84, 86, 98, 110
Zabaglione	101
Zafeen	77, 103
Zindabad	112
Zinziberine	77

Sponsored by Stan James